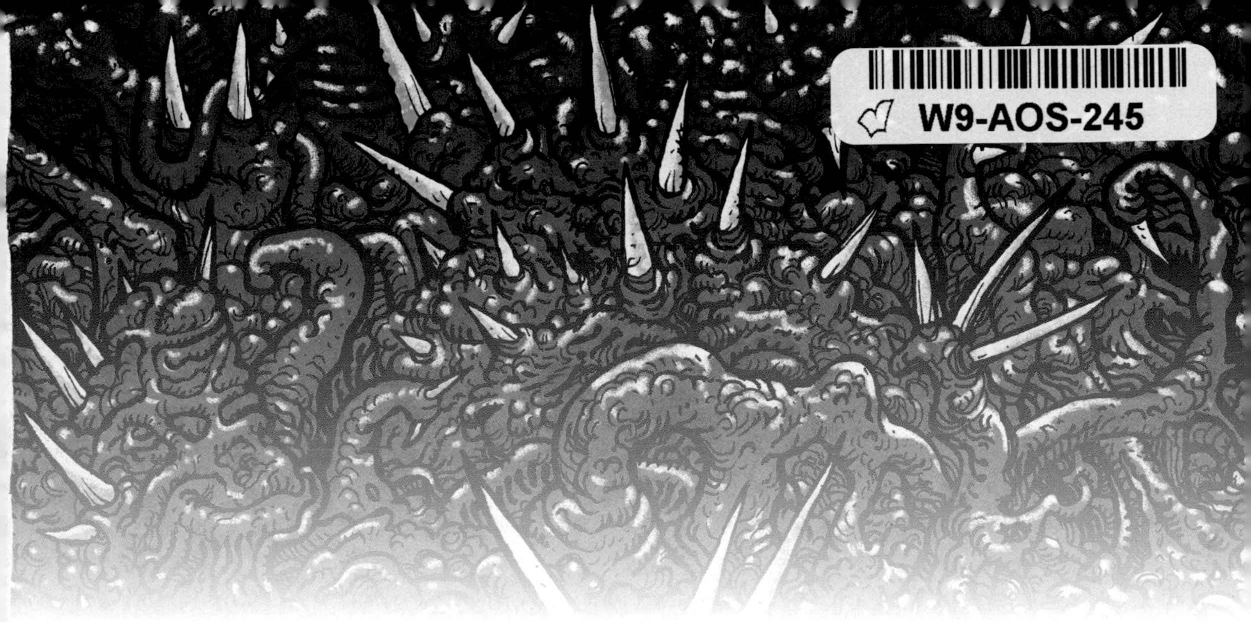

SPREAD™

VOL. 1: NO HOPE

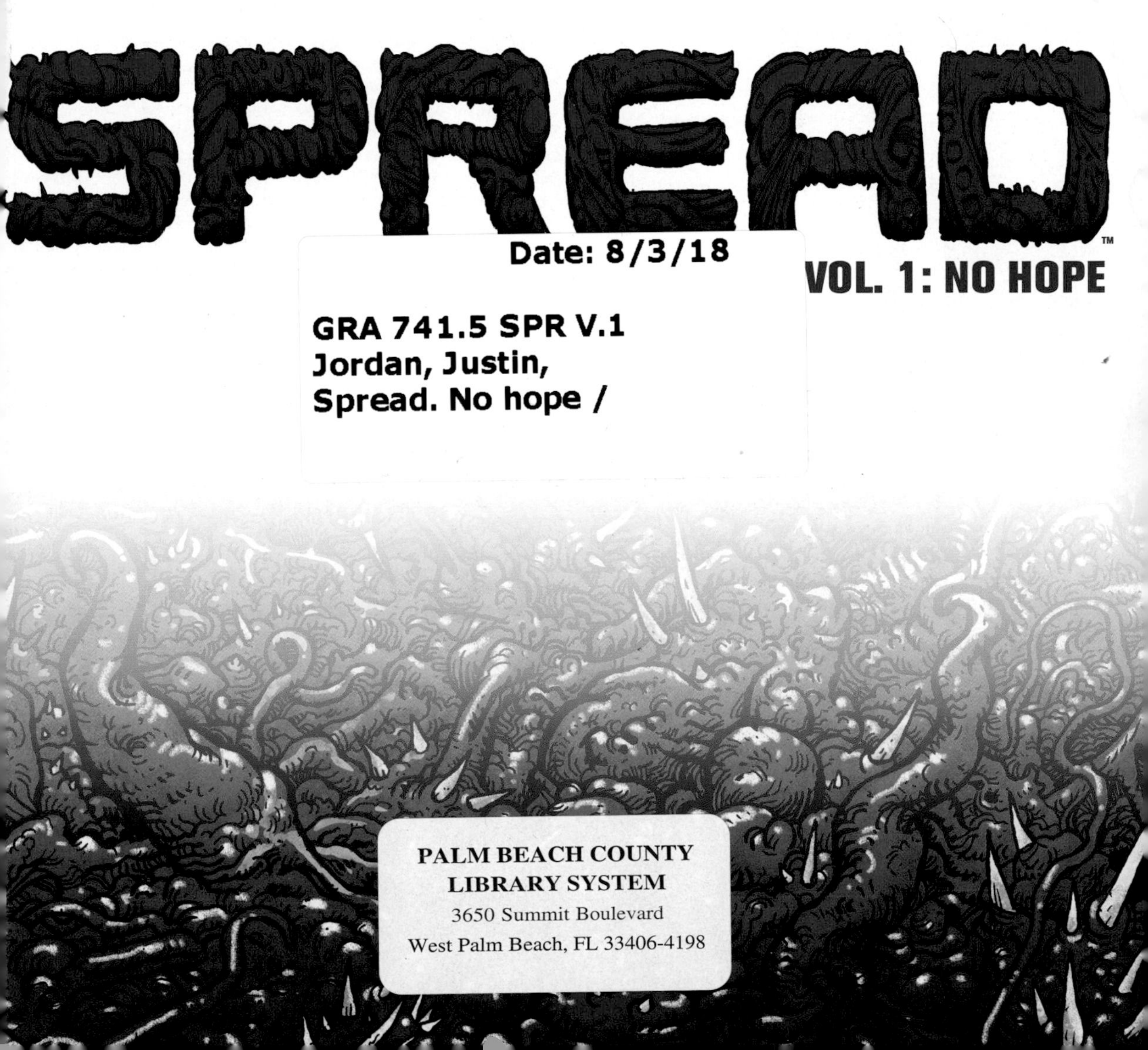

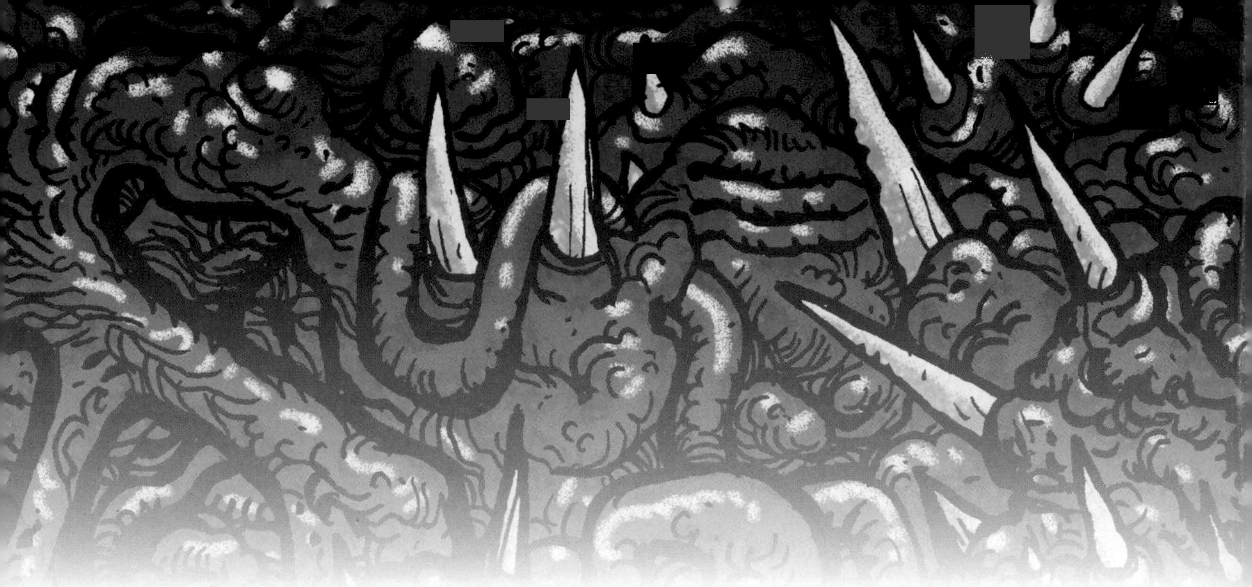

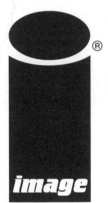

IMAGE COMICS, INC.
Robert Kirkman – Chief Operating Officer
Erik Larsen – Chief Financial Officer
Todd McFarlane – President
Marc Silvestri – Chief Executive Officer
Jim Valentino – Vice-President

Eric Stephenson – Publisher
Ron Richards – Director of Business Development
Jennifer de Guzman – Director of Trade Book Sales
Kat Salazar – Director of PR & Marketing
Corey Murphy – Director of Retail Sales
Jeremy Sullivan – Director of Digital Sales
Randy Okamura – Marketing Production Designer
Emilio Bautista – Sales Assistant
Branwyn Bigglestone – Senior Accounts Manager
Emily Miller – Accounts Manager
Jessica Ambriz – Administrative Assistant
David Brothers – Content Manager
Jonathan Chan – Production Manager
Drew Gill – Art Director
Meredith Wallace – Print Manager
Addison Duke – Production Artist
Vincent Kukua – Production Artist
Sasha Head – Production Artist
Tricia Ramos – Production Assistant
IMAGECOMICS.COM

SPREAD VOL. 1. FIRST PRINTING. APRIL 2015.
ISBN# 978-1-63215-256-5

Published by Image Comics, Inc. Office of publication: 2001 Center Street, 6th Floor, Berkeley, CA 94704. PRINTED IN THE U.S.A. For information regarding the CPSIA on this printed material call: 203-595-3636 and provide reference # RICH – 608428

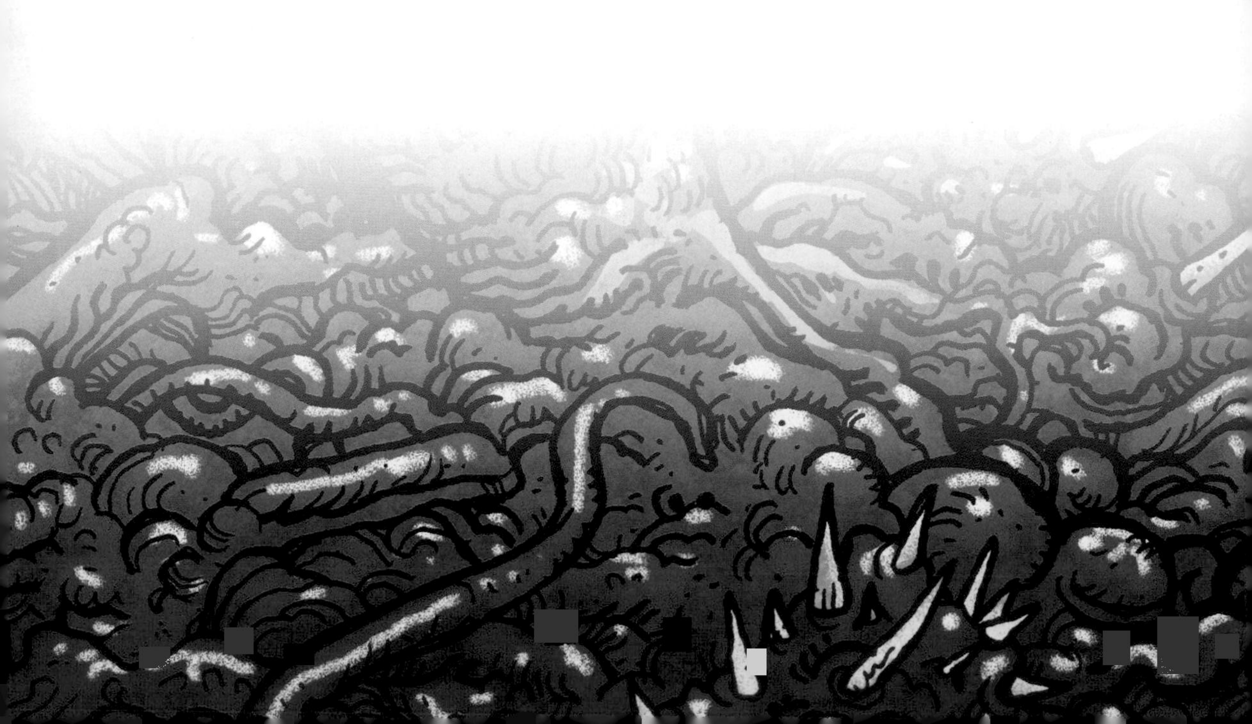

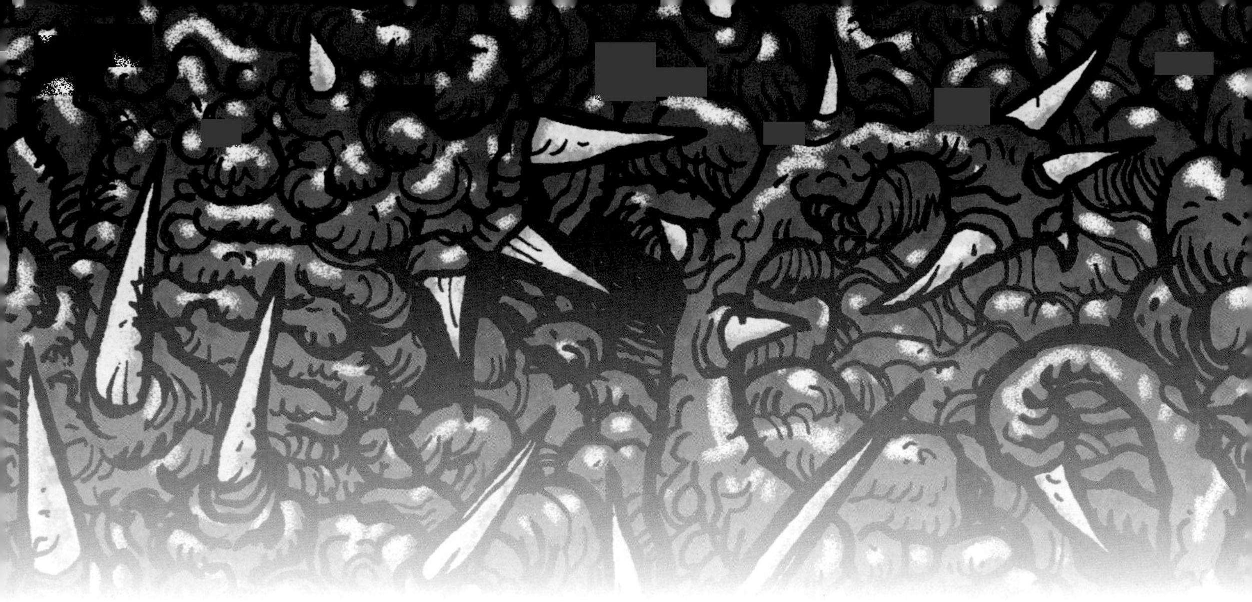

CO-CREATED BY

JUSTIN JORDAN and KYLE STRAHM

SCRIPT BY
JUSTIN JORDAN

ART BY
KYLE STRAHM

COLOR BY
FELIPE SOBREIRO

LETTERS BY
CRANK!

EDITED BY
SEBASTIAN GIRNER

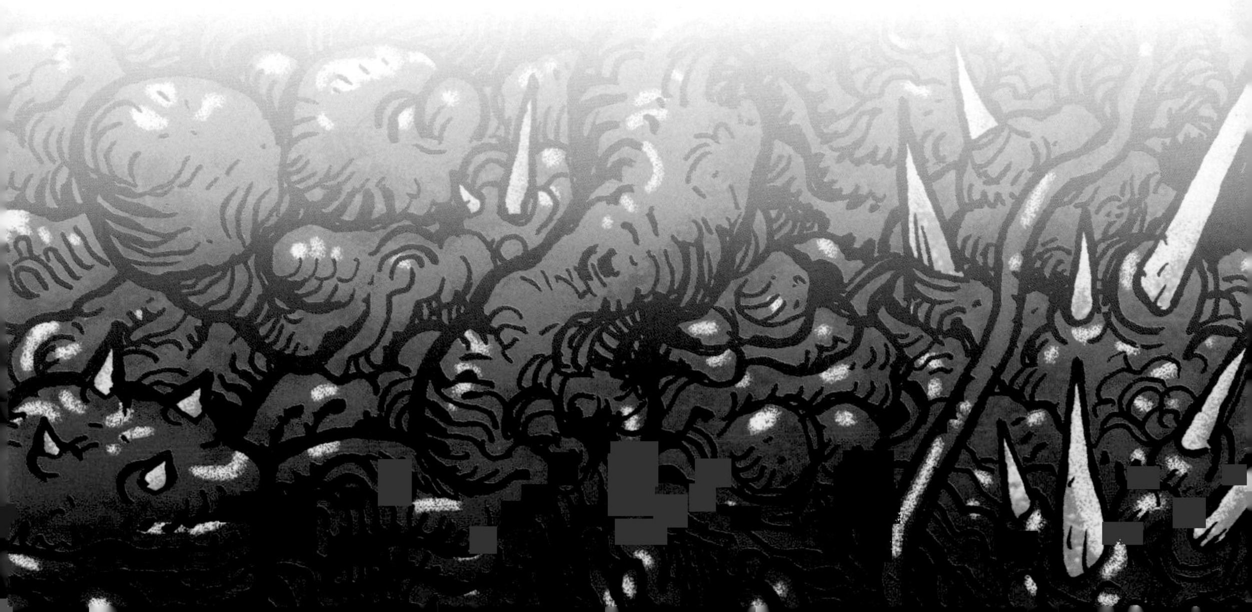

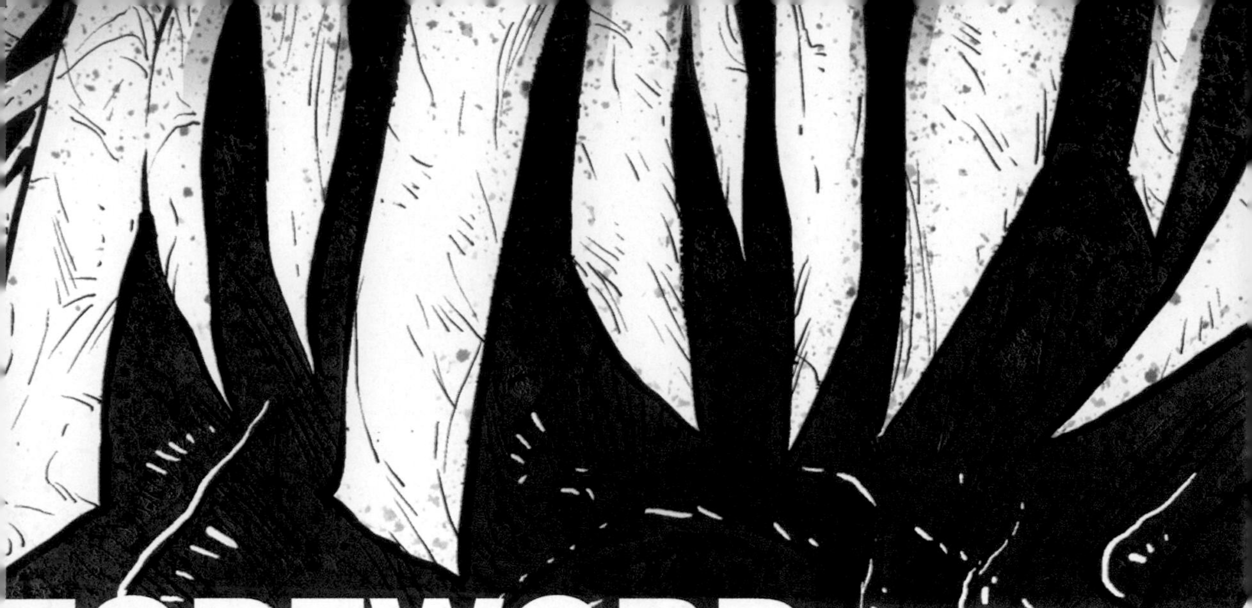

FOREWORD

I like to make a drawing so gross it makes me chuckle.

I grew up in the '80s and '90s watching Gremlins turning into spiders, Klopeks killing their neighbors and Graboids breaking in to the wrong goddamn rec room. My favorite Ninja Turtle was made of garbage and vomited ooze. To me, a villain getting his comeuppance in an action movie meant his head would melt away and explode by the power of God. And a hitchhiker could shock the diners at a truck stop by telling them that Large Marge sent him.

When I was older and starting to publish my own comics, I was labelled a "horror artist". The label doesn't bother me, but I've never embraced it. I draw stories and some of them have gross subject matter. It's never been the horror that interests me because when I was watching those movies I loved as a kid, I wasn't hiding behind a blanket; I was grinning from ear to ear.

The book you're holding is pretty gross. A lot of gruesome things happen to well-intentioned people. It has more than its fair share of dripping monster orifices, eyeballs with teeth, gallons of pus and just a lot of sphincters. I hope it all makes you cringe, but more than that, I hope it makes you chuckle.

-Kyle Strahm

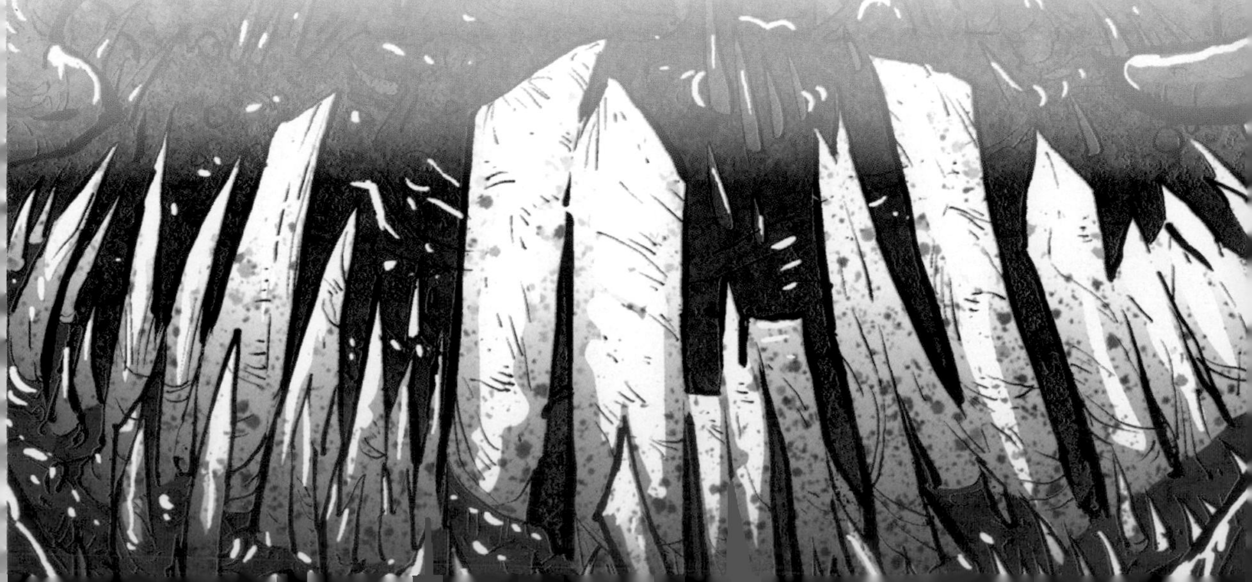

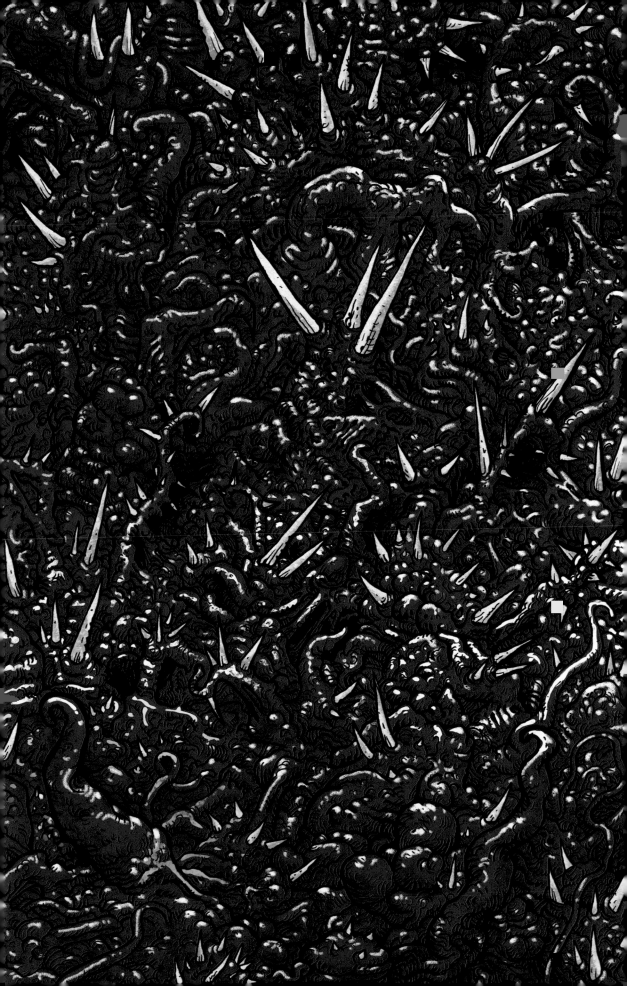

CHAPTER ONE

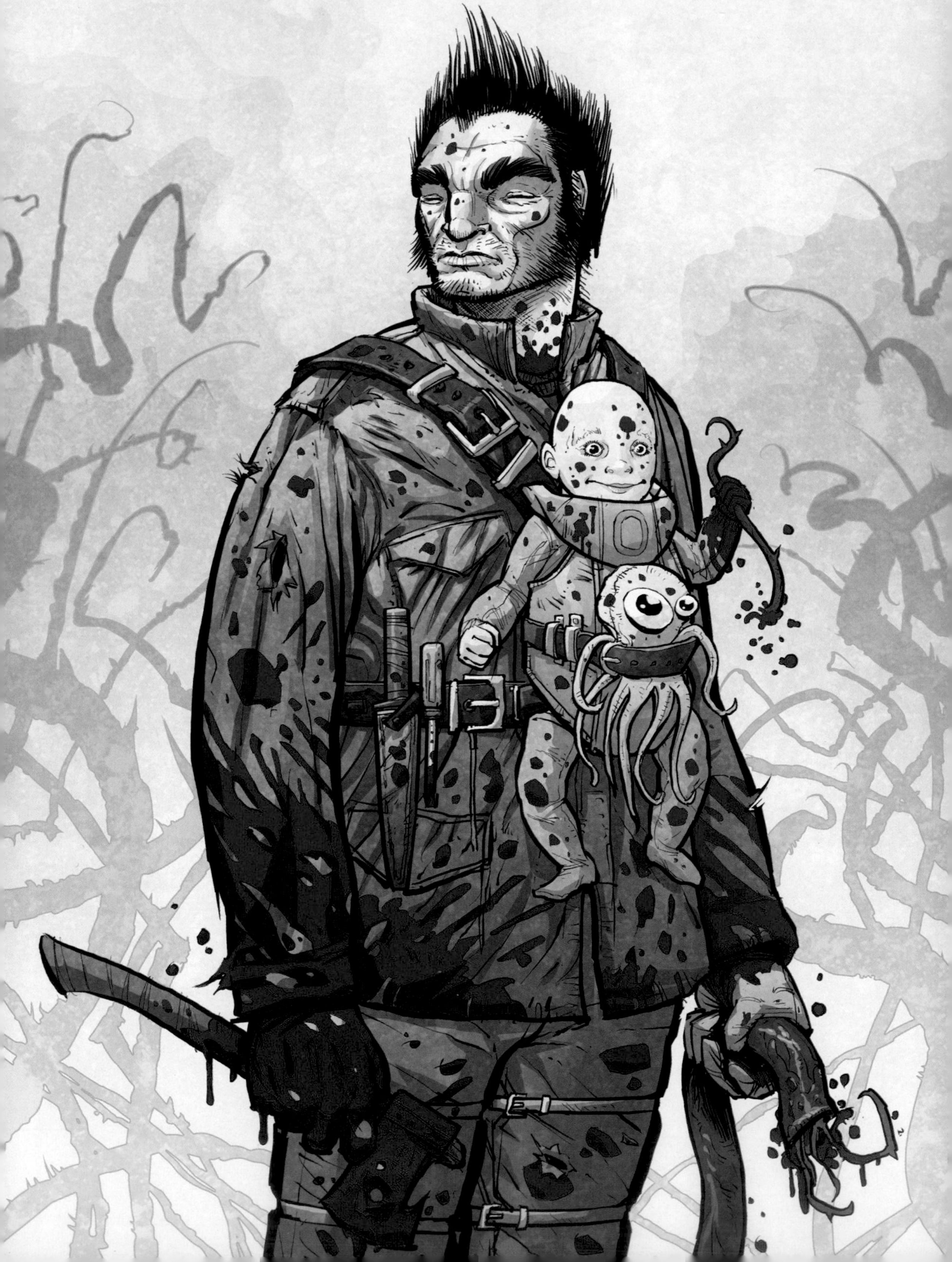

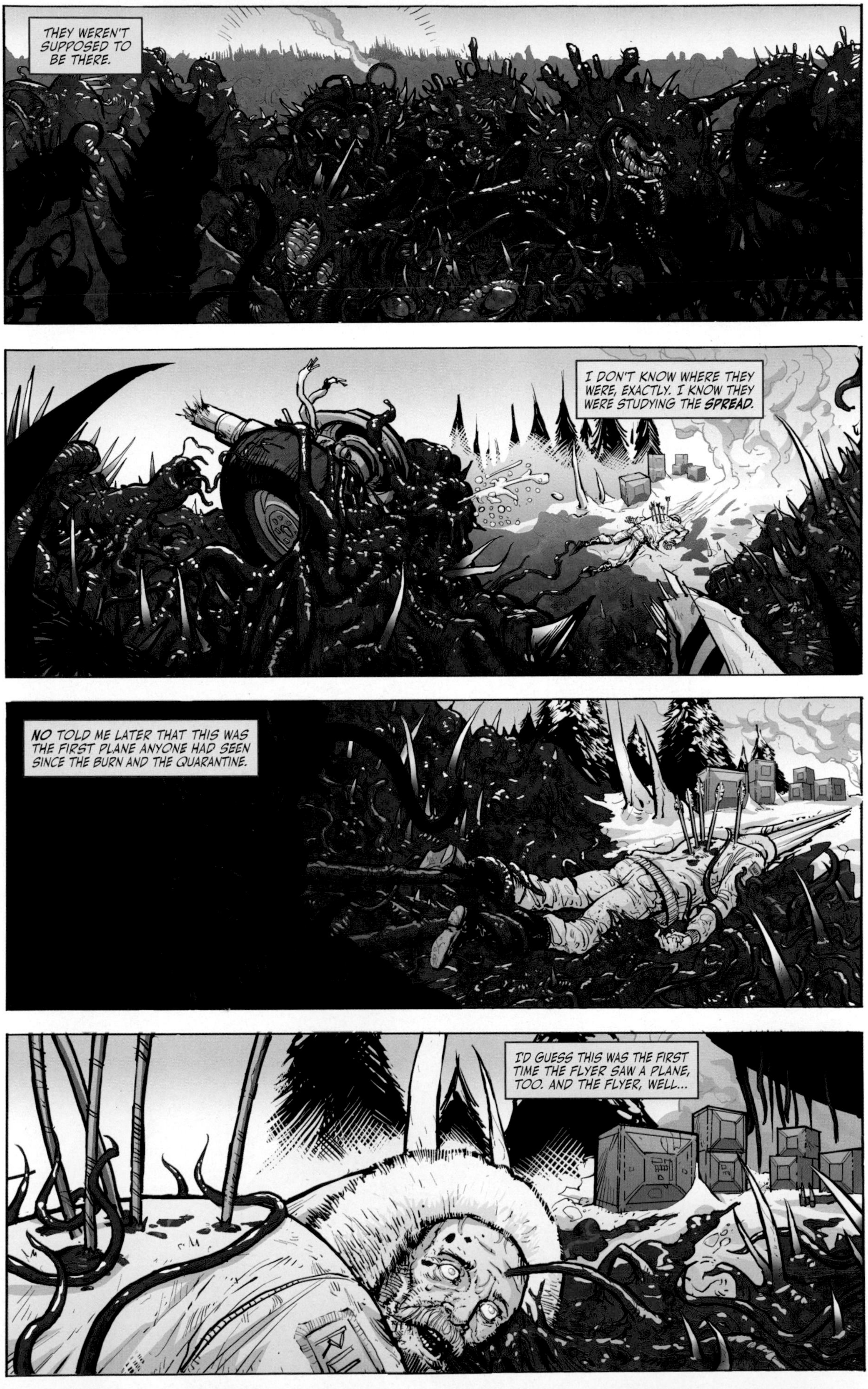
THEY WEREN'T SUPPOSED TO BE THERE.
I DON'T KNOW WHERE THEY WERE, EXACTLY. I KNOW THEY WERE STUDYING THE SPREAD.
NO TOLD ME LATER THAT THIS WAS THE FIRST PLANE ANYONE HAD SEEN SINCE THE BURN AND THE QUARANTINE.
I'D GUESS THIS WAS THE FIRST TIME THE FLYER SAW A PLANE, TOO. AND THE FLYER, WELL...

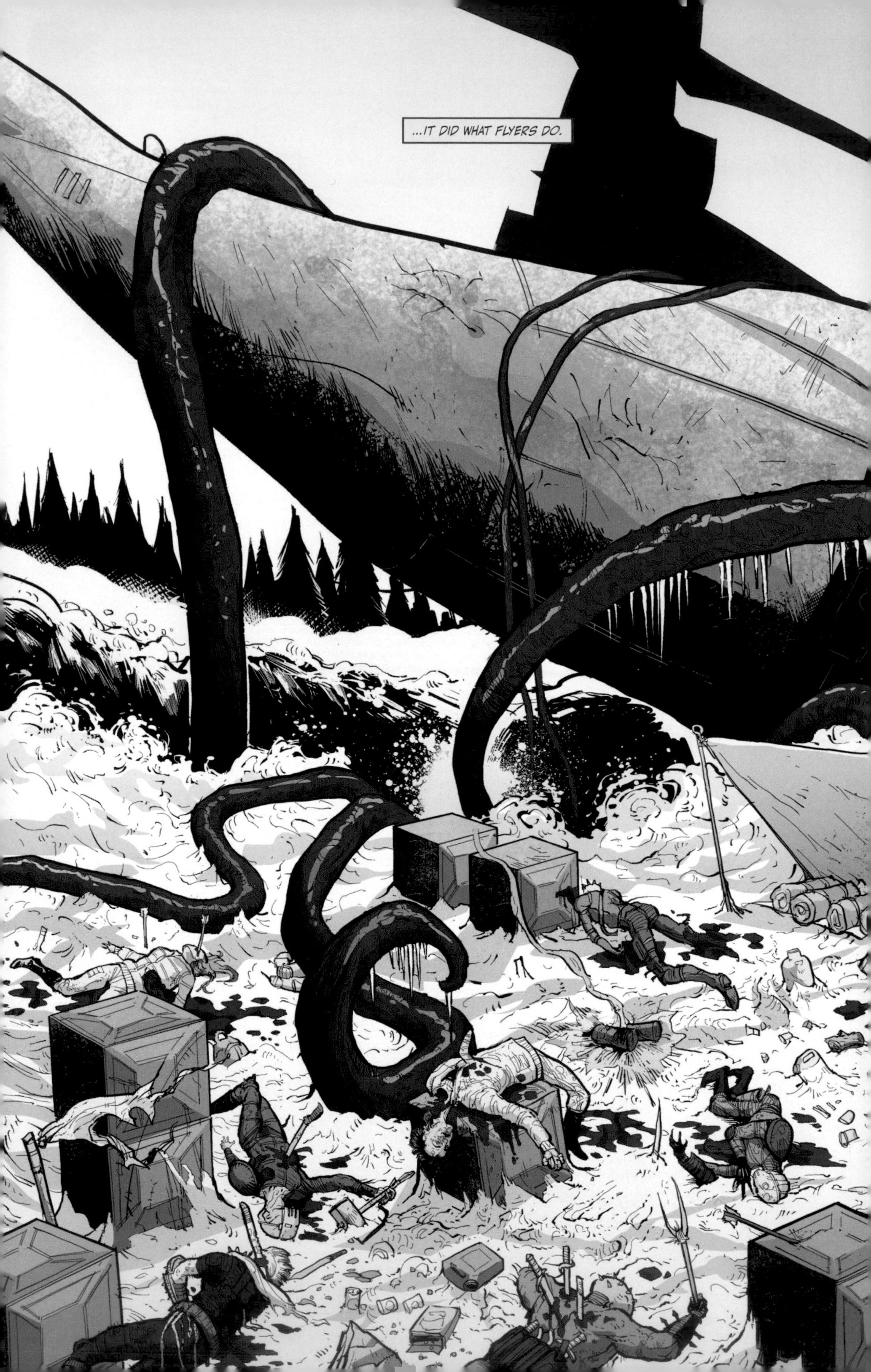
...IT DID WHAT FLYERS DO.

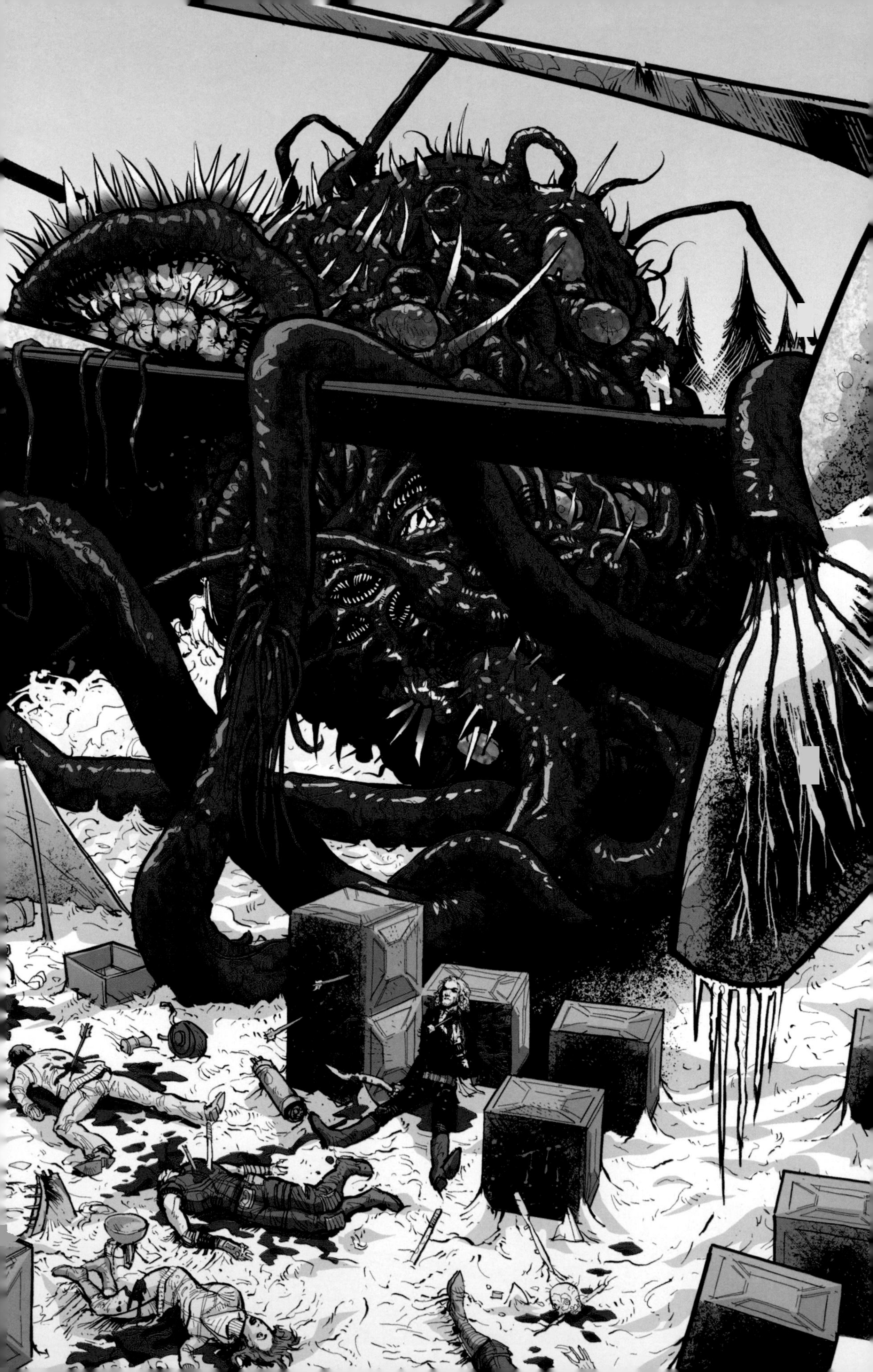

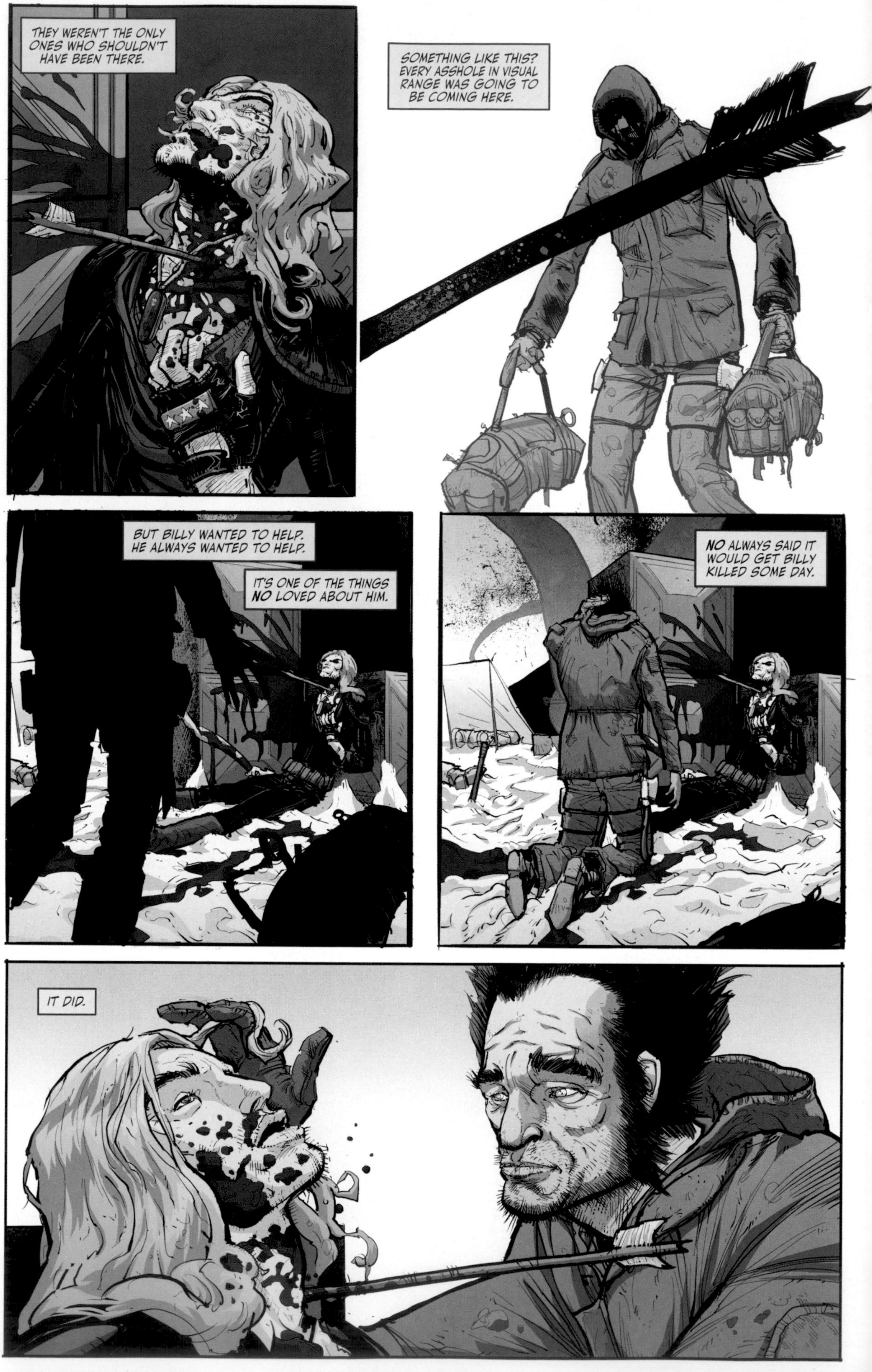
THEY WEREN'T THE ONLY ONES WHO SHOULDN'T HAVE BEEN THERE.
SOMETHING LIKE THIS? EVERY ASSHOLE IN VISUAL RANGE WAS GOING TO BE COMING HERE.
BUT BILLY WANTED TO HELP. HE ALWAYS WANTED TO HELP.
IT'S ONE OF THE THINGS **NO** LOVED ABOUT HIM.
NO ALWAYS SAID IT WOULD GET BILLY KILLED SOME DAY.
IT DID.

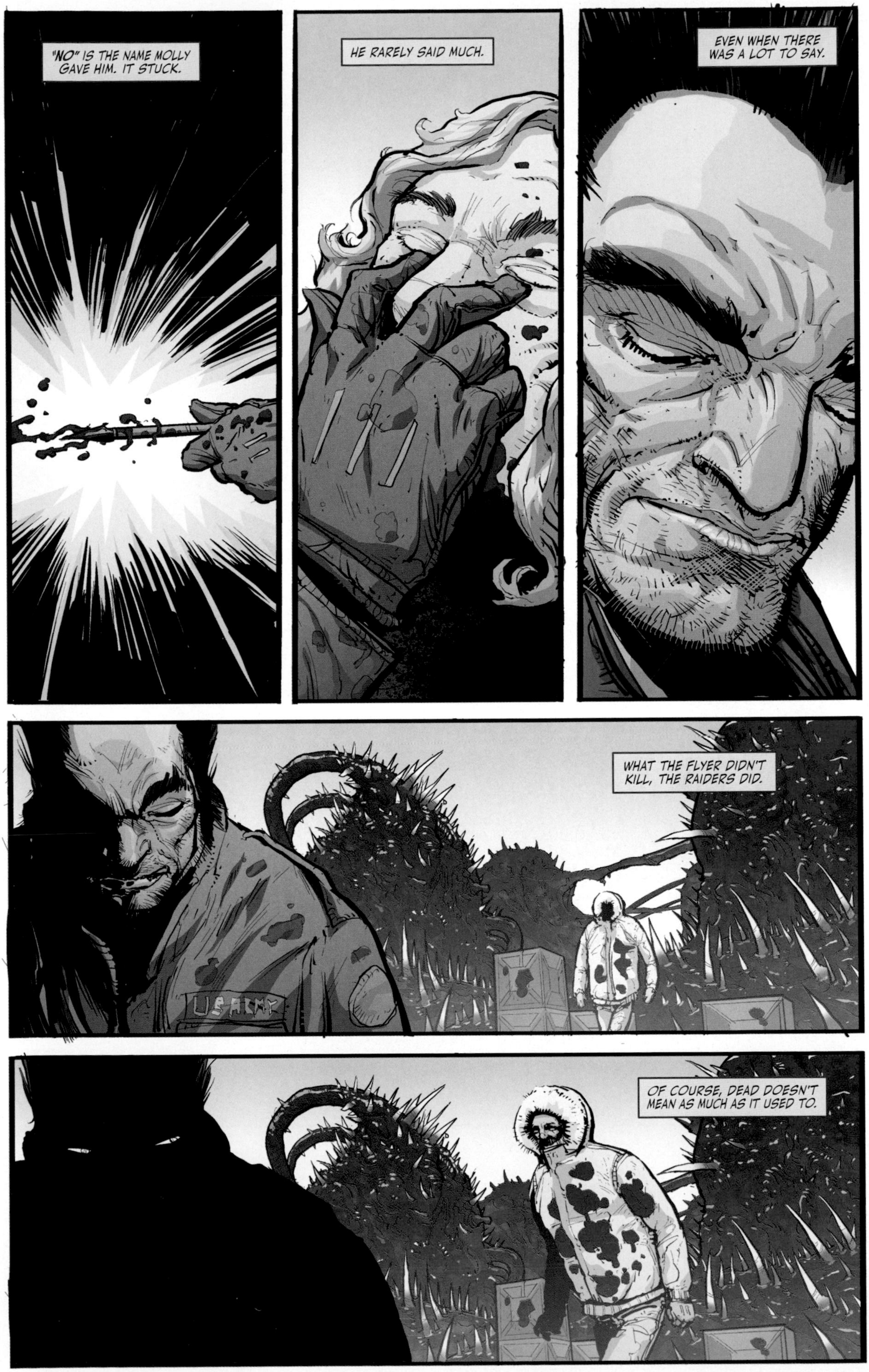
"NO" IS THE NAME MOLLY GAVE HIM. IT STUCK.
HE RARELY SAID MUCH.
EVEN WHEN THERE WAS A LOT TO SAY.
WHAT THE FLYER DIDN'T KILL, THE RAIDERS DID.
U.S. ARMY
OF COURSE, DEAD DOESN'T MEAN AS MUCH AS IT USED TO.

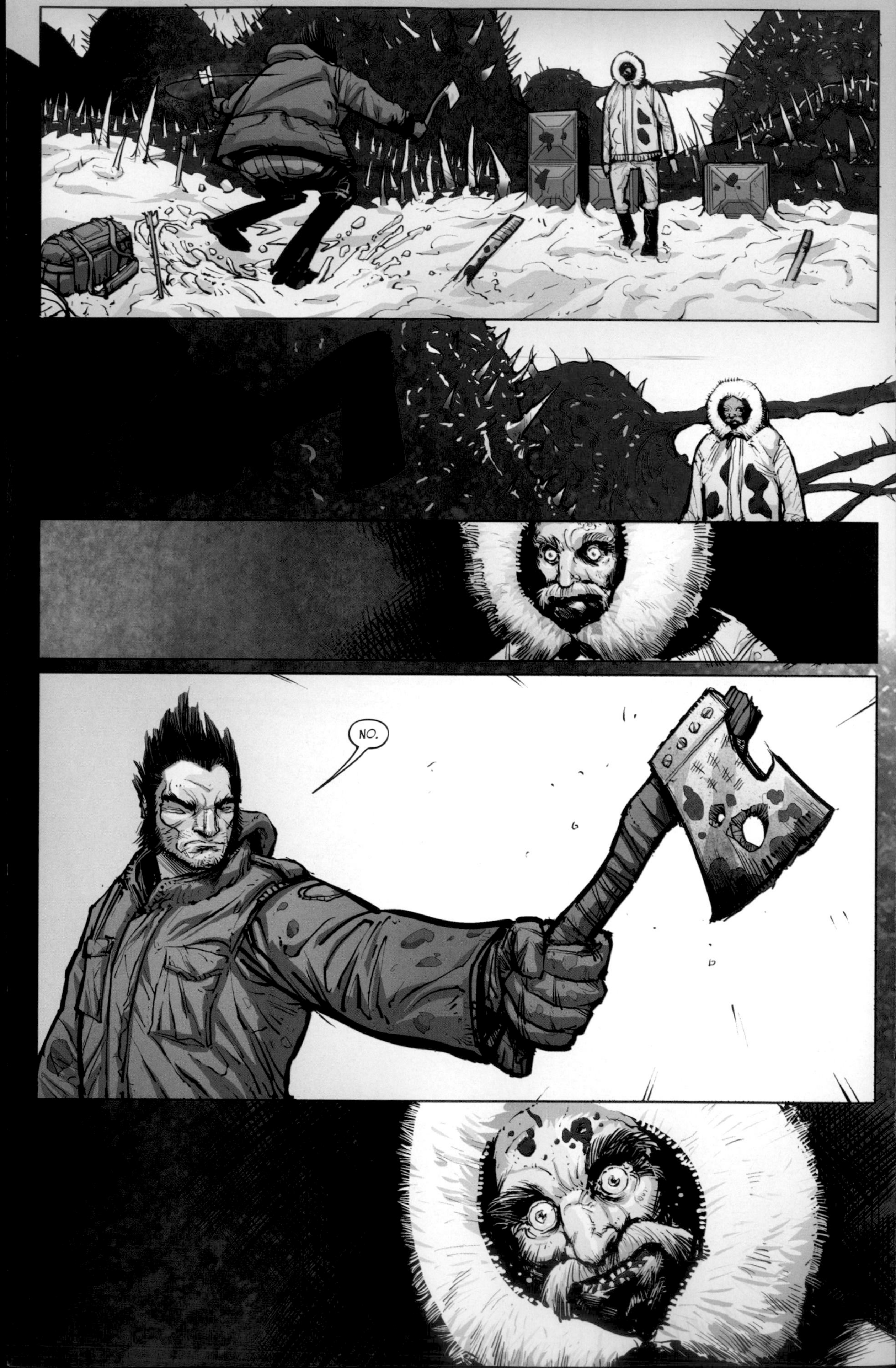
NO.

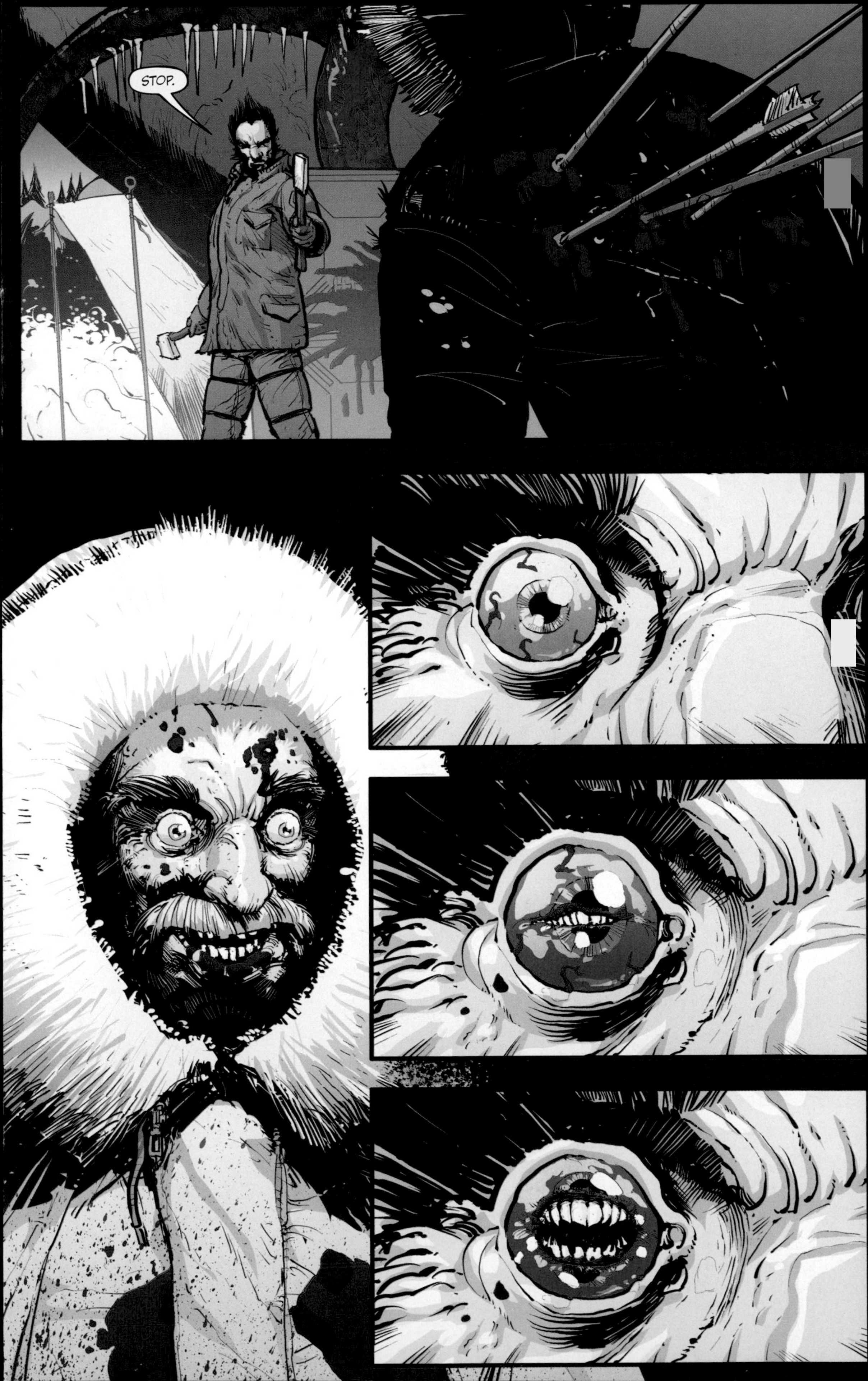
STOP.

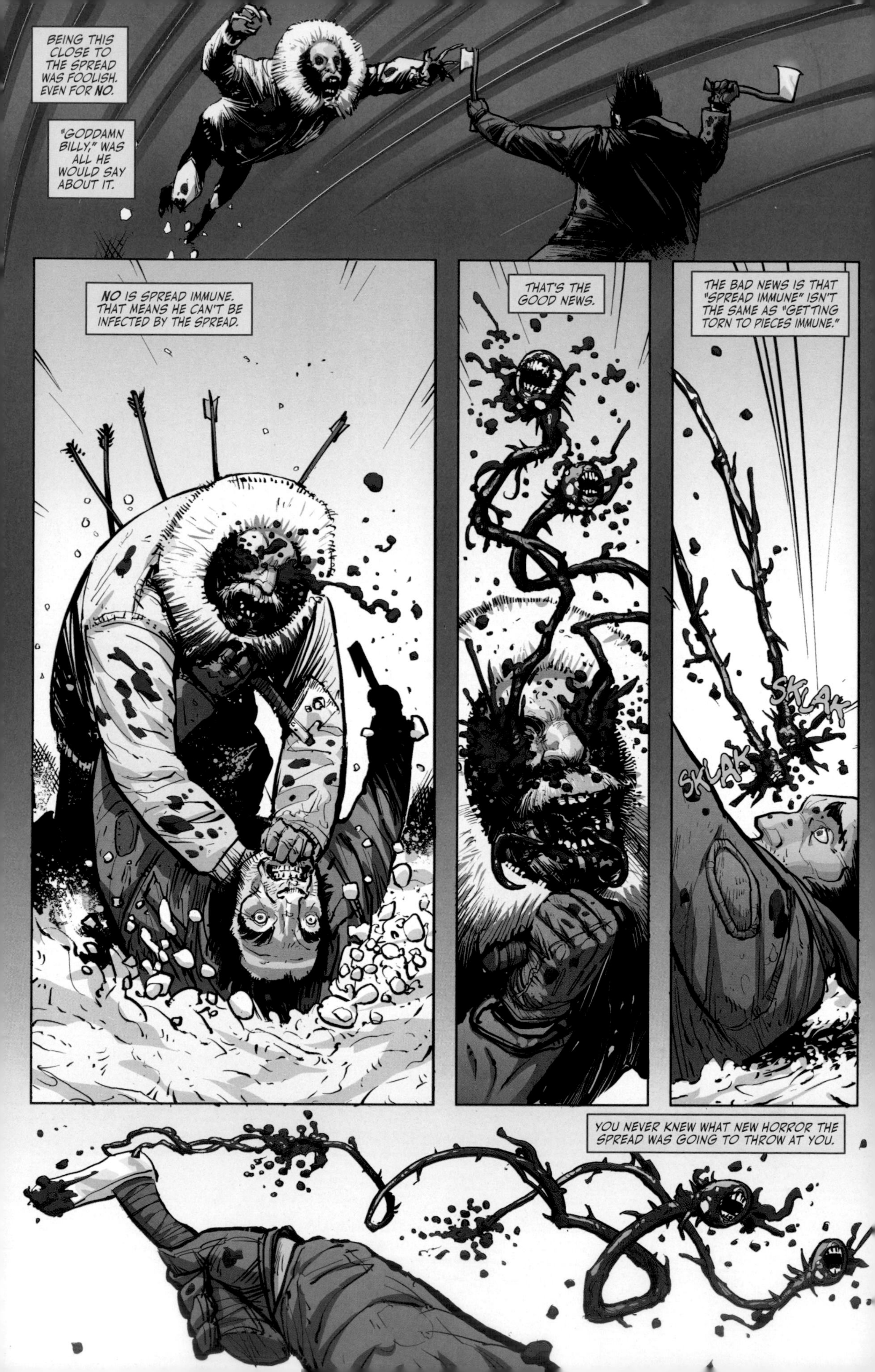
BEING THIS CLOSE TO THE SPREAD WAS FOOLISH. EVEN FOR NO.
"GODDAMN BILLY," WAS ALL HE WOULD SAY ABOUT IT.
NO IS SPREAD IMMUNE. THAT MEANS HE CAN'T BE INFECTED BY THE SPREAD.
THAT'S THE GOOD NEWS.
THE BAD NEWS IS THAT "SPREAD IMMUNE" ISN'T THE SAME AS "GETTING TORN TO PIECES IMMUNE."
SKLAK
SKLAK
YOU NEVER KNEW WHAT NEW HORROR THE SPREAD WAS GOING TO THROW AT YOU.

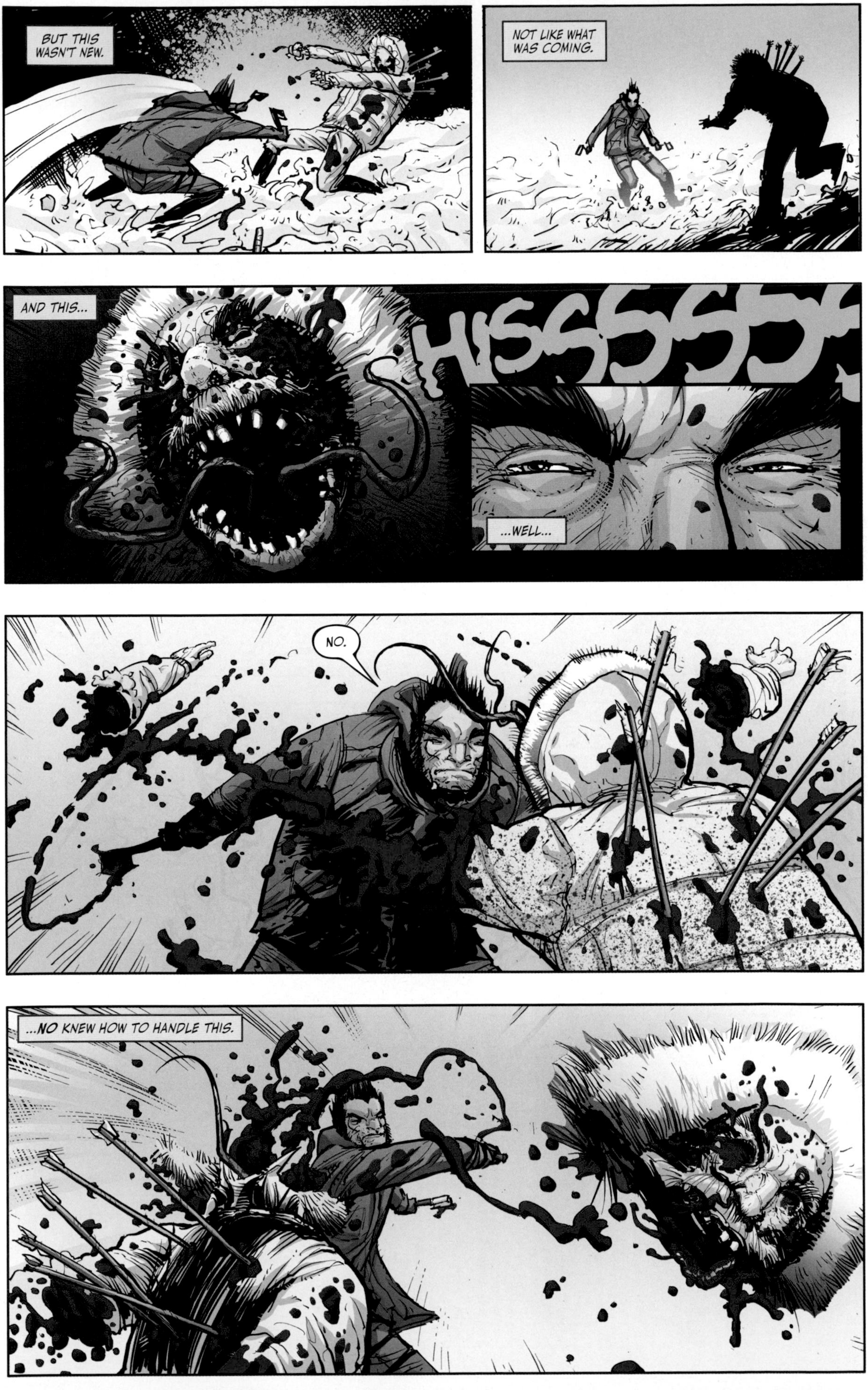
BUT THIS WASN'T NEW.
NOT LIKE WHAT WAS COMING.
AND THIS...
HISSSSS
...WELL...
NO.
...NO KNEW HOW TO HANDLE THIS.

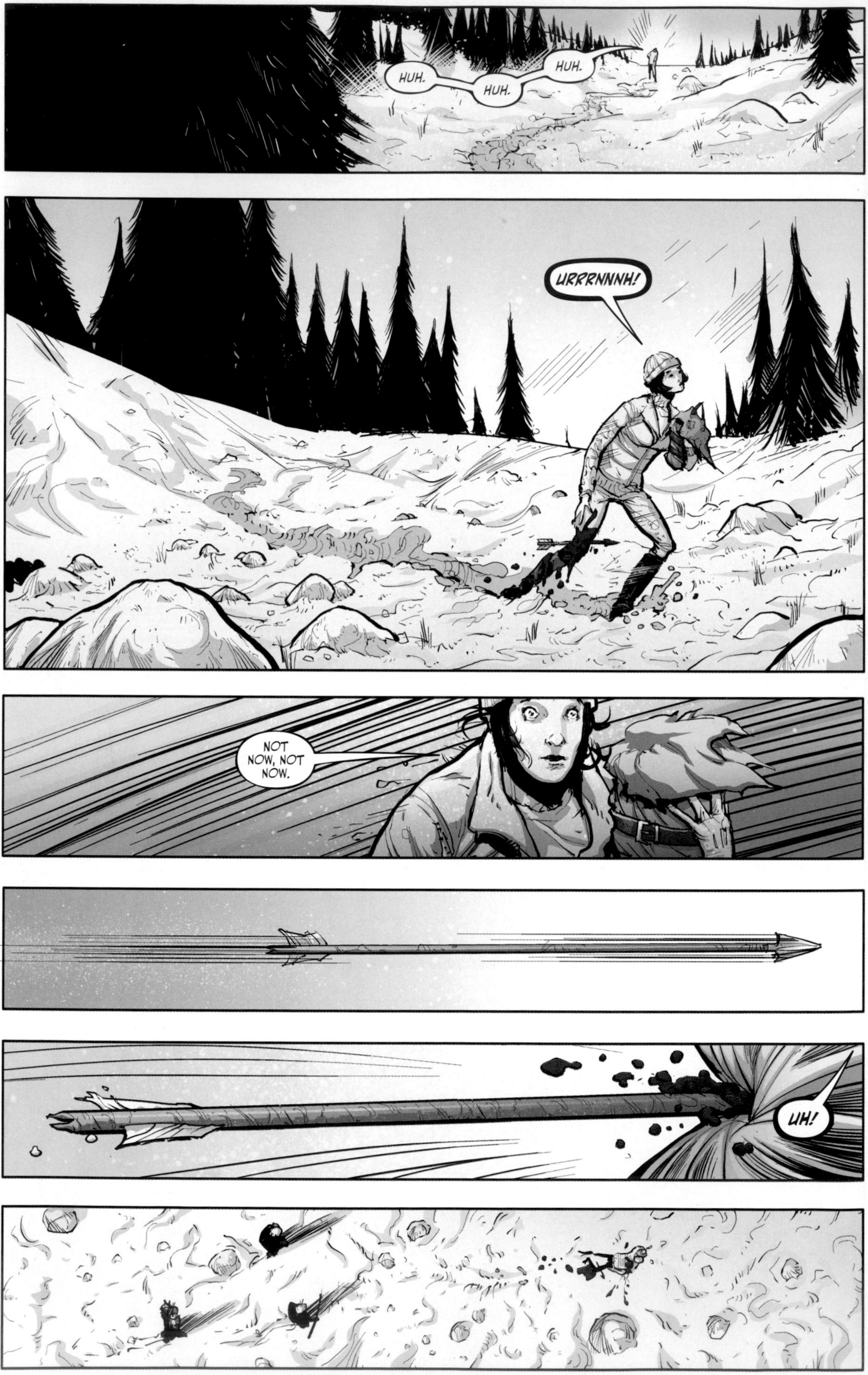

HUH.
HUH.
HUH.
URRRNNNH!
NOT NOW, NOT NOW.
UH!

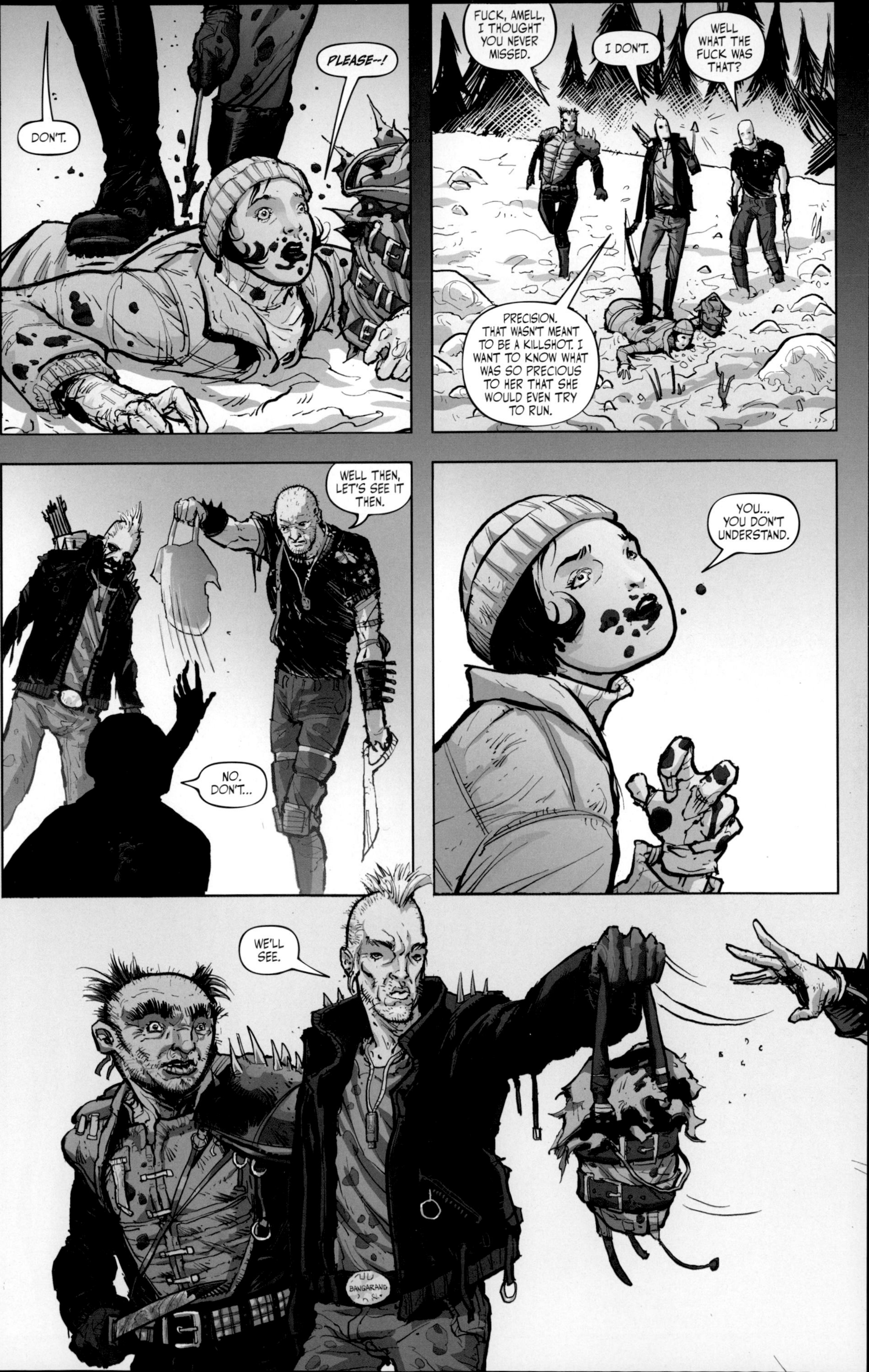
DON'T.
PLEASE--!
FUCK, AMELL, I THOUGHT YOU NEVER MISSED.
I DON'T.
WELL WHAT THE FUCK WAS THAT?
PRECISION. THAT WASN'T MEANT TO BE A KILLSHOT. I WANT TO KNOW WHAT WAS SO PRECIOUS TO HER THAT SHE WOULD EVEN TRY TO RUN.
WELL THEN, LET'S SEE IT THEN.
NO. DON'T...
YOU... YOU DON'T UNDERSTAND.
WE'LL SEE.
BANGARANG

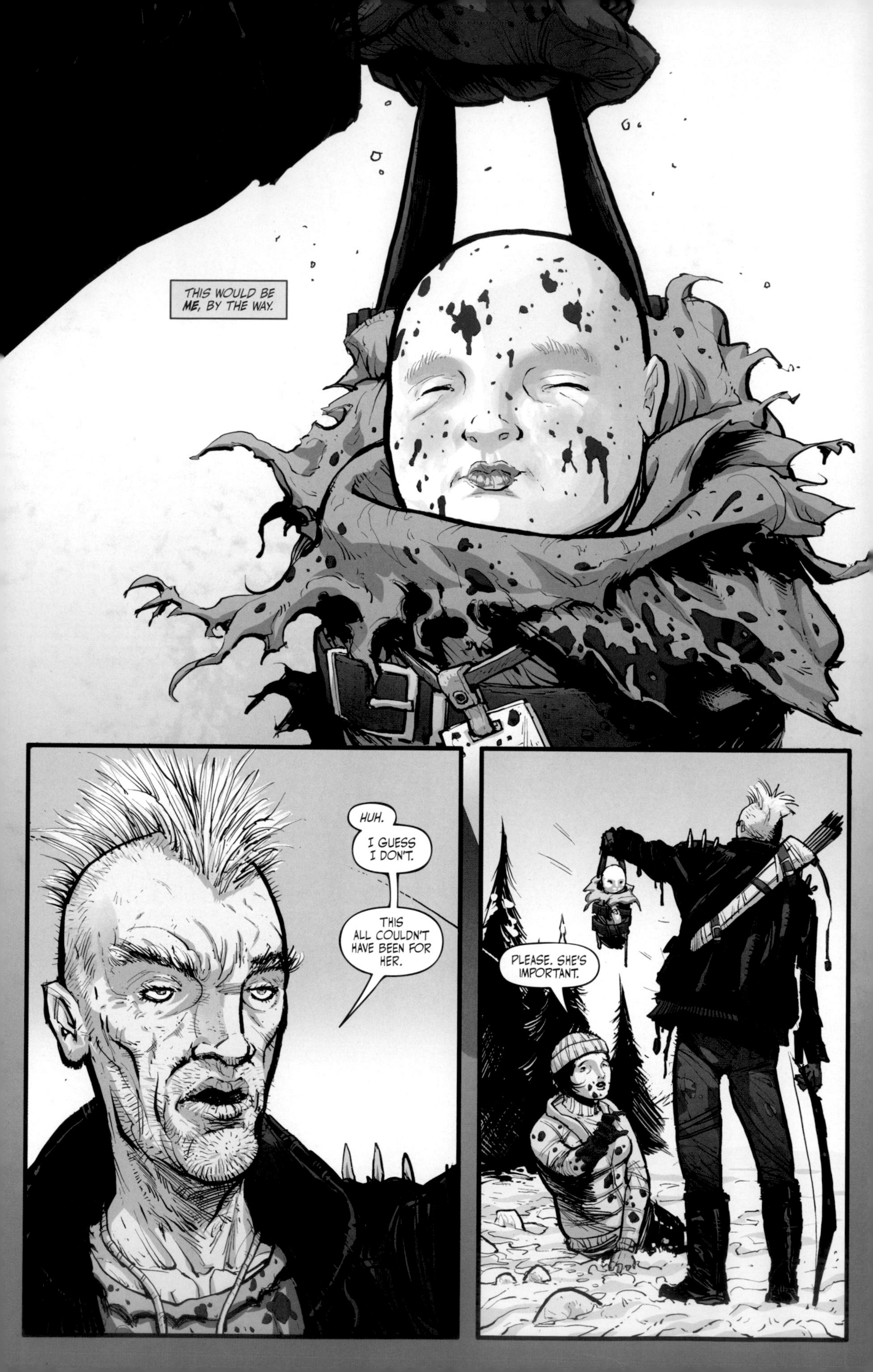
THIS WOULD BE *ME*, BY THE WAY.
HUH.
I GUESS I DON'T.
THIS ALL COULDN'T HAVE BEEN FOR HER.
PLEASE. SHE'S IMPORTANT.

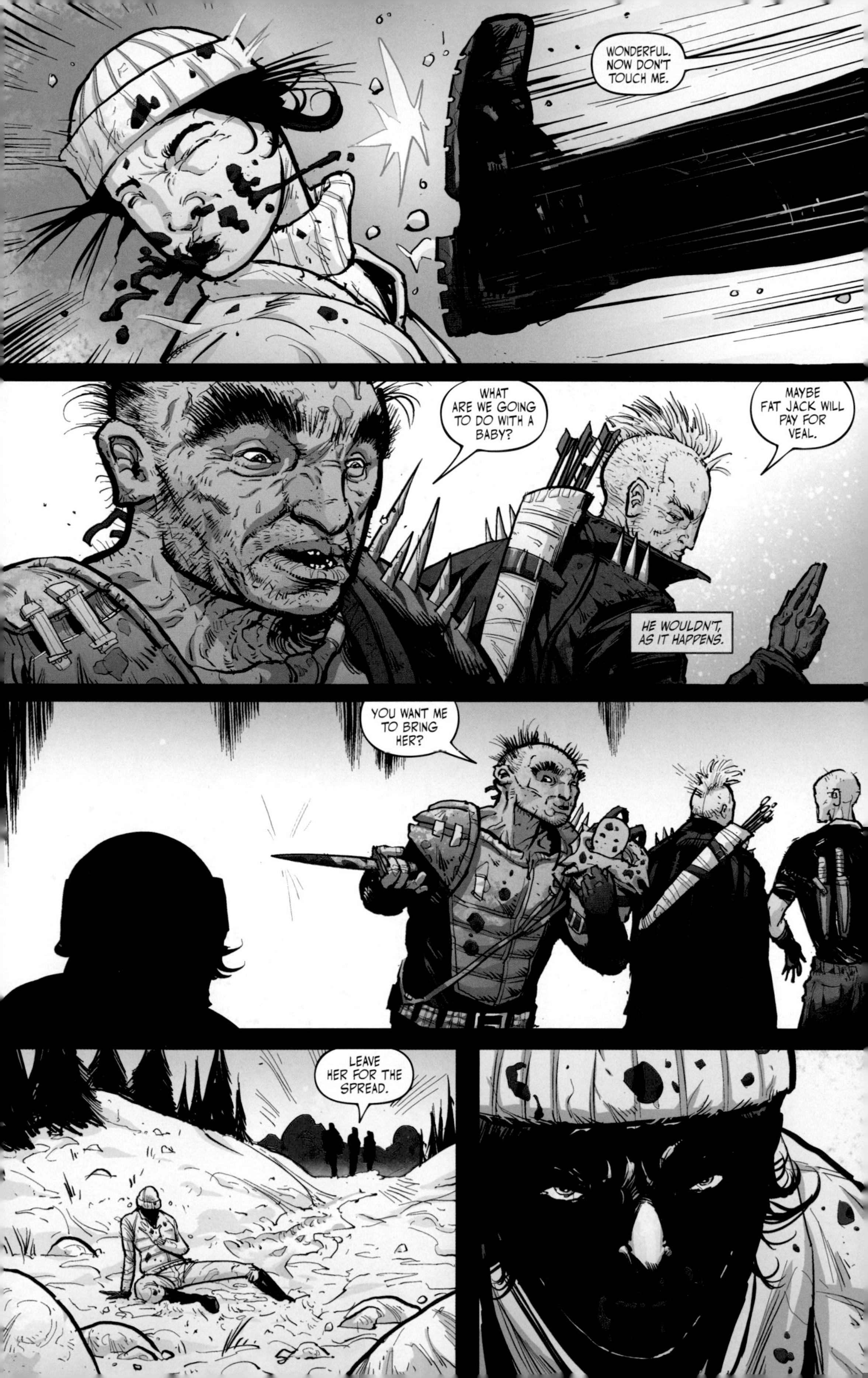
WONDERFUL. NOW DON'T TOUCH ME.
WHAT ARE WE GOING TO DO WITH A BABY?
MAYBE FAT JACK WILL PAY FOR VEAL.
HE WOULDN'T, AS IT HAPPENS.
YOU WANT ME TO BRING HER?
LEAVE HER FOR THE SPREAD.

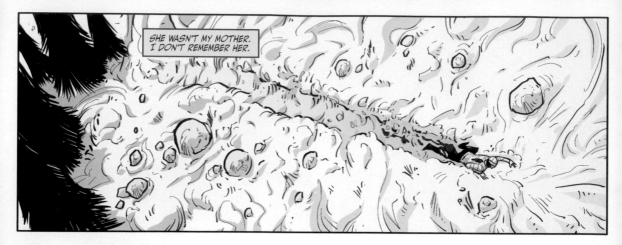

SHE WASN'T MY MOTHER. I DON'T REMEMBER HER.

ONLY ONE PERSON DID.

THE PEOPLE WHO DID THIS TO YOU.

HOW MANY WERE THERE?

DON'T... DON'T KNOW... PLEASE.

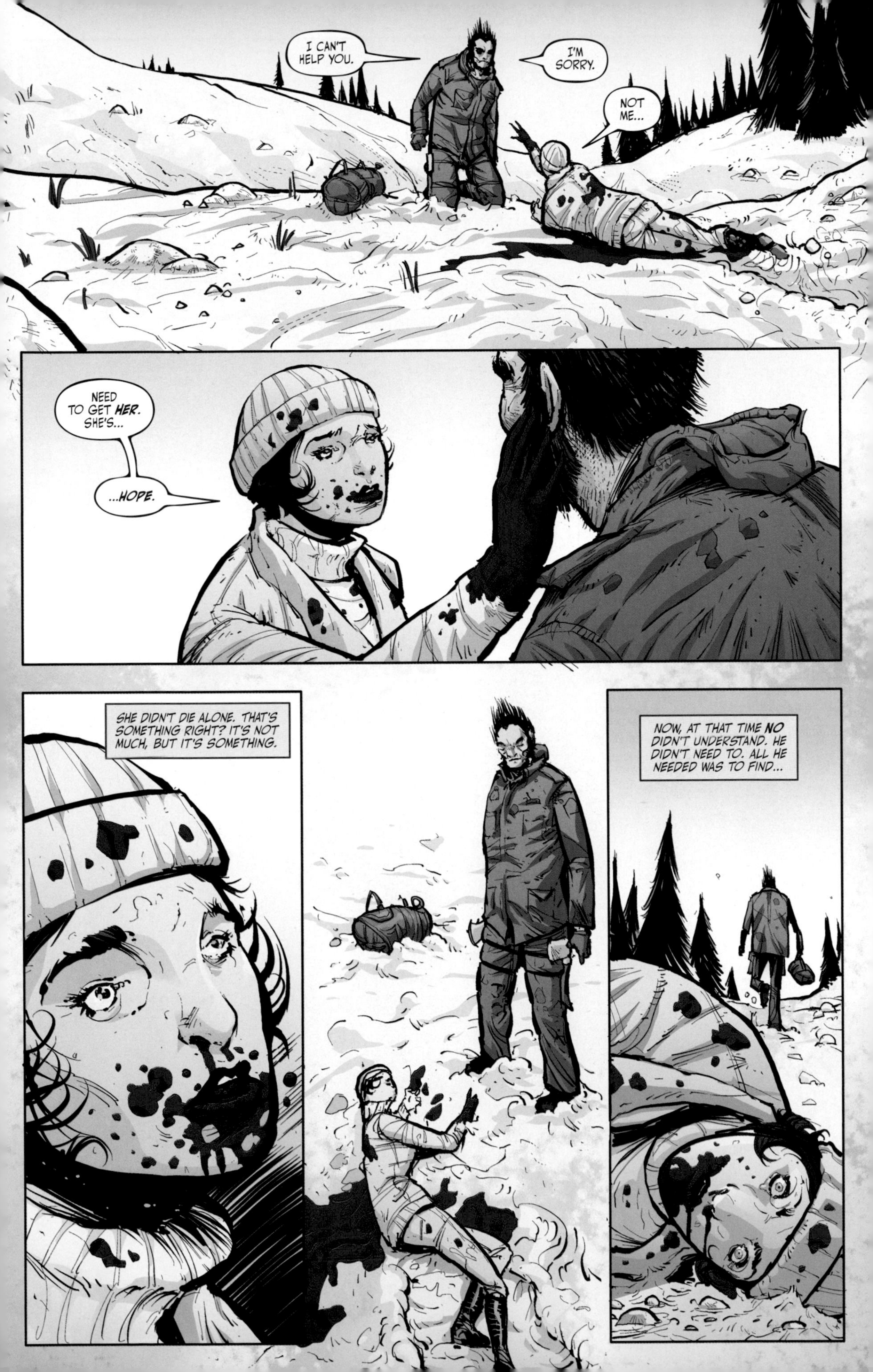
I CAN'T HELP YOU.
I'M SORRY.
NOT ME...
NEED TO GET ***HER***. SHE'S...
...HOPE.
SHE DIDN'T DIE ALONE. THAT'S SOMETHING RIGHT? IT'S NOT MUCH, BUT IT'S SOMETHING.
*NOW, AT THAT TIME **NO** DIDN'T UNDERSTAND. HE DIDN'T NEED TO. ALL HE NEEDED WAS TO FIND...*

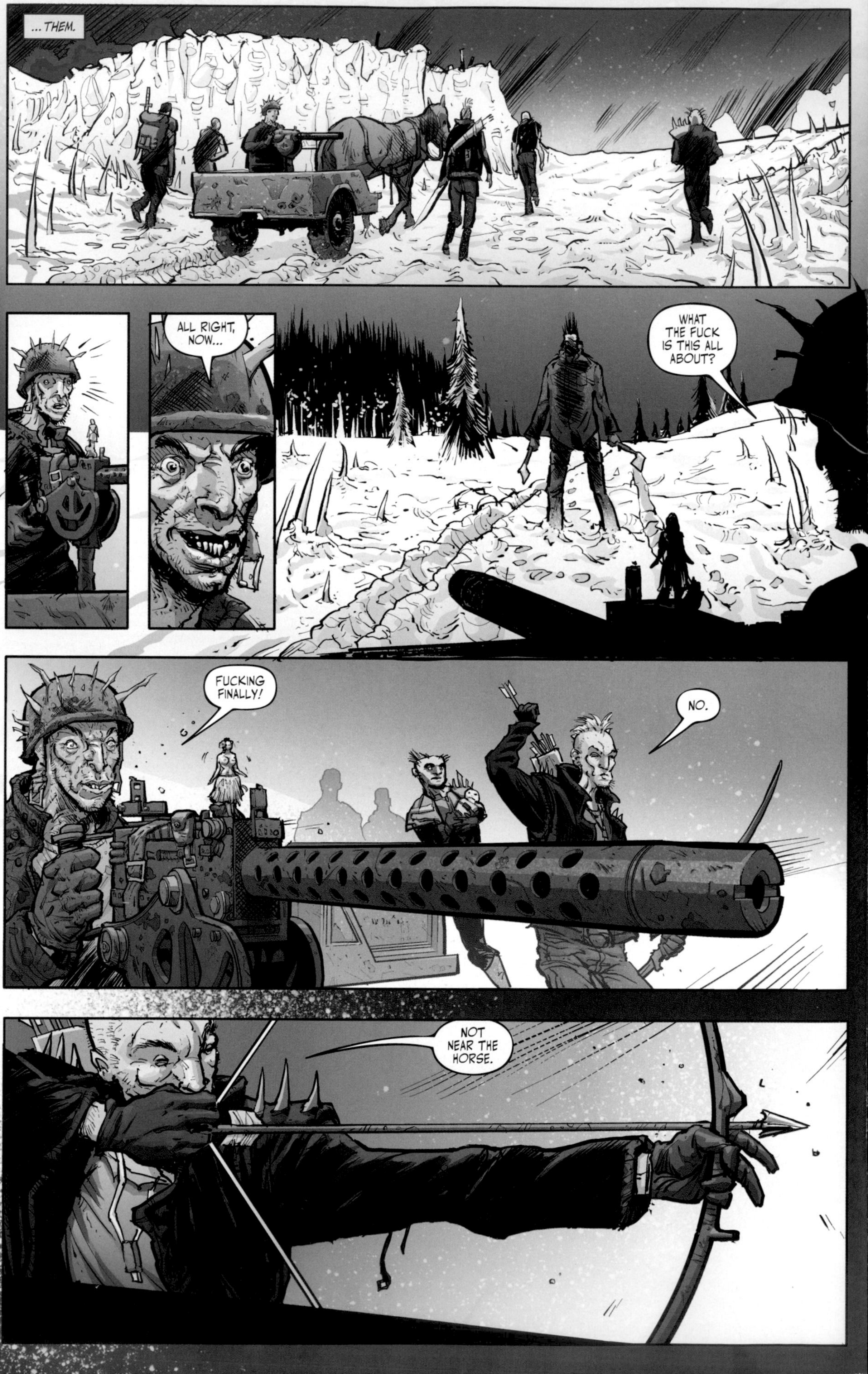
...THEM.
ALL RIGHT, NOW...
WHAT THE FUCK IS THIS ALL ABOUT?
FUCKING FINALLY!
NO.
NOT NEAR THE HORSE.

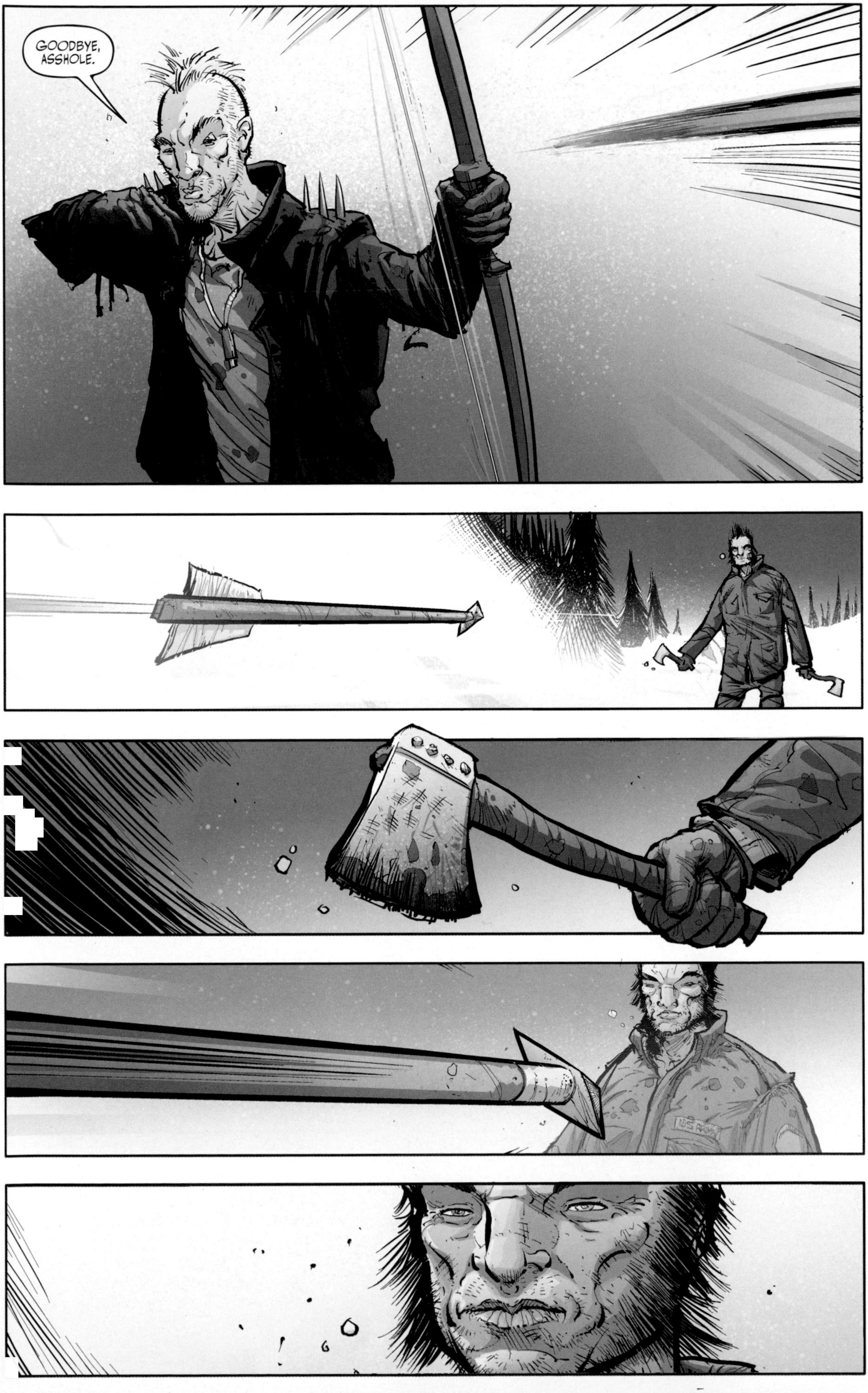
GOODBYE, ASSHOLE.

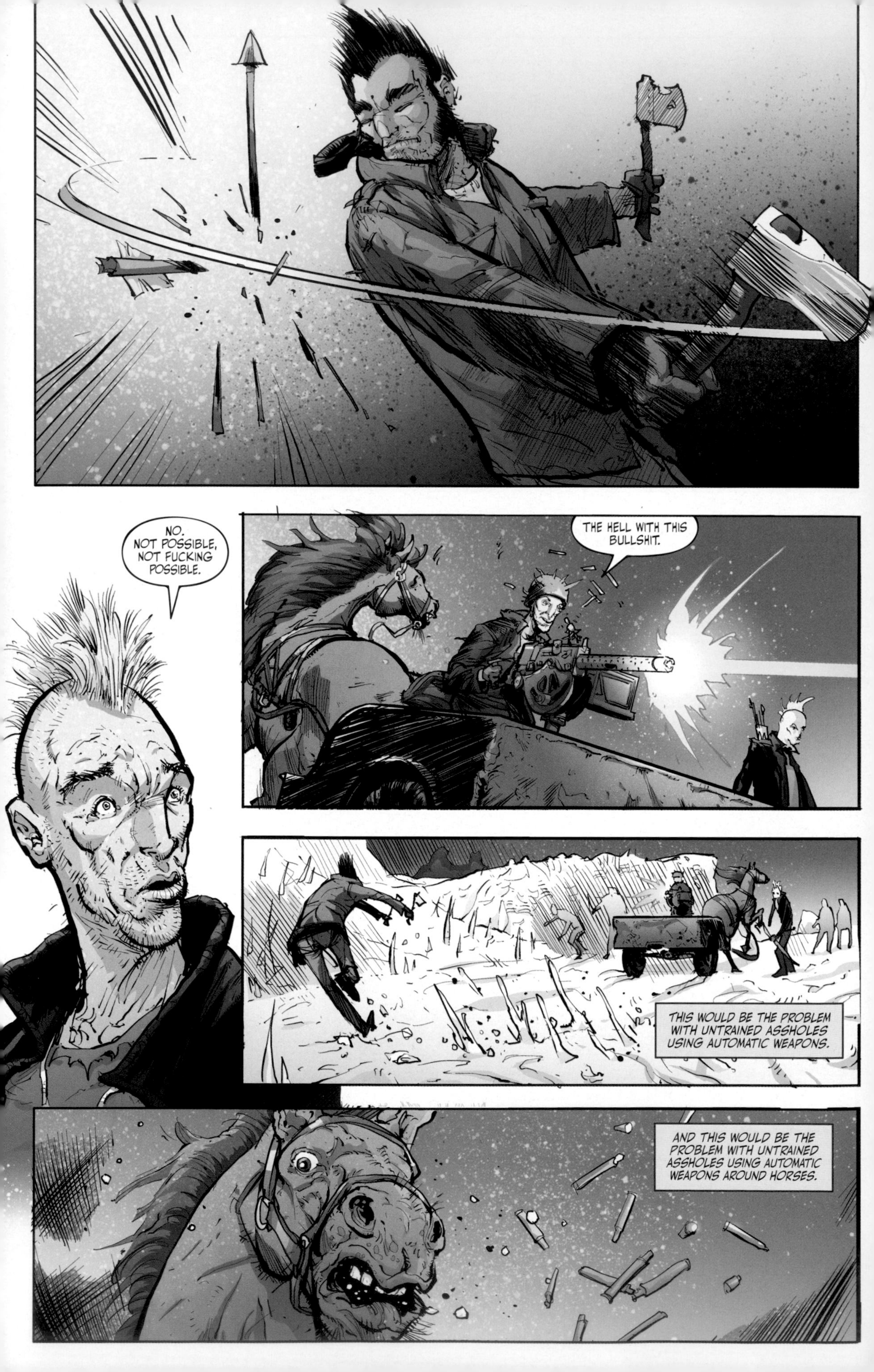
NO. NOT POSSIBLE, NOT FUCKING POSSIBLE.
THE HELL WITH THIS BULLSHIT.
THIS WOULD BE THE PROBLEM WITH UNTRAINED ASSHOLES USING AUTOMATIC WEAPONS.
AND THIS WOULD BE THE PROBLEM WITH UNTRAINED ASSHOLES USING AUTOMATIC WEAPONS AROUND HORSES.

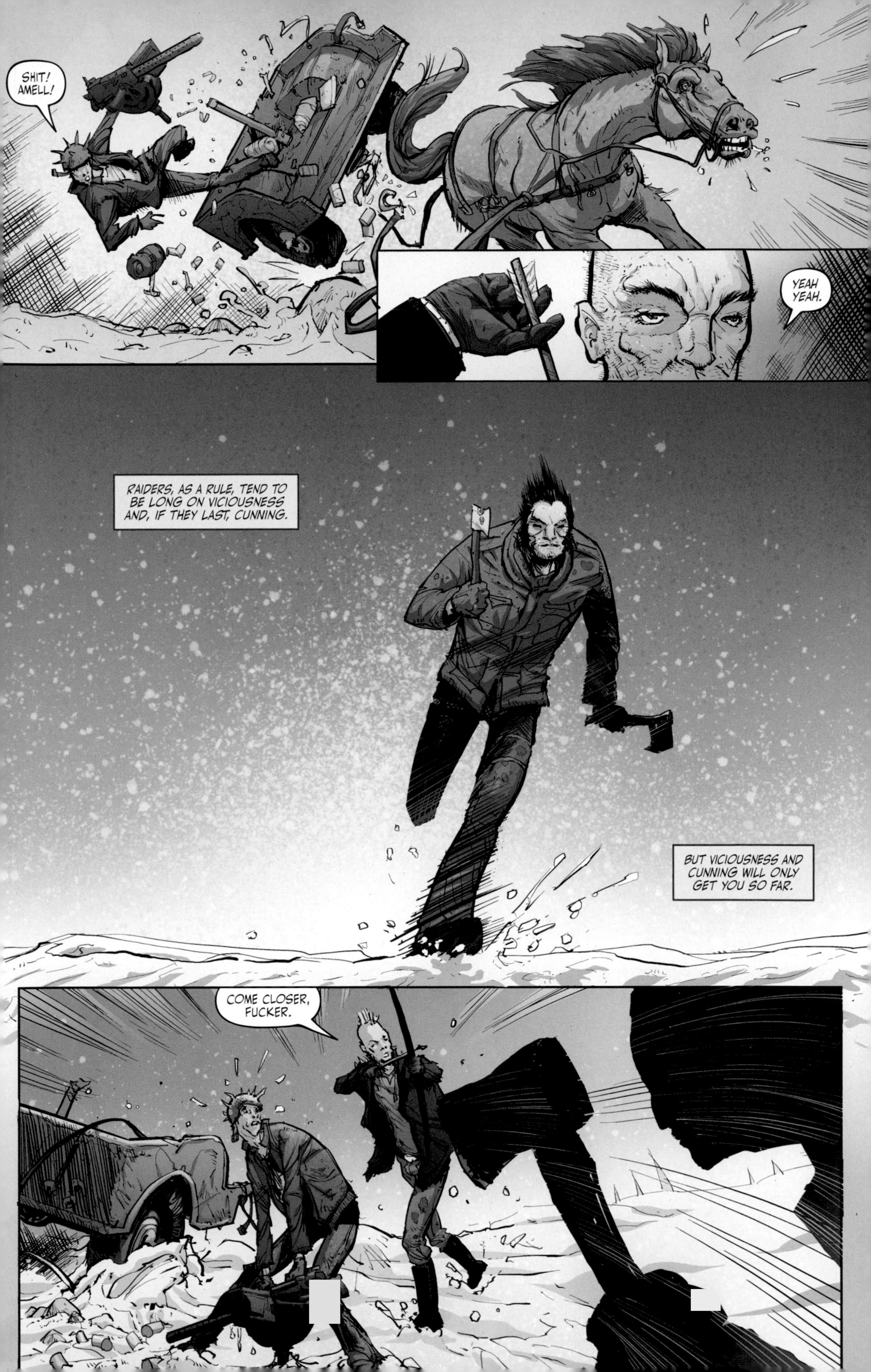
SHIT! AMELL!
YEAH YEAH.
RAIDERS, AS A RULE, TEND TO BE LONG ON VICIOUSNESS AND, IF THEY LAST, CUNNING.
BUT VICIOUSNESS AND CUNNING WILL ONLY GET YOU SO FAR.
COME CLOSER, FUCKER.

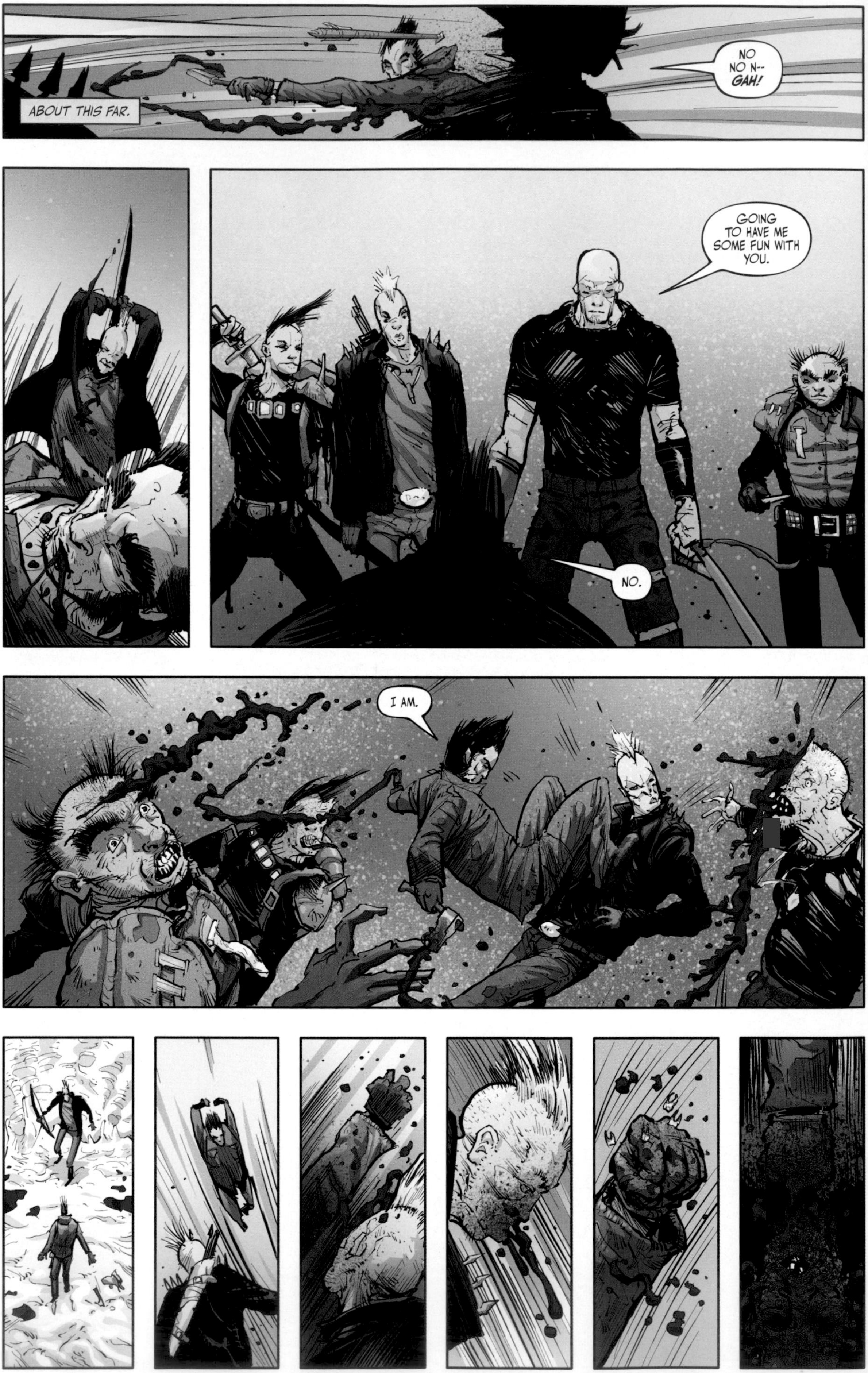
ABOUT THIS FAR.
NO NO N-- GAH!
GOING TO HAVE ME SOME FUN WITH YOU.
NO.
I AM.

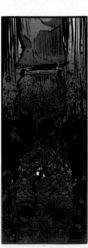

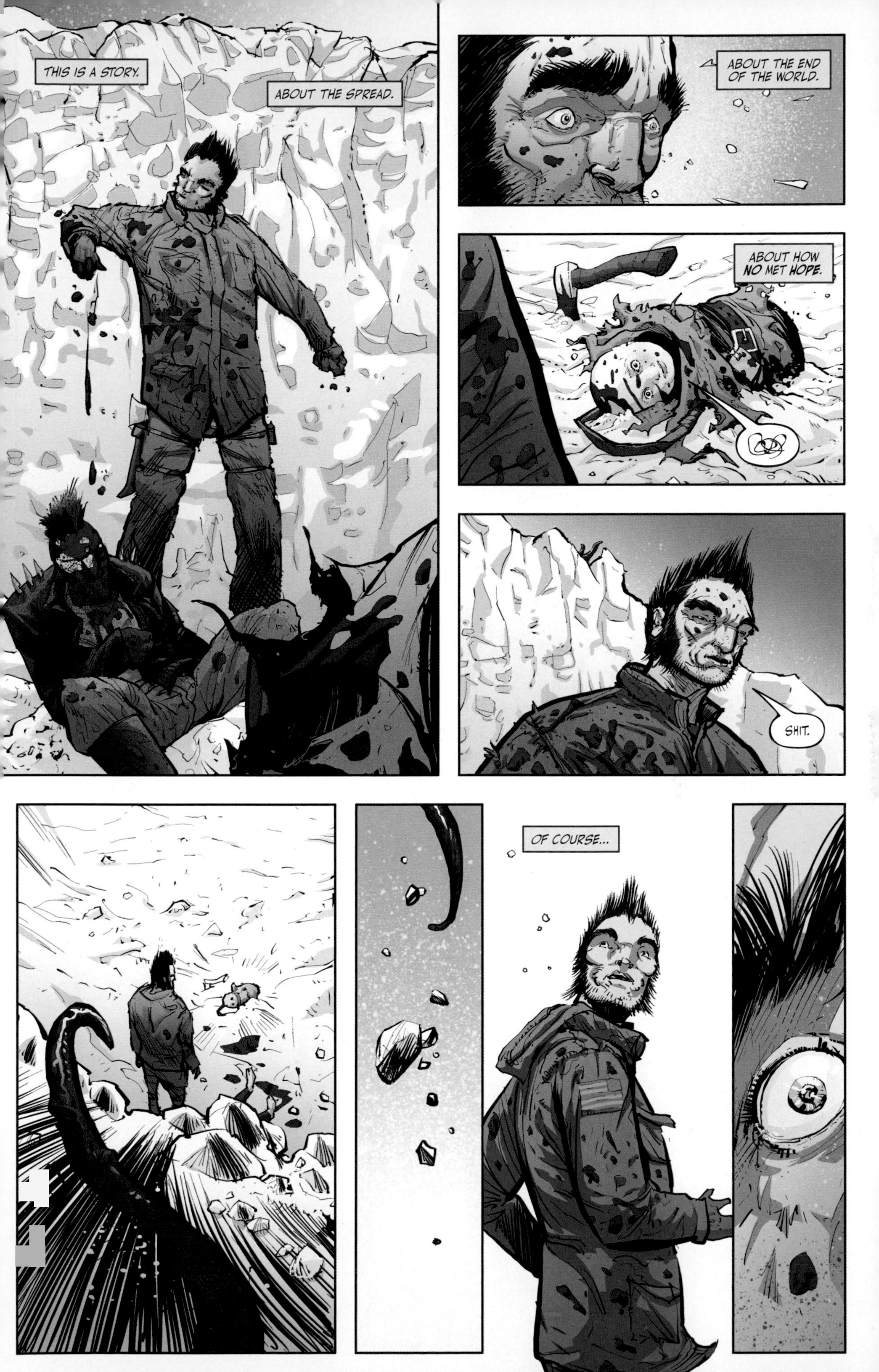
THIS IS A STORY.
ABOUT THE SPREAD.
ABOUT THE END OF THE WORLD.
ABOUT HOW NO MET HOPE.
SHIT.
OF COURSE...

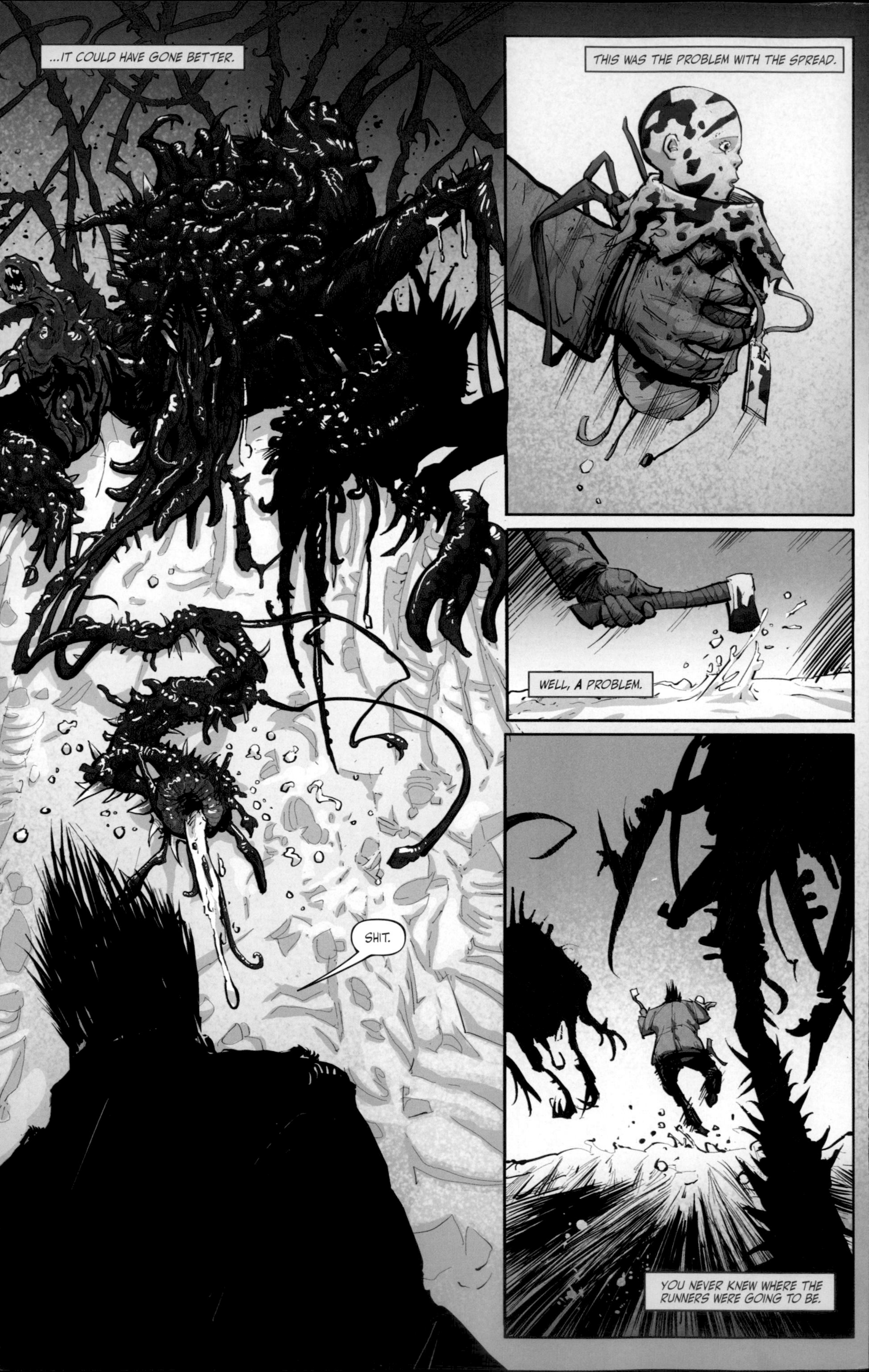
...IT COULD HAVE GONE BETTER.
SHIT.
THIS WAS THE PROBLEM WITH THE SPREAD.
WELL, A PROBLEM.
YOU NEVER KNEW WHERE THE RUNNERS WERE GOING TO BE.

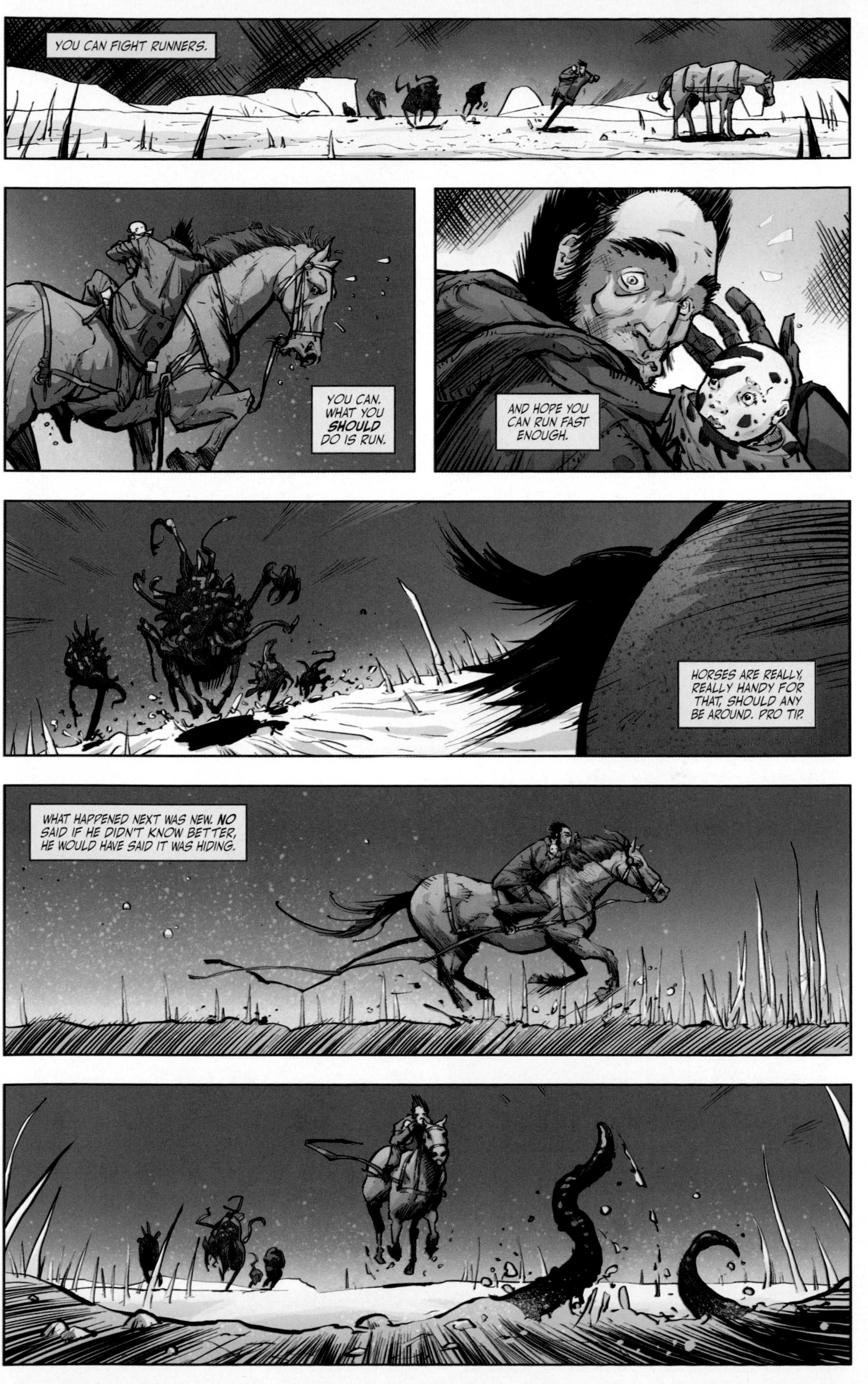
YOU CAN FIGHT RUNNERS.
YOU CAN. WHAT YOU SHOULD DO IS RUN.
AND HOPE YOU CAN RUN FAST ENOUGH.
HORSES ARE REALLY, REALLY HANDY FOR THAT, SHOULD ANY BE AROUND. PRO TIP.
WHAT HAPPENED NEXT WAS NEW. NO SAID IF HE DIDN'T KNOW BETTER, HE WOULD HAVE SAID IT WAS HIDING.

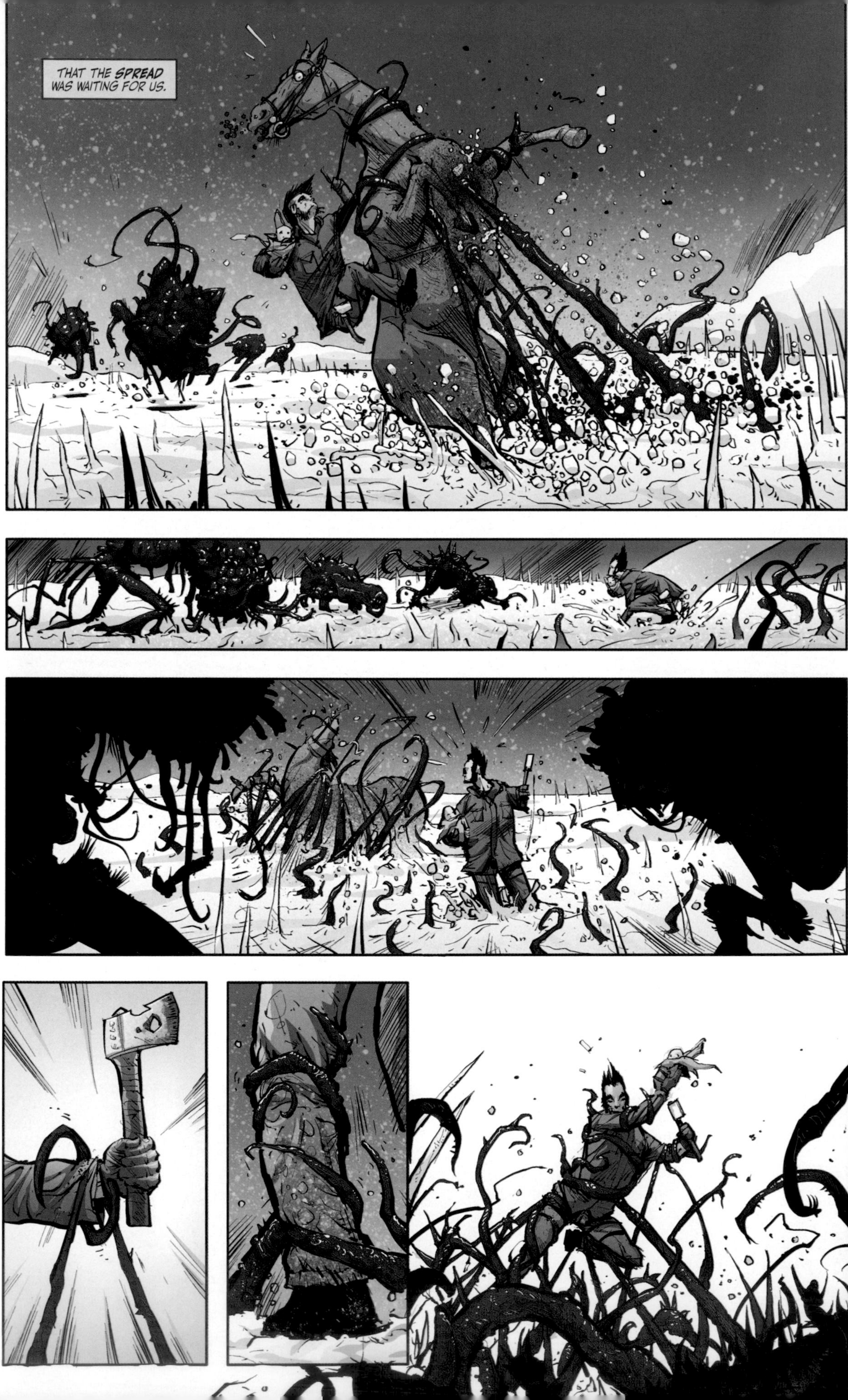
THAT THE SPREAD WAS WAITING FOR US.

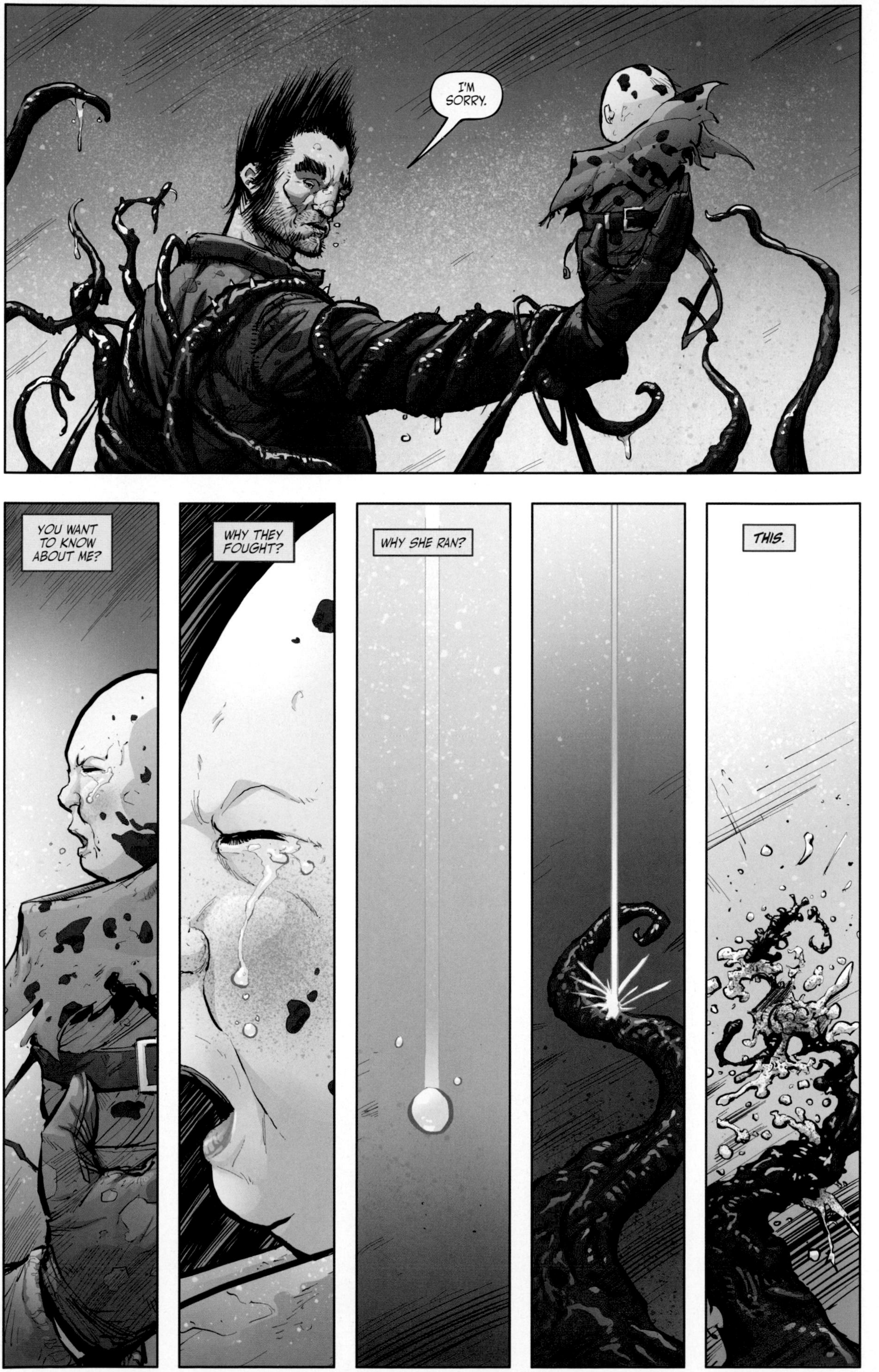
I'M SORRY.
YOU WANT TO KNOW ABOUT ME?
WHY THEY FOUGHT?
WHY SHE RAN?
THIS.

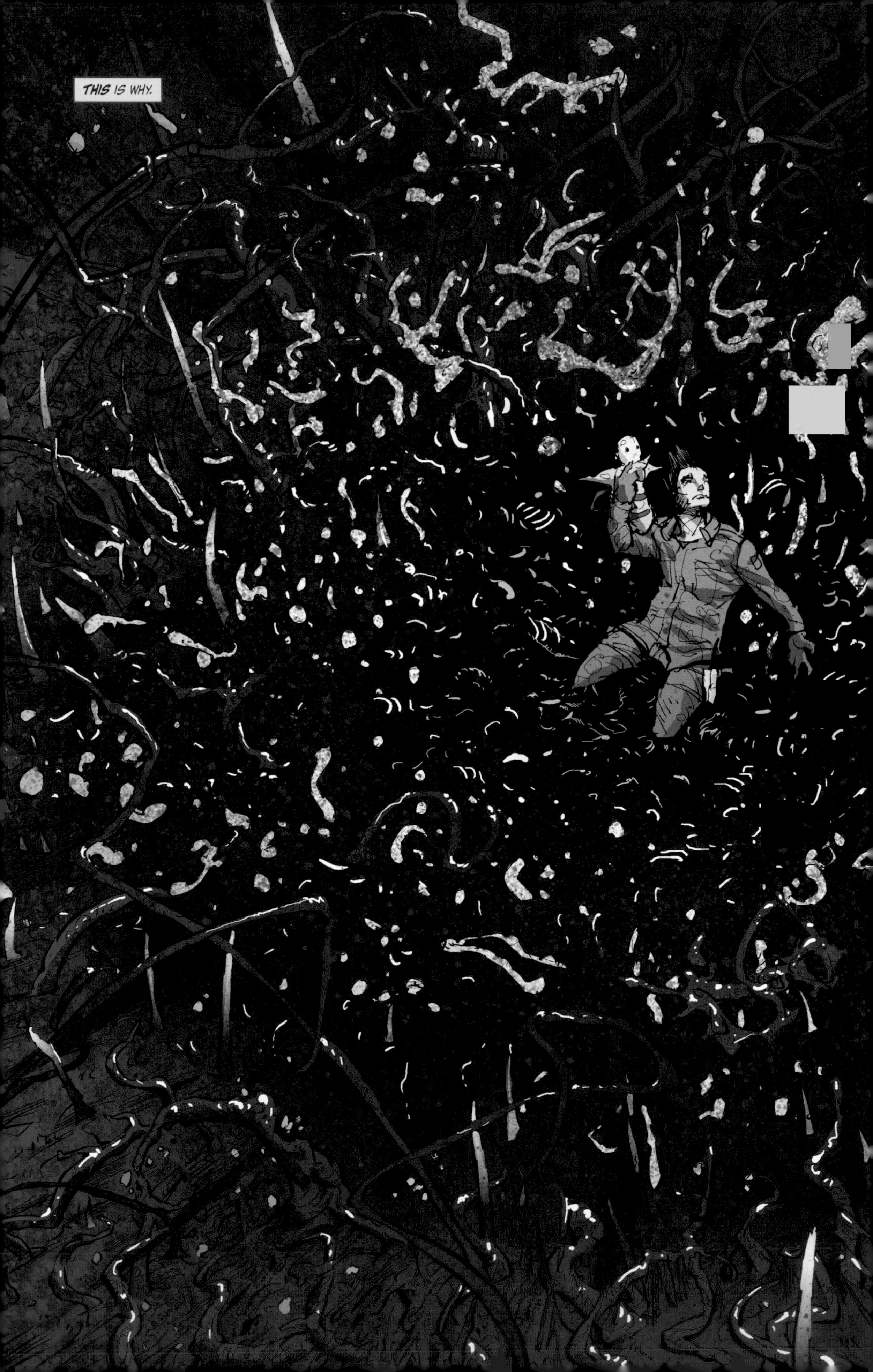
THIS IS WHY.

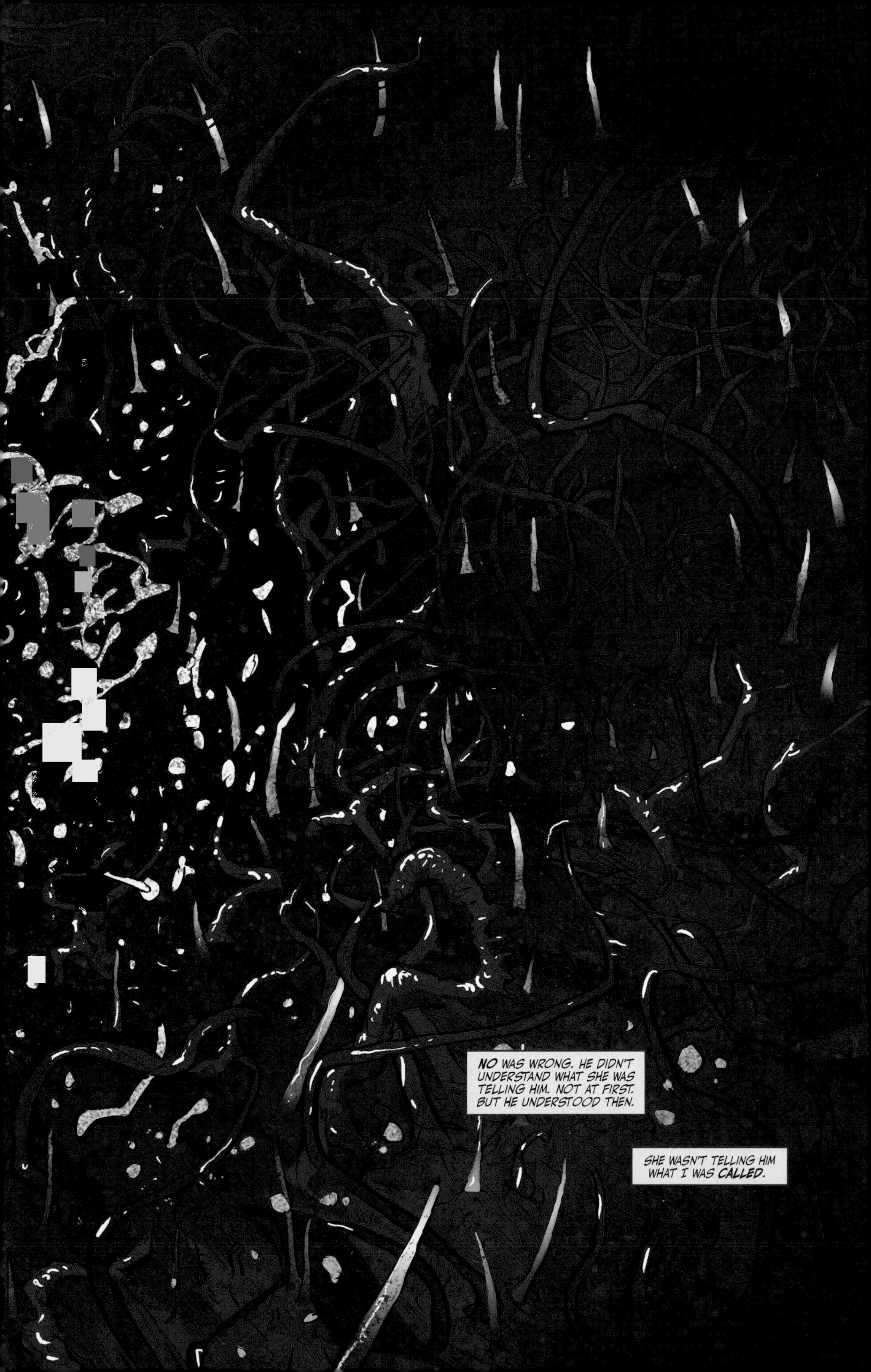
NO WAS WRONG. HE DIDN'T UNDERSTAND WHAT SHE WAS TELLING HIM. NOT AT FIRST. BUT HE UNDERSTOOD THEN.
SHE WASN'T TELLING HIM WHAT I WAS CALLED.

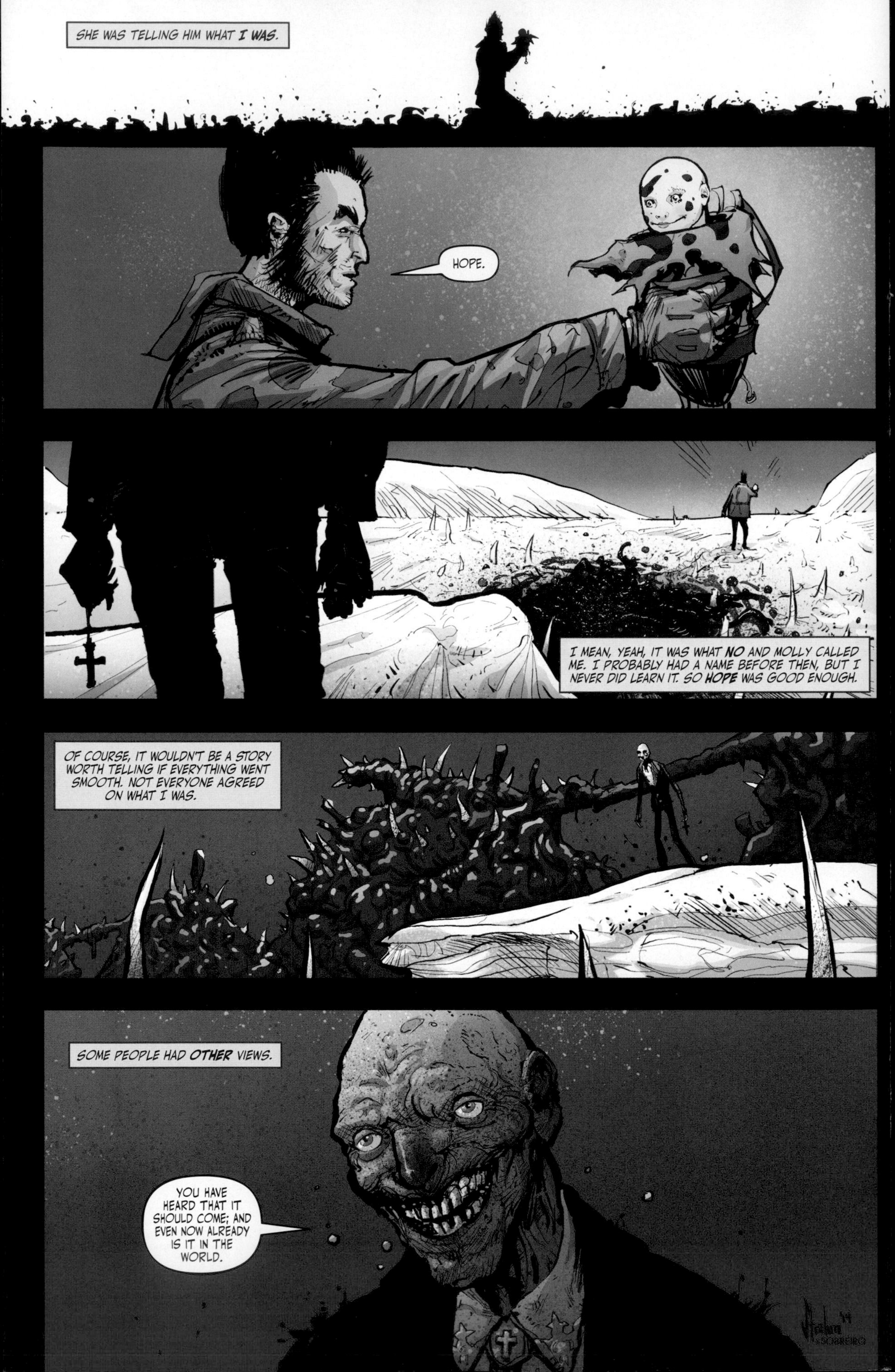
SHE WAS TELLING HIM WHAT I WAS.
HOPE.
I MEAN, YEAH, IT WAS WHAT NO AND MOLLY CALLED ME. I PROBABLY HAD A NAME BEFORE THEN, BUT I NEVER DID LEARN IT. SO HOPE WAS GOOD ENOUGH.
OF COURSE, IT WOULDN'T BE A STORY WORTH TELLING IF EVERYTHING WENT SMOOTH. NOT EVERYONE AGREED ON WHAT I WAS.
SOME PEOPLE HAD OTHER VIEWS.
YOU HAVE HEARD THAT IT SHOULD COME; AND EVEN NOW ALREADY IS IT IN THE WORLD.

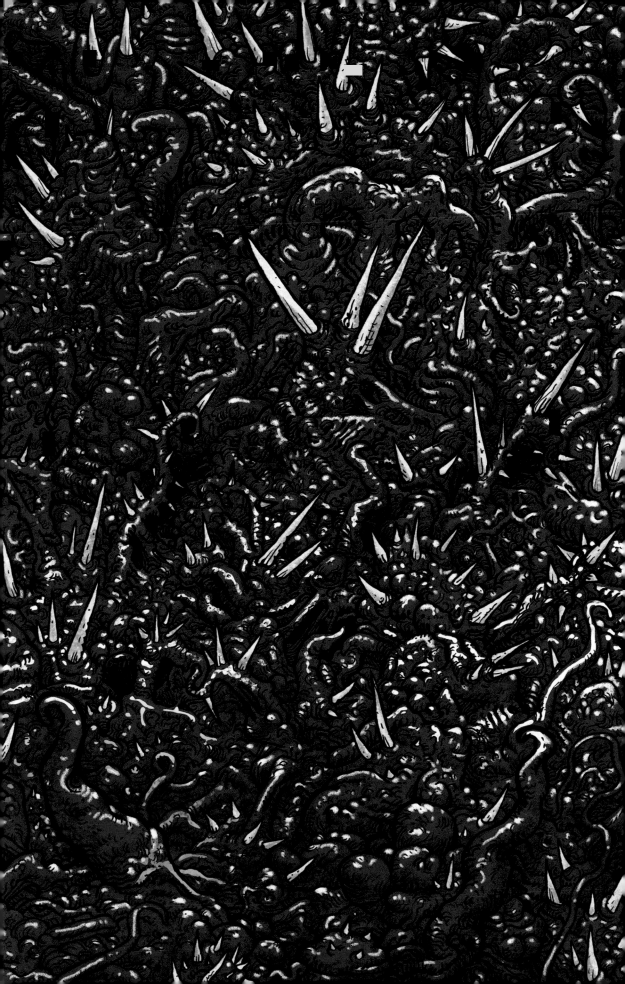

CHAPTER TWO

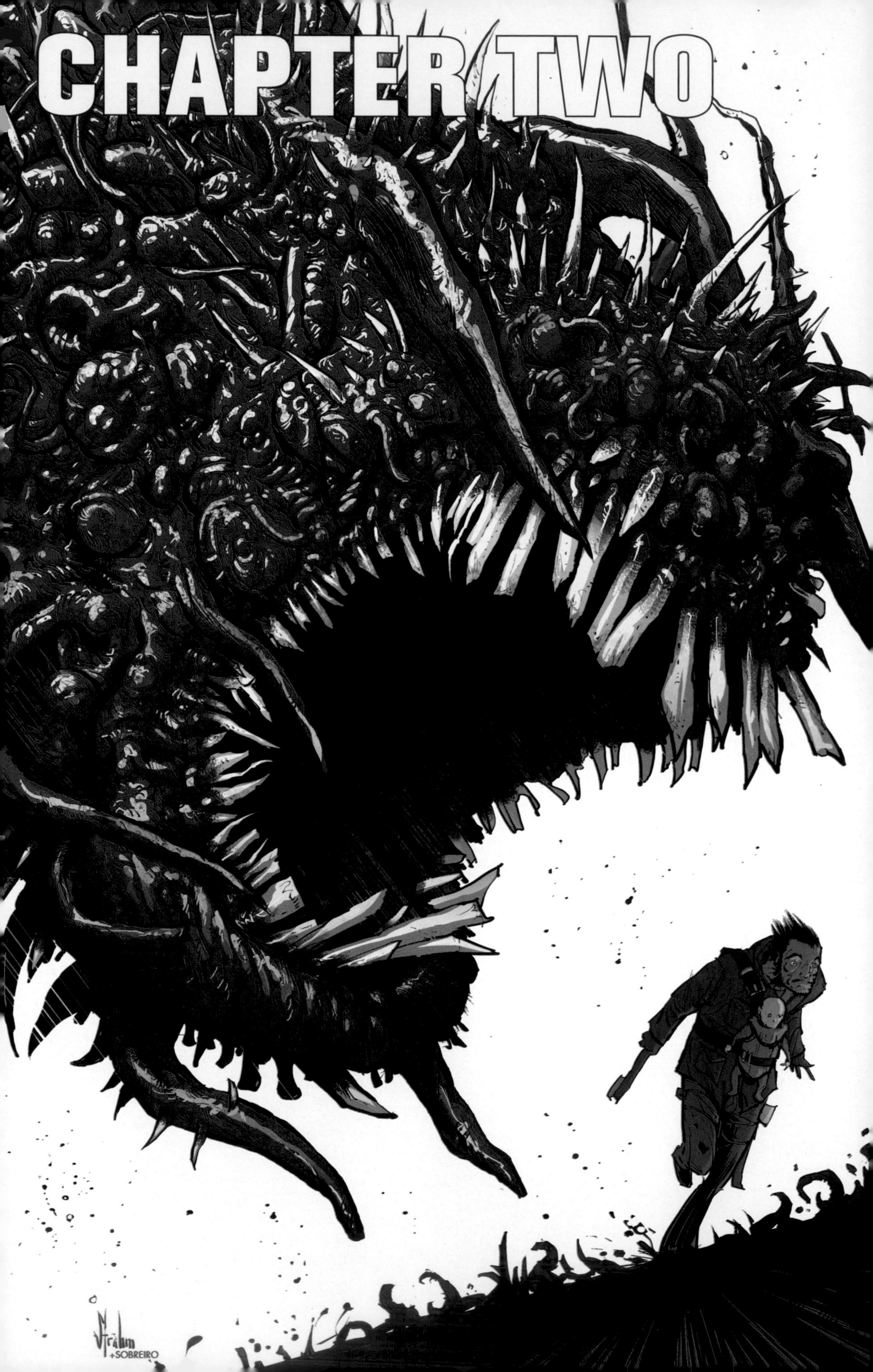
+SOBREIRO

YOU MIGHT BE THINKING THAT OUR LITTLE CHUNK OF THE WORLD WAS PRETTY MUCH A HOLE.

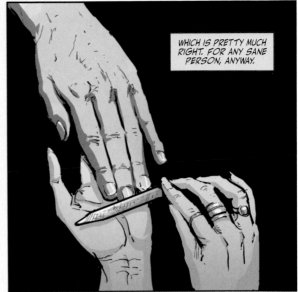

WHICH IS PRETTY MUCH RIGHT. FOR ANY SANE PERSON, ANYWAY.

BUT SOME PEOPLE CAN FIND HEAVEN IN MOST PEOPLE'S HELL.

IF YOU'RE THE RIGHT SORT OF PERSON...

...LIFE IS BEAUTIFUL.

WELL AREN'T I JUST SO GODDAMN PRETTY.

LET'S GET THIS SHOW ON THE ROAD.

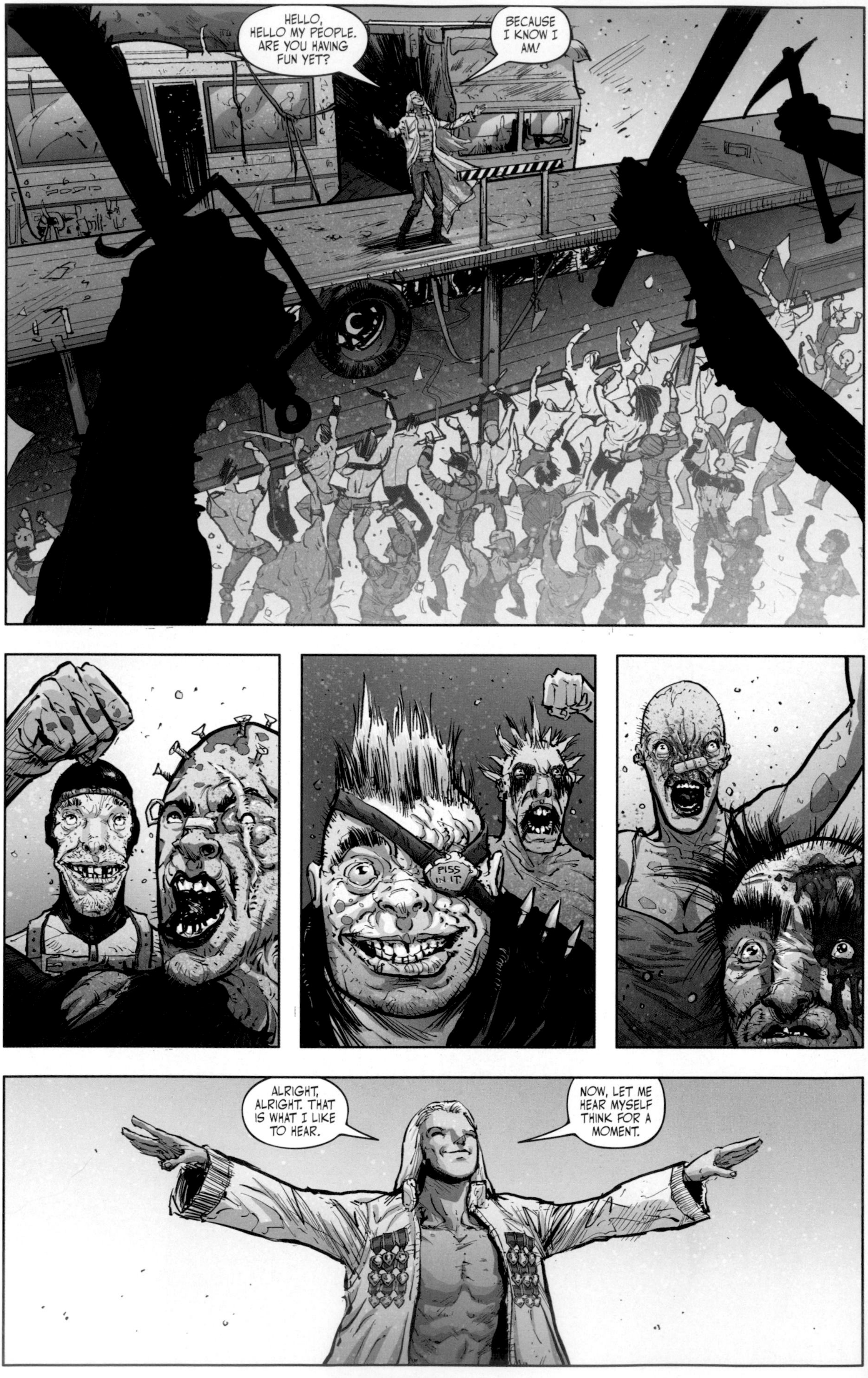
HELLO, HELLO MY PEOPLE. ARE YOU HAVING FUN YET?
BECAUSE I KNOW I AM!
PISS IN IT.
ALRIGHT, ALRIGHT. THAT IS WHAT I LIKE TO HEAR.
NOW, LET ME HEAR MYSELF THINK FOR A MOMENT.

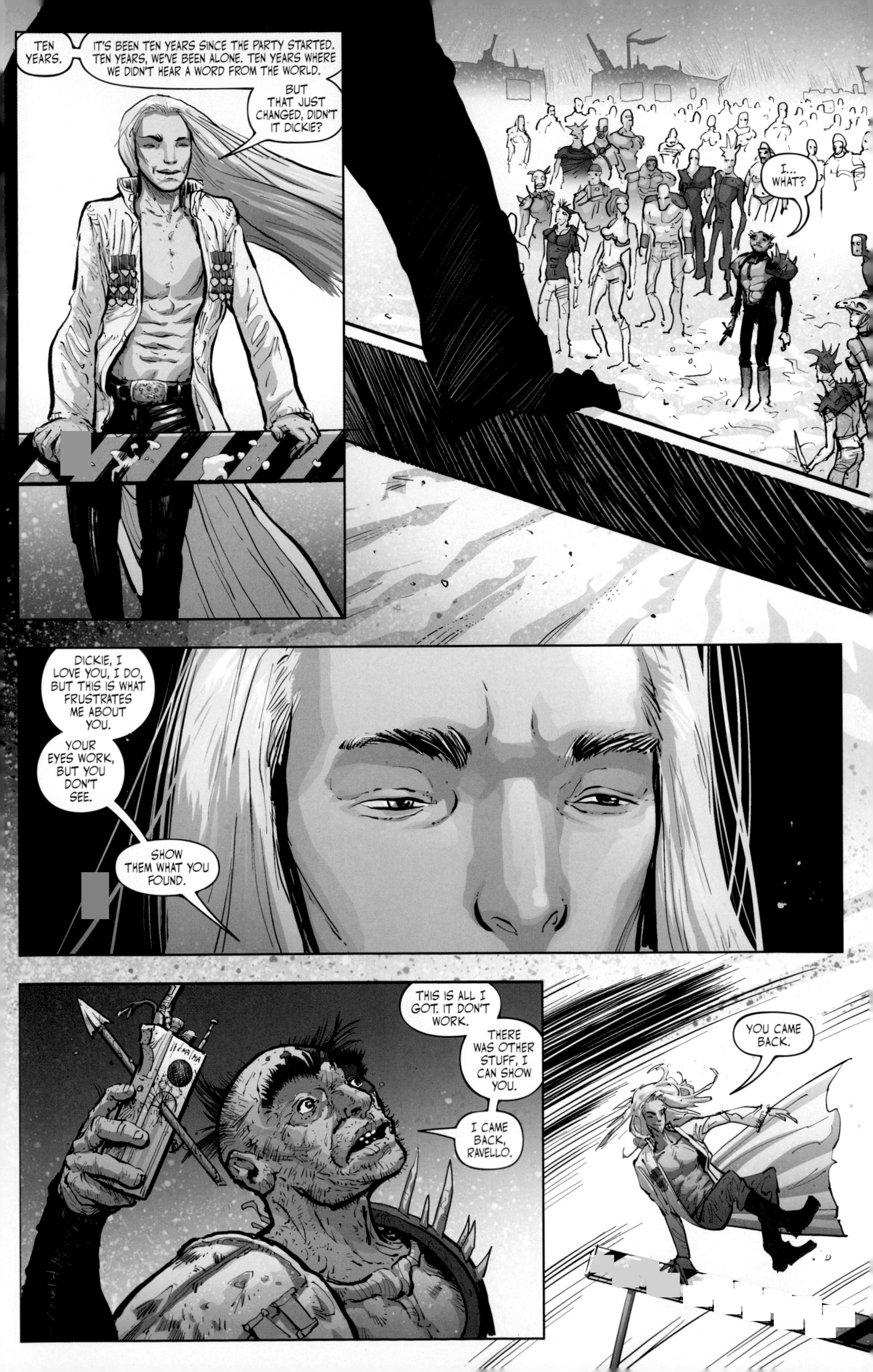
TEN YEARS.
IT'S BEEN TEN YEARS SINCE THE PARTY STARTED. TEN YEARS, WE'VE BEEN ALONE. TEN YEARS WHERE WE DIDN'T HEAR A WORD FROM THE WORLD.
BUT THAT JUST CHANGED, DIDN'T IT DICKIE?
I... WHAT?
DICKIE, I LOVE YOU, I DO, BUT THIS IS WHAT FRUSTRATES ME ABOUT YOU.
YOUR EYES WORK, BUT YOU DON'T SEE.
SHOW THEM WHAT YOU FOUND.
THIS IS ALL I GOT. IT DON'T WORK.
THERE WAS OTHER STUFF, I CAN SHOW YOU.
I CAME BACK, RAVELLO.
YOU CAME BACK.

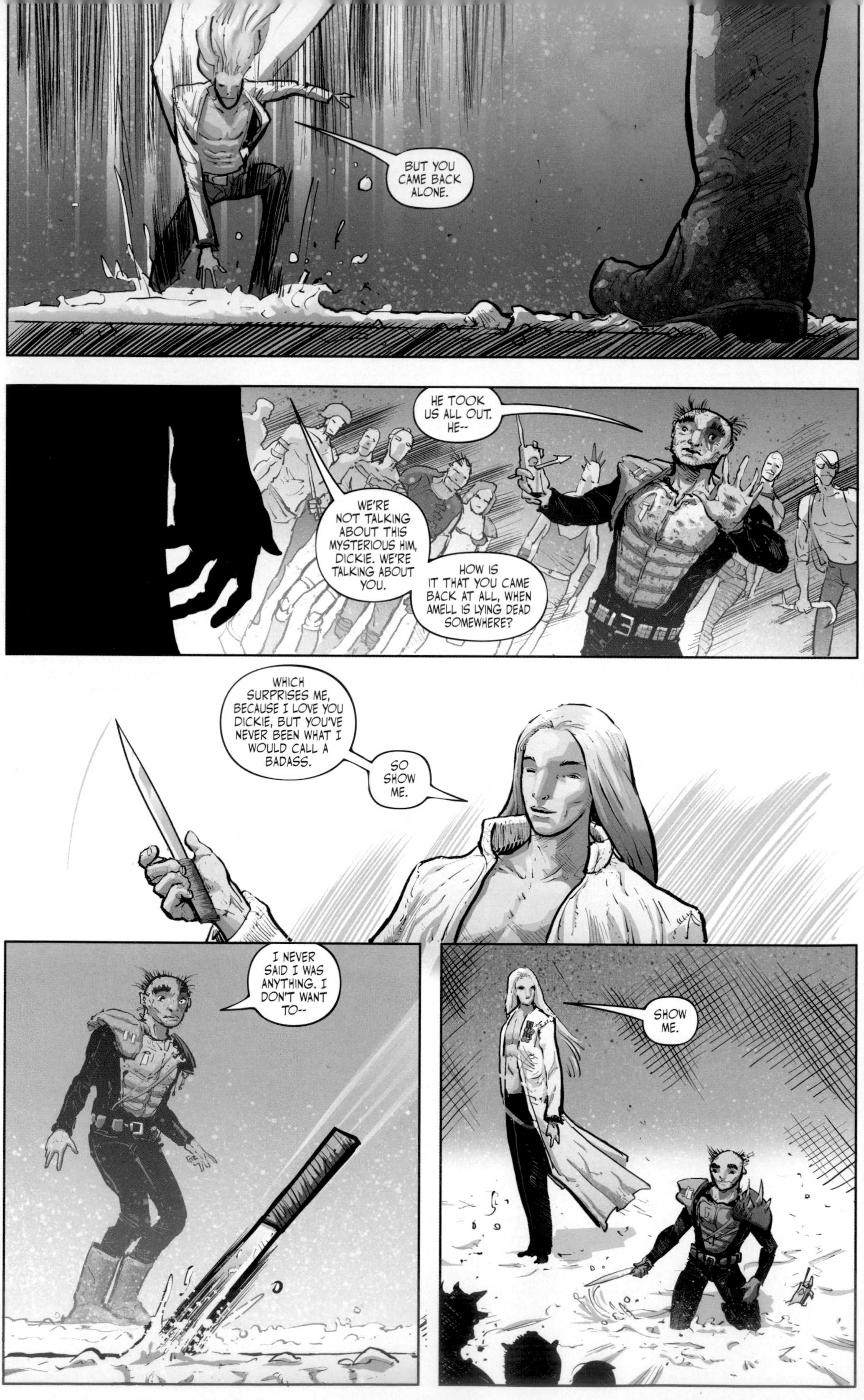
BUT YOU CAME BACK ALONE.
HE TOOK US ALL OUT. HE--
WE'RE NOT TALKING ABOUT THIS MYSTERIOUS HIM, DICKIE. WE'RE TALKING ABOUT YOU.
HOW IS IT THAT YOU CAME BACK AT ALL, WHEN AMELL IS LYING DEAD SOMEWHERE?
WHICH SURPRISES ME, BECAUSE I LOVE YOU DICKIE, BUT YOU'VE NEVER BEEN WHAT I WOULD CALL A BADASS.
SO SHOW ME.
I NEVER SAID I WAS ANYTHING. I DON'T WANT TO--
SHOW ME.

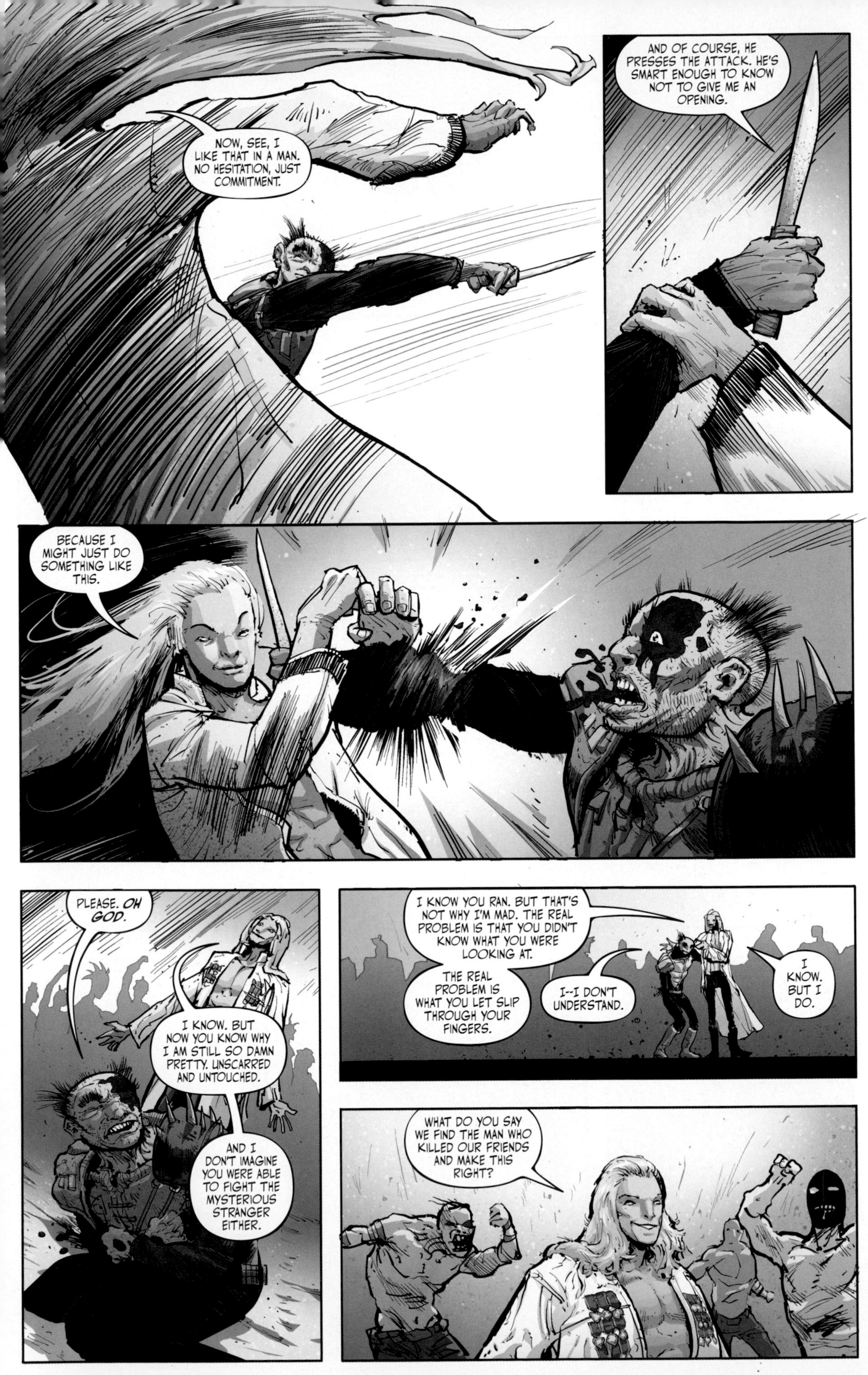

NOW, SEE, I LIKE THAT IN A MAN. NO HESITATION, JUST COMMITMENT.
AND OF COURSE, HE PRESSES THE ATTACK. HE'S SMART ENOUGH TO KNOW NOT TO GIVE ME AN OPENING.
BECAUSE I MIGHT JUST DO SOMETHING LIKE THIS.
PLEASE. OH GOD.
I KNOW. BUT NOW YOU KNOW WHY I AM STILL SO DAMN PRETTY. UNSCARRED AND UNTOUCHED.
AND I DON'T IMAGINE YOU WERE ABLE TO FIGHT THE MYSTERIOUS STRANGER EITHER.
I KNOW YOU RAN. BUT THAT'S NOT WHY I'M MAD. THE REAL PROBLEM IS THAT YOU DIDN'T KNOW WHAT YOU WERE LOOKING AT.
THE REAL PROBLEM IS WHAT YOU LET SLIP THROUGH YOUR FINGERS.
I--I DON'T UNDERSTAND.
I KNOW. BUT I DO.
WHAT DO YOU SAY WE FIND THE MAN WHO KILLED OUR FRIENDS AND MAKE THIS RIGHT?

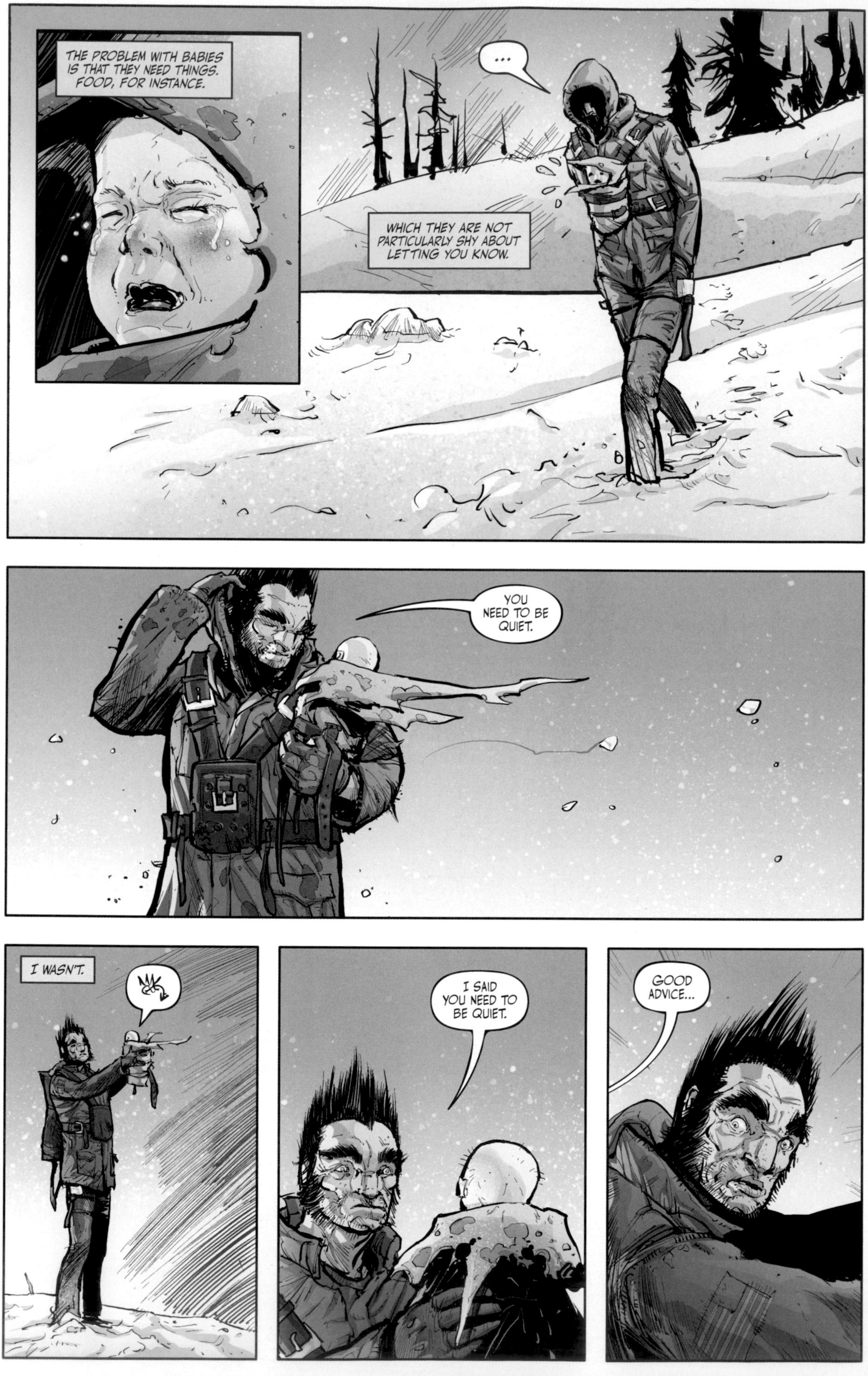
THE PROBLEM WITH BABIES IS THAT THEY NEED THINGS. FOOD, FOR INSTANCE.
...
WHICH THEY ARE NOT PARTICULARLY SHY ABOUT LETTING YOU KNOW.
YOU NEED TO BE QUIET.
I WASN'T.
I SAID YOU NEED TO BE QUIET.
GOOD ADVICE...

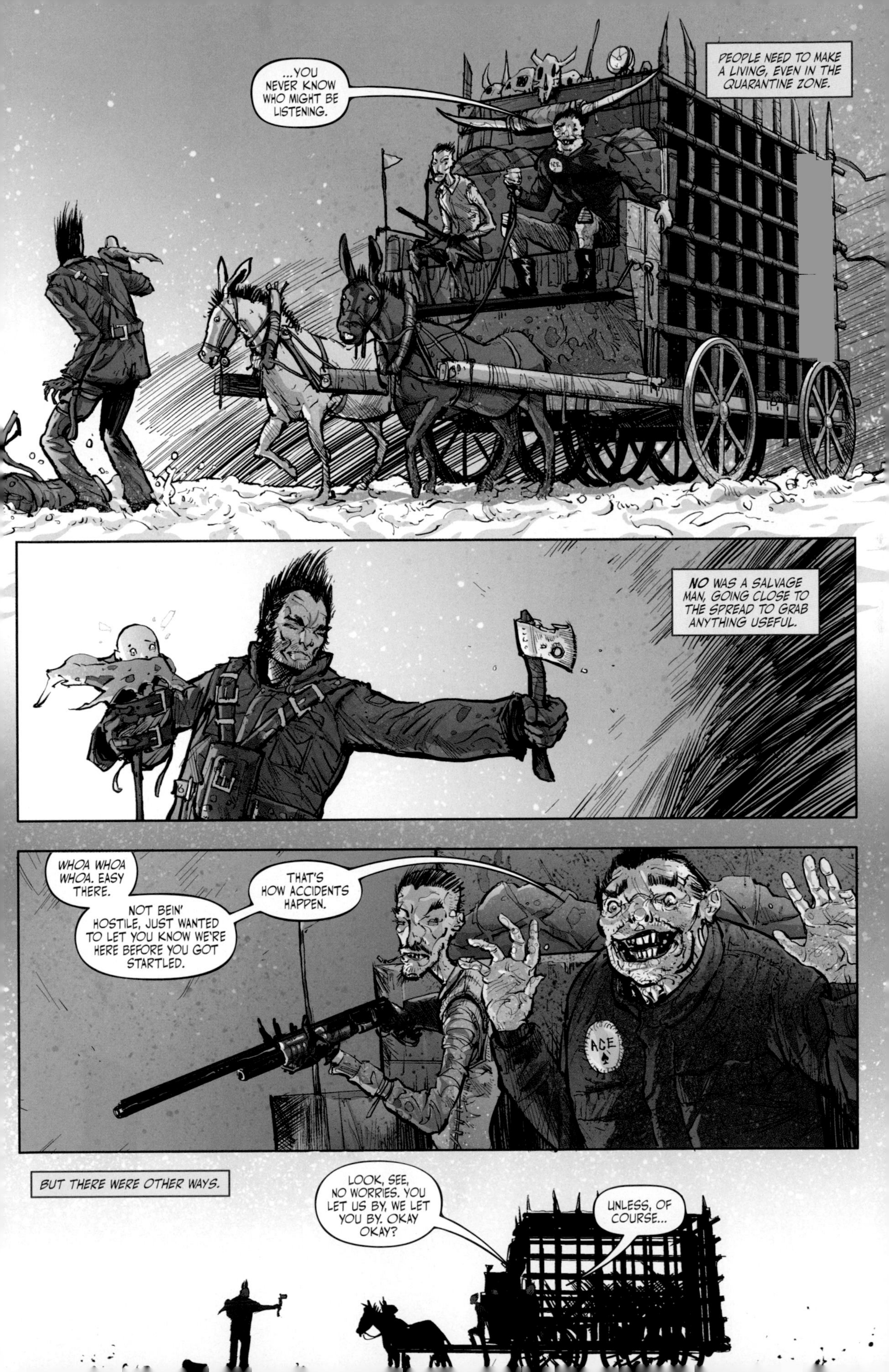
PEOPLE NEED TO MAKE A LIVING, EVEN IN THE QUARANTINE ZONE.
...YOU NEVER KNOW WHO MIGHT BE LISTENING.
NO WAS A SALVAGE MAN, GOING CLOSE TO THE SPREAD TO GRAB ANYTHING USEFUL.
WHOA WHOA WHOA. EASY THERE.
NOT BEIN' HOSTILE, JUST WANTED TO LET YOU KNOW WE'RE HERE BEFORE YOU GOT STARTLED.
THAT'S HOW ACCIDENTS HAPPEN.
ACE
BUT THERE WERE OTHER WAYS.
LOOK, SEE, NO WORRIES. YOU LET US BY, WE LET YOU BY. OKAY OKAY?
UNLESS, OF COURSE...

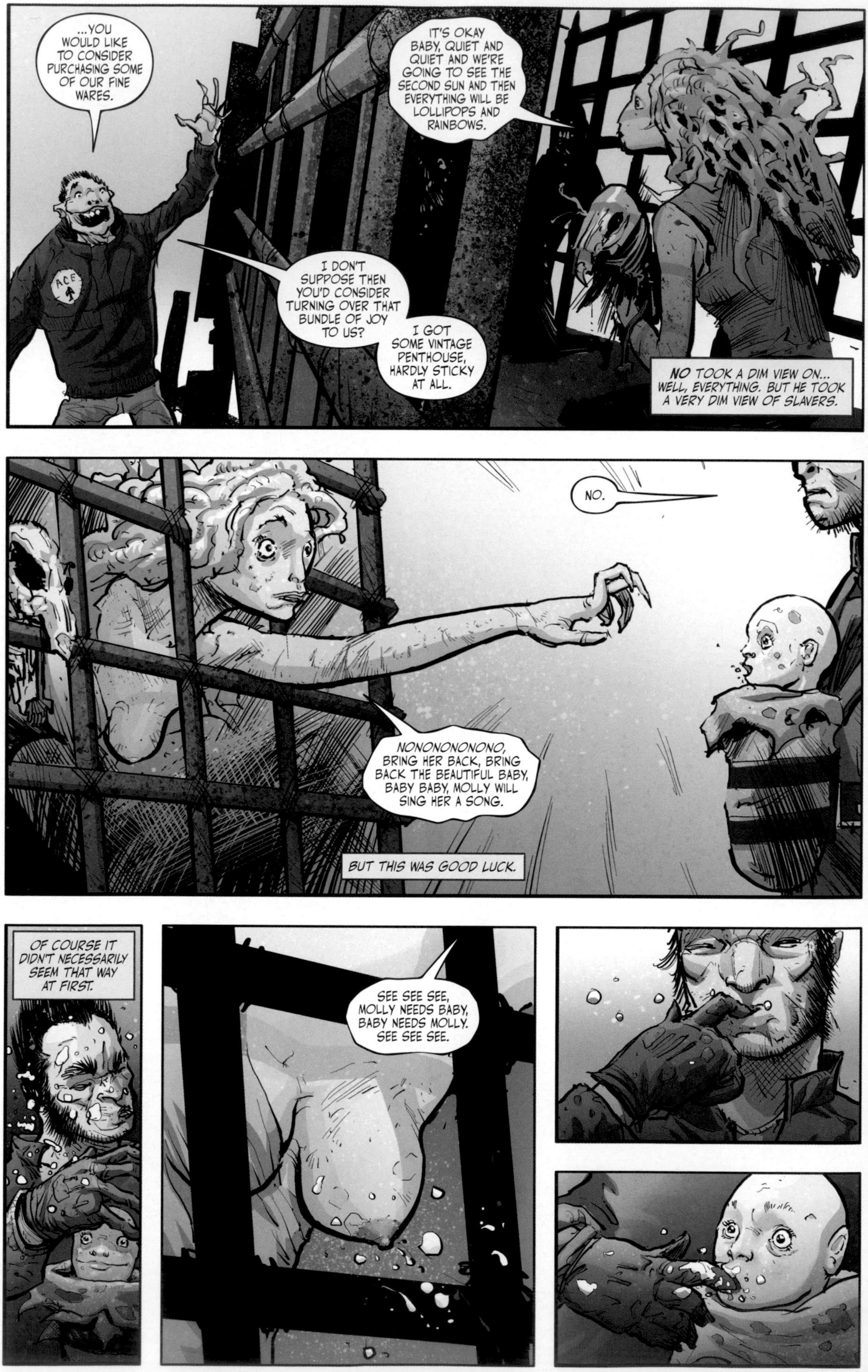
...YOU WOULD LIKE TO CONSIDER PURCHASING SOME OF OUR FINE WARES.
IT'S OKAY BABY, QUIET AND QUIET AND WE'RE GOING TO SEE THE SECOND SUN AND THEN EVERYTHING WILL BE LOLLIPOPS AND RAINBOWS.
ACE
I DON'T SUPPOSE THEN YOU'D CONSIDER TURNING OVER THAT BUNDLE OF JOY TO US?
I GOT SOME VINTAGE PENTHOUSE, HARDLY STICKY AT ALL.
NO TOOK A DIM VIEW ON... WELL, EVERYTHING. BUT HE TOOK A VERY DIM VIEW OF SLAVERS.
NO.
NONONONONONO, BRING HER BACK, BRING BACK THE BEAUTIFUL BABY, BABY BABY, MOLLY WILL SING HER A SONG.
BUT THIS WAS GOOD LUCK.
OF COURSE IT DIDN'T NECESSARILY SEEM THAT WAY AT FIRST.
SEE SEE SEE, MOLLY NEEDS BABY, BABY NEEDS MOLLY. SEE SEE SEE.

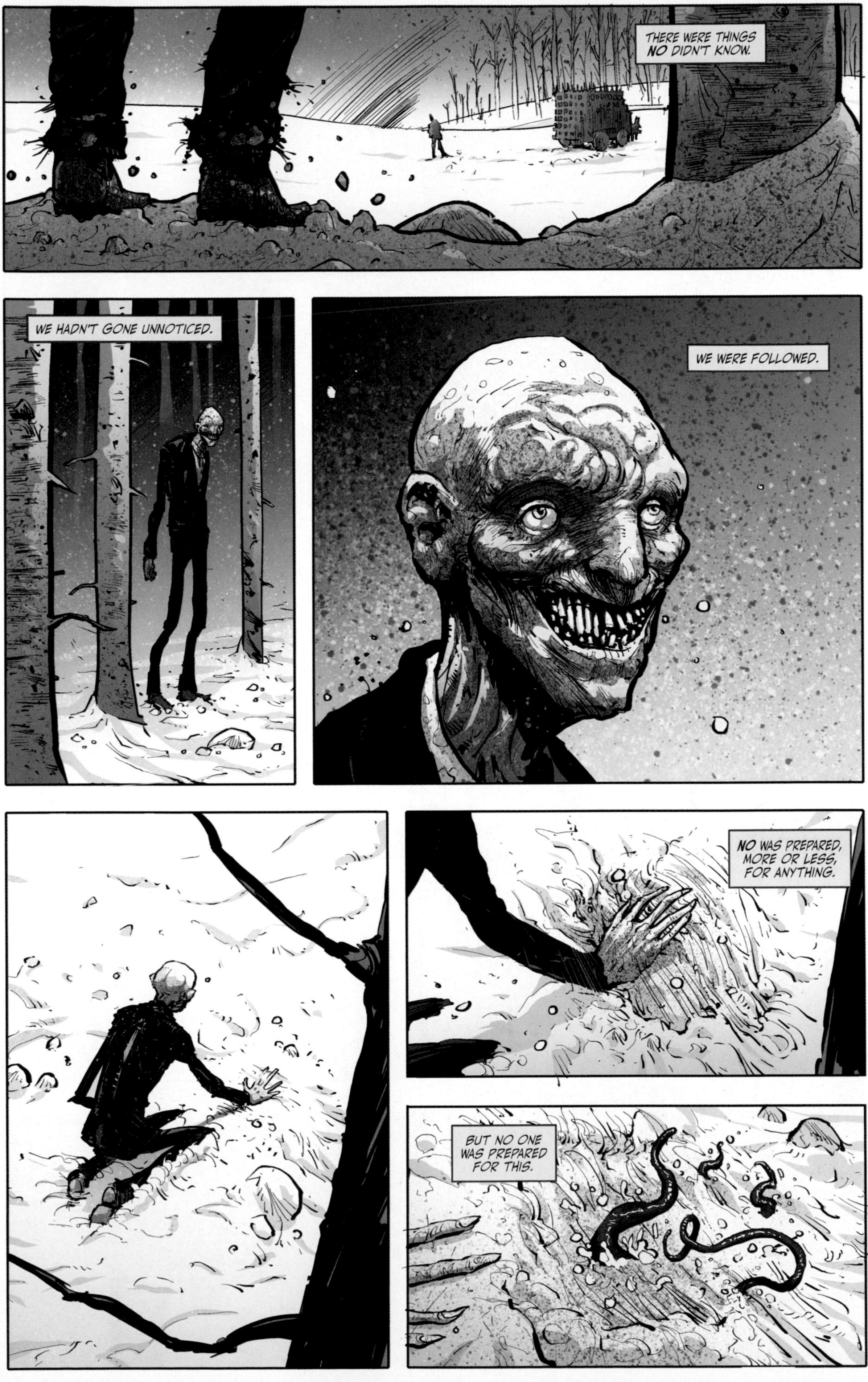
THERE WERE THINGS NO DIDN'T KNOW.
WE HADN'T GONE UNNOTICED.
WE WERE FOLLOWED.
NO WAS PREPARED, MORE OR LESS, FOR ANYTHING.
BUT NO ONE WAS PREPARED FOR THIS.

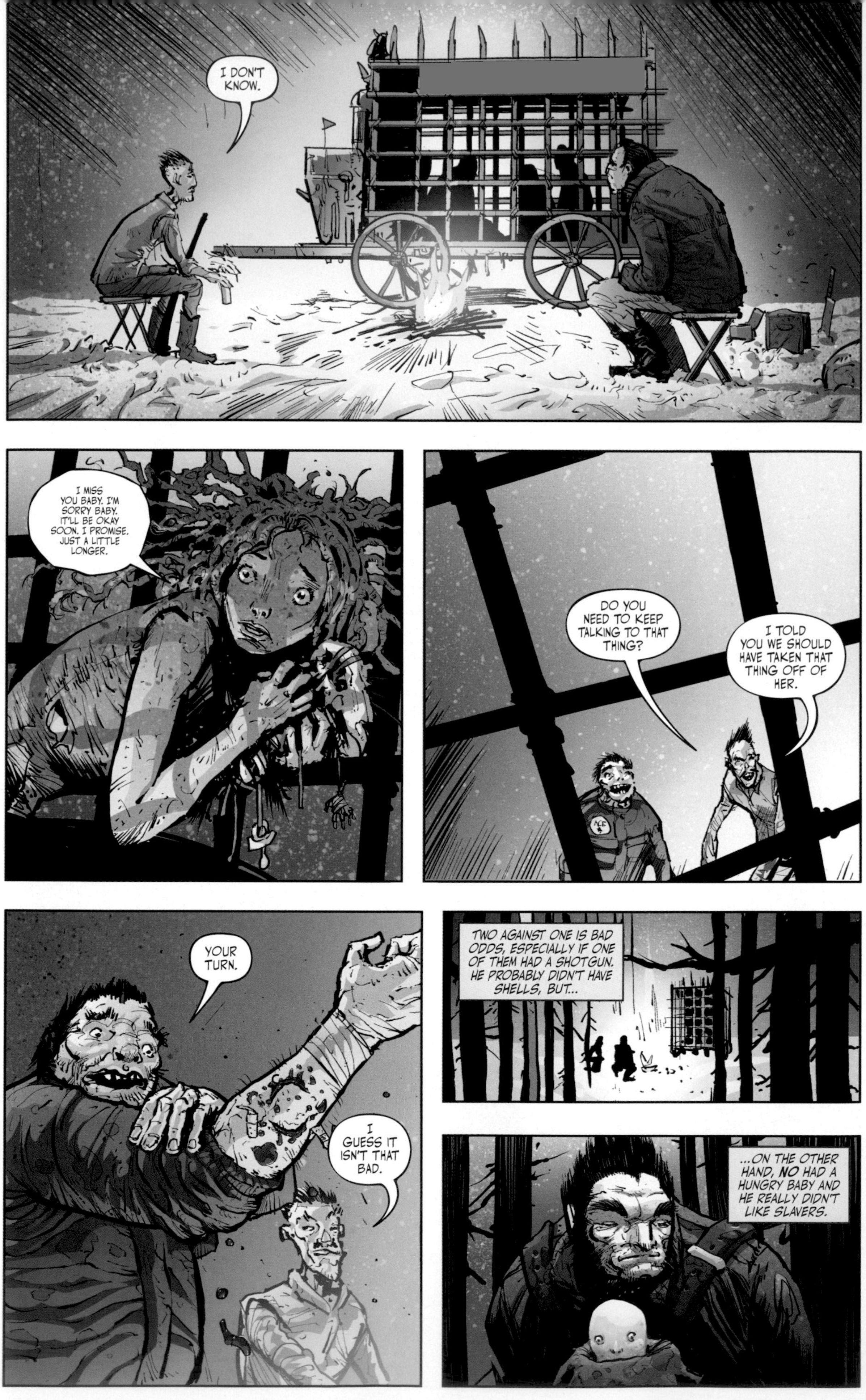
I DON'T KNOW.
I MISS YOU BABY. I'M SORRY BABY. IT'LL BE OKAY SOON. I PROMISE. JUST A LITTLE LONGER.
DO YOU NEED TO KEEP TALKING TO THAT THING?
I TOLD YOU WE SHOULD HAVE TAKEN THAT THING OFF OF HER.
YOUR TURN.
I GUESS IT ISN'T THAT BAD.
TWO AGAINST ONE IS BAD ODDS, ESPECIALLY IF ONE OF THEM HAD A SHOTGUN. HE PROBABLY DIDN'T HAVE SHELLS, BUT...
...ON THE OTHER HAND, NO HAD A HUNGRY BABY AND HE REALLY DIDN'T LIKE SLAVERS.

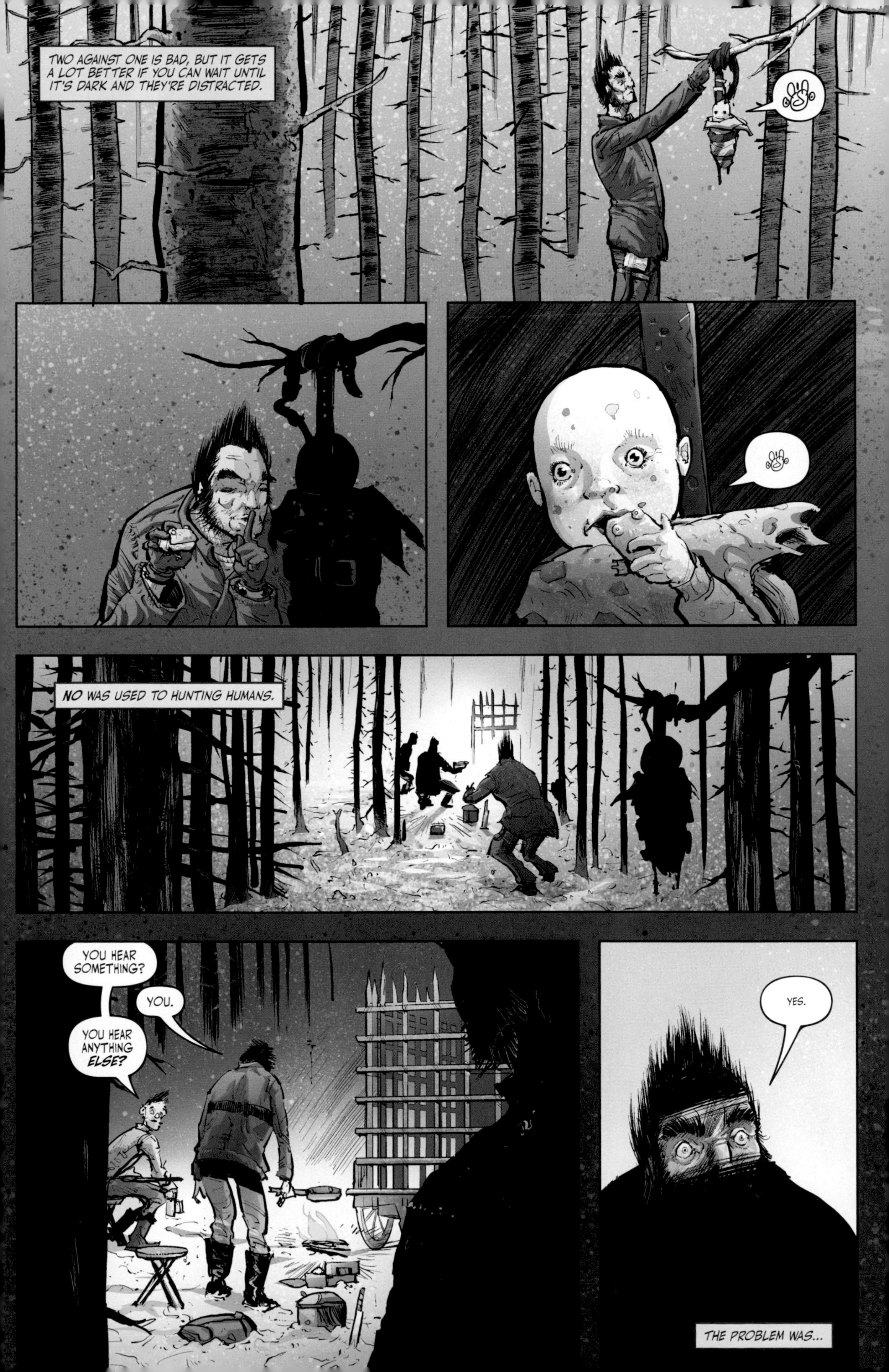
TWO AGAINST ONE IS BAD, BUT IT GETS A LOT BETTER IF YOU CAN WAIT UNTIL IT'S DARK AND THEY'RE DISTRACTED.
NO WAS USED TO HUNTING HUMANS.
YOU HEAR SOMETHING?
YOU.
YOU HEAR ANYTHING ELSE?
YES.
THE PROBLEM WAS...

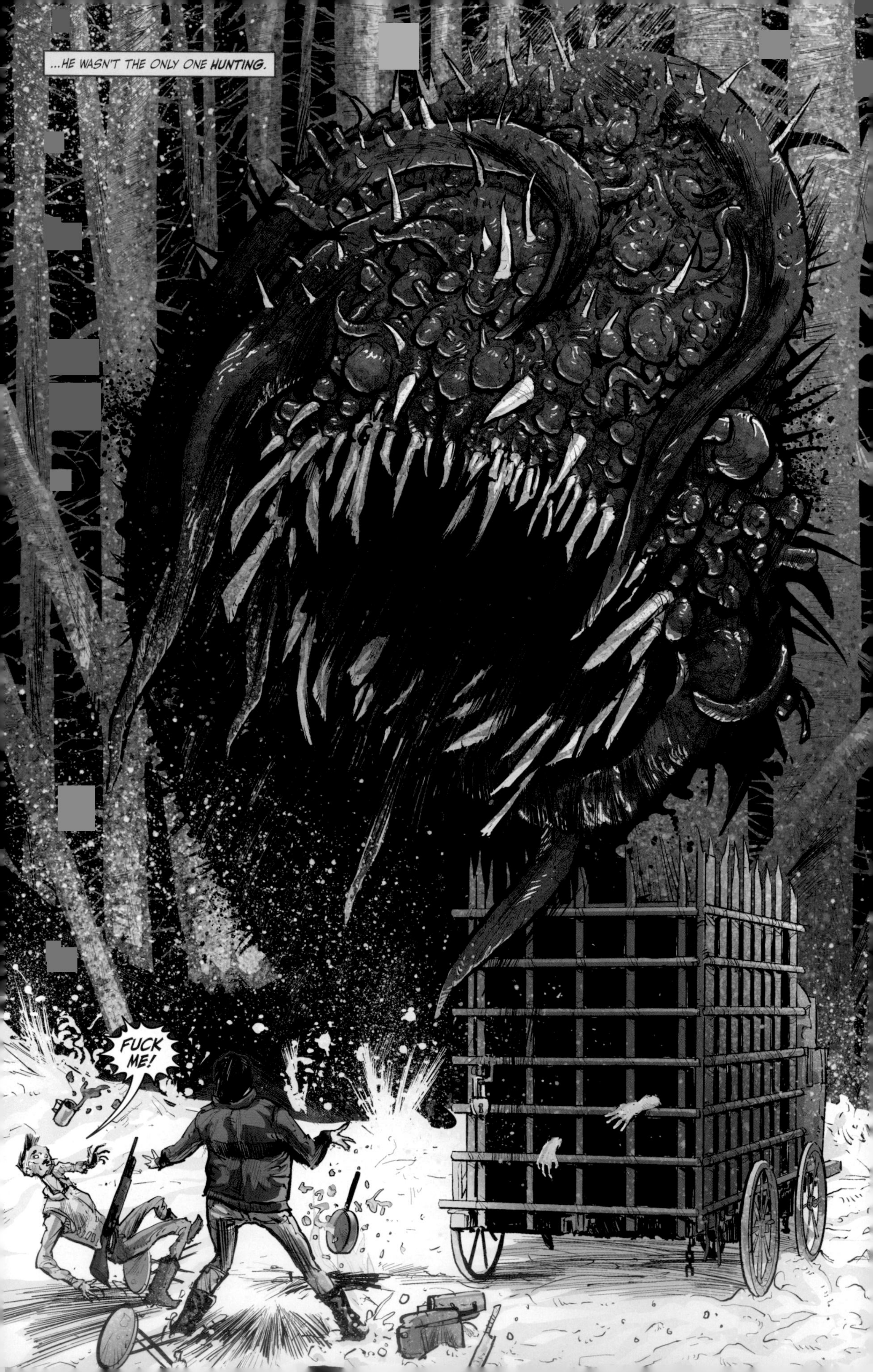
...HE WASN'T THE ONLY ONE HUNTING.
FUCK ME!

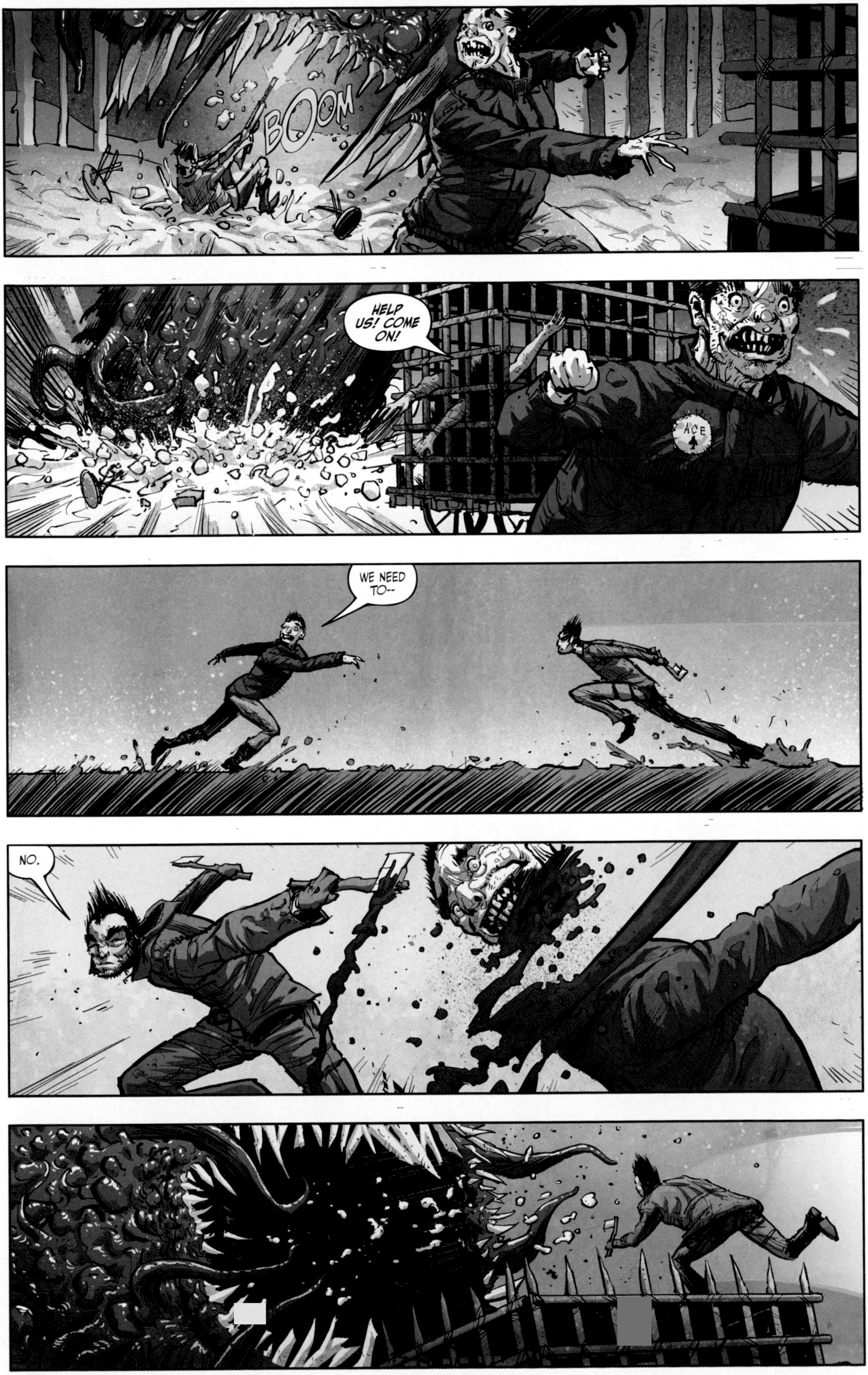
BOOM
HELP US! COME ON!
WE NEED TO--
NO.

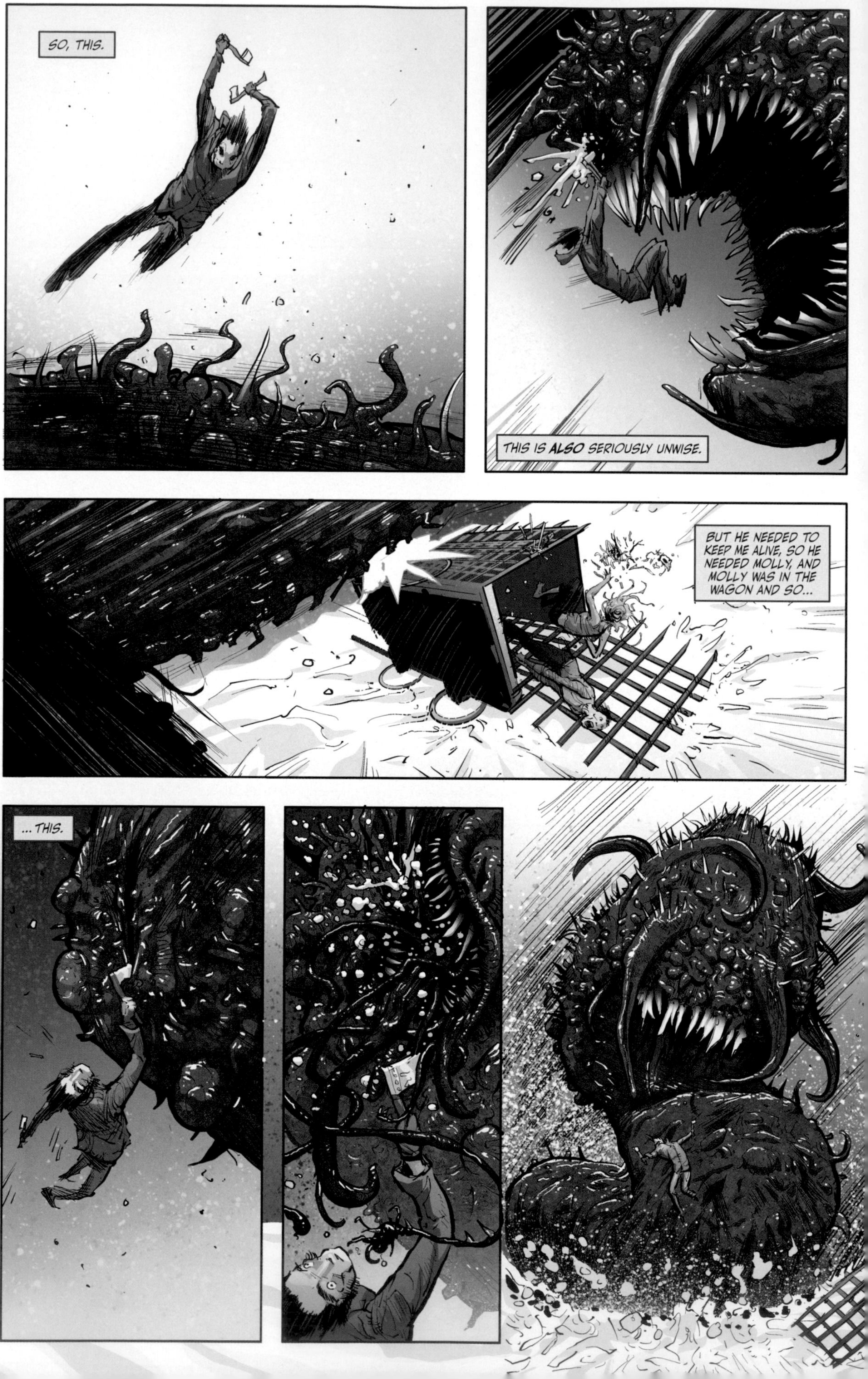
SO, THIS.
THIS IS ALSO SERIOUSLY UNWISE.
BUT HE NEEDED TO KEEP ME ALIVE, SO HE NEEDED MOLLY, AND MOLLY WAS IN THE WAGON AND SO...
...THIS.

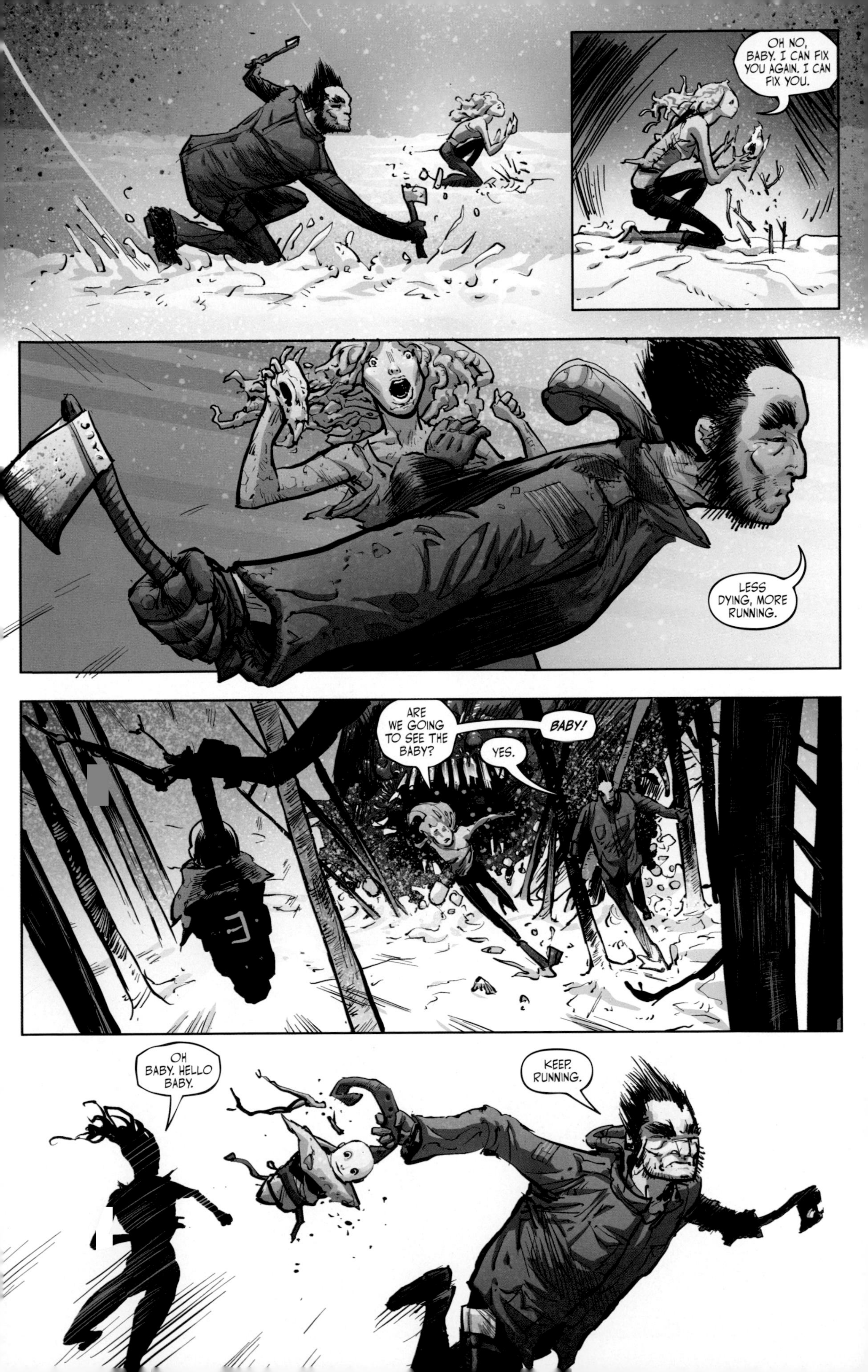
OH NO, BABY. I CAN FIX YOU AGAIN. I CAN FIX YOU.
LESS DYING, MORE RUNNING.
ARE WE GOING TO SEE THE BABY?
BABY!
YES.
OH BABY. HELLO BABY.
KEEP. RUNNING.

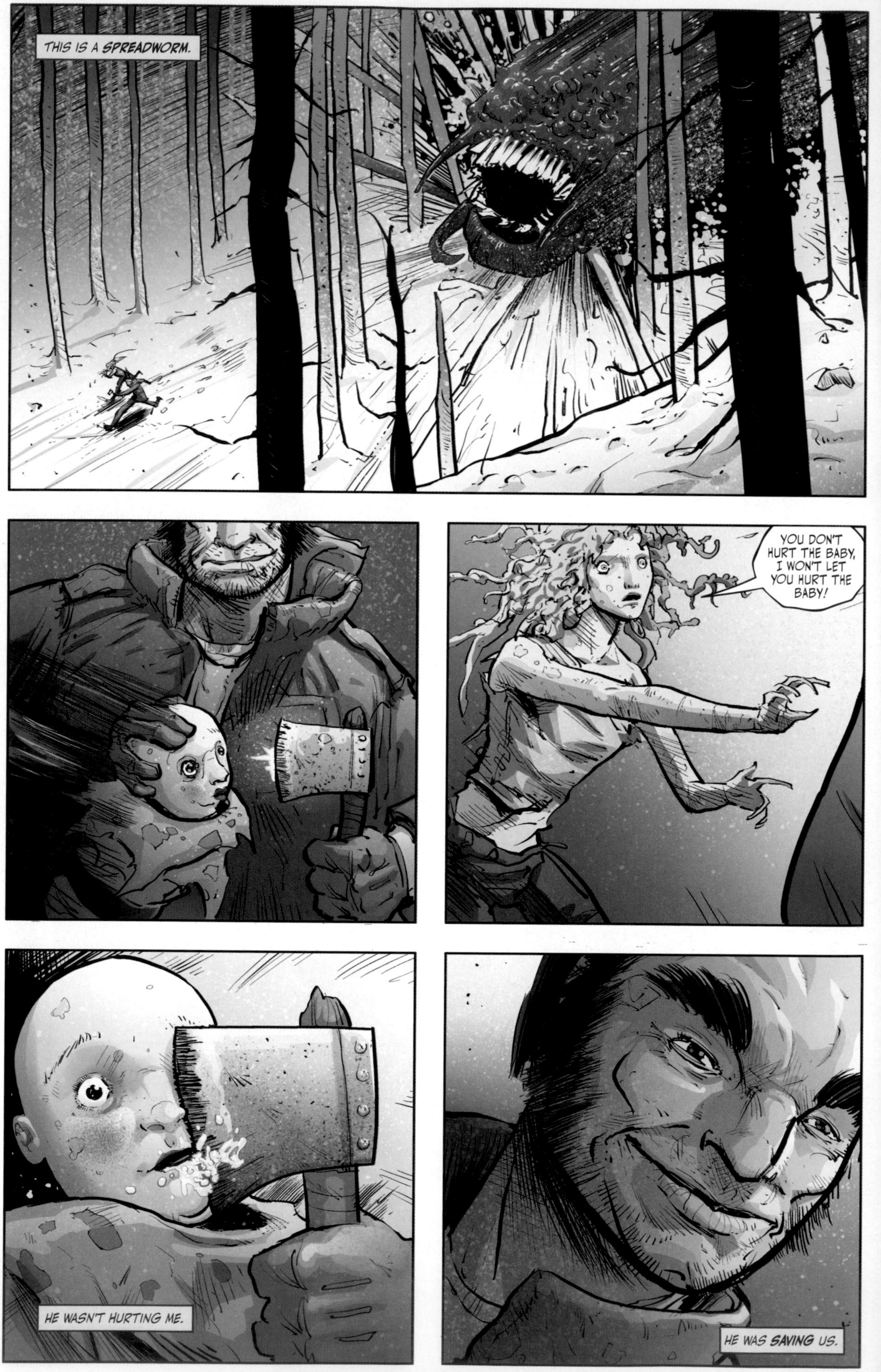

THIS IS A SPREADWORM.
YOU DON'T HURT THE BABY, I WON'T LET YOU HURT THE BABY!
HE WASN'T HURTING ME.
HE WAS SAVING US.

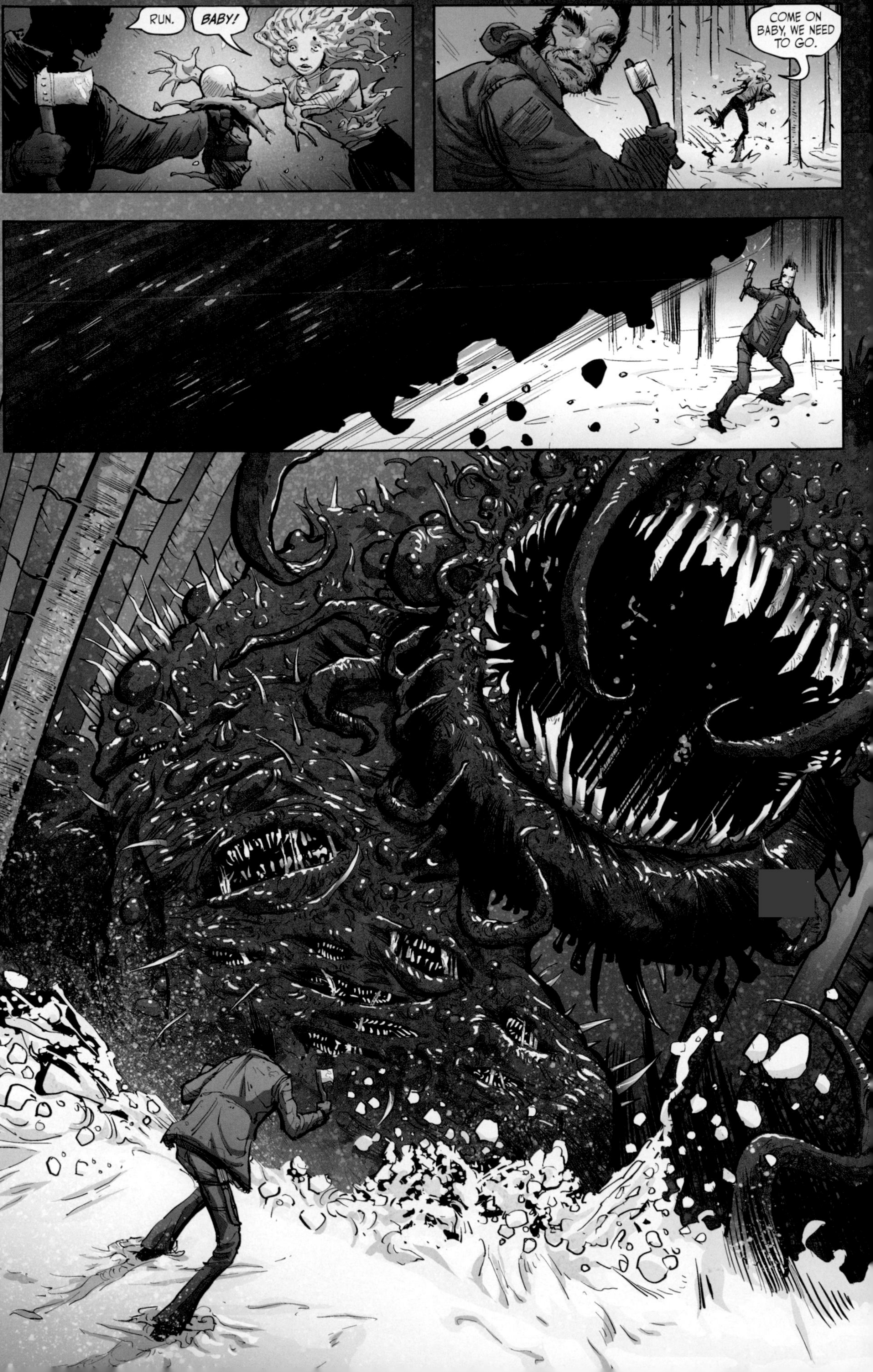
RUN.
BABY!
COME ON BABY, WE NEED TO GO.

THEY'RE THE END RESULT OF *SPREAD INFECTION,* WHEN RUNNERS AND ROAMERS AND WHATEVER ELSE COMBINE INTO SOMETHING AWFUL. THIS ONE COULD BE DESCRIBED AS SMALL.

AS FAR AS **NO** KNEW, NO ONE HAD EVER KILLED ONE BEFORE.

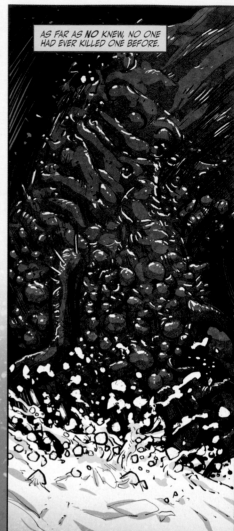

BEFORE.

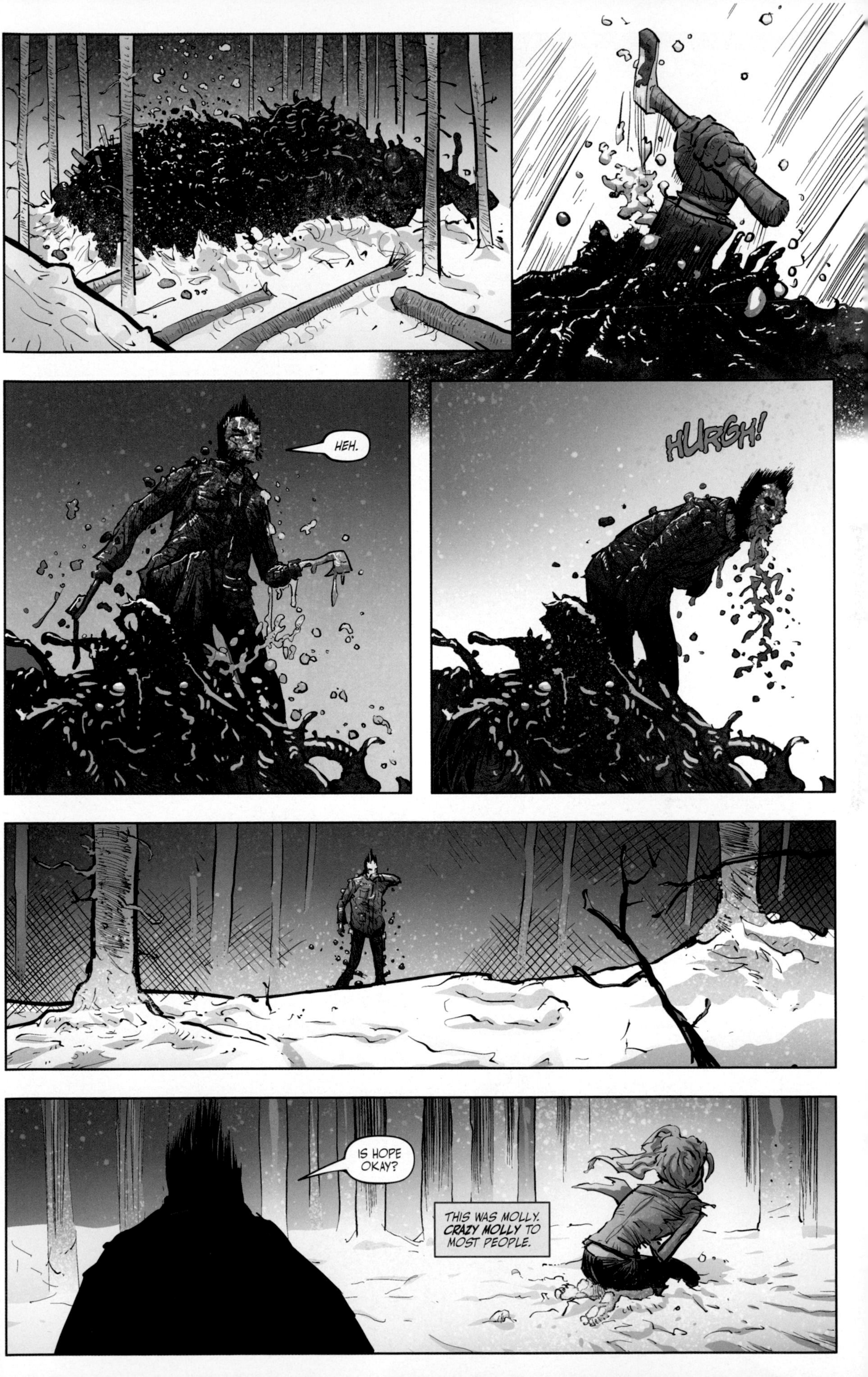
HEH.
HURGH!
IS HOPE OKAY?
THIS WAS MOLLY. CRAZY MOLLY TO MOST PEOPLE.

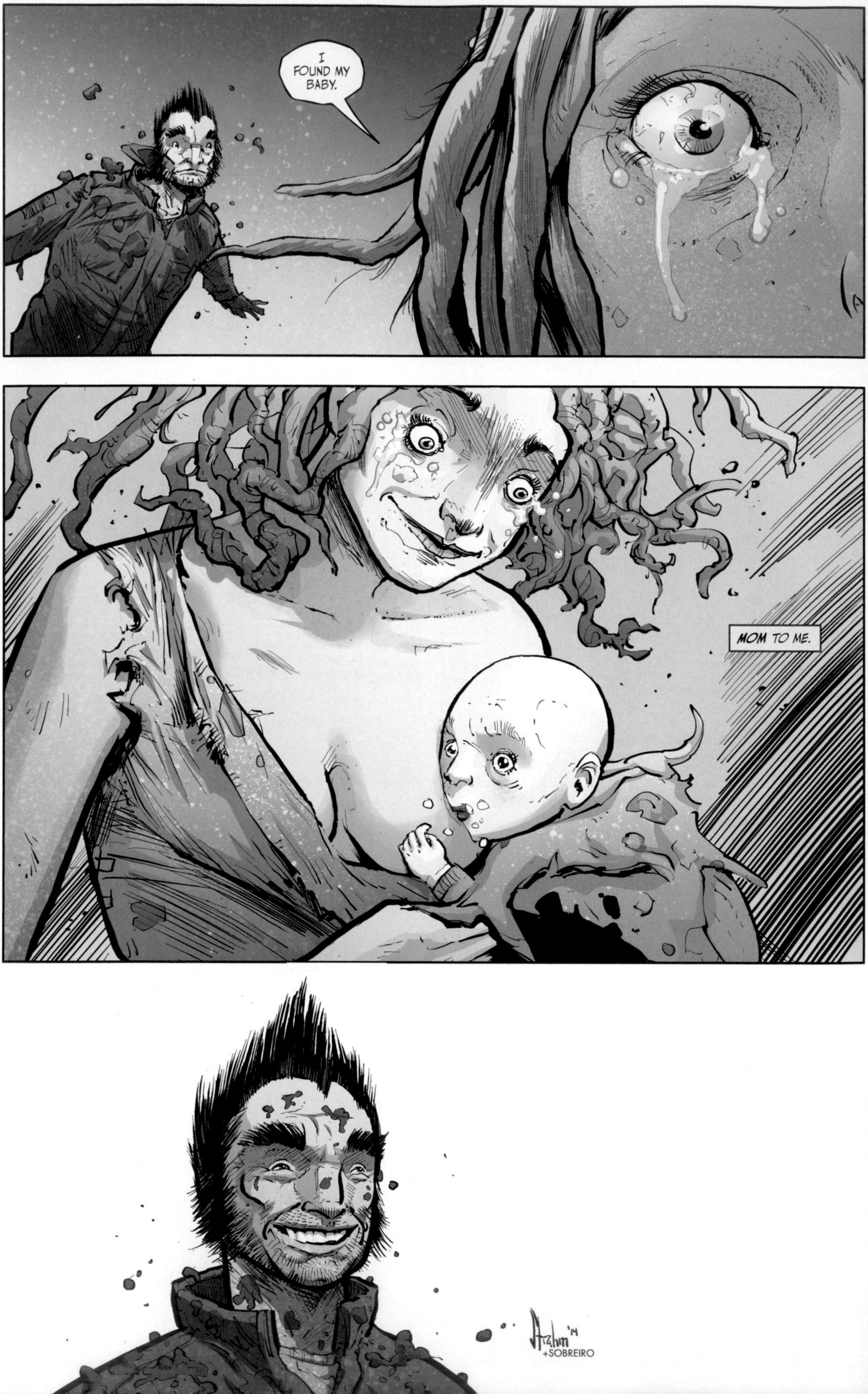
I FOUND MY BABY.
MOM TO ME.
Azahm '14 +SOBREIRO

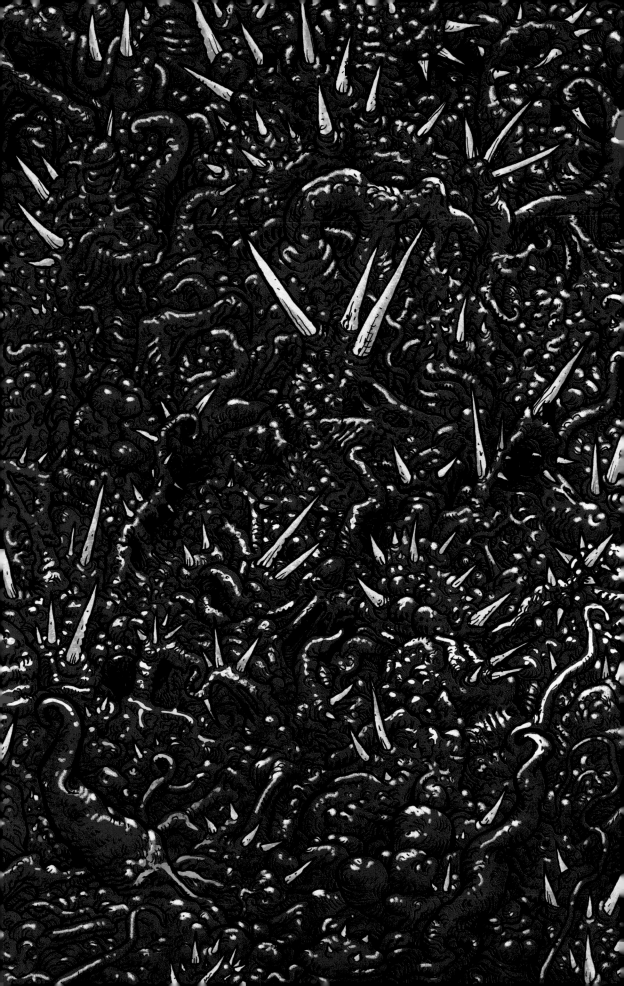

CHAPTER THREE

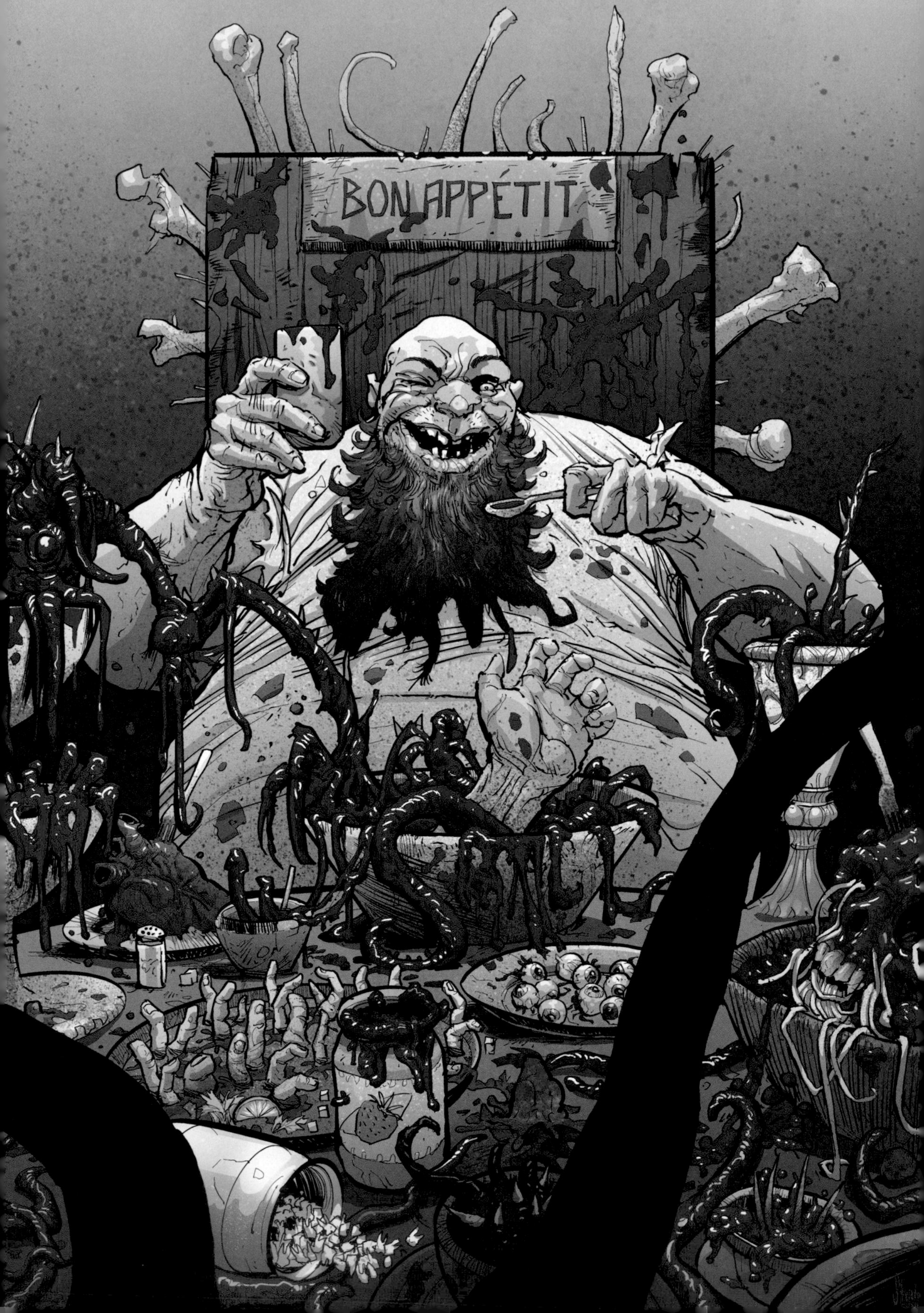
BON APPÉTIT

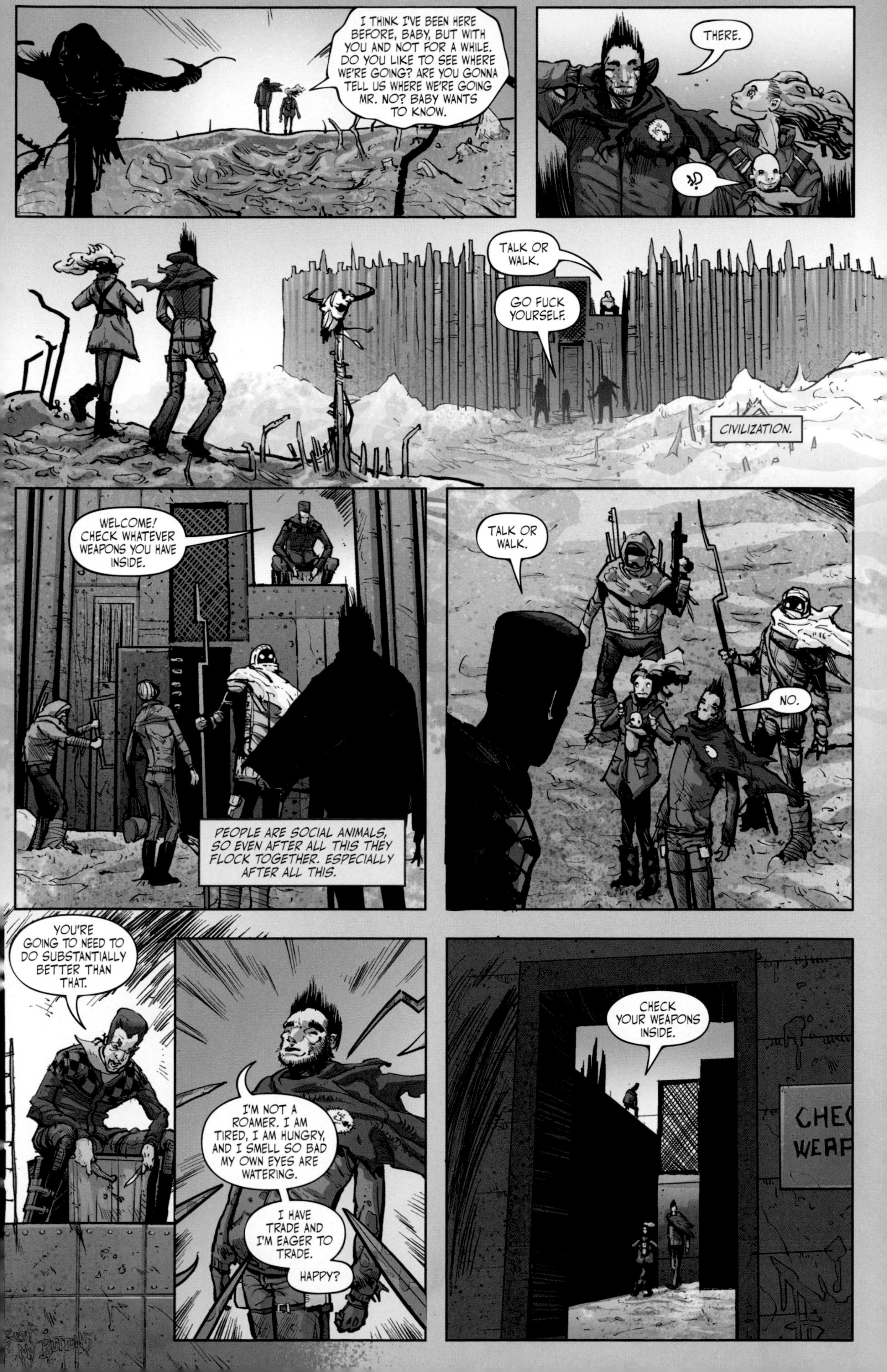
I THINK I'VE BEEN HERE BEFORE, BABY, BUT WITH YOU AND NOT FOR A WHILE. DO YOU LIKE TO SEE WHERE WE'RE GOING? ARE YOU GONNA TELL US WHERE WE'RE GOING MR. NO? BABY WANTS TO KNOW.
THERE.
TALK OR WALK.
GO FUCK YOURSELF.
CIVILIZATION.
WELCOME! CHECK WHATEVER WEAPONS YOU HAVE INSIDE.
PEOPLE ARE SOCIAL ANIMALS, SO EVEN AFTER ALL THIS THEY FLOCK TOGETHER. ESPECIALLY AFTER ALL THIS.
TALK OR WALK.
NO.
YOU'RE GOING TO NEED TO DO SUBSTANTIALLY BETTER THAN THAT.
I'M NOT A ROAMER. I AM TIRED, I AM HUNGRY, AND I SMELL SO BAD MY OWN EYES ARE WATERING.
I HAVE TRADE AND I'M EAGER TO TRADE.
HAPPY?
MY BUTTONS
CHECK YOUR WEAPONS INSIDE.
CHEC
WEAP

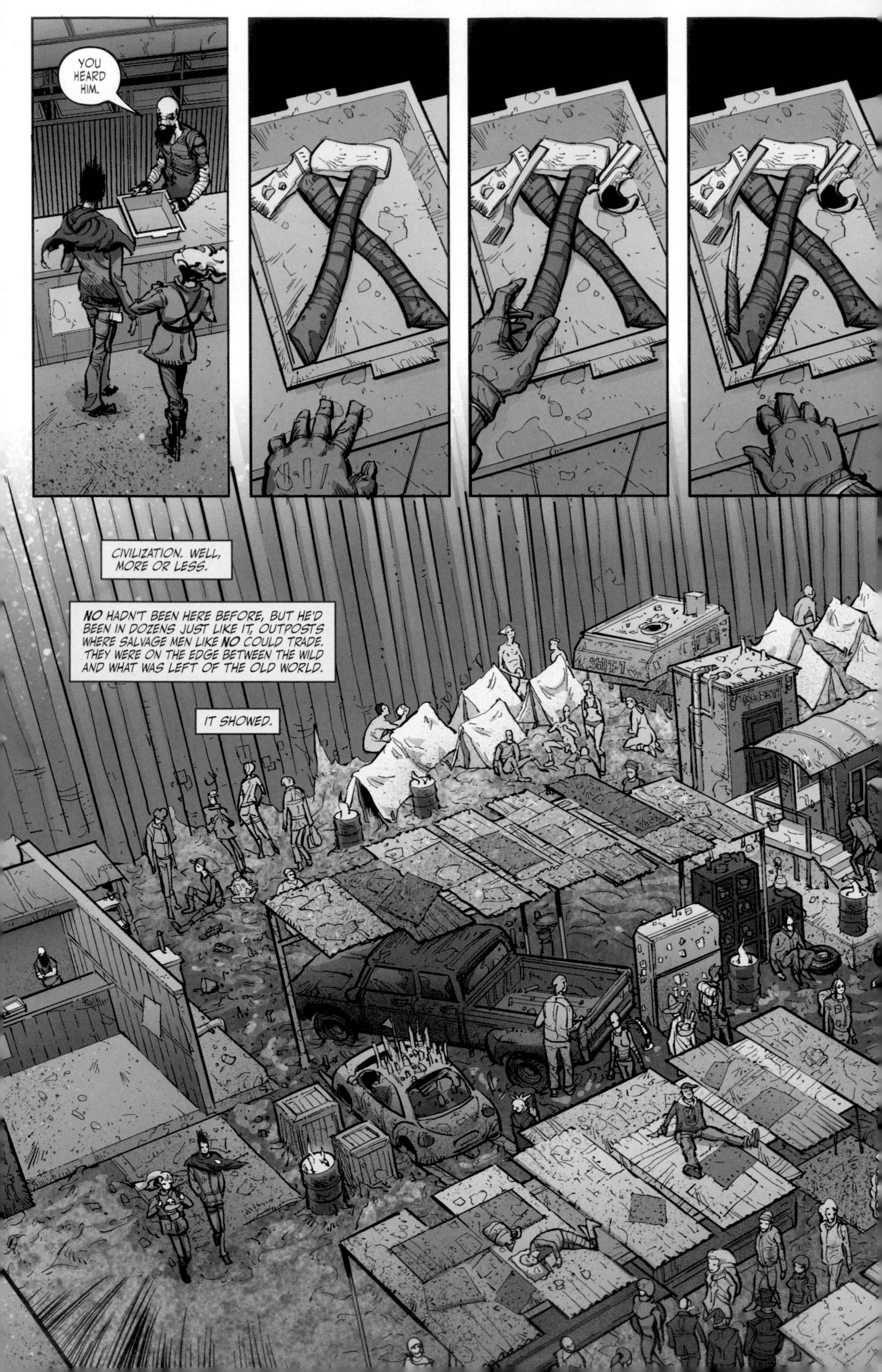
YOU HEARD HIM.
CIVILIZATION. WELL, MORE OR LESS.
NO HADN'T BEEN HERE BEFORE, BUT HE'D BEEN IN DOZENS JUST LIKE IT, OUTPOSTS WHERE SALVAGE MEN LIKE **NO** COULD TRADE. THEY WERE ON THE EDGE BETWEEN THE WILD AND WHAT WAS LEFT OF THE OLD WORLD.
IT SHOWED.

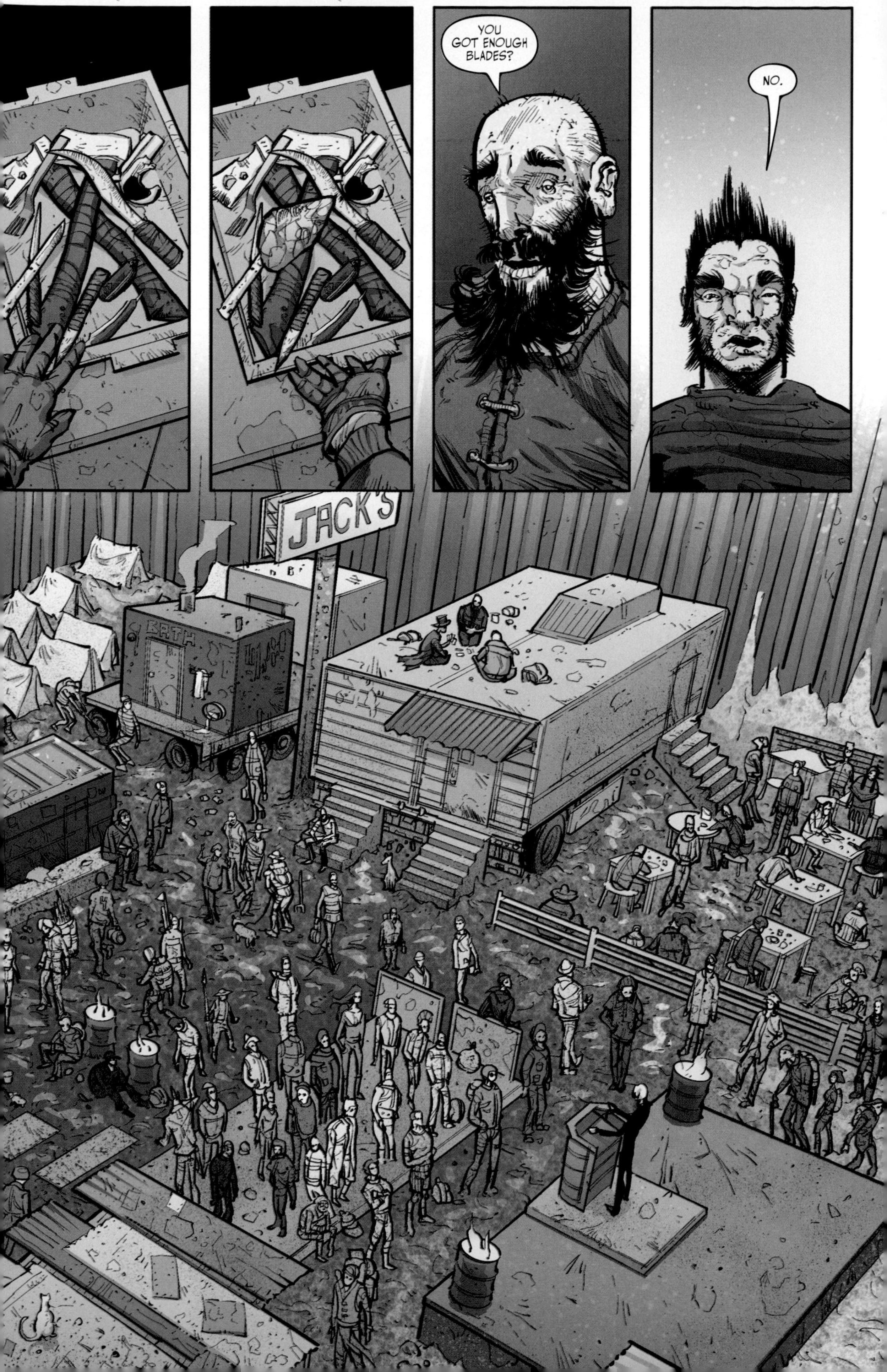
YOU GOT ENOUGH BLADES?
NO.
JACK'S
BATH

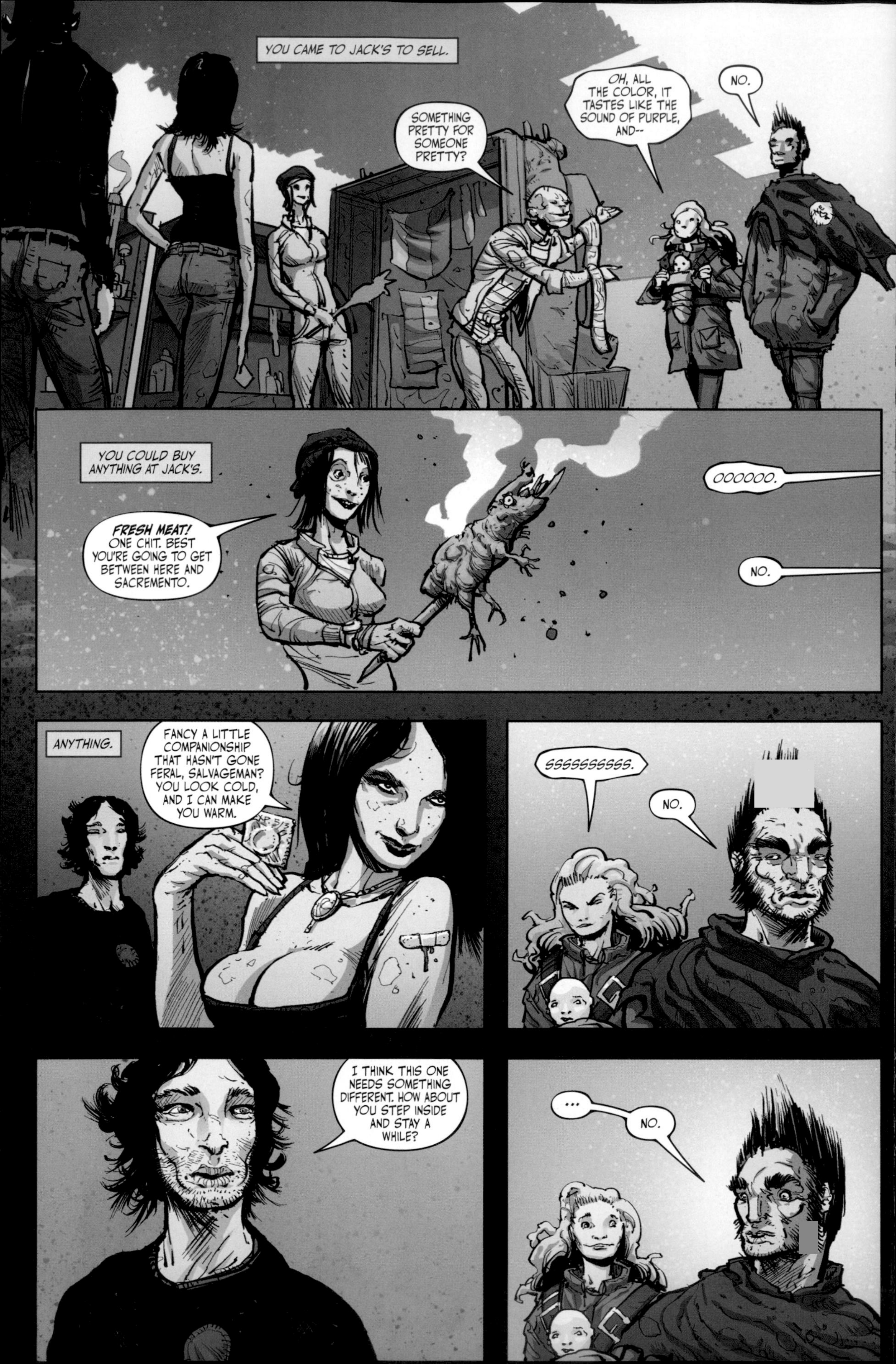

YOU CAME TO JACK'S TO SELL.
SOMETHING PRETTY FOR SOMEONE PRETTY?
OH, ALL THE COLOR, IT TASTES LIKE THE SOUND OF PURPLE, AND--
NO.
YOU COULD BUY ANYTHING AT JACK'S.
FRESH MEAT! ONE CHIT. BEST YOU'RE GOING TO GET BETWEEN HERE AND SACREMENTO.
OOOOOO.
NO.
ANYTHING.
FANCY A LITTLE COMPANIONSHIP THAT HASN'T GONE FERAL, SALVAGEMAN? YOU LOOK COLD, AND I CAN MAKE YOU WARM.
SSSSSSSSSS.
NO.
I THINK THIS ONE NEEDS SOMETHING DIFFERENT. HOW ABOUT YOU STEP INSIDE AND STAY A WHILE?
...
NO.

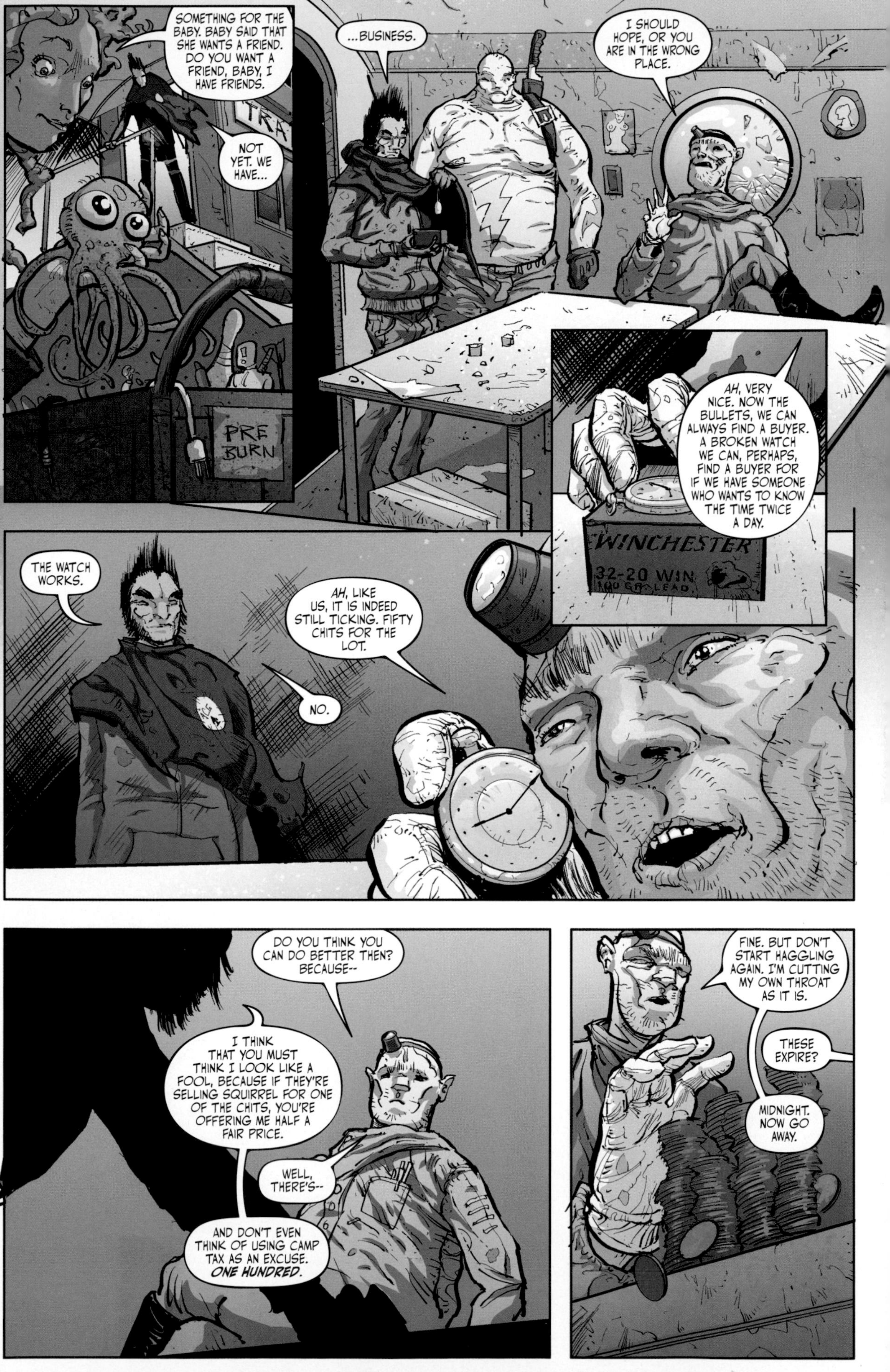
SOMETHING FOR THE BABY. BABY SAID THAT SHE WANTS A FRIEND. DO YOU WANT A FRIEND, BABY, I HAVE FRIENDS.
NOT YET. WE HAVE...
TRA
PRE BURN
...BUSINESS.
I SHOULD HOPE, OR YOU ARE IN THE WRONG PLACE.
AH, VERY NICE. NOW THE BULLETS, WE CAN ALWAYS FIND A BUYER. A BROKEN WATCH WE CAN, PERHAPS, FIND A BUYER FOR IF WE HAVE SOMEONE WHO WANTS TO KNOW THE TIME TWICE A DAY.
WINCHESTER
32-20 WIN
THE WATCH WORKS.
AH, LIKE US, IT IS INDEED STILL TICKING. FIFTY CHITS FOR THE LOT.
NO.
DO YOU THINK YOU CAN DO BETTER THEN? BECAUSE--
I THINK THAT YOU MUST THINK I LOOK LIKE A FOOL, BECAUSE IF THEY'RE SELLING SQUIRREL FOR ONE OF THE CHITS, YOU'RE OFFERING ME HALF A FAIR PRICE.
WELL, THERE'S--
AND DON'T EVEN THINK OF USING CAMP TAX AS AN EXCUSE. ONE HUNDRED.
FINE. BUT DON'T START HAGGLING AGAIN. I'M CUTTING MY OWN THROAT AS IT IS.
THESE EXPIRE?
MIDNIGHT. NOW GO AWAY.

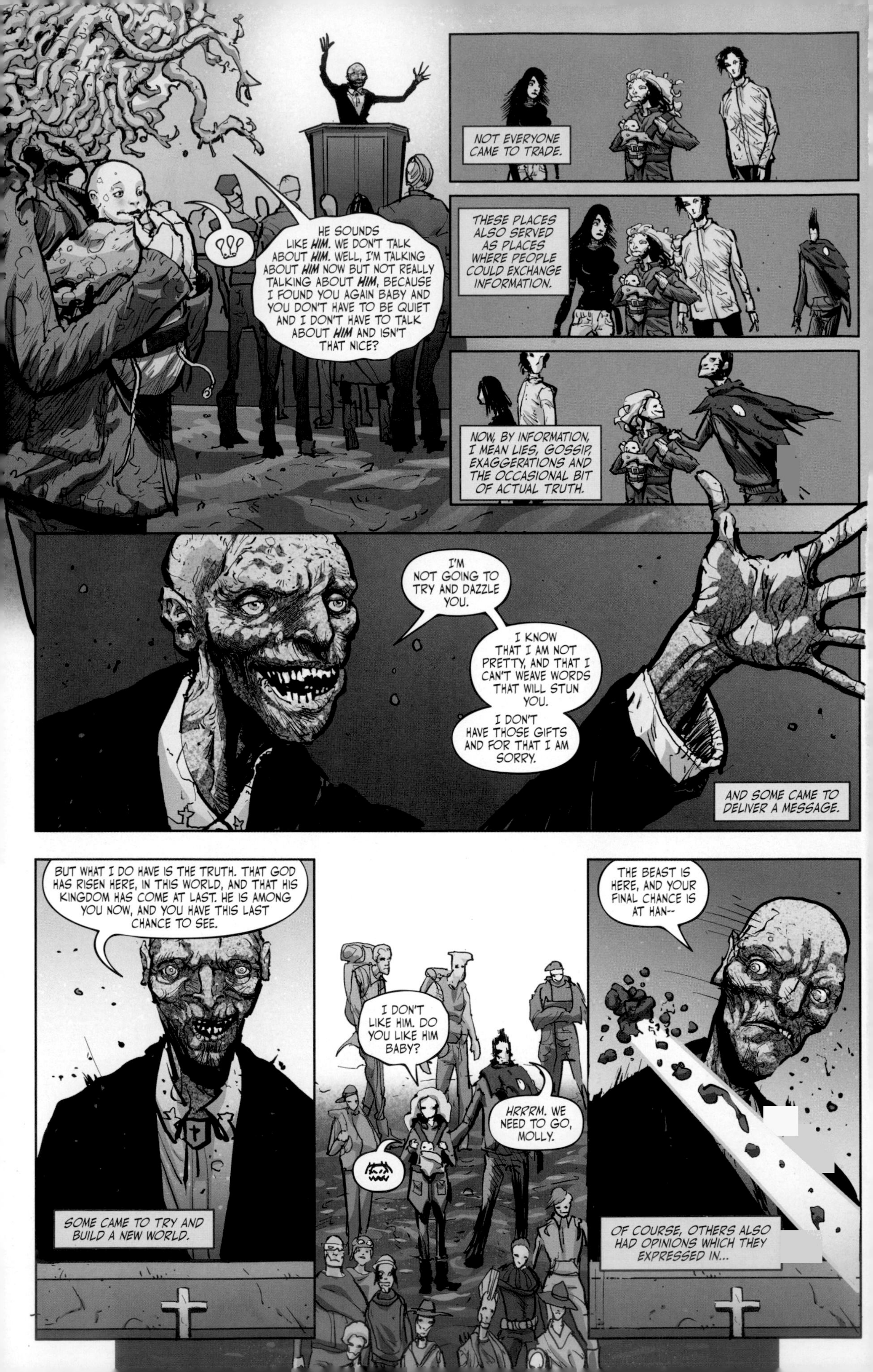
HE SOUNDS LIKE HIM. WE DON'T TALK ABOUT HIM. WELL, I'M TALKING ABOUT HIM NOW BUT NOT REALLY TALKING ABOUT HIM, BECAUSE I FOUND YOU AGAIN BABY AND YOU DON'T HAVE TO BE QUIET AND I DON'T HAVE TO TALK ABOUT HIM AND ISN'T THAT NICE?
NOT EVERYONE CAME TO TRADE.
THESE PLACES ALSO SERVED AS PLACES WHERE PEOPLE COULD EXCHANGE INFORMATION.
NOW, BY INFORMATION, I MEAN LIES, GOSSIP, EXAGGERATIONS AND THE OCCASIONAL BIT OF ACTUAL TRUTH.
I'M NOT GOING TO TRY AND DAZZLE YOU.
I KNOW THAT I AM NOT PRETTY, AND THAT I CAN'T WEAVE WORDS THAT WILL STUN YOU.
I DON'T HAVE THOSE GIFTS AND FOR THAT I AM SORRY.
AND SOME CAME TO DELIVER A MESSAGE.
BUT WHAT I DO HAVE IS THE TRUTH. THAT GOD HAS RISEN HERE, IN THIS WORLD, AND THAT HIS KINGDOM HAS COME AT LAST. HE IS AMONG YOU NOW, AND YOU HAVE THIS LAST CHANCE TO SEE.
SOME CAME TO TRY AND BUILD A NEW WORLD.
I DON'T LIKE HIM. DO YOU LIKE HIM BABY?
HRRRM. WE NEED TO GO, MOLLY.
THE BEAST IS HERE, AND YOUR FINAL CHANCE IS AT HAN--
OF COURSE, OTHERS ALSO HAD OPINIONS WHICH THEY EXPRESSED IN...

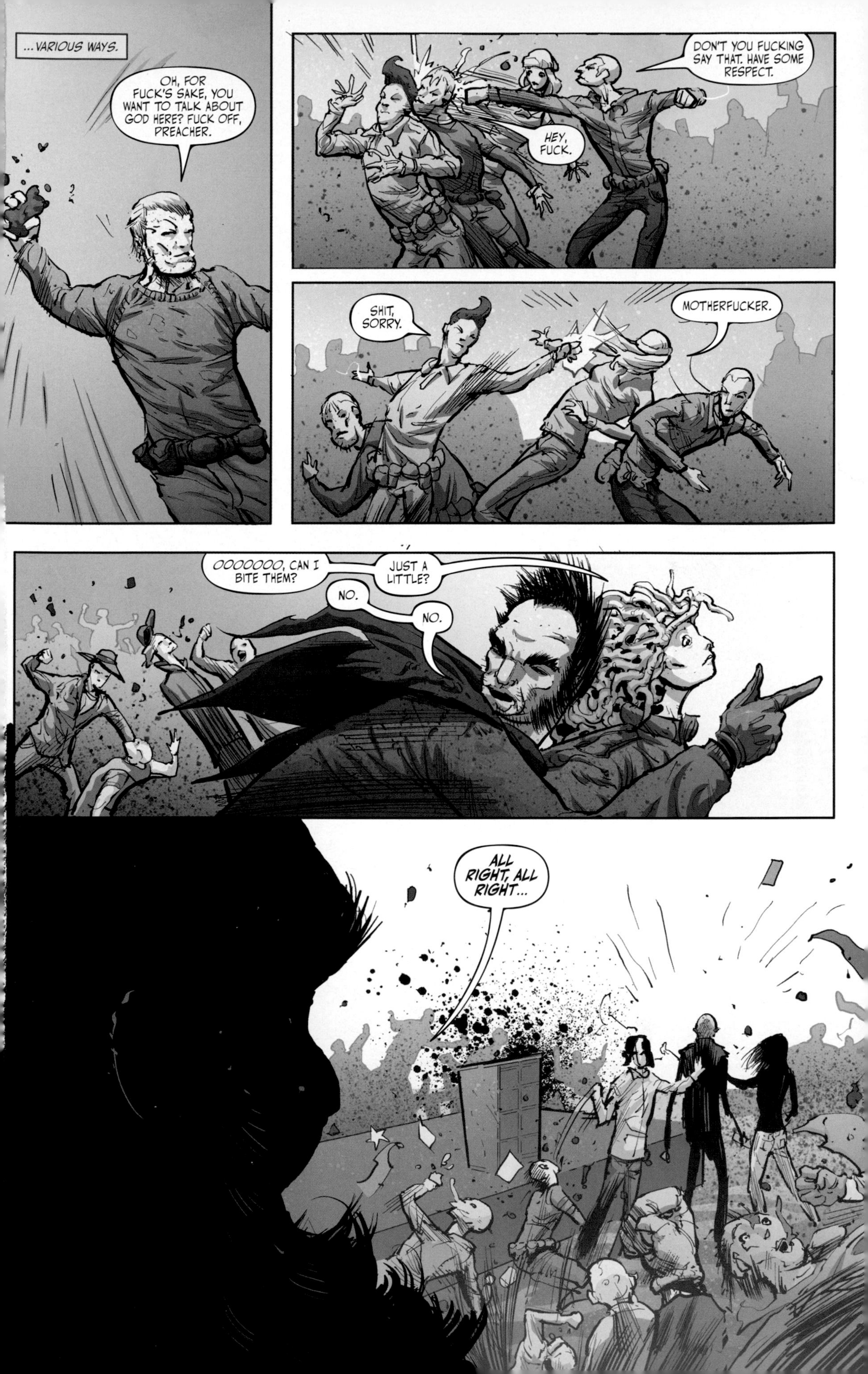
...VARIOUS WAYS.
OH, FOR FUCK'S SAKE, YOU WANT TO TALK ABOUT GOD HERE? FUCK OFF, PREACHER.
DON'T YOU FUCKING SAY THAT. HAVE SOME RESPECT.
HEY, FUCK.
SHIT, SORRY.
MOTHERFUCKER.
OOOOOOO, CAN I BITE THEM?
NO.
JUST A LITTLE?
NO.
ALL RIGHT, ALL RIGHT...

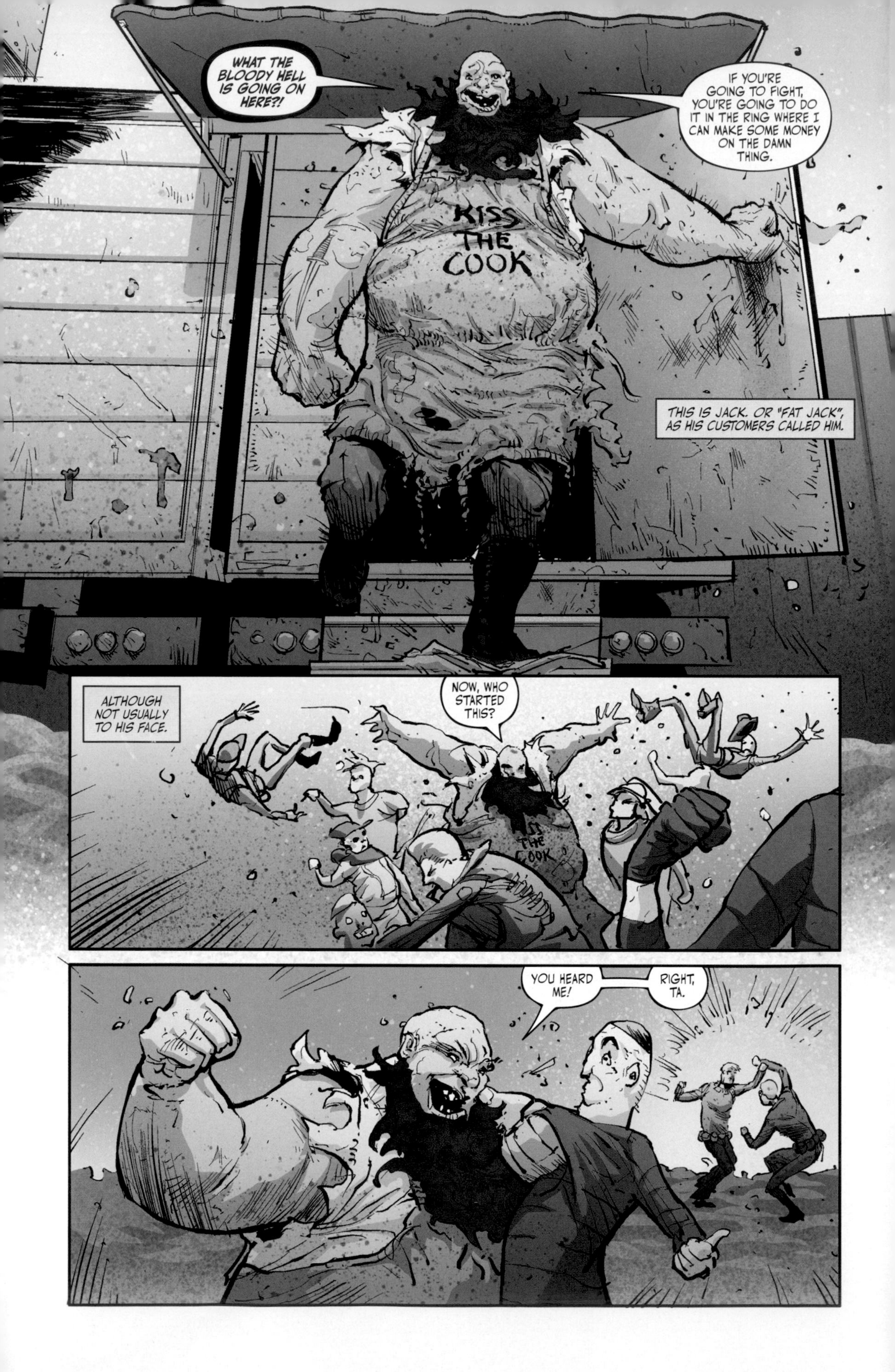
WHAT THE BLOODY HELL IS GOING ON HERE?!
IF YOU'RE GOING TO FIGHT, YOU'RE GOING TO DO IT IN THE RING WHERE I CAN MAKE SOME MONEY ON THE DAMN THING.
KISS THE COOK
THIS IS JACK. OR "FAT JACK", AS HIS CUSTOMERS CALLED HIM.
ALTHOUGH NOT USUALLY TO HIS FACE.
NOW, WHO STARTED THIS?
YOU HEARD ME!
RIGHT, TA.

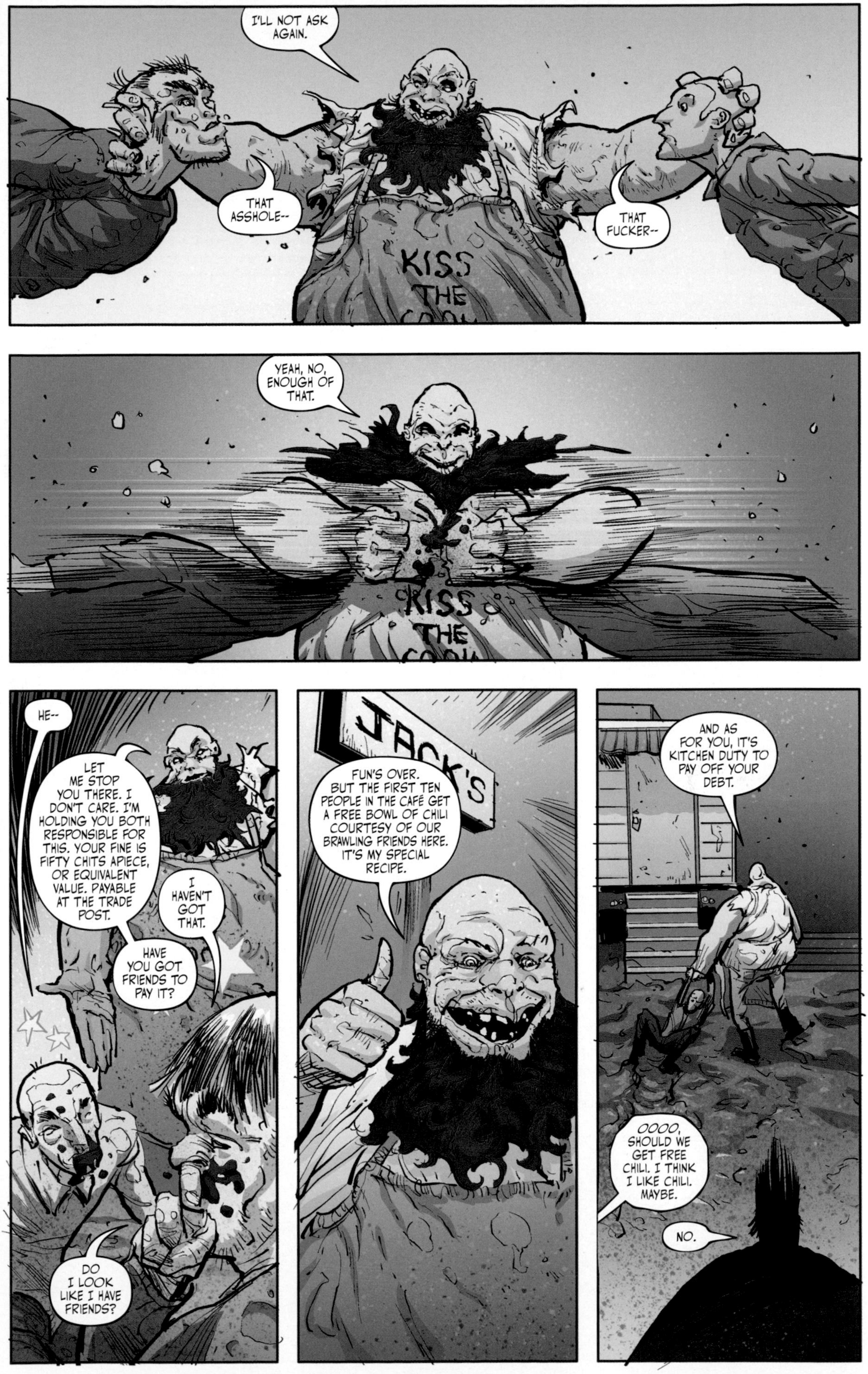
I'LL NOT ASK AGAIN.
THAT ASSHOLE--
THAT FUCKER--
KISS THE COOK
YEAH, NO, ENOUGH OF THAT.
KISS THE
HE--
LET ME STOP YOU THERE. I DON'T CARE. I'M HOLDING YOU BOTH RESPONSIBLE FOR THIS. YOUR FINE IS FIFTY CHITS APIECE, OR EQUIVALENT VALUE. PAYABLE AT THE TRADE POST.
I HAVEN'T GOT THAT.
HAVE YOU GOT FRIENDS TO PAY IT?
DO I LOOK LIKE I HAVE FRIENDS?
JACK'S
FUN'S OVER. BUT THE FIRST TEN PEOPLE IN THE CAFÉ GET A FREE BOWL OF CHILI COURTESY OF OUR BRAWLING FRIENDS HERE. IT'S MY SPECIAL RECIPE.
AND AS FOR YOU, IT'S KITCHEN DUTY TO PAY OFF YOUR DEBT.
OOOO, SHOULD WE GET FREE CHILI. I THINK I LIKE CHILI. MAYBE.
NO.

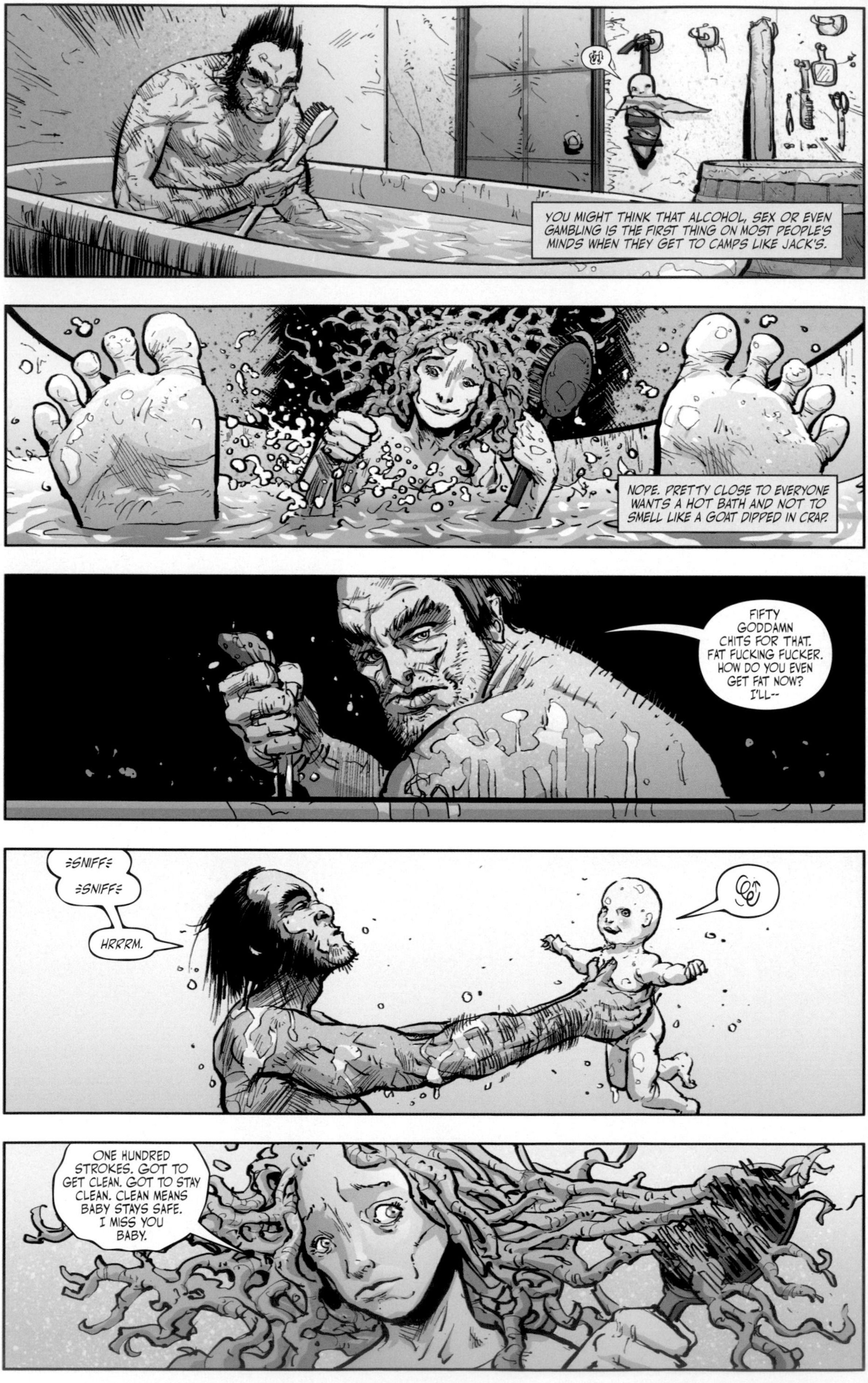
YOU MIGHT THINK THAT ALCOHOL, SEX OR EVEN GAMBLING IS THE FIRST THING ON MOST PEOPLE'S MINDS WHEN THEY GET TO CAMPS LIKE JACK'S.
NOPE. PRETTY CLOSE TO EVERYONE WANTS A HOT BATH AND NOT TO SMELL LIKE A GOAT DIPPED IN CRAP.
FIFTY GODDAMN CHITS FOR THAT. FAT FUCKING FUCKER. HOW DO YOU EVEN GET FAT NOW? I'LL--
SNIFF
SNIFF
HRRRM.
ONE HUNDRED STROKES. GOT TO GET CLEAN. GOT TO STAY CLEAN. CLEAN MEANS BABY STAYS SAFE. I MISS YOU BABY.

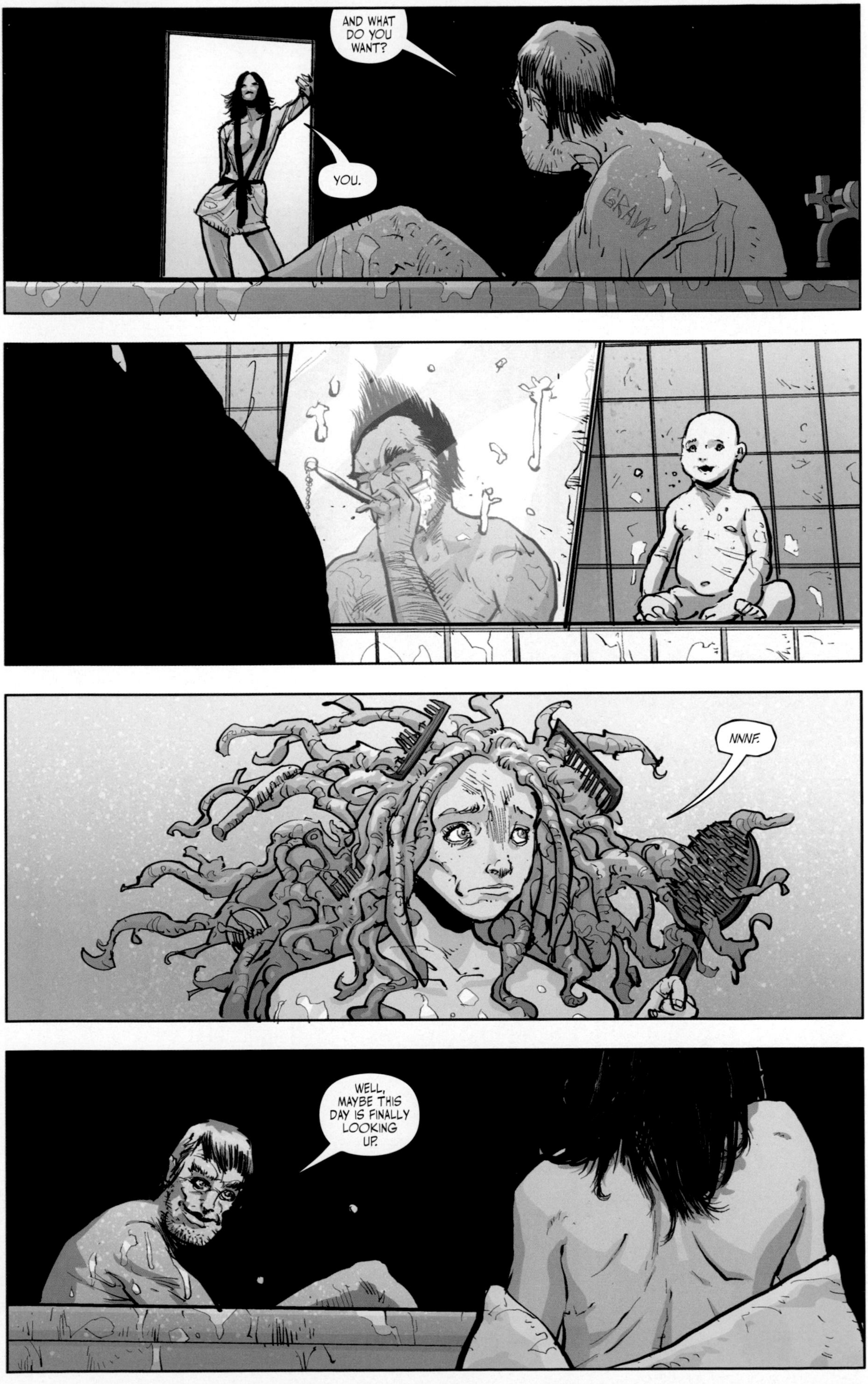
AND WHAT DO YOU WANT?
YOU.
NNNF.
WELL, MAYBE THIS DAY IS FINALLY LOOKING UP.

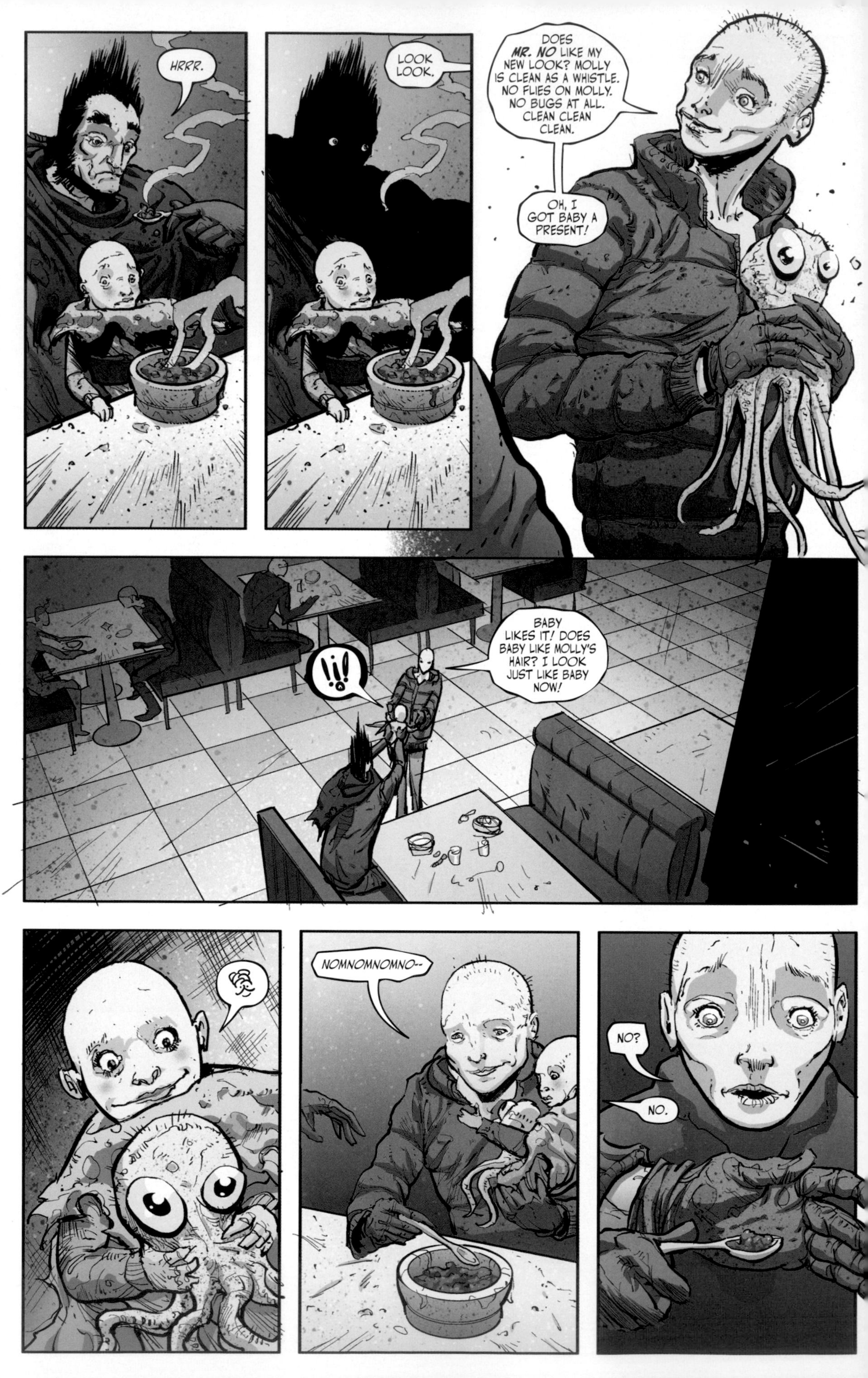
HRRR.
LOOK LOOK.
DOES MR. NO LIKE MY NEW LOOK? MOLLY IS CLEAN AS A WHISTLE. NO FLIES ON MOLLY. NO BUGS AT ALL. CLEAN CLEAN CLEAN.
OH, I GOT BABY A PRESENT!
!¡!
BABY LIKES IT! DOES BABY LIKE MOLLY'S HAIR? I LOOK JUST LIKE BABY NOW!
NOMNOMNOMNO--
NO?
NO.

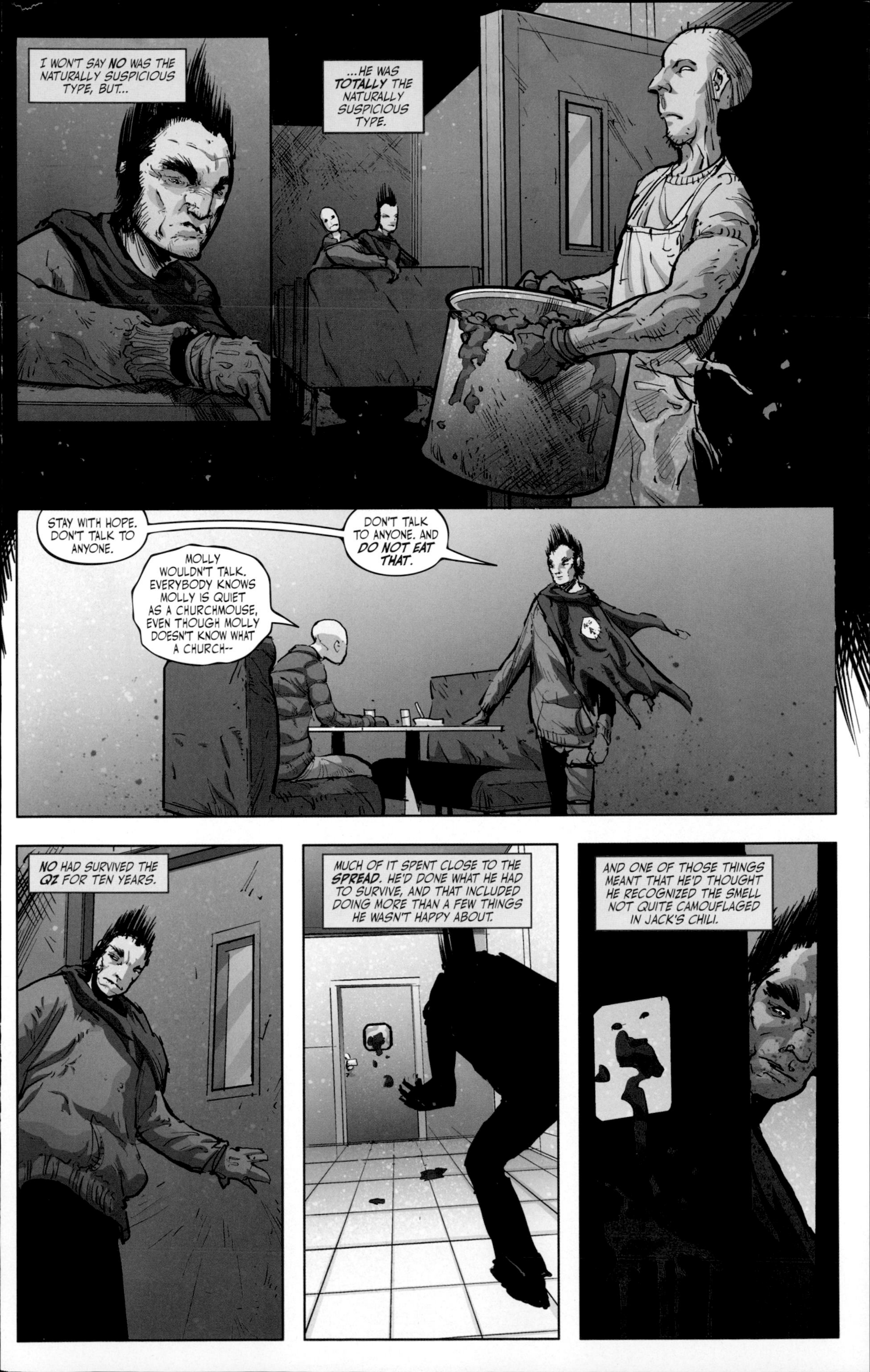
I WON'T SAY NO WAS THE NATURALLY SUSPICIOUS TYPE, BUT...
...HE WAS TOTALLY THE NATURALLY SUSPICIOUS TYPE.
STAY WITH HOPE. DON'T TALK TO ANYONE.
DON'T TALK TO ANYONE. AND DO NOT EAT THAT.
MOLLY WOULDN'T TALK. EVERYBODY KNOWS MOLLY IS QUIET AS A CHURCHMOUSE, EVEN THOUGH MOLLY DOESN'T KNOW WHAT A CHURCH--
NO HAD SURVIVED THE QZ FOR TEN YEARS.
MUCH OF IT SPENT CLOSE TO THE SPREAD. HE'D DONE WHAT HE HAD TO SURVIVE, AND THAT INCLUDED DOING MORE THAN A FEW THINGS HE WASN'T HAPPY ABOUT.
AND ONE OF THOSE THINGS MEANT THAT HE'D THOUGHT HE RECOGNIZED THE SMELL NOT QUITE CAMOUFLAGED IN JACK'S CHILI.

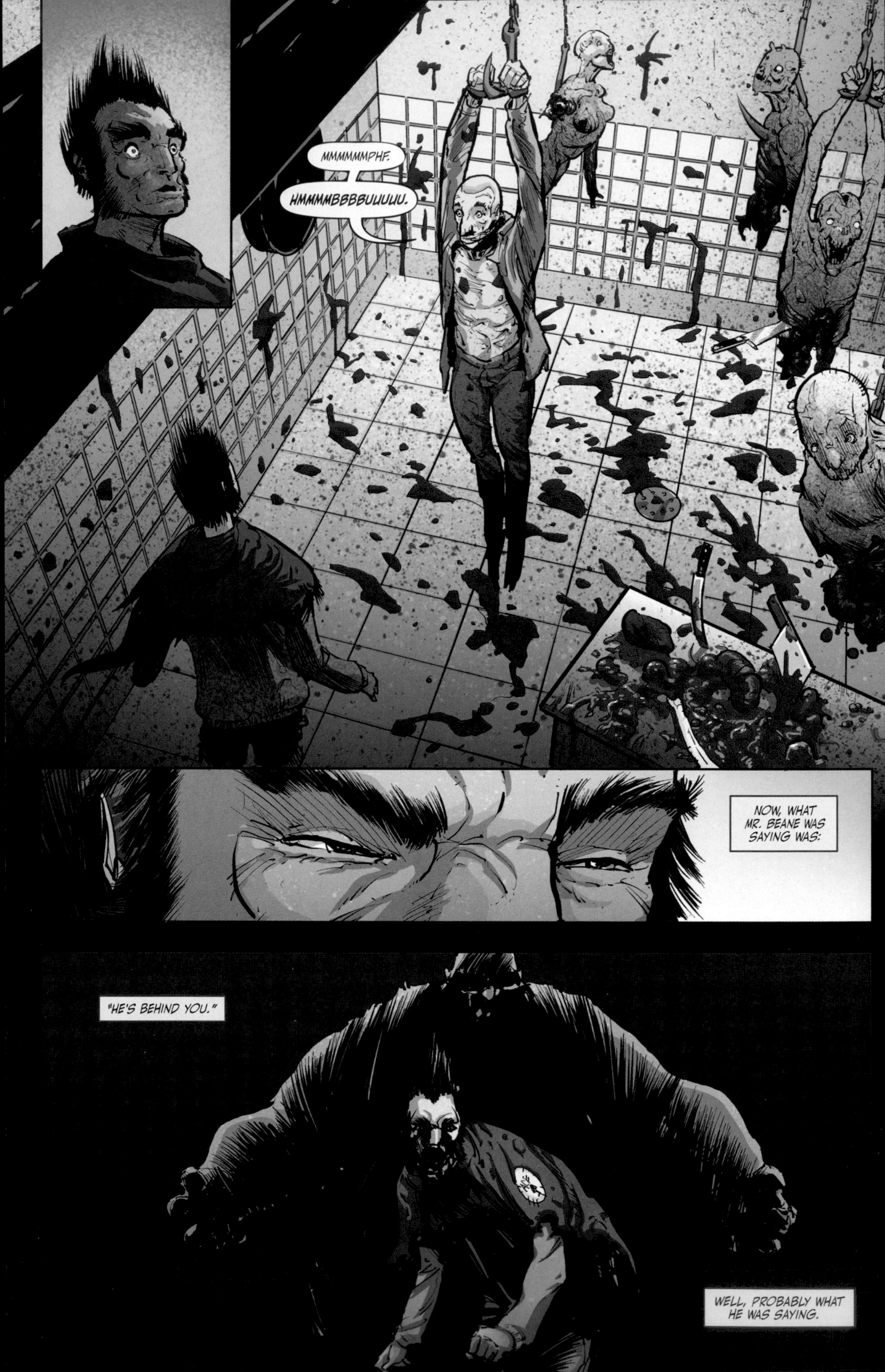
MMMMMMPHF.
HMMMMBBBUUUUU.
NOW, WHAT MR. BEANE WAS SAYING WAS:
"HE'S BEHIND YOU."
WELL, PROBABLY WHAT HE WAS SAYING.

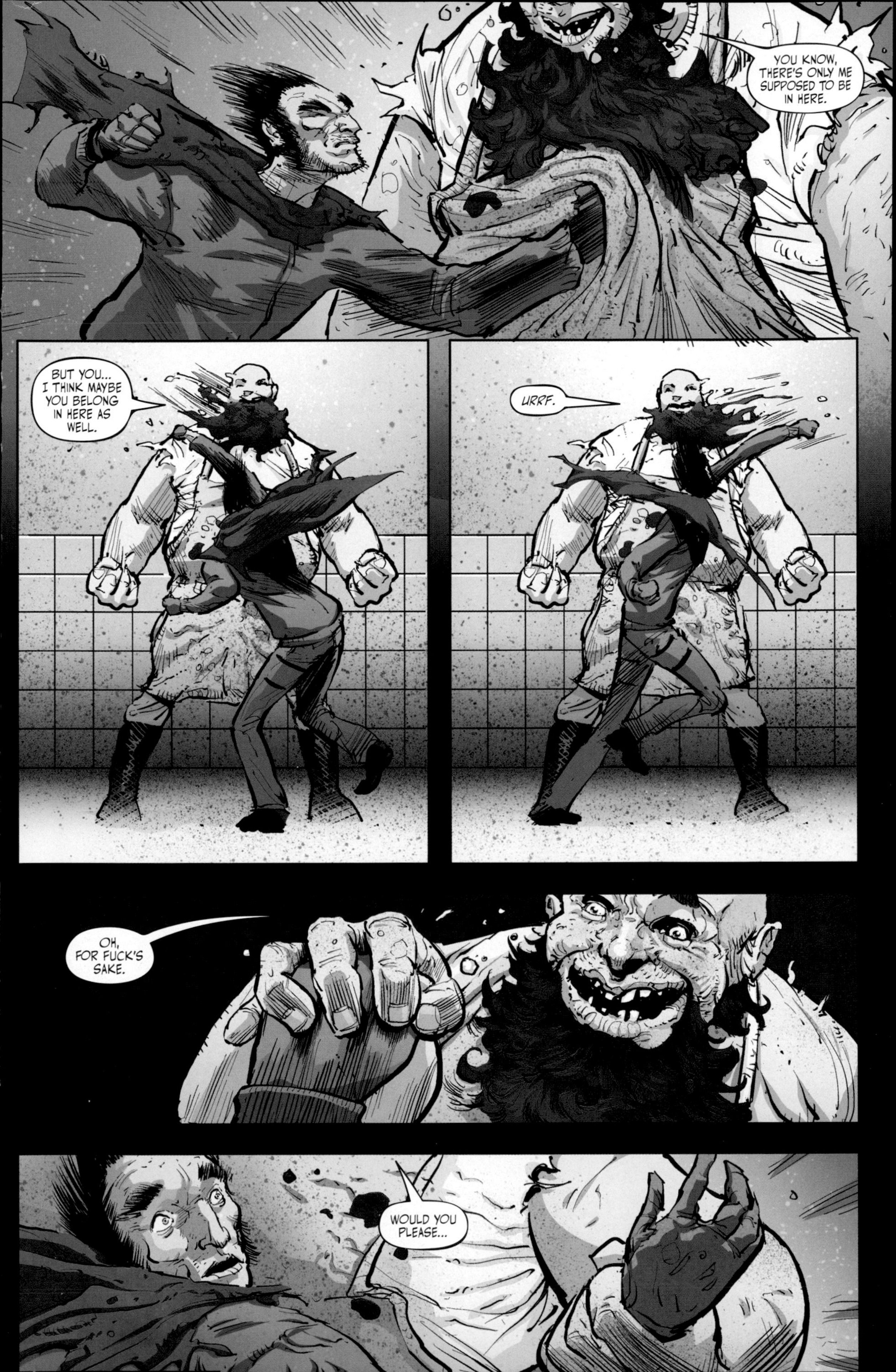
YOU KNOW, THERE'S ONLY ME SUPPOSED TO BE IN HERE.
BUT YOU... I THINK MAYBE YOU BELONG IN HERE AS WELL.
URRF.
OH, FOR FUCK'S SAKE.
WOULD YOU PLEASE...

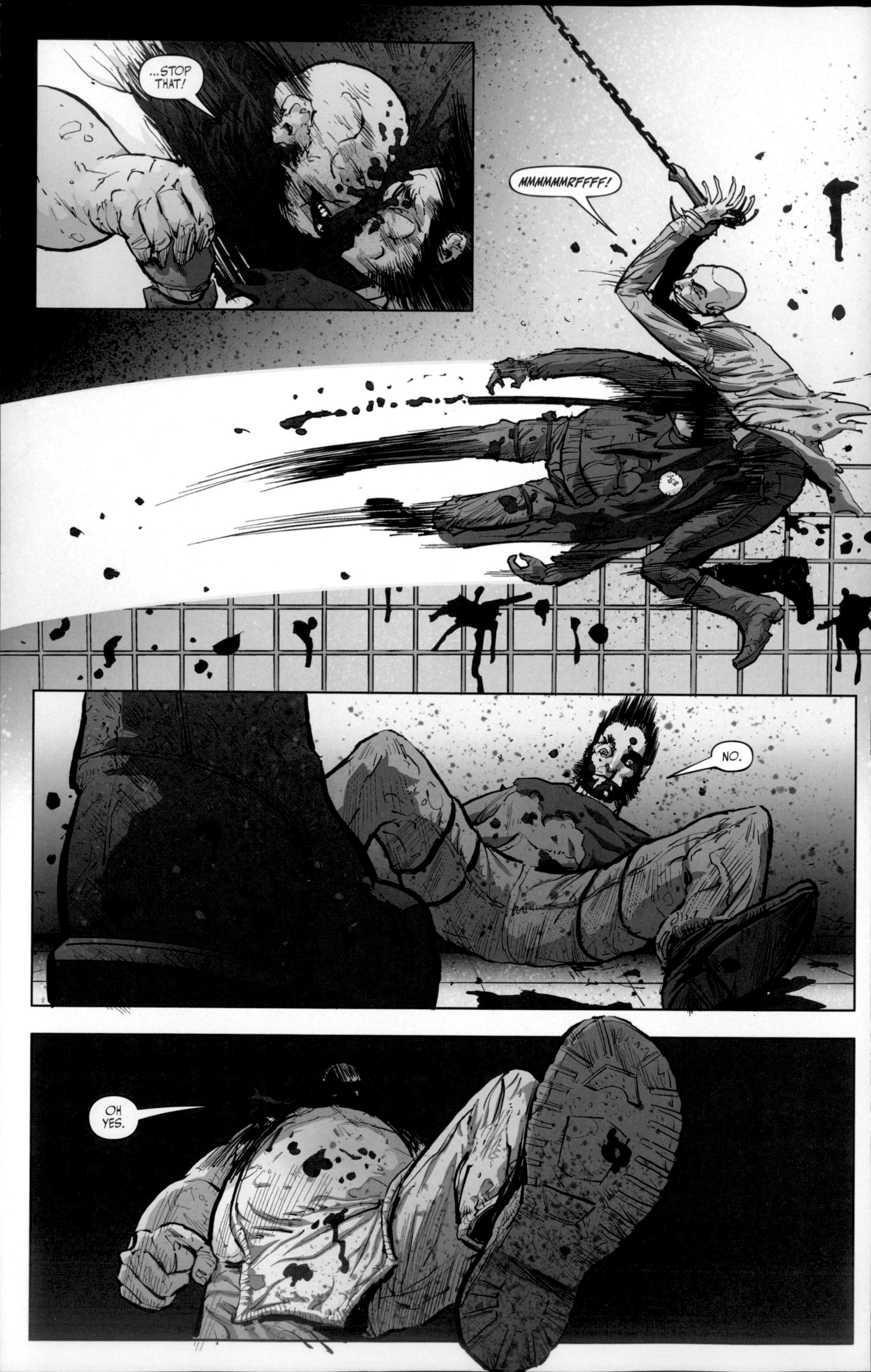
...STOP THAT!
MMMMMMRFFFF!
NO.
OH YES.

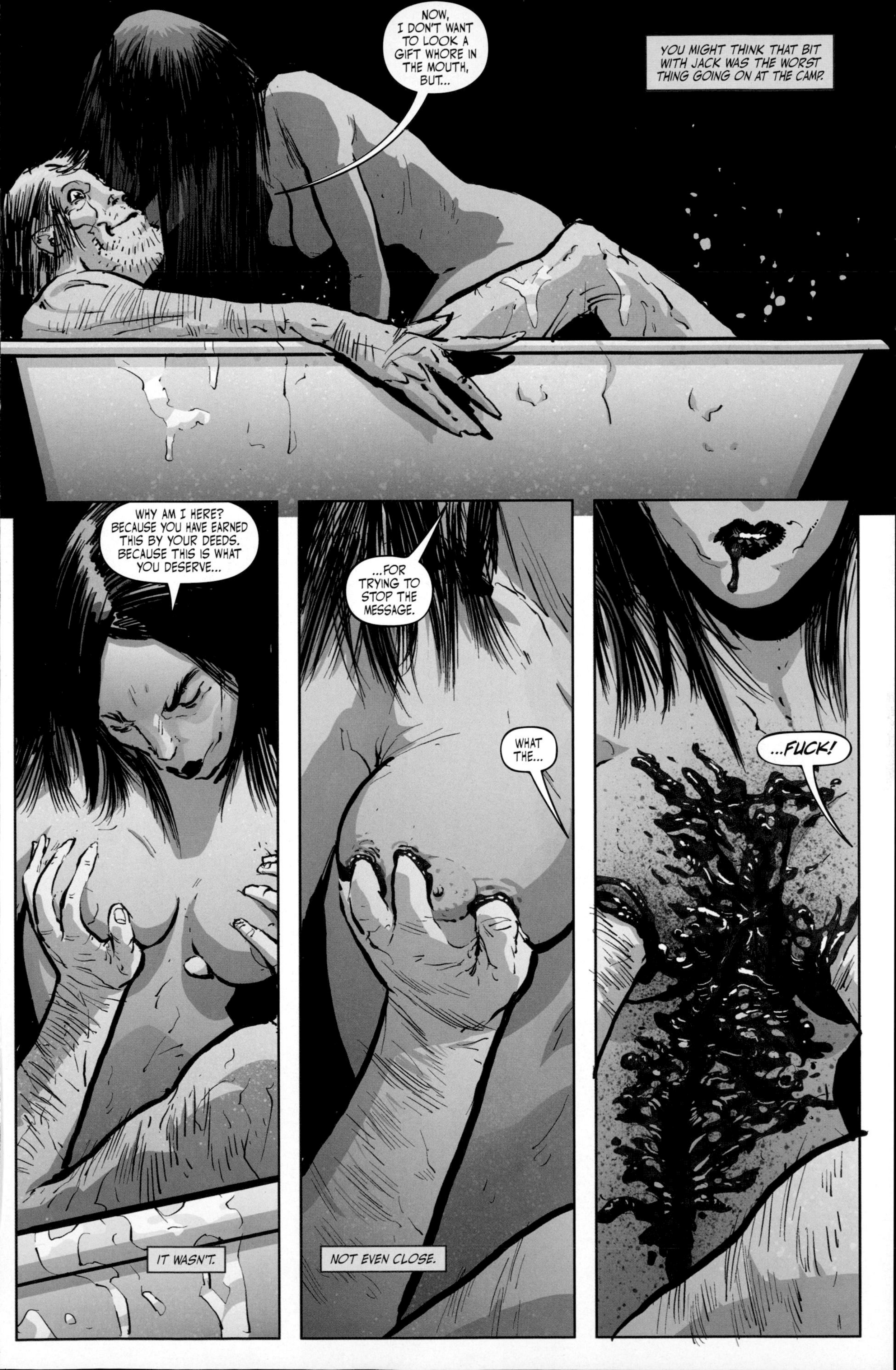
NOW, I DON'T WANT TO LOOK A GIFT WHORE IN THE MOUTH, BUT...
YOU MIGHT THINK THAT BIT WITH JACK WAS THE WORST THING GOING ON AT THE CAMP.
WHY AM I HERE? BECAUSE YOU HAVE EARNED THIS BY YOUR DEEDS. BECAUSE THIS IS WHAT YOU DESERVE...
IT WASN'T.
...FOR TRYING TO STOP THE MESSAGE.
WHAT THE...
NOT EVEN CLOSE.
...FUCK!

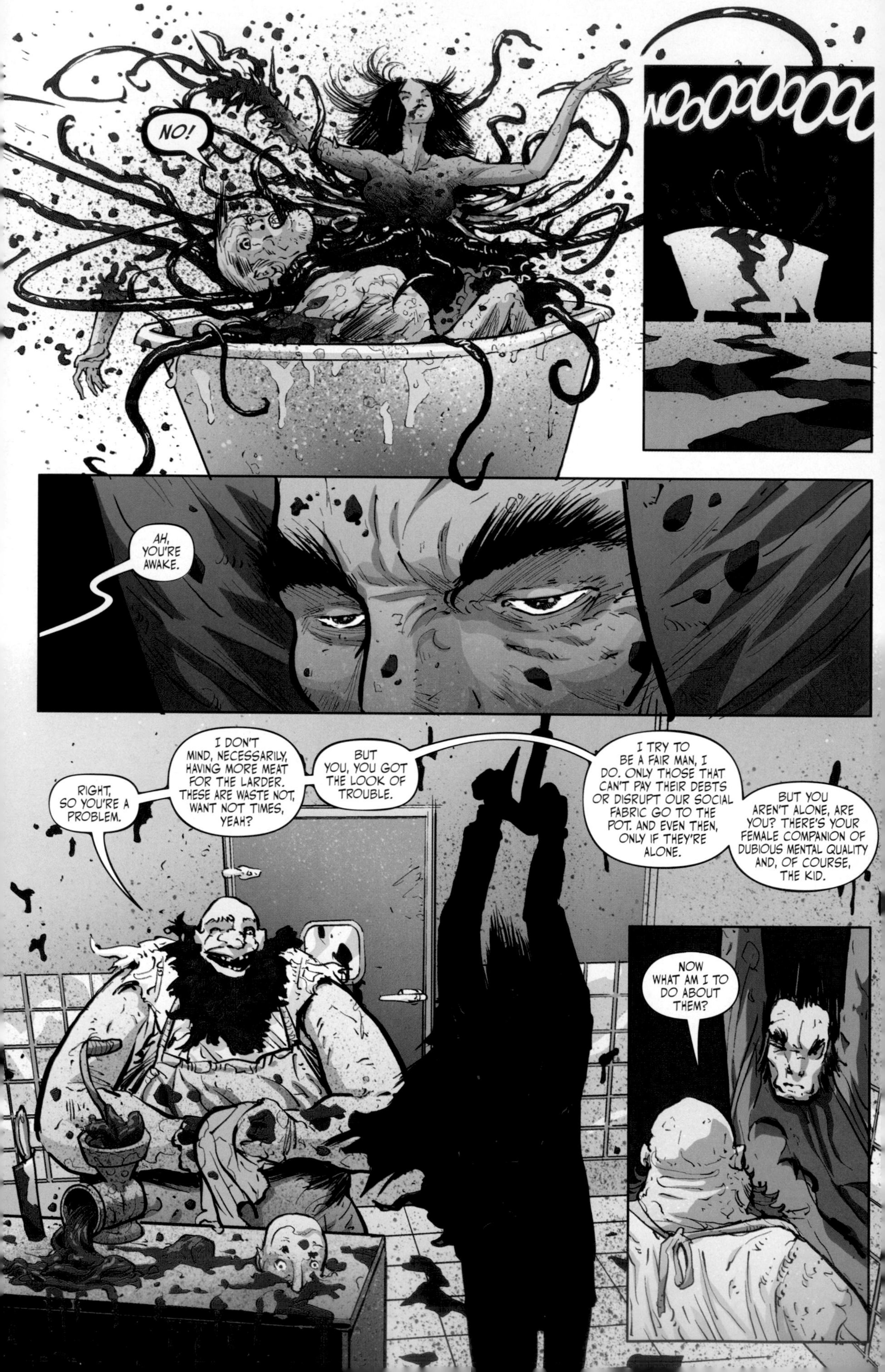
NO!
NOOOOOOOOOO
AH, YOU'RE AWAKE.
RIGHT, SO YOU'RE A PROBLEM.
I DON'T MIND, NECESSARILY, HAVING MORE MEAT FOR THE LARDER. THESE ARE WASTE NOT, WANT NOT TIMES, YEAH?
BUT YOU, YOU GOT THE LOOK OF TROUBLE.
I TRY TO BE A FAIR MAN, I DO. ONLY THOSE THAT CAN'T PAY THEIR DEBTS OR DISRUPT OUR SOCIAL FABRIC GO TO THE POT. AND EVEN THEN, ONLY IF THEY'RE ALONE.
BUT YOU AREN'T ALONE, ARE YOU? THERE'S YOUR FEMALE COMPANION OF DUBIOUS MENTAL QUALITY AND, OF COURSE, THE KID.
NOW WHAT AM I TO DO ABOUT THEM?

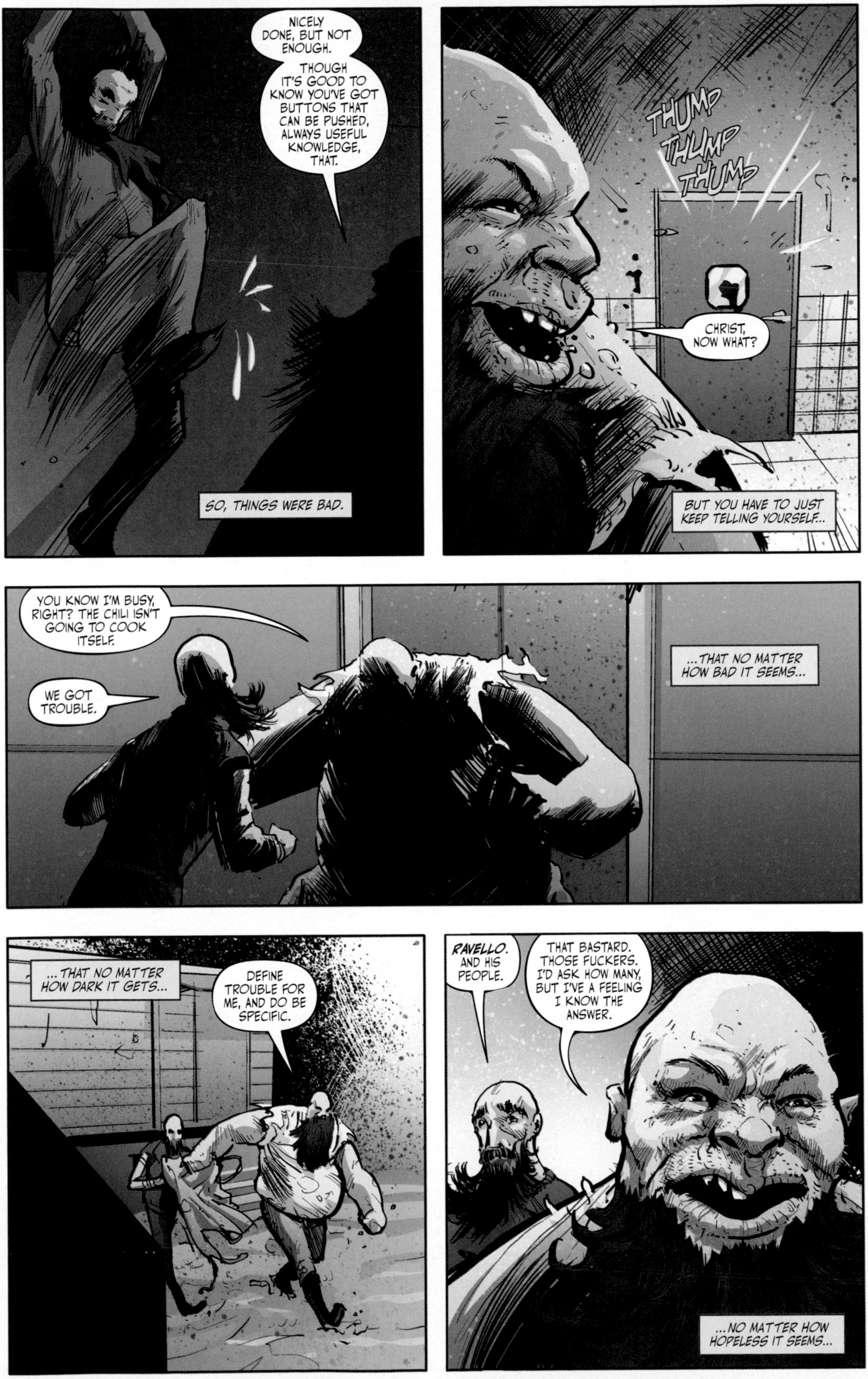
NICELY DONE, BUT NOT ENOUGH.
THOUGH IT'S GOOD TO KNOW YOU'VE GOT BUTTONS THAT CAN BE PUSHED, ALWAYS USEFUL KNOWLEDGE, THAT.
SO, THINGS WERE BAD.
THUMP THUMP THUMP
CHRIST, NOW WHAT?
BUT YOU HAVE TO JUST KEEP TELLING YOURSELF...
YOU KNOW I'M BUSY, RIGHT? THE CHILI ISN'T GOING TO COOK ITSELF.
WE GOT TROUBLE.
...THAT NO MATTER HOW BAD IT SEEMS...
...THAT NO MATTER HOW DARK IT GETS...
DEFINE TROUBLE FOR ME, AND DO BE SPECIFIC.
RAVELLO. AND HIS PEOPLE.
THAT BASTARD. THOSE FUCKERS. I'D ASK HOW MANY, BUT I'VE A FEELING I KNOW THE ANSWER.
...NO MATTER HOW HOPELESS IT SEEMS...

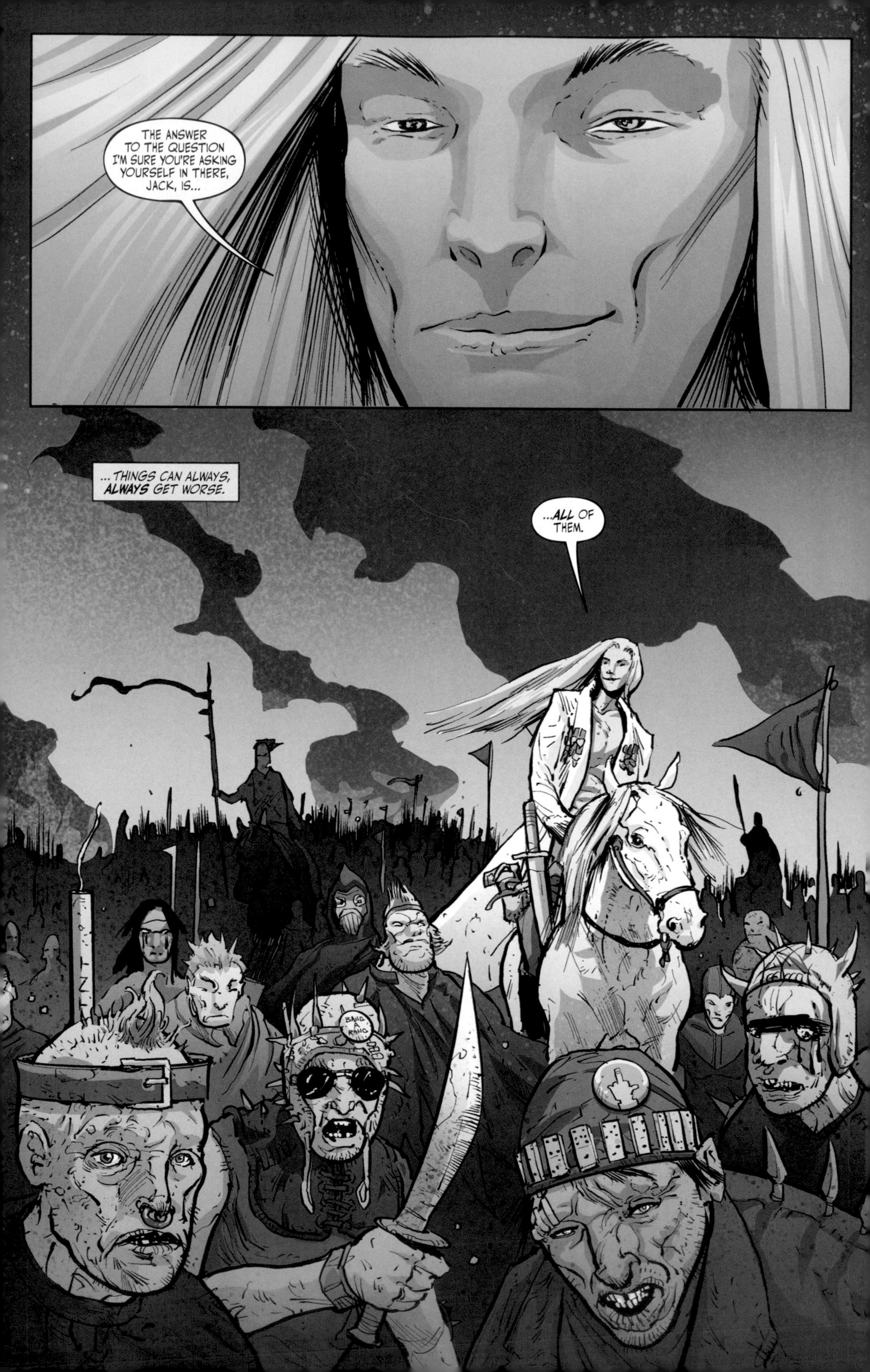
THE ANSWER TO THE QUESTION I'M SURE YOU'RE ASKING YOURSELF IN THERE, JACK, IS...
...THINGS CAN ALWAYS, ALWAYS GET WORSE.
...ALL OF THEM.
BANG A RANG

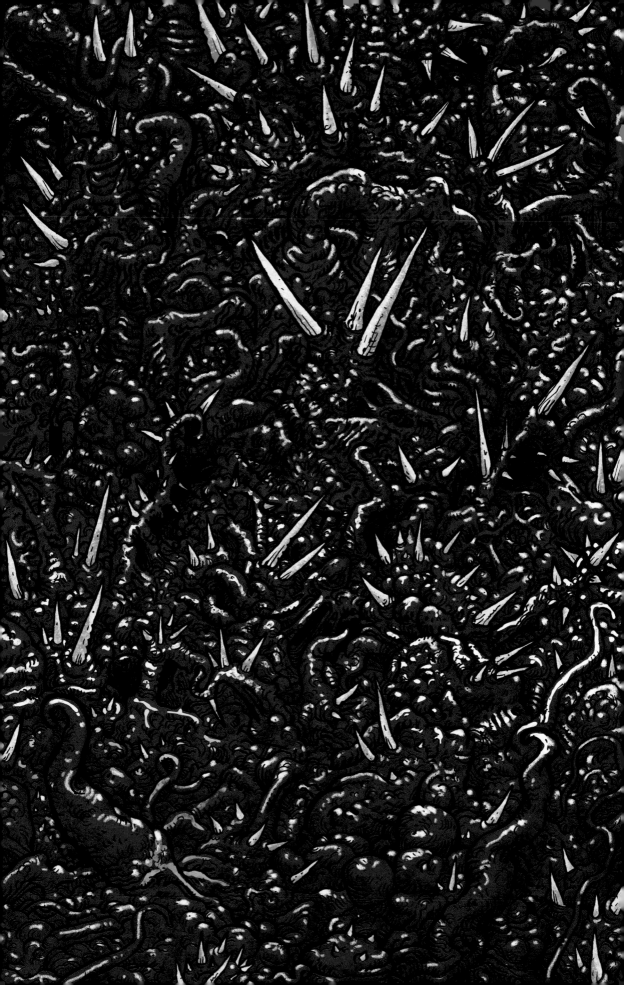

CHAPTER FOUR

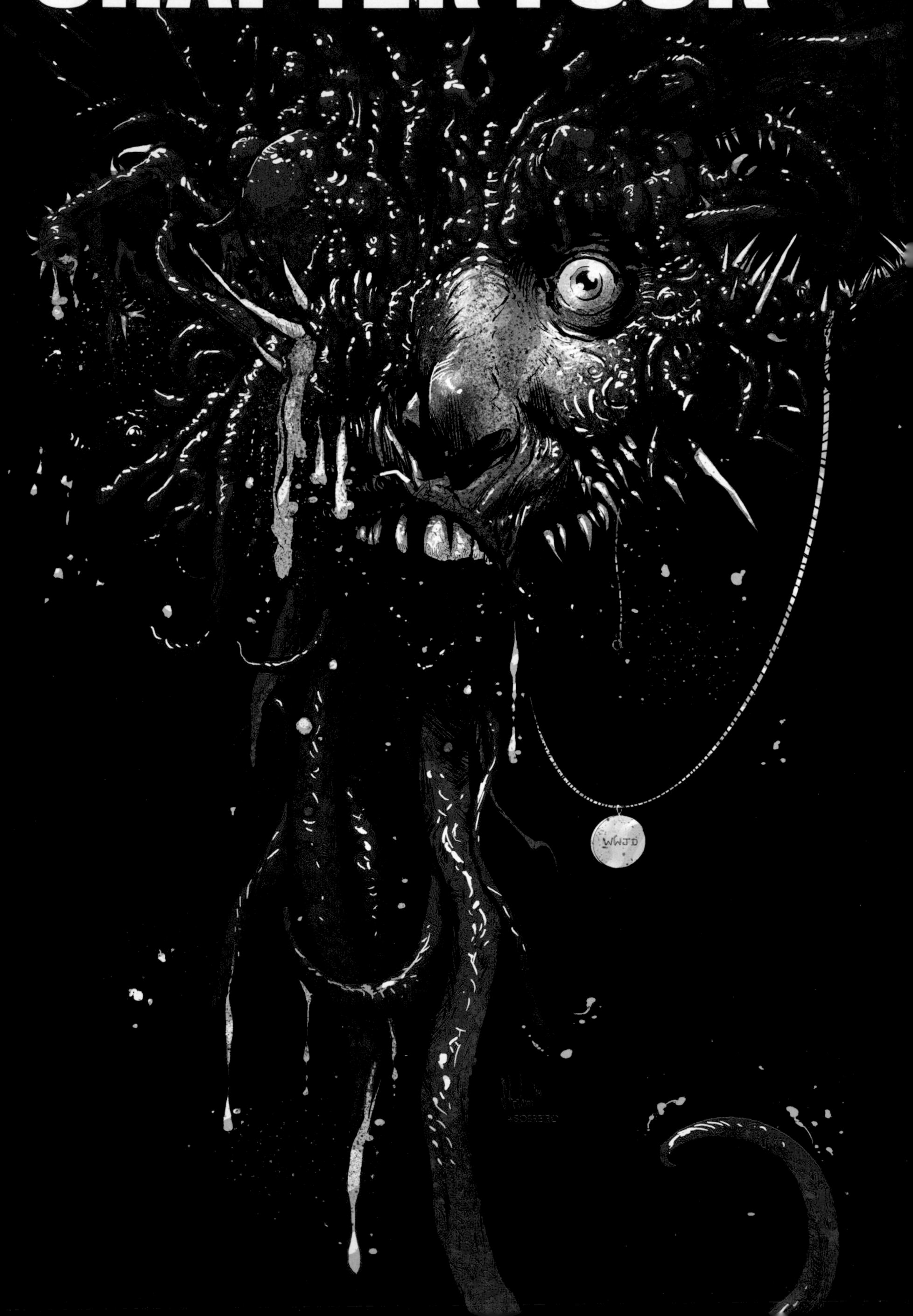

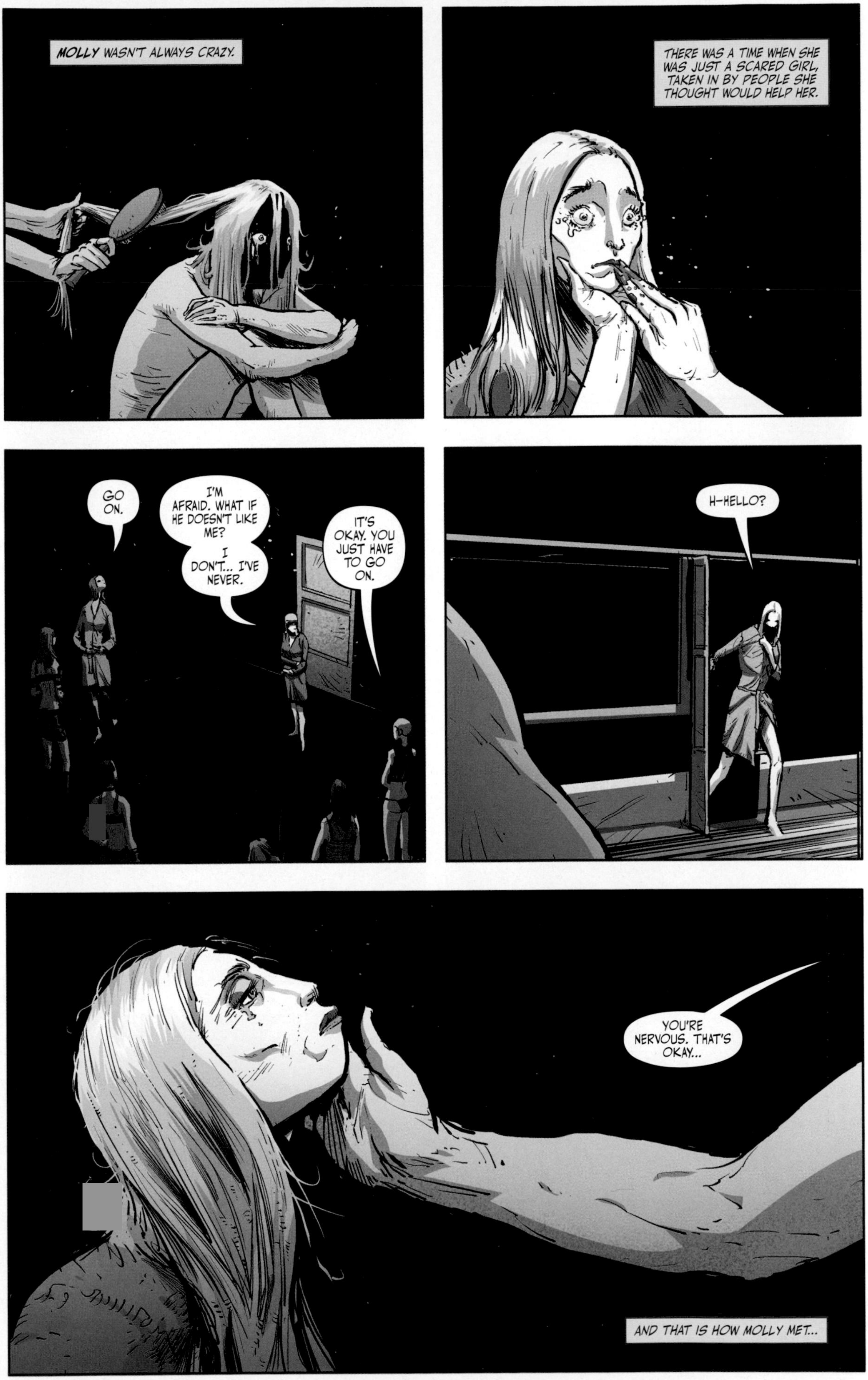
MOLLY WASN'T ALWAYS CRAZY.
THERE WAS A TIME WHEN SHE WAS JUST A SCARED GIRL, TAKEN IN BY PEOPLE SHE THOUGHT WOULD HELP HER.
GO ON.
I'M AFRAID. WHAT IF HE DOESN'T LIKE ME?
I DON'T... I'VE NEVER.
IT'S OKAY. YOU JUST HAVE TO GO ON.
H-HELLO?
YOU'RE NERVOUS. THAT'S OKAY...
AND THAT IS HOW MOLLY MET...

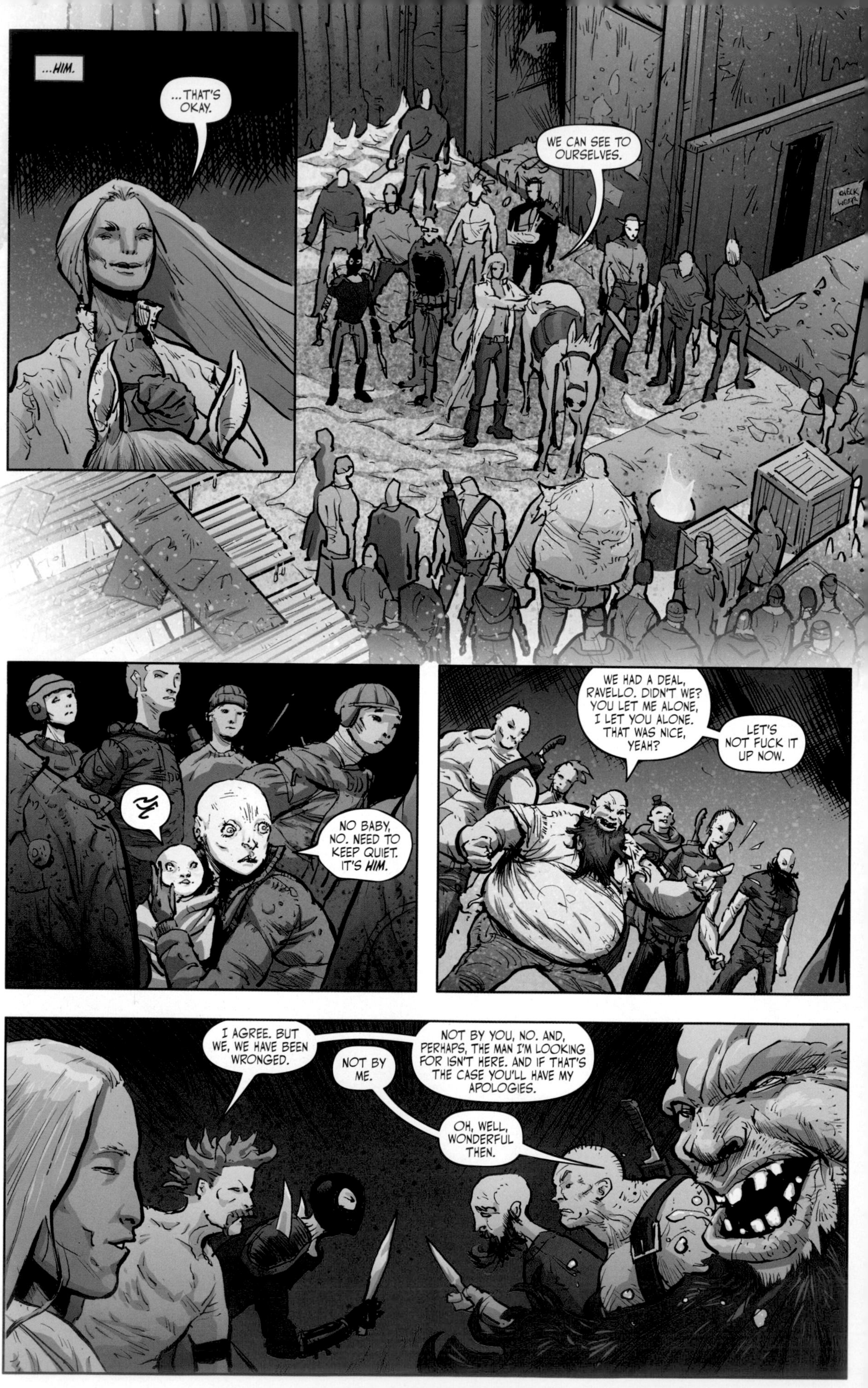
...HIM.
...THAT'S OKAY.
WE CAN SEE TO OURSELVES.
NO BABY, NO. NEED TO KEEP QUIET. IT'S HIM.
WE HAD A DEAL, RAVELLO. DIDN'T WE? YOU LET ME ALONE, I LET YOU ALONE. THAT WAS NICE, YEAH?
LET'S NOT FUCK IT UP NOW.
I AGREE. BUT WE, WE HAVE BEEN WRONGED.
NOT BY ME.
NOT BY YOU, NO. AND, PERHAPS, THE MAN I'M LOOKING FOR ISN'T HERE. AND IF THAT'S THE CASE YOU'LL HAVE MY APOLOGIES.
OH, WELL, WONDERFUL THEN.

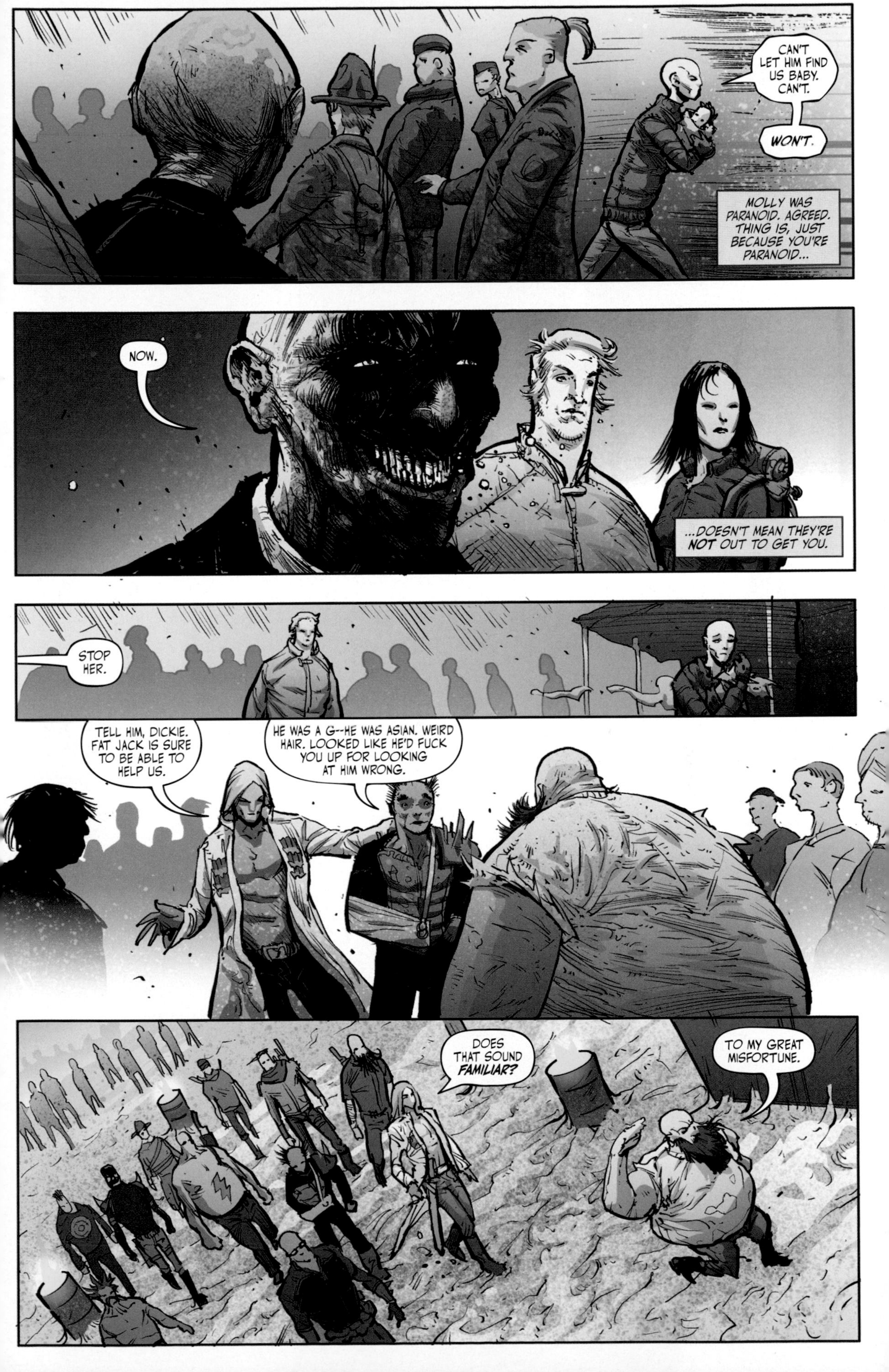
CAN'T LET HIM FIND US BABY. CAN'T.
WON'T.
MOLLY WAS PARANOID. AGREED. THING IS, JUST BECAUSE YOU'RE PARANOID...
NOW.
...DOESN'T MEAN THEY'RE NOT OUT TO GET YOU.
STOP HER.
TELL HIM, DICKIE. FAT JACK IS SURE TO BE ABLE TO HELP US.
HE WAS A G--HE WAS ASIAN. WEIRD HAIR. LOOKED LIKE HE'D FUCK YOU UP FOR LOOKING AT HIM WRONG.
DOES THAT SOUND FAMILIAR?
TO MY GREAT MISFORTUNE.

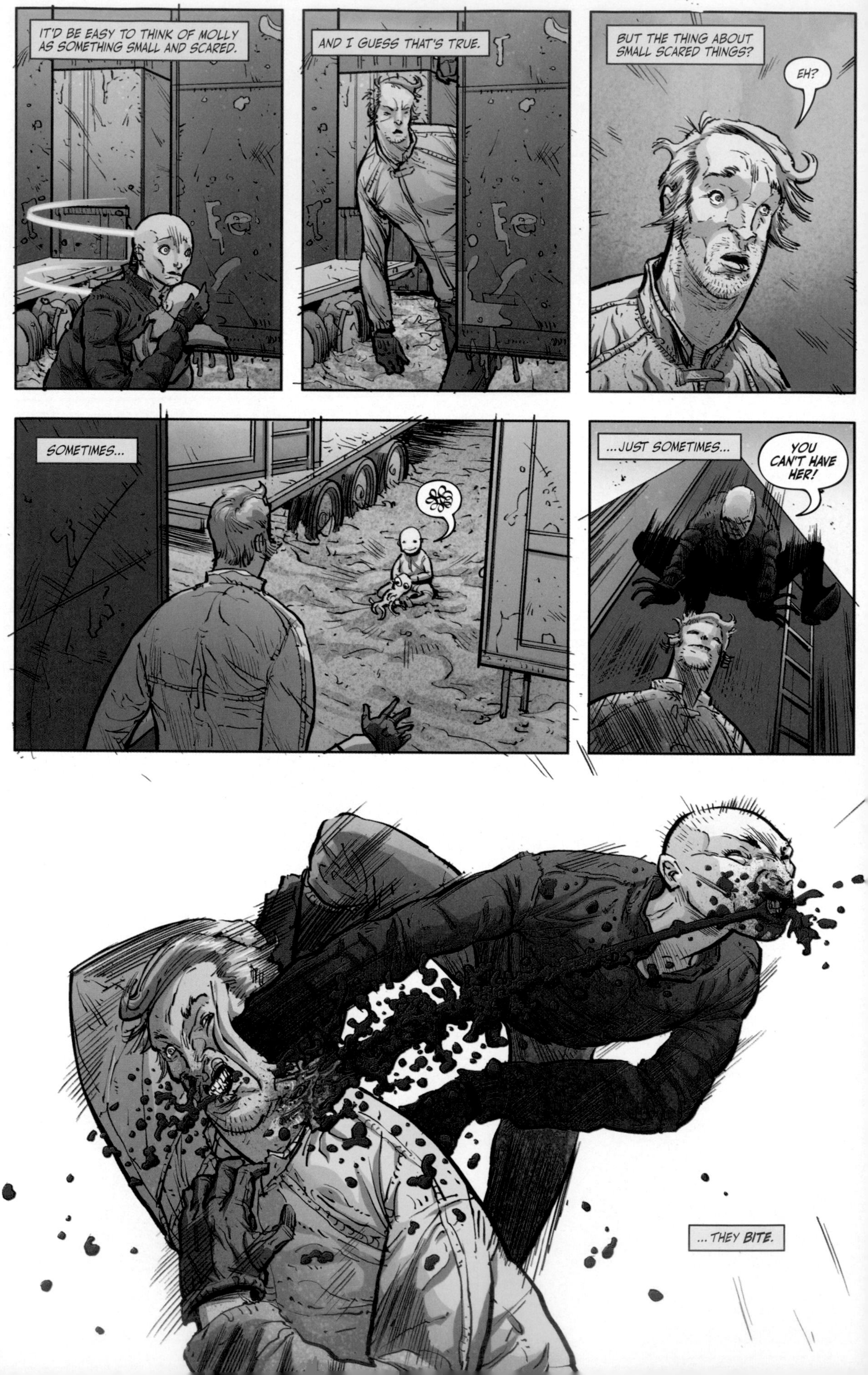
IT'D BE EASY TO THINK OF MOLLY AS SOMETHING SMALL AND SCARED.
AND I GUESS THAT'S TRUE.
BUT THE THING ABOUT SMALL SCARED THINGS?
EH?
SOMETIMES...
...JUST SOMETIMES...
YOU CAN'T HAVE HER!
...THEY BITE.

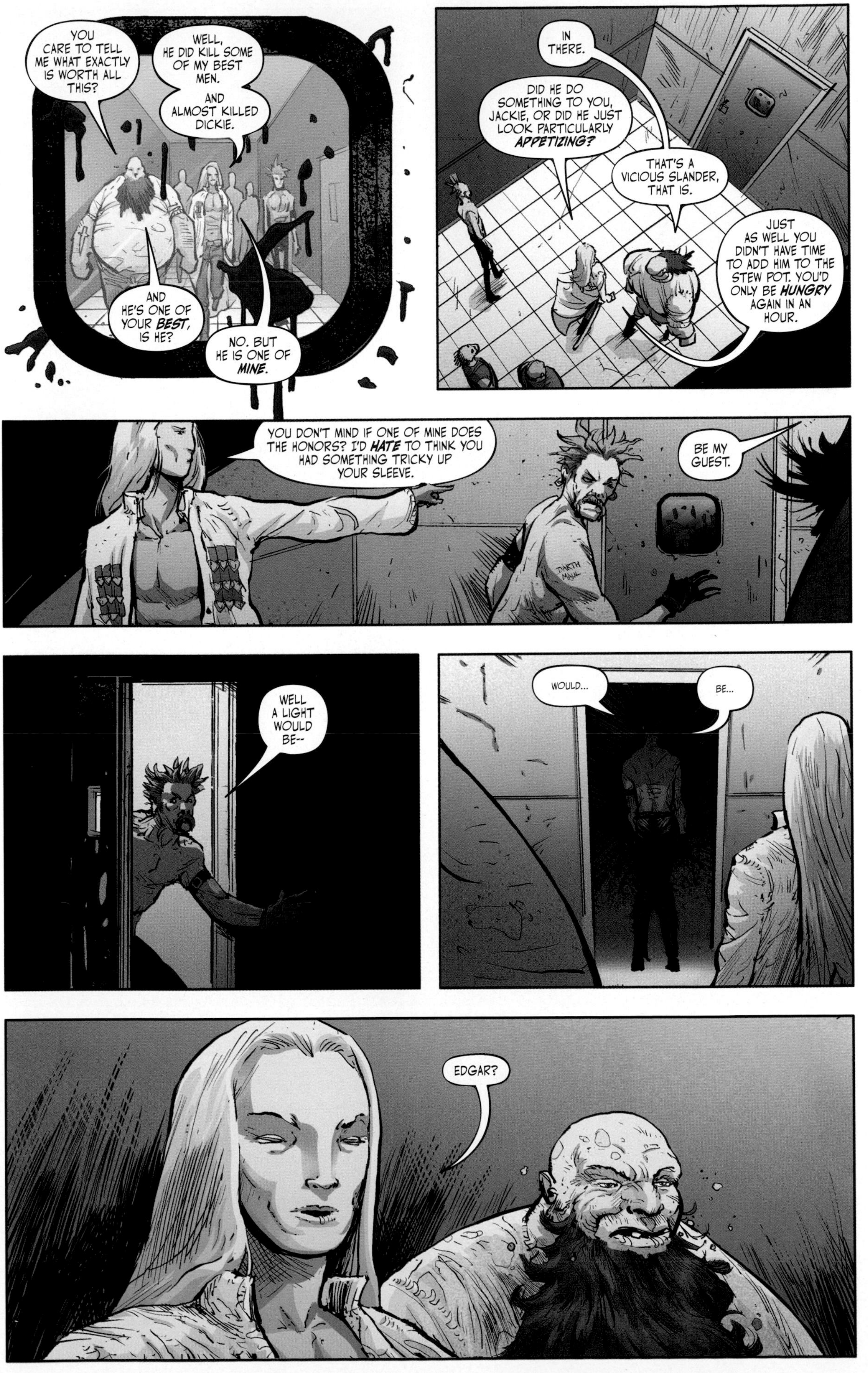
YOU CARE TO TELL ME WHAT EXACTLY IS WORTH ALL THIS?
WELL, HE DID KILL SOME OF MY BEST MEN.
AND ALMOST KILLED DICKIE.
AND HE'S ONE OF YOUR BEST, IS HE?
NO. BUT HE IS ONE OF MINE.
IN THERE.
DID HE DO SOMETHING TO YOU, JACKIE, OR DID HE JUST LOOK PARTICULARLY APPETIZING?
THAT'S A VICIOUS SLANDER, THAT IS.
JUST AS WELL YOU DIDN'T HAVE TIME TO ADD HIM TO THE STEW POT. YOU'D ONLY BE HUNGRY AGAIN IN AN HOUR.
YOU DON'T MIND IF ONE OF MINE DOES THE HONORS? I'D HATE TO THINK YOU HAD SOMETHING TRICKY UP YOUR SLEEVE.
BE MY GUEST.
DARTH MAUL
WELL A LIGHT WOULD BE--
WOULD...
BE...
EDGAR?

...NICE.

FUCKING WONDERFUL.

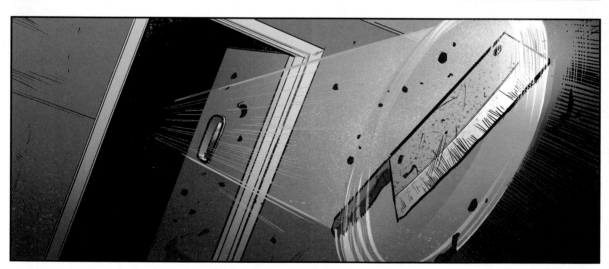

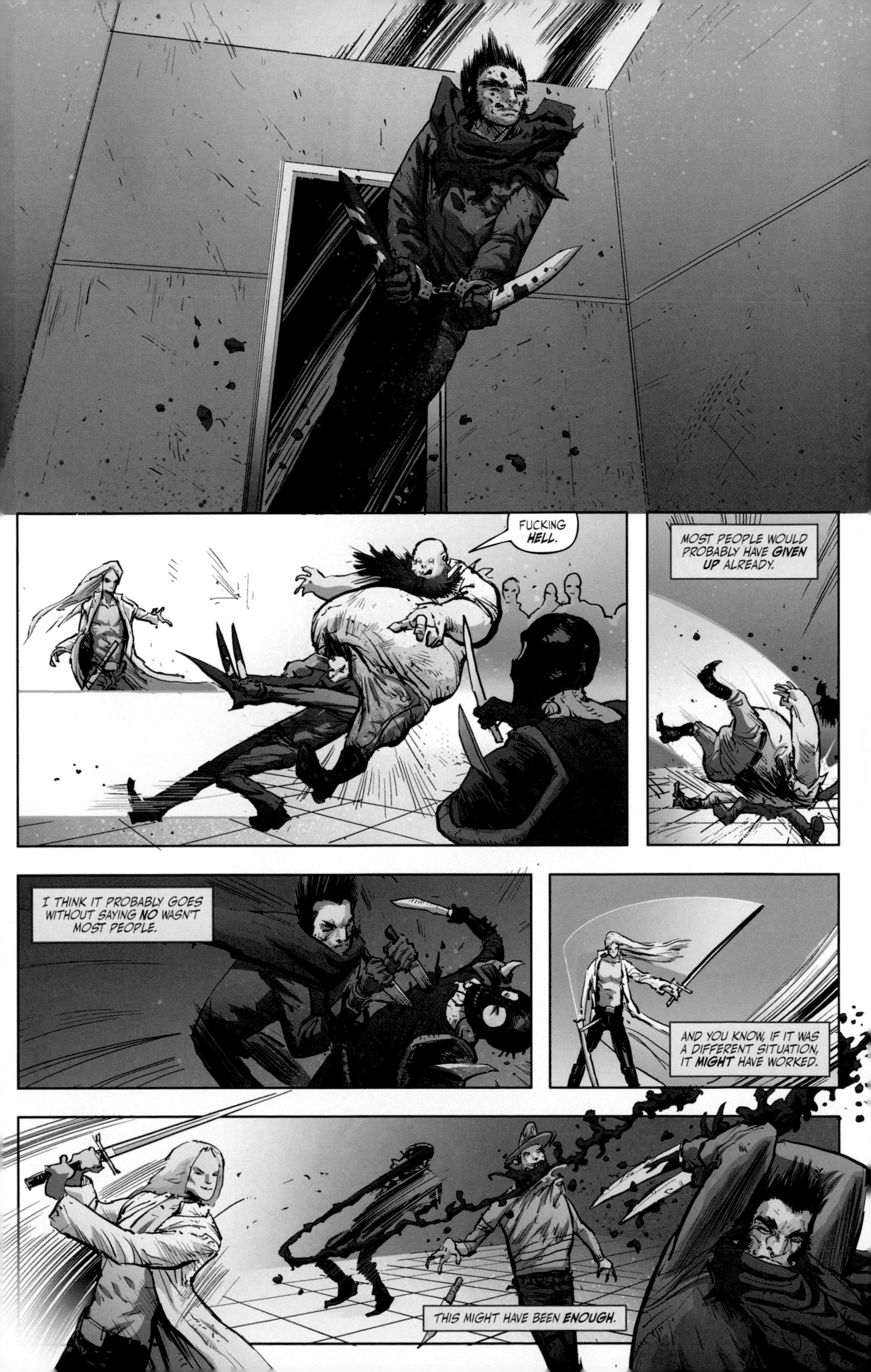
FUCKING HELL.
MOST PEOPLE WOULD PROBABLY HAVE GIVEN UP ALREADY.
I THINK IT PROBABLY GOES WITHOUT SAYING NO WASN'T MOST PEOPLE.
AND YOU KNOW, IF IT WAS A DIFFERENT SITUATION, IT MIGHT HAVE WORKED.
THIS MIGHT HAVE BEEN ENOUGH.

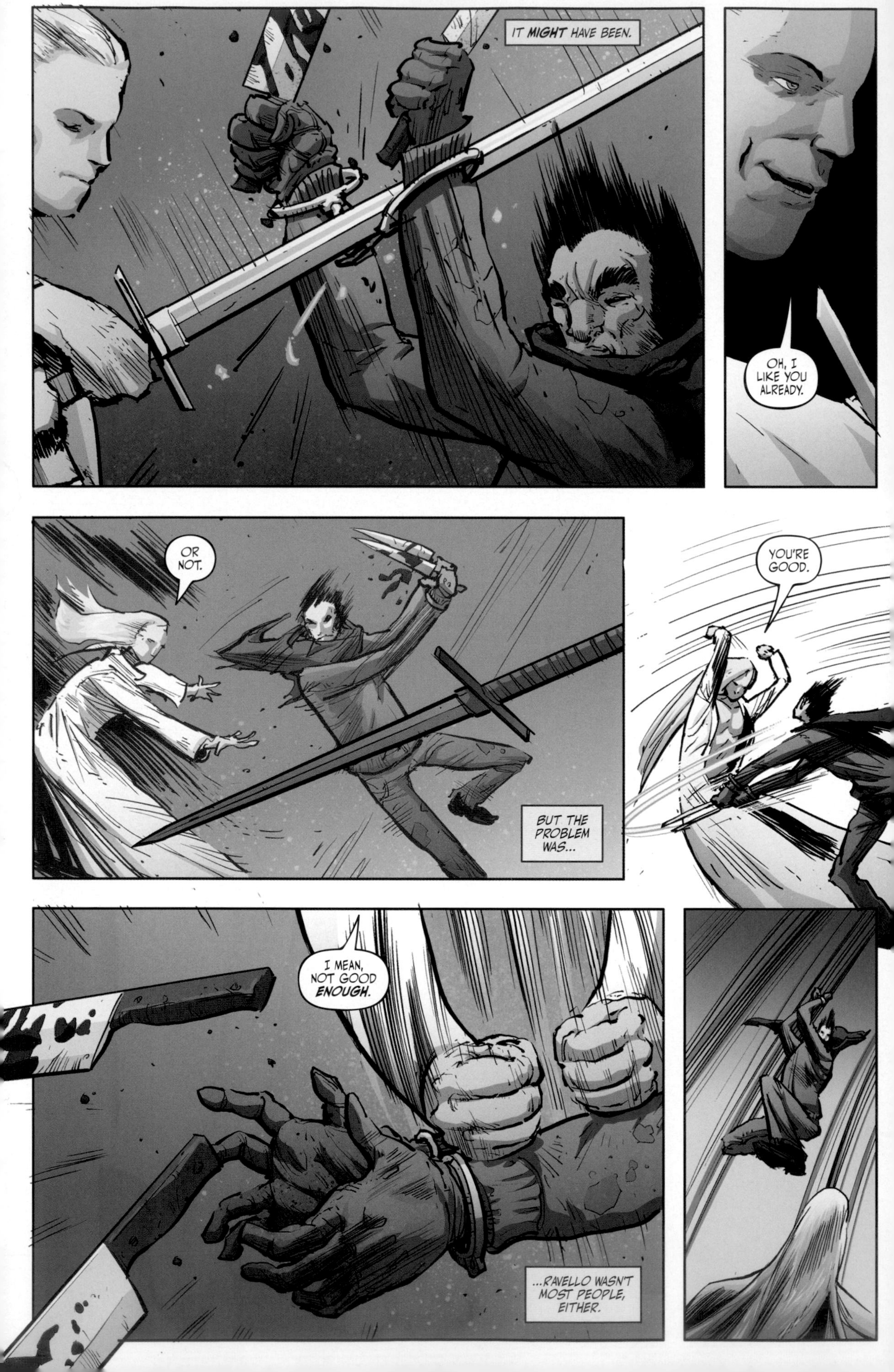
IT MIGHT HAVE BEEN.
OH, I LIKE YOU ALREADY.
OR NOT.
BUT THE PROBLEM WAS...
YOU'RE GOOD.
I MEAN, NOT GOOD ENOUGH.
...RAVELLO WASN'T MOST PEOPLE, EITHER.

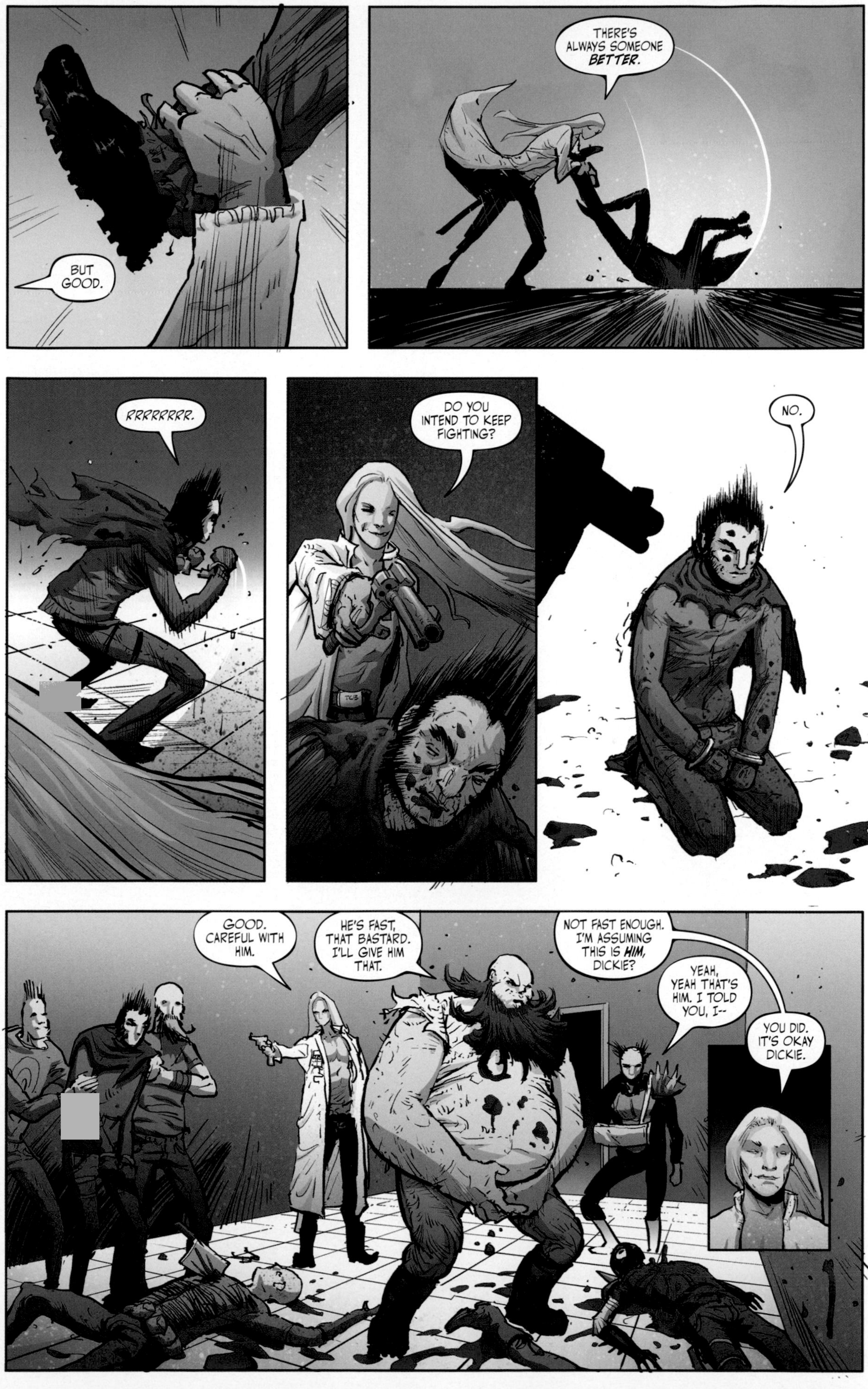

BUT GOOD.
THERE'S ALWAYS SOMEONE *BETTER*.
RRRRRRRR.
DO YOU INTEND TO KEEP FIGHTING?
NO.
GOOD. CAREFUL WITH HIM.
HE'S FAST, THAT BASTARD. I'LL GIVE HIM THAT.
NOT FAST ENOUGH. I'M ASSUMING THIS IS *HIM*, DICKIE?
YEAH, YEAH THAT'S HIM. I TOLD YOU, I--
YOU DID. IT'S OKAY DICKIE.

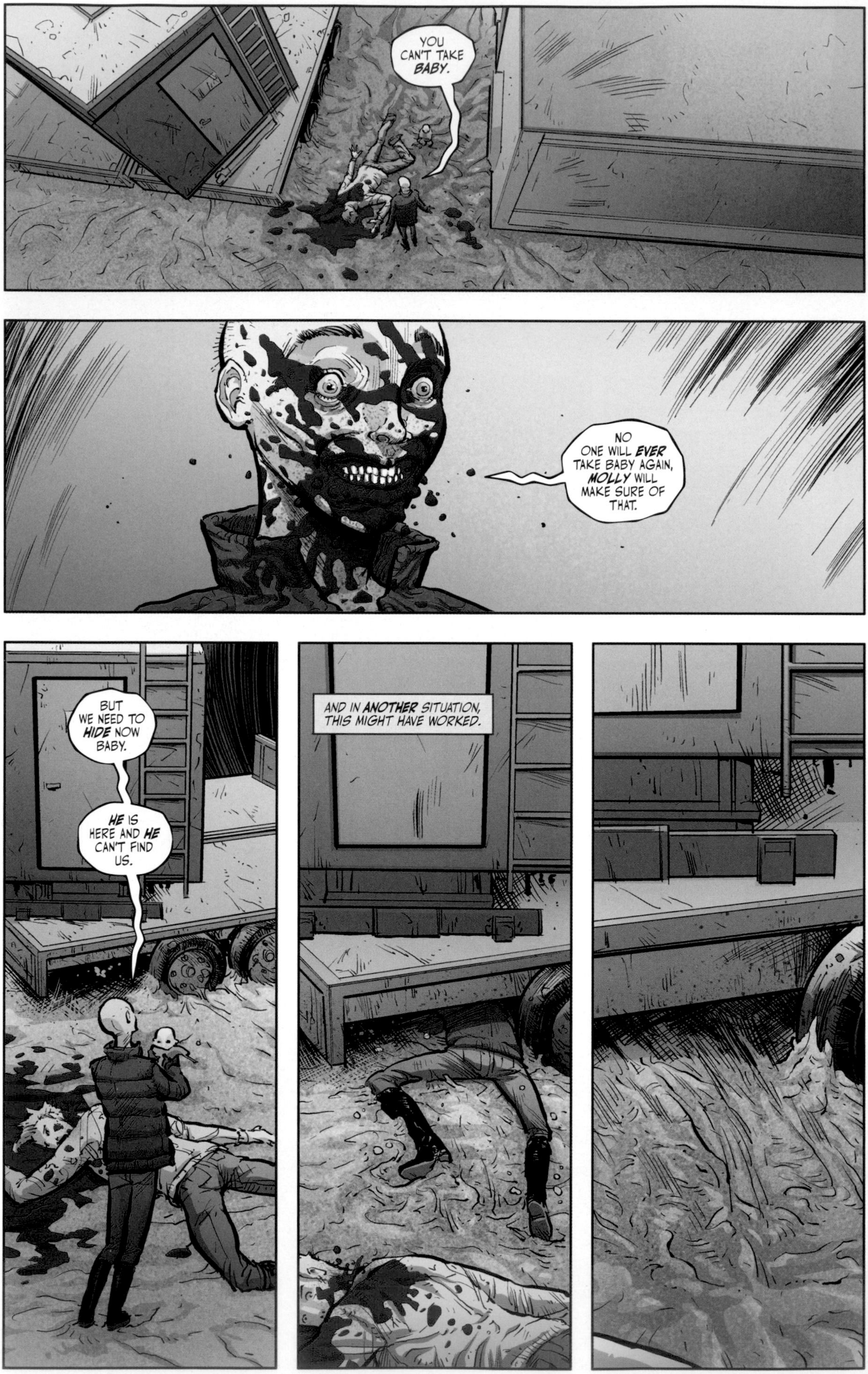
YOU CAN'T TAKE BABY.
NO ONE WILL EVER TAKE BABY AGAIN, MOLLY WILL MAKE SURE OF THAT.
BUT WE NEED TO HIDE NOW BABY.
HE IS HERE AND HE CAN'T FIND US.
AND IN ANOTHER SITUATION, THIS MIGHT HAVE WORKED.

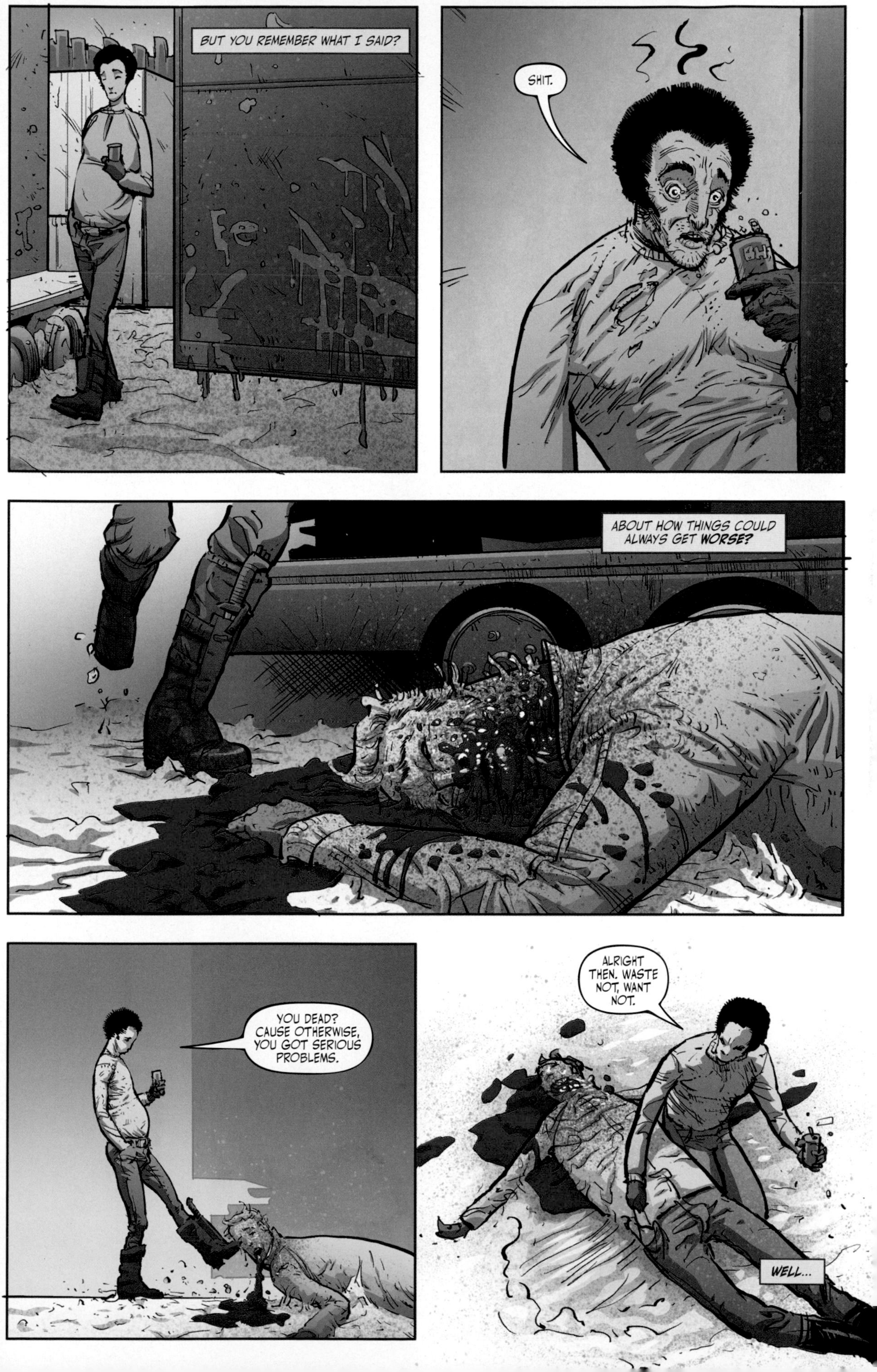

BUT YOU REMEMBER WHAT I SAID?
SHIT.
ABOUT HOW THINGS COULD ALWAYS GET **WORSE?**
YOU DEAD? CAUSE OTHERWISE, YOU GOT SERIOUS PROBLEMS.
ALRIGHT THEN. WASTE NOT, WANT NOT.
WELL...

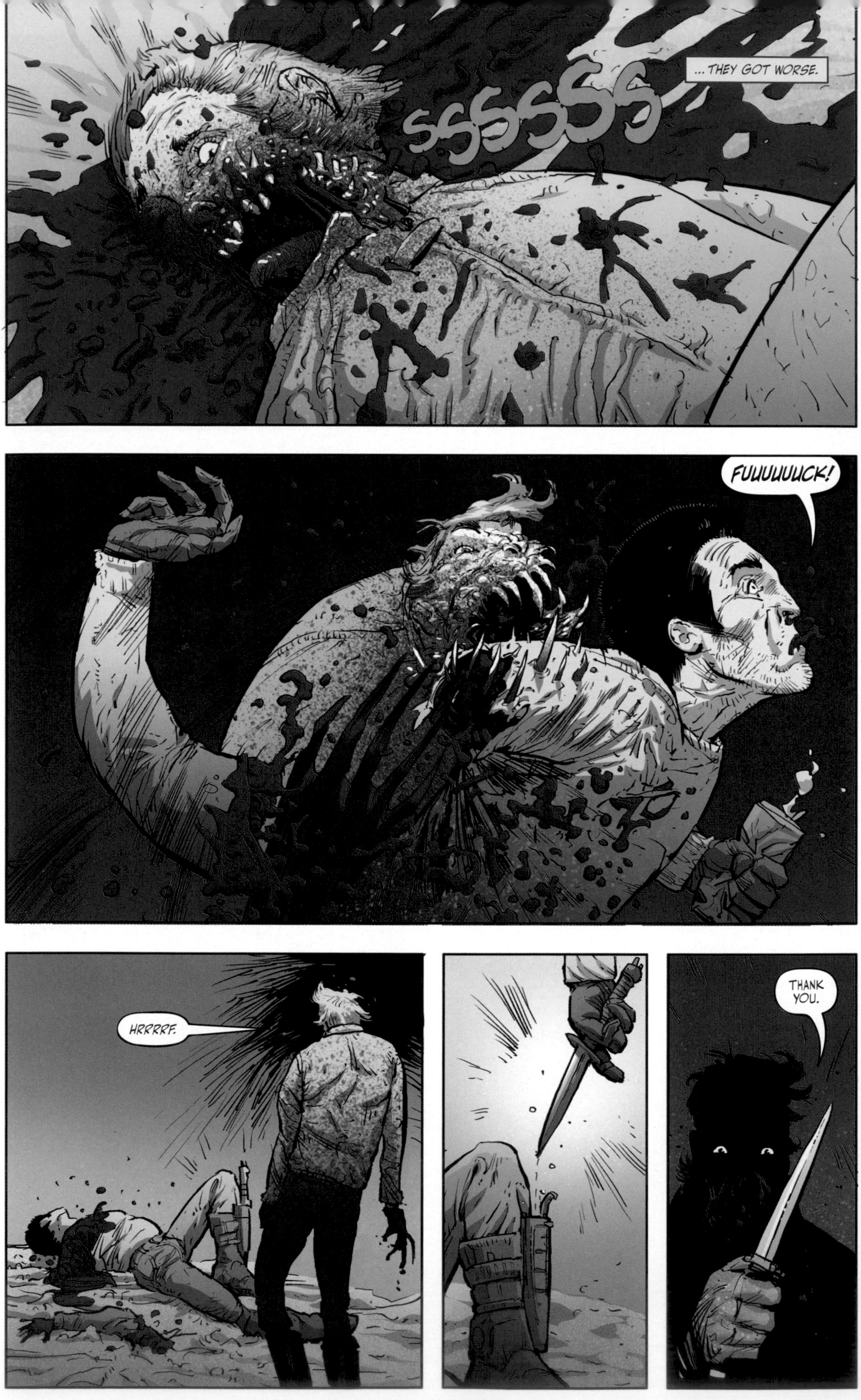
...THEY GOT WORSE.
SSSSSSS
FUUUUUUCK!
HRRRRF.
THANK YOU.

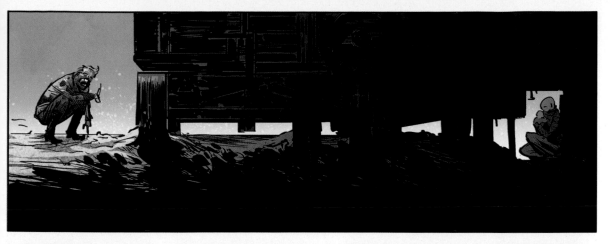

HELLO.

HELLO. HELLO. HELLO.

MUCH WORSE.

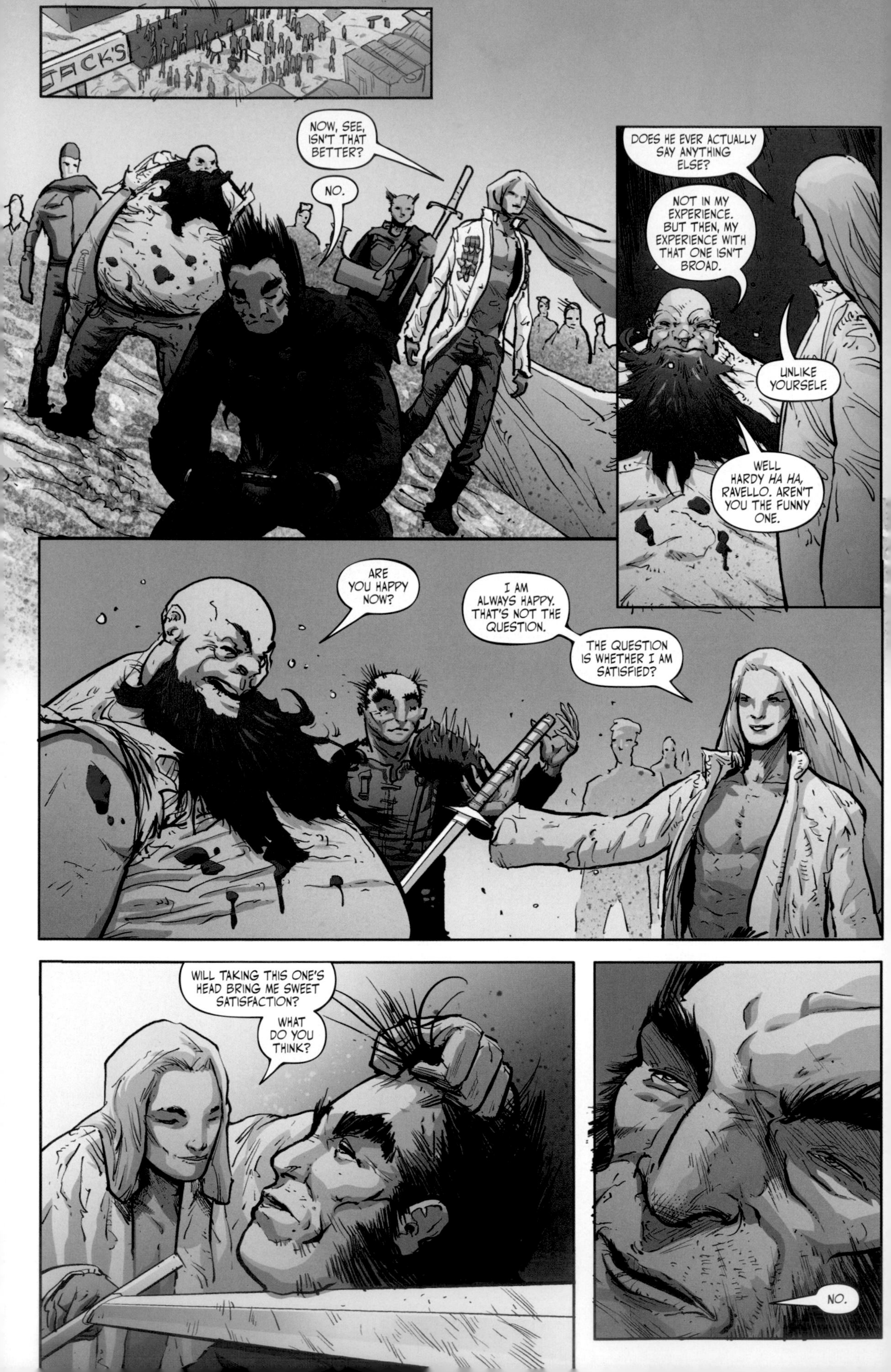
JACK'S
NOW, SEE, ISN'T THAT BETTER?
NO.
DOES HE EVER ACTUALLY SAY ANYTHING ELSE?
NOT IN MY EXPERIENCE. BUT THEN, MY EXPERIENCE WITH THAT ONE ISN'T BROAD.
UNLIKE YOURSELF.
WELL HARDY *HA HA*, RAVELLO. AREN'T YOU THE FUNNY ONE.
ARE YOU HAPPY NOW?
I AM ALWAYS HAPPY. THAT'S NOT THE QUESTION.
THE QUESTION IS WHETHER I AM SATISFIED?
WILL TAKING THIS ONE'S HEAD BRING ME SWEET SATISFACTION?
WHAT DO YOU THINK?
NO.

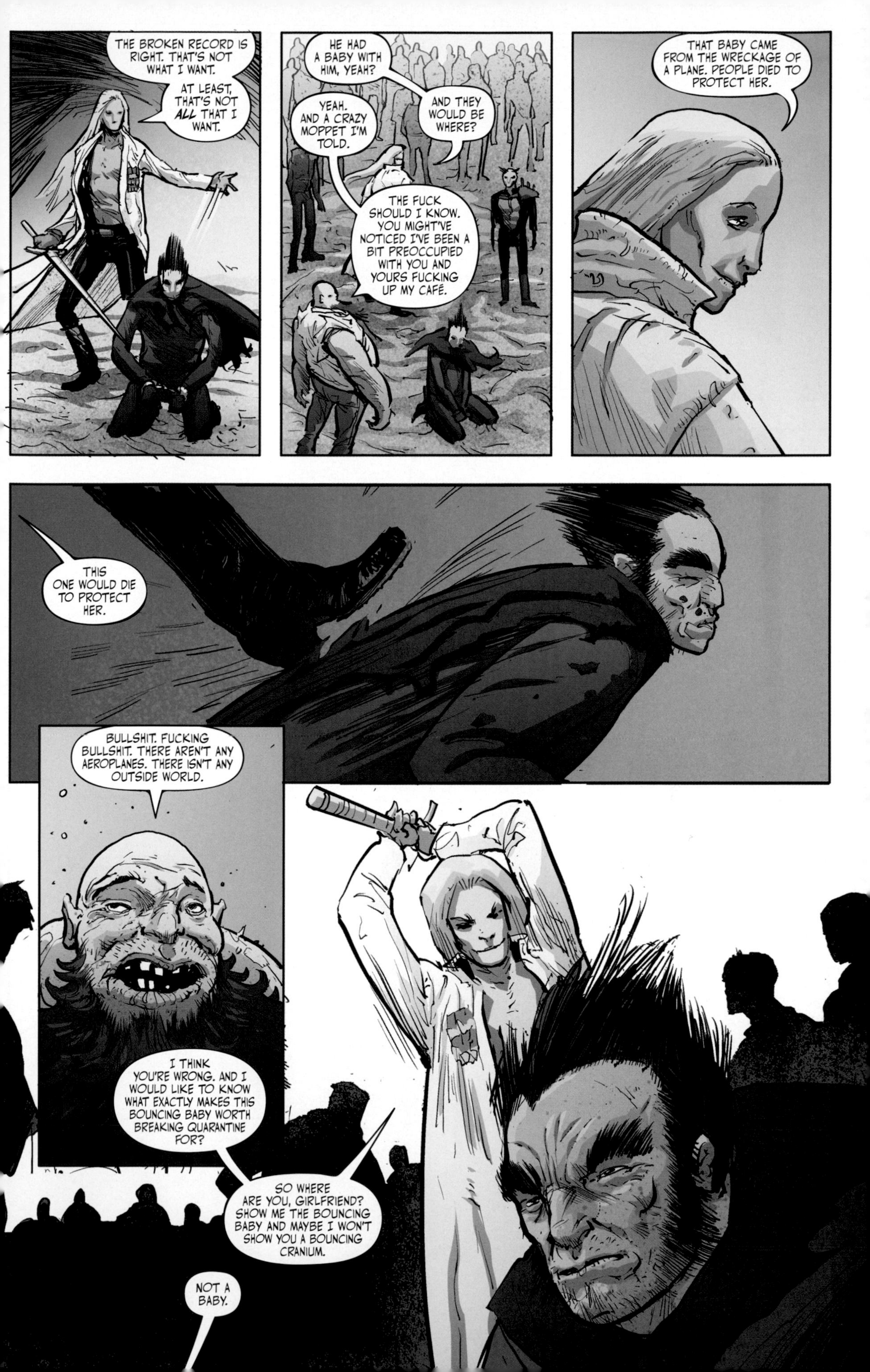
THE BROKEN RECORD IS RIGHT. THAT'S NOT WHAT I WANT.
AT LEAST, THAT'S NOT *ALL* THAT I WANT.
HE HAD A BABY WITH HIM, YEAH?
YEAH. AND A CRAZY MOPPET I'M TOLD.
AND THEY WOULD BE WHERE?
THE FUCK SHOULD I KNOW. YOU MIGHT'VE NOTICED I'VE BEEN A BIT PREOCCUPIED WITH YOU AND YOURS FUCKING UP MY CAFÉ.
THAT BABY CAME FROM THE WRECKAGE OF A PLANE. PEOPLE DIED TO PROTECT HER.
THIS ONE WOULD DIE TO PROTECT HER.
BULLSHIT. FUCKING BULLSHIT. THERE AREN'T ANY AEROPLANES. THERE ISN'T ANY OUTSIDE WORLD.
I THINK YOU'RE WRONG. AND I WOULD LIKE TO KNOW WHAT EXACTLY MAKES THIS BOUNCING BABY WORTH BREAKING QUARANTINE FOR?
SO WHERE ARE YOU, GIRLFRIEND? SHOW ME THE BOUNCING BABY AND MAYBE I WON'T SHOW YOU A BOUNCING CRANIUM.
NOT A BABY.

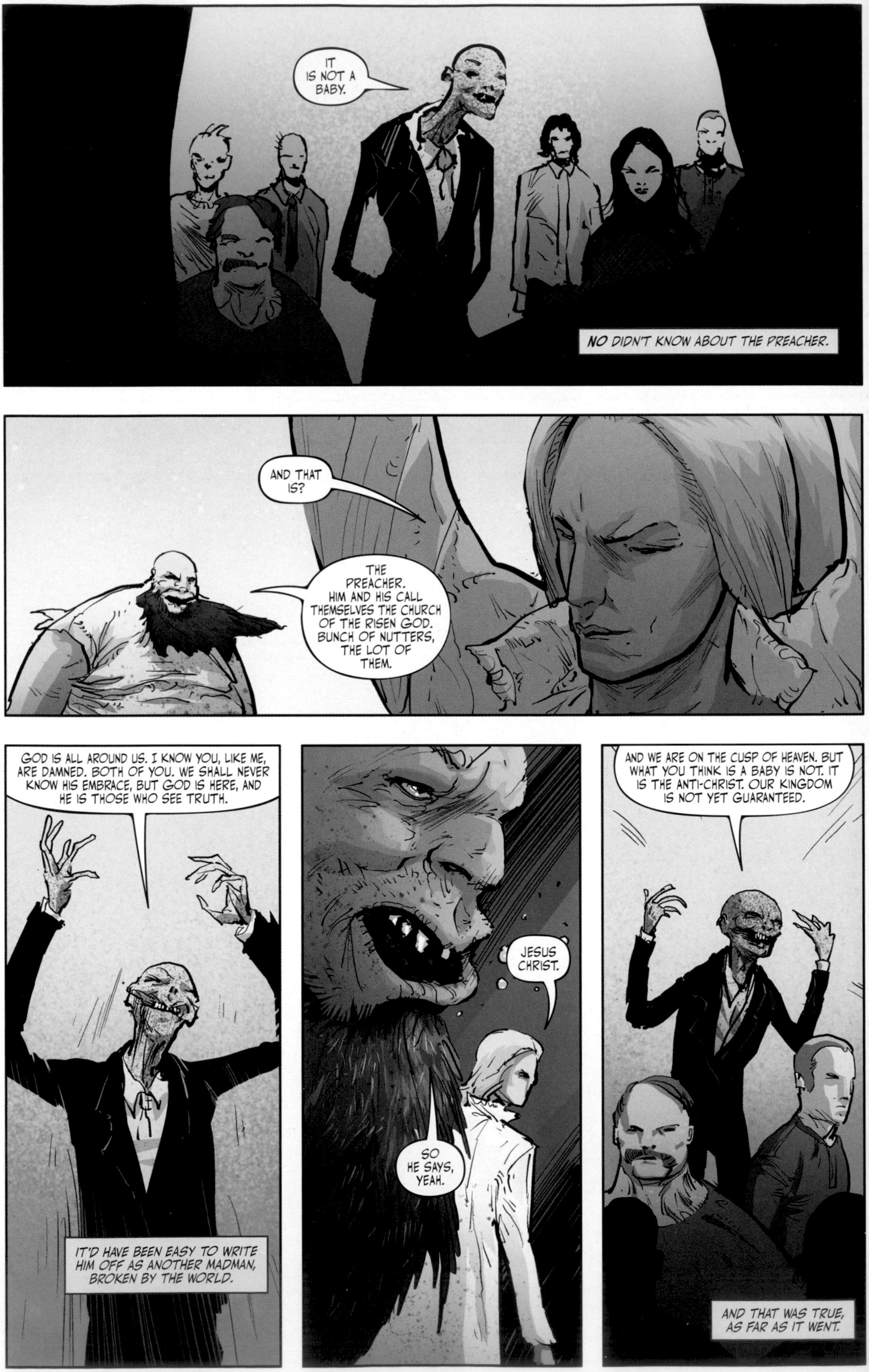
IT IS NOT A BABY.
NO DIDN'T KNOW ABOUT THE PREACHER.
AND THAT IS?
THE PREACHER. HIM AND HIS CALL THEMSELVES THE CHURCH OF THE RISEN GOD. BUNCH OF NUTTERS, THE LOT OF THEM.
GOD IS ALL AROUND US. I KNOW YOU, LIKE ME, ARE DAMNED. BOTH OF YOU. WE SHALL NEVER KNOW HIS EMBRACE, BUT GOD IS HERE, AND HE IS THOSE WHO SEE TRUTH.
IT'D HAVE BEEN EASY TO WRITE HIM OFF AS ANOTHER MADMAN, BROKEN BY THE WORLD.
JESUS CHRIST.
SO HE SAYS, YEAH.
AND WE ARE ON THE CUSP OF HEAVEN. BUT WHAT YOU THINK IS A BABY IS NOT. IT IS THE ANTI-CHRIST. OUR KINGDOM IS NOT YET GUARANTEED.
AND THAT WAS TRUE, AS FAR AS IT WENT.

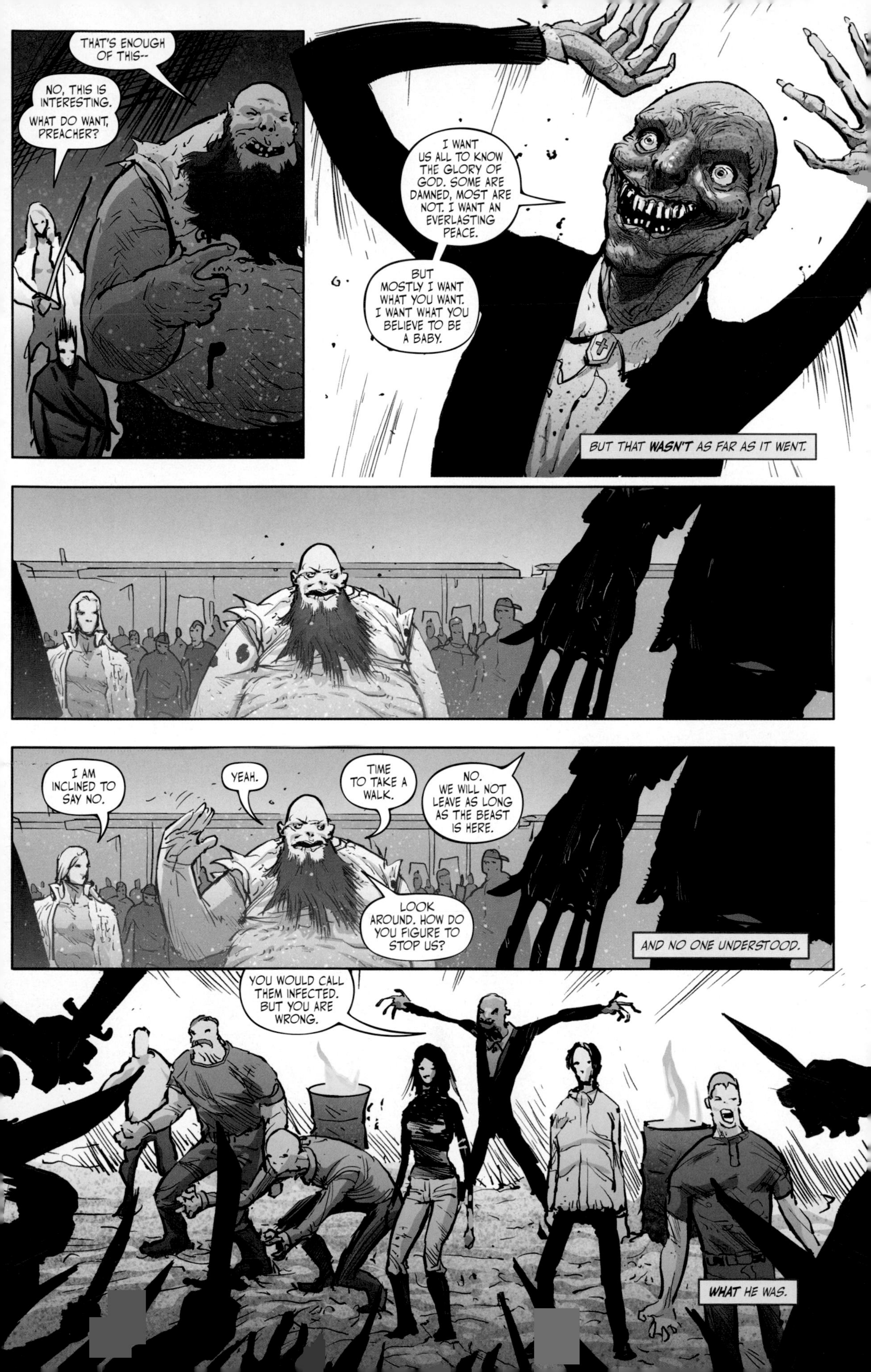
THAT'S ENOUGH OF THIS--
NO, THIS IS INTERESTING.
WHAT DO WANT, PREACHER?
I WANT US ALL TO KNOW THE GLORY OF GOD. SOME ARE DAMNED, MOST ARE NOT. I WANT AN EVERLASTING PEACE.
BUT MOSTLY I WANT WHAT YOU WANT. I WANT WHAT YOU BELIEVE TO BE A BABY.
BUT THAT WASN'T AS FAR AS IT WENT.
I AM INCLINED TO SAY NO.
YEAH.
TIME TO TAKE A WALK.
NO. WE WILL NOT LEAVE AS LONG AS THE BEAST IS HERE.
LOOK AROUND. HOW DO YOU FIGURE TO STOP US?
AND NO ONE UNDERSTOOD.
YOU WOULD CALL THEM INFECTED. BUT YOU ARE WRONG.
WHAT HE WAS.

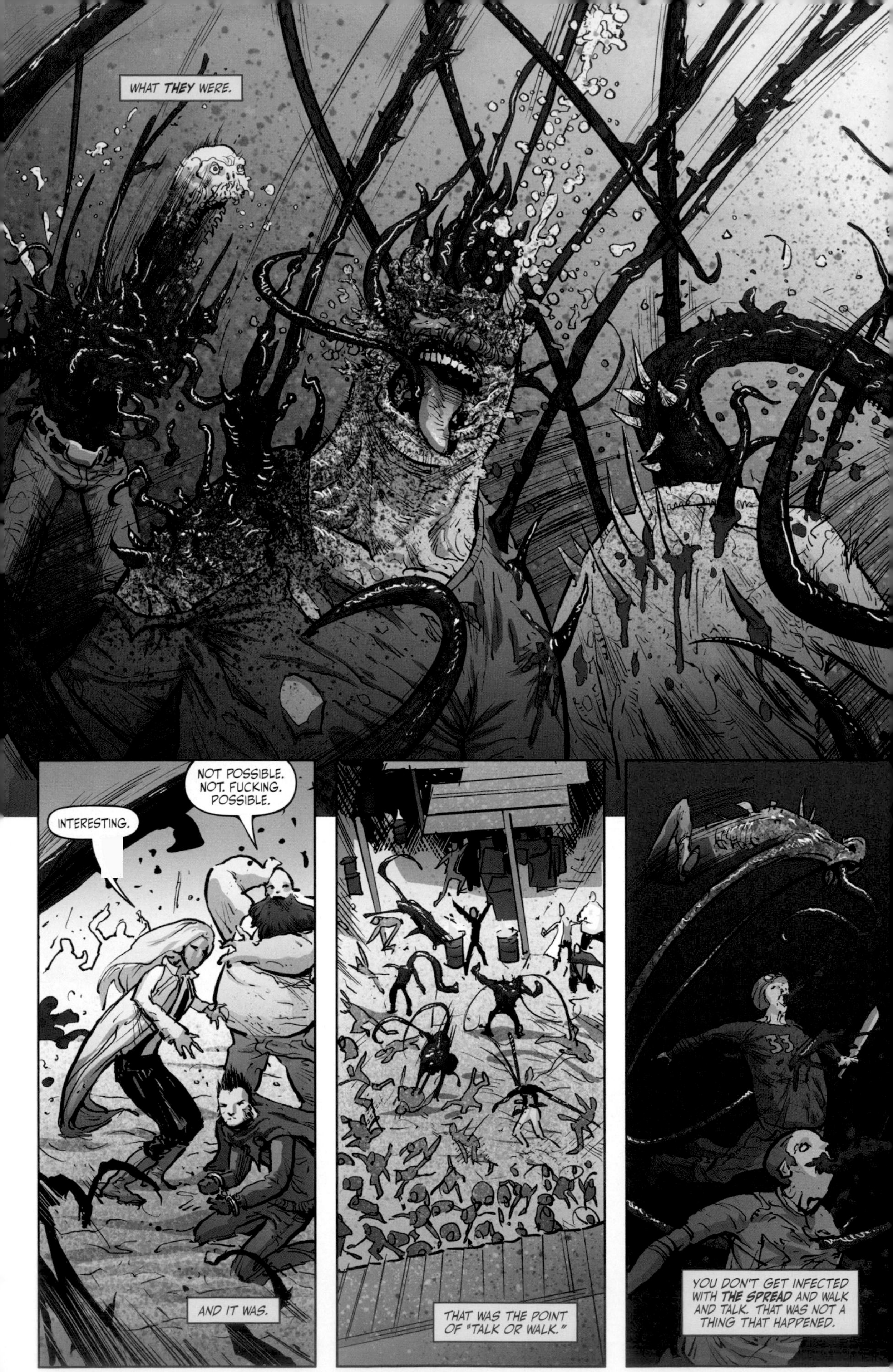
WHAT THEY WERE.
INTERESTING.
NOT POSSIBLE. NOT. FUCKING. POSSIBLE.
AND IT WAS.
THAT WAS THE POINT OF "TALK OR WALK."
YOU DON'T GET INFECTED WITH THE SPREAD AND WALK AND TALK. THAT WAS NOT A THING THAT HAPPENED.

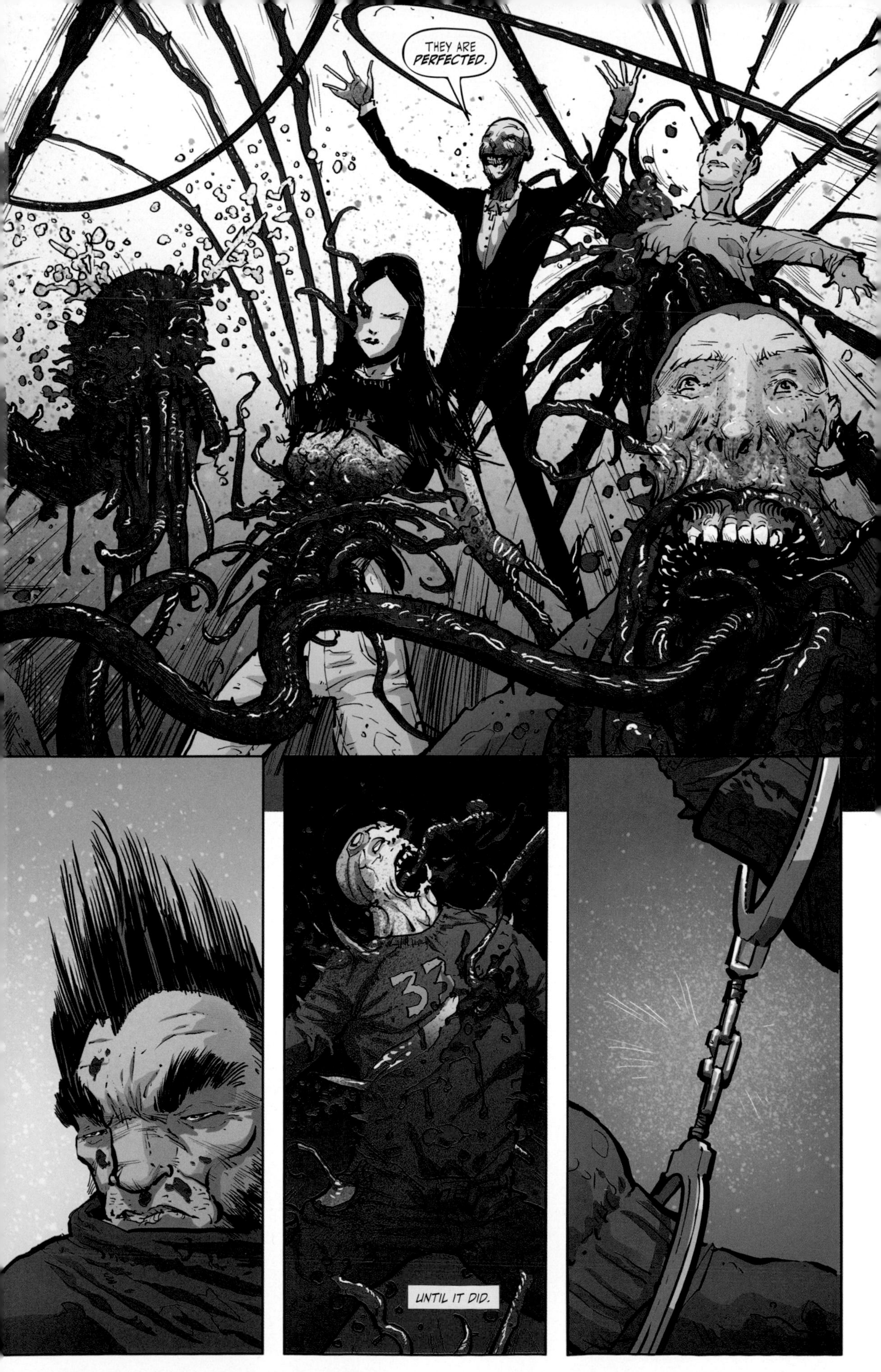
THEY ARE PERFECTED.
UNTIL IT DID.

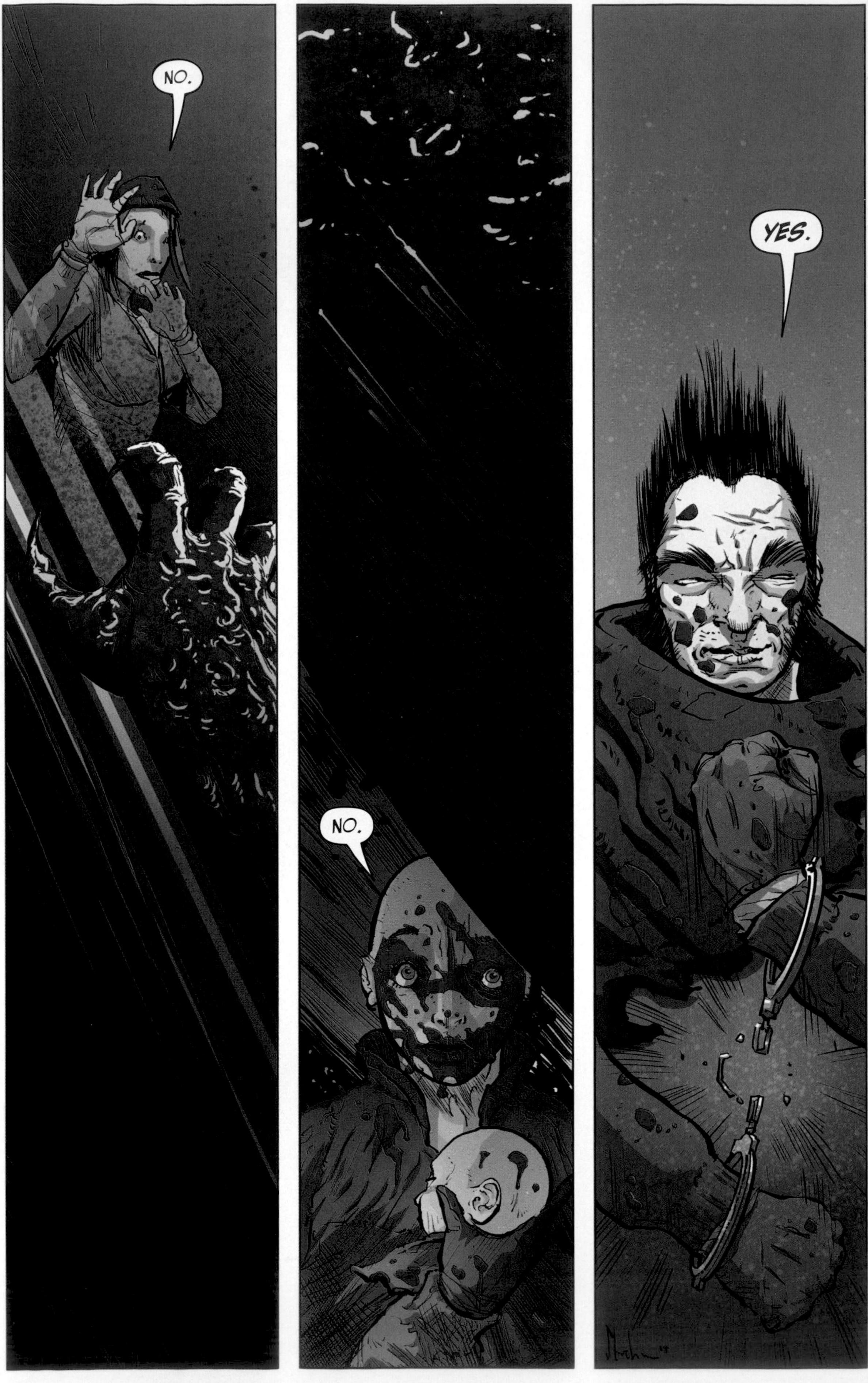
NO.
NO.
YES.

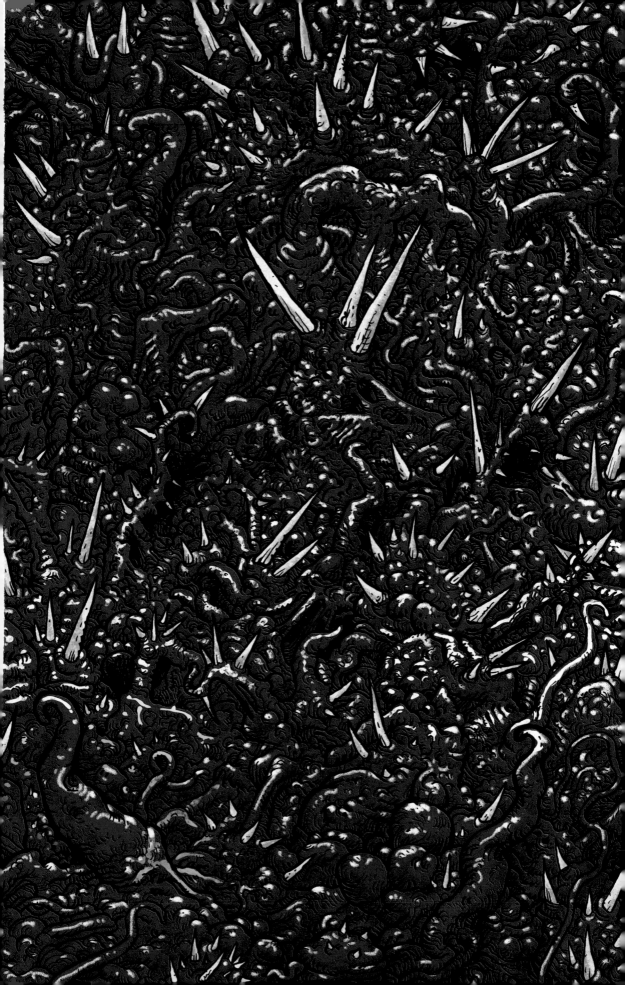

CHAPTER FIVE

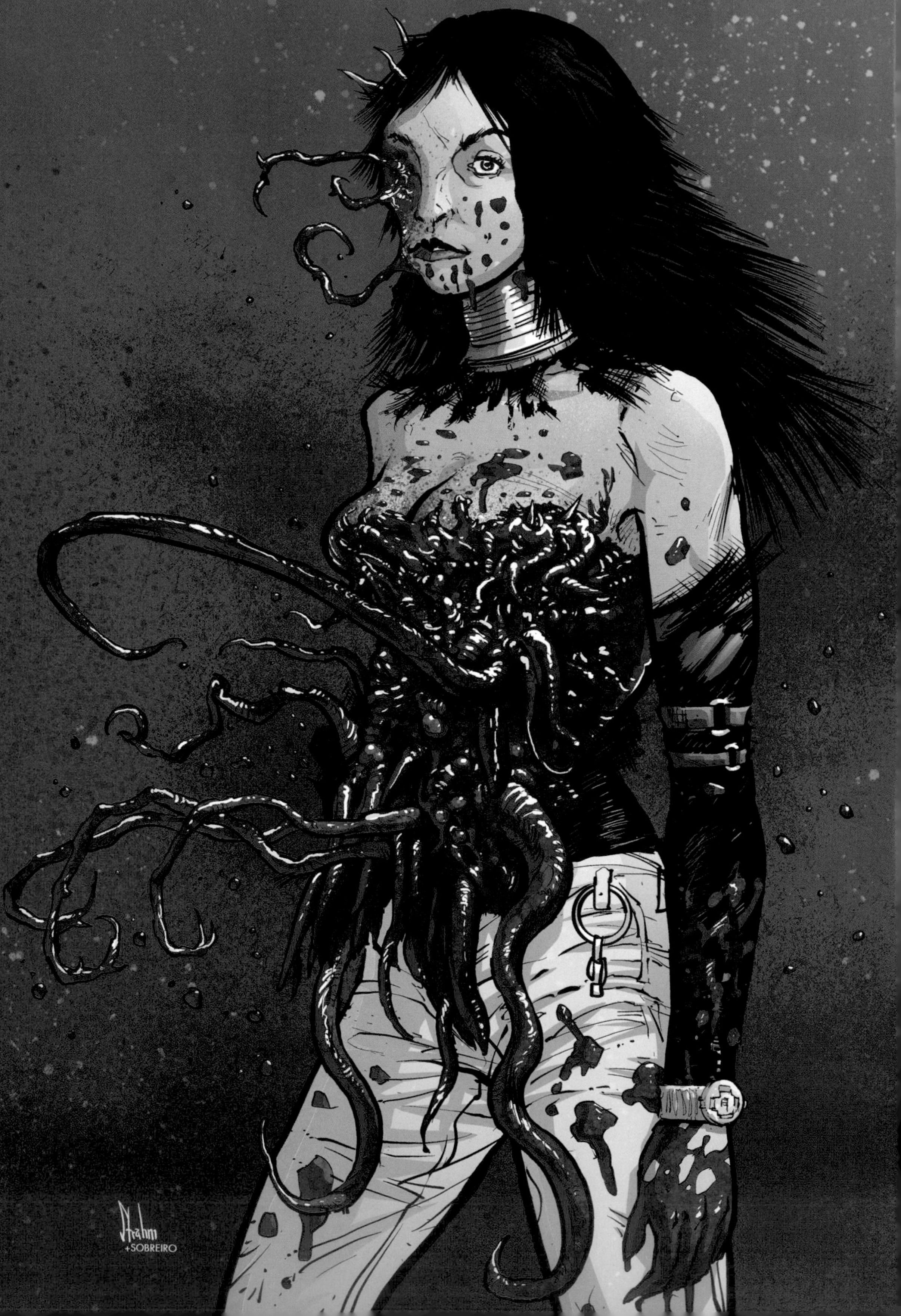
+SOBREIRO

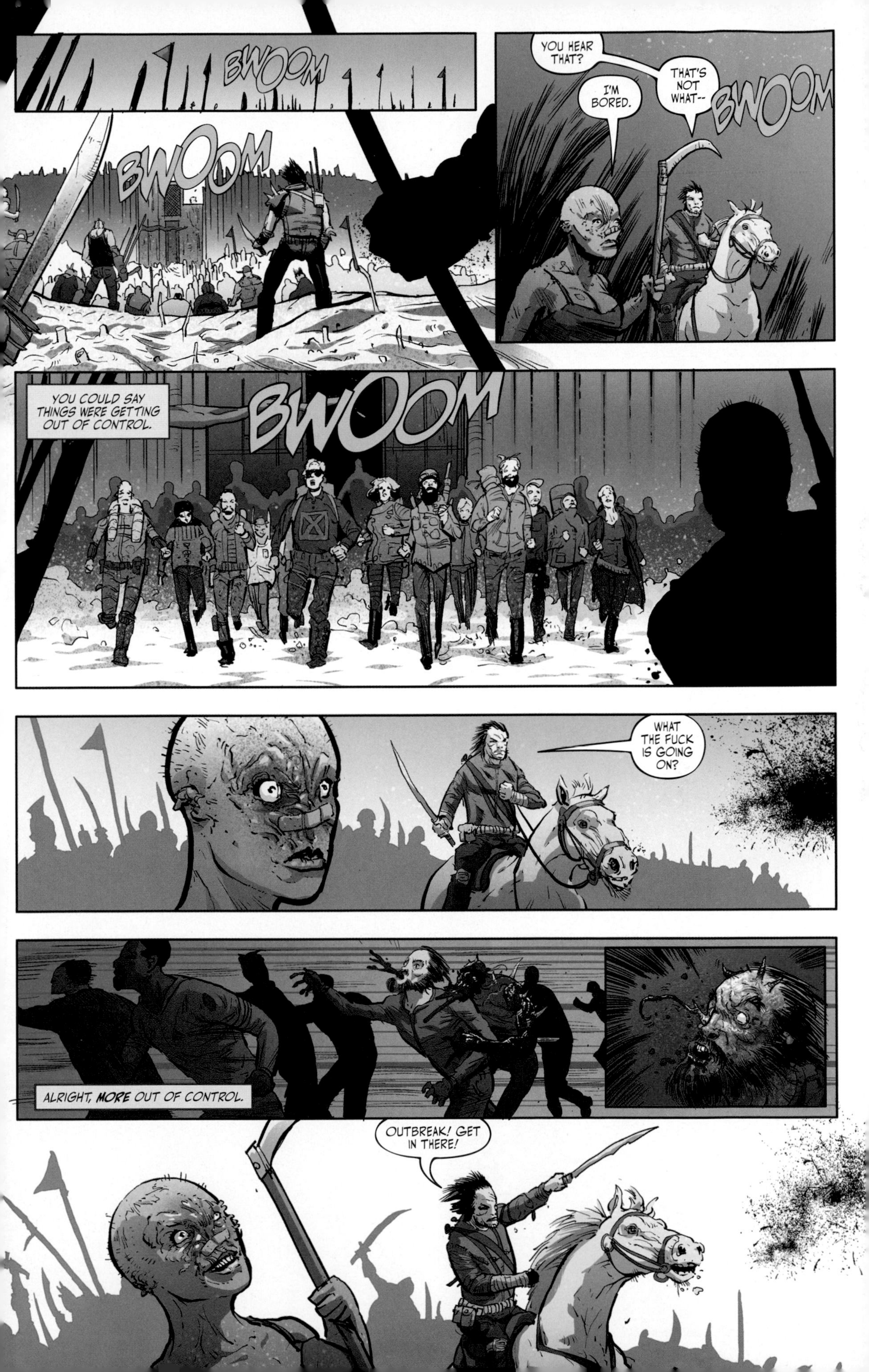
BWOOM
BWOOM
YOU HEAR THAT?
I'M BORED.
THAT'S NOT WHAT--
BWOOM
YOU COULD SAY THINGS WERE GETTING OUT OF CONTROL.
BWOOM
WHAT THE FUCK IS GOING ON?
ALRIGHT, **MORE** OUT OF CONTROL.
OUTBREAK! GET IN THERE!

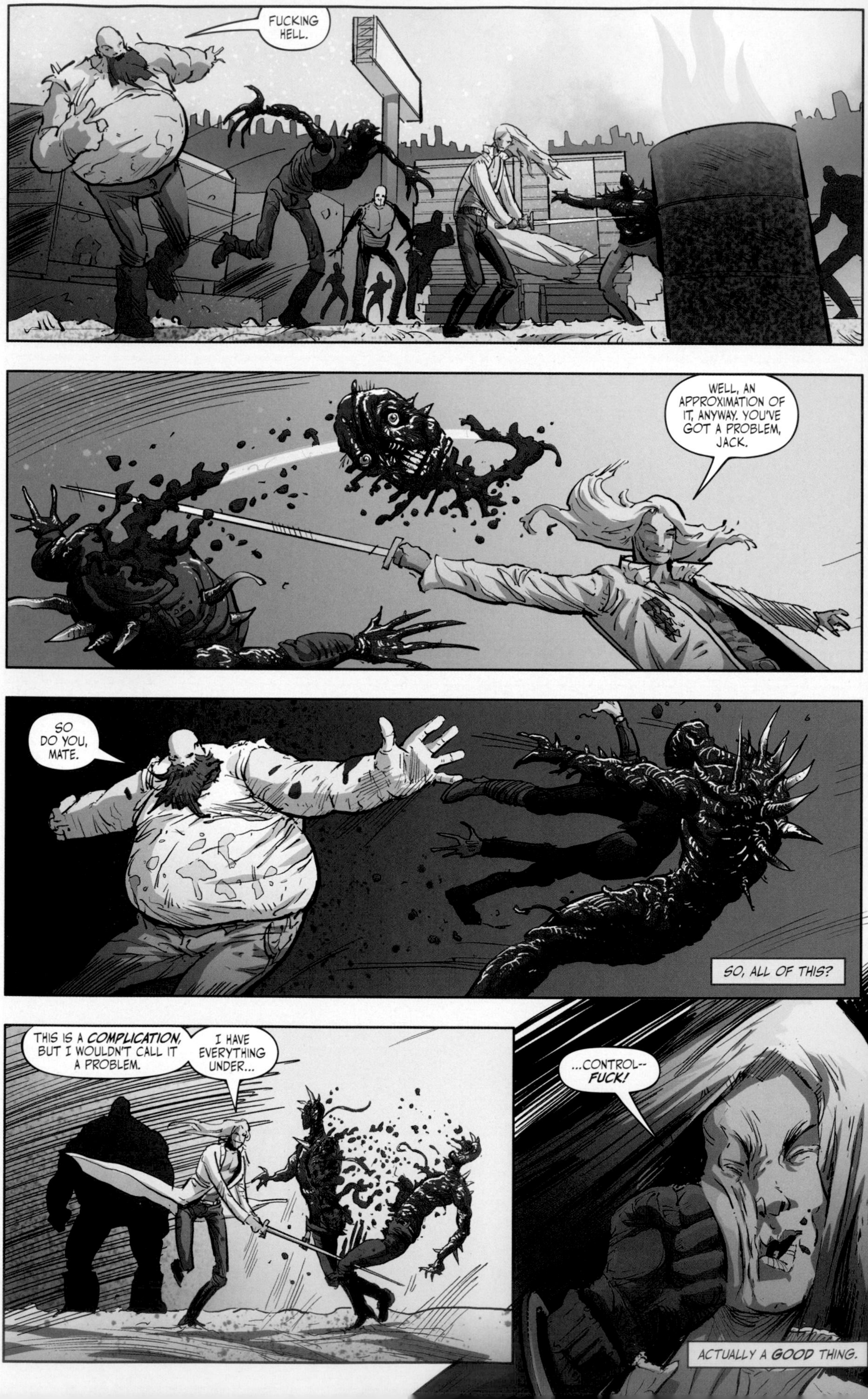
FUCKING HELL.
WELL, AN APPROXIMATION OF IT, ANYWAY. YOU'VE GOT A PROBLEM, JACK.
SO DO YOU, MATE.
SO, ALL OF THIS?
THIS IS A COMPLICATION, BUT I WOULDN'T CALL IT A PROBLEM.
I HAVE EVERYTHING UNDER...
...CONTROL-- FUCK!
ACTUALLY A GOOD THING.

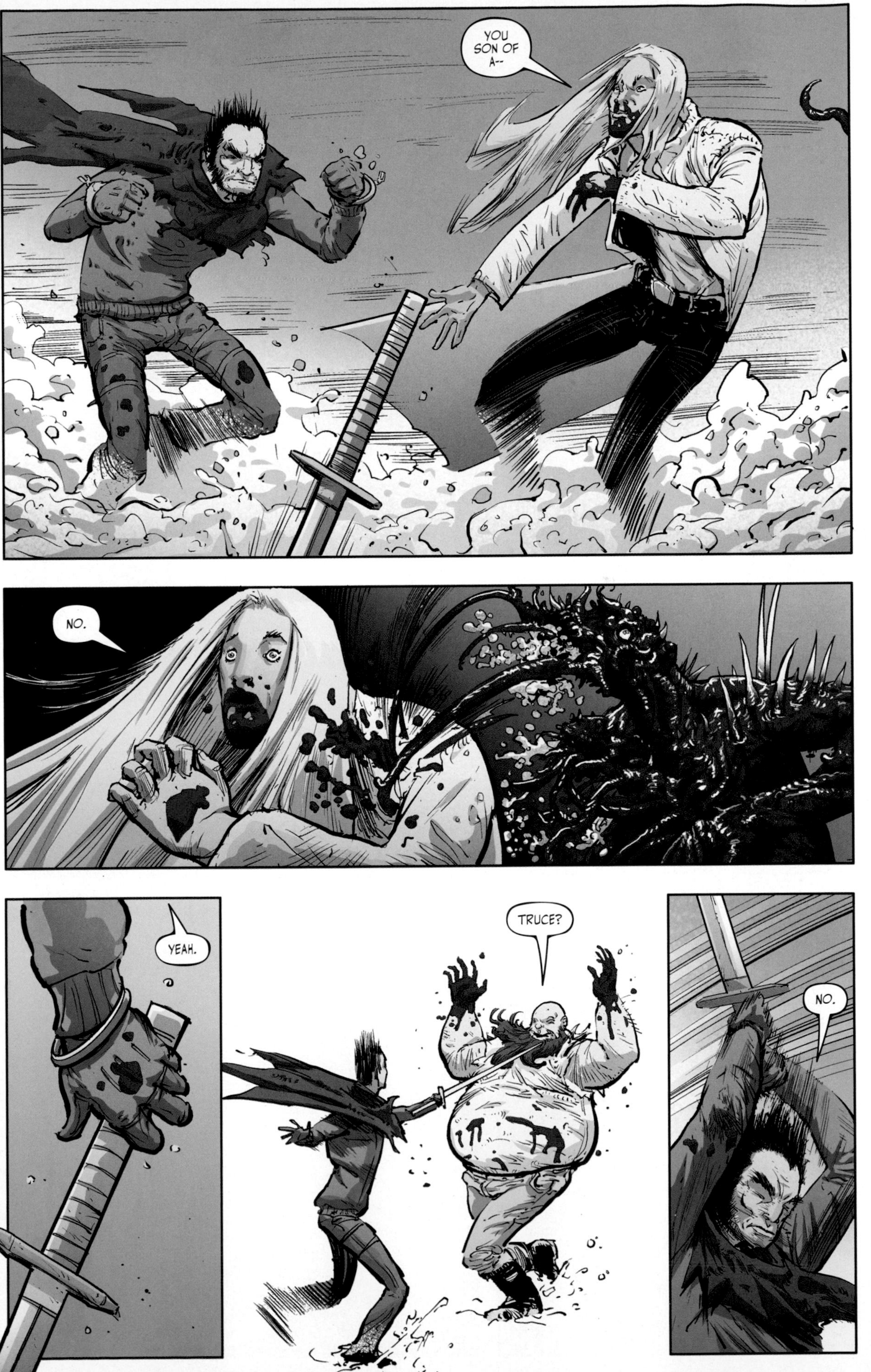
YOU SON OF A--
NO.
YEAH.
TRUCE?
NO.

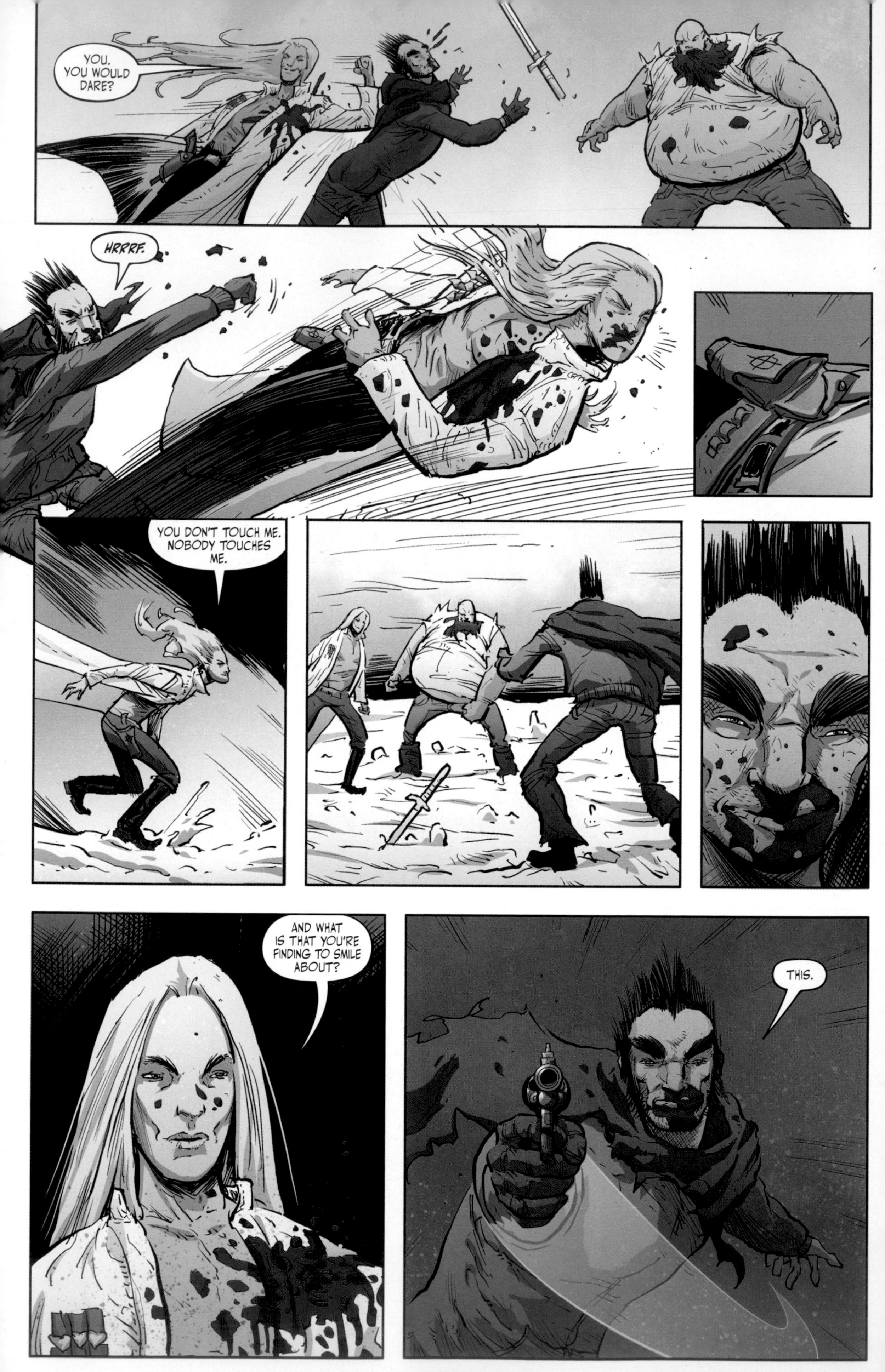
YOU. YOU WOULD DARE?
HRRRF.
YOU DON'T TOUCH ME. NOBODY TOUCHES ME.
AND WHAT IS THAT YOU'RE FINDING TO SMILE ABOUT?
THIS.

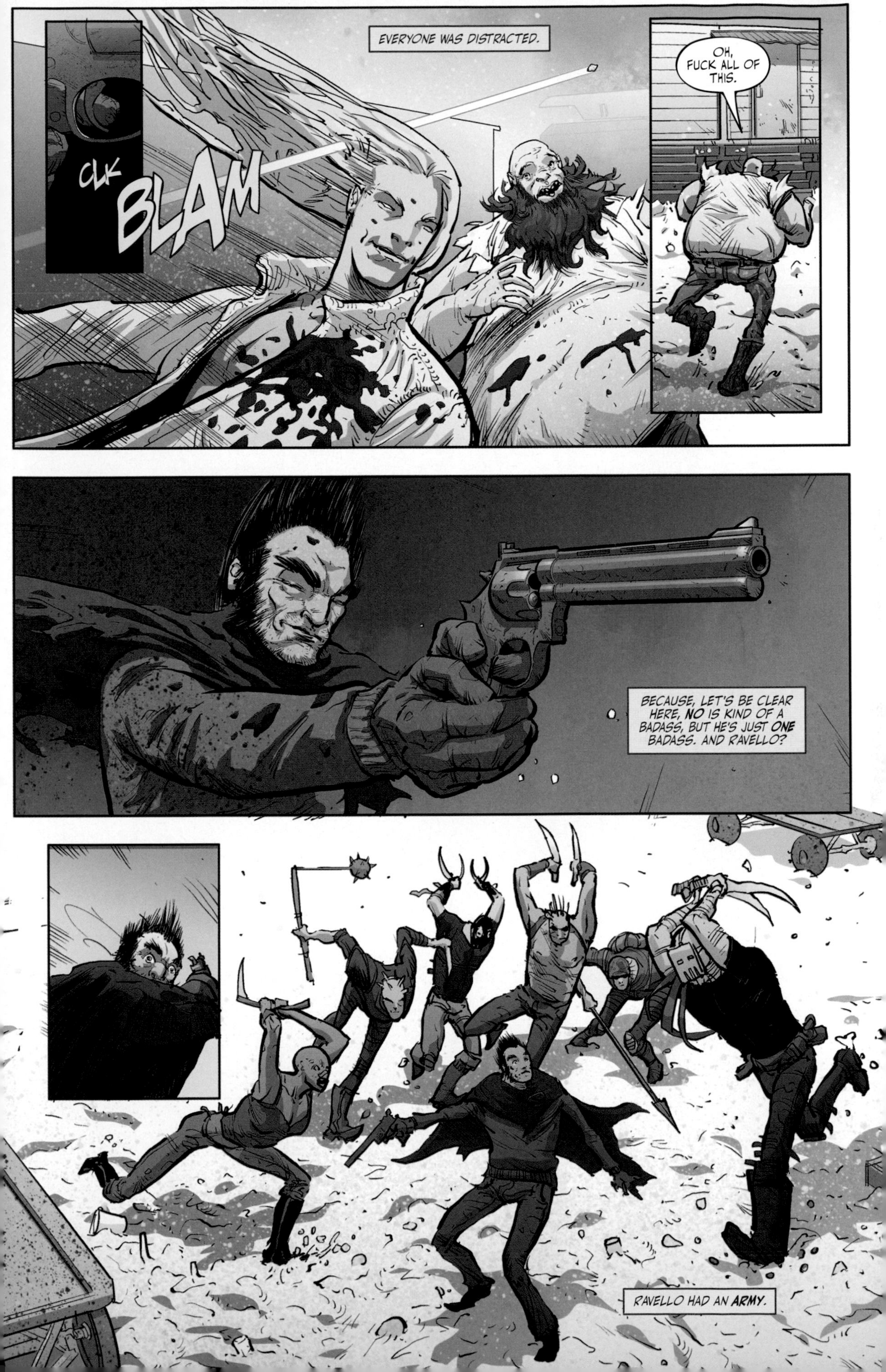
EVERYONE WAS DISTRACTED.
CLK
BLAM
OH, FUCK ALL OF THIS.
BECAUSE, LET'S BE CLEAR HERE, **NO** IS KIND OF A BADASS, BUT HE'S JUST **ONE** BADASS. AND RAVELLO?
RAVELLO HAD AN **ARMY**.

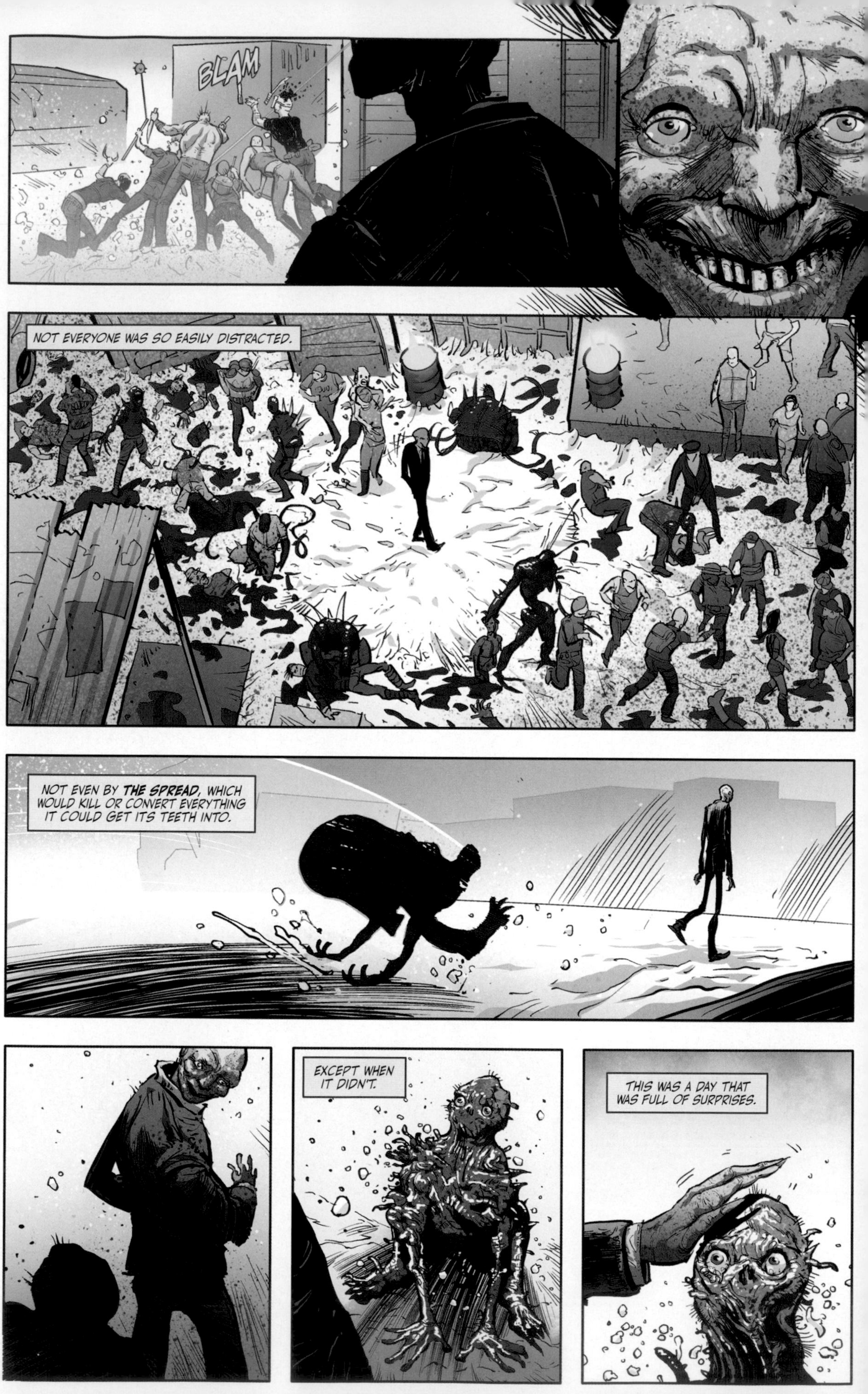
BLAM
NOT EVERYONE WAS SO EASILY DISTRACTED.
NOT EVEN BY **THE SPREAD**, WHICH WOULD KILL OR CONVERT EVERYTHING IT COULD GET ITS TEETH INTO.
EXCEPT WHEN IT DIDN'T.
THIS WAS A DAY THAT WAS FULL OF SURPRISES.

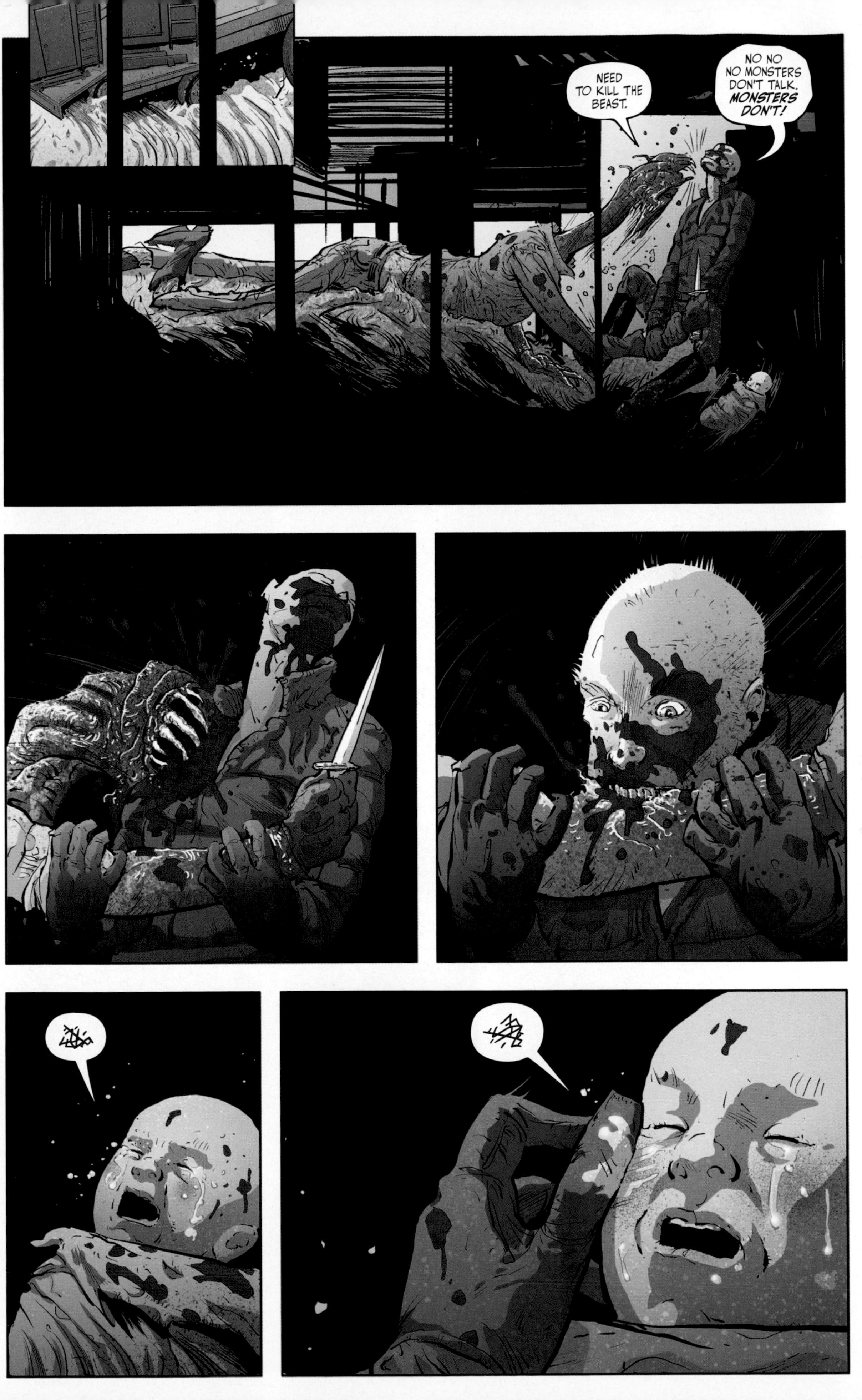
NEED TO KILL THE BEAST.
NO NO NO MONSTERS DON'T TALK. MONSTERS DON'T!

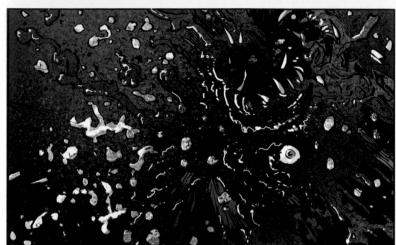

IT'S OKAY, BABY, IT'S OKAY. *MOLLY* IS GOING TO KEEP YOU SAFE.

MOLLY WILL SAVE YOU.

OKAY, BABY...

...OKAY?

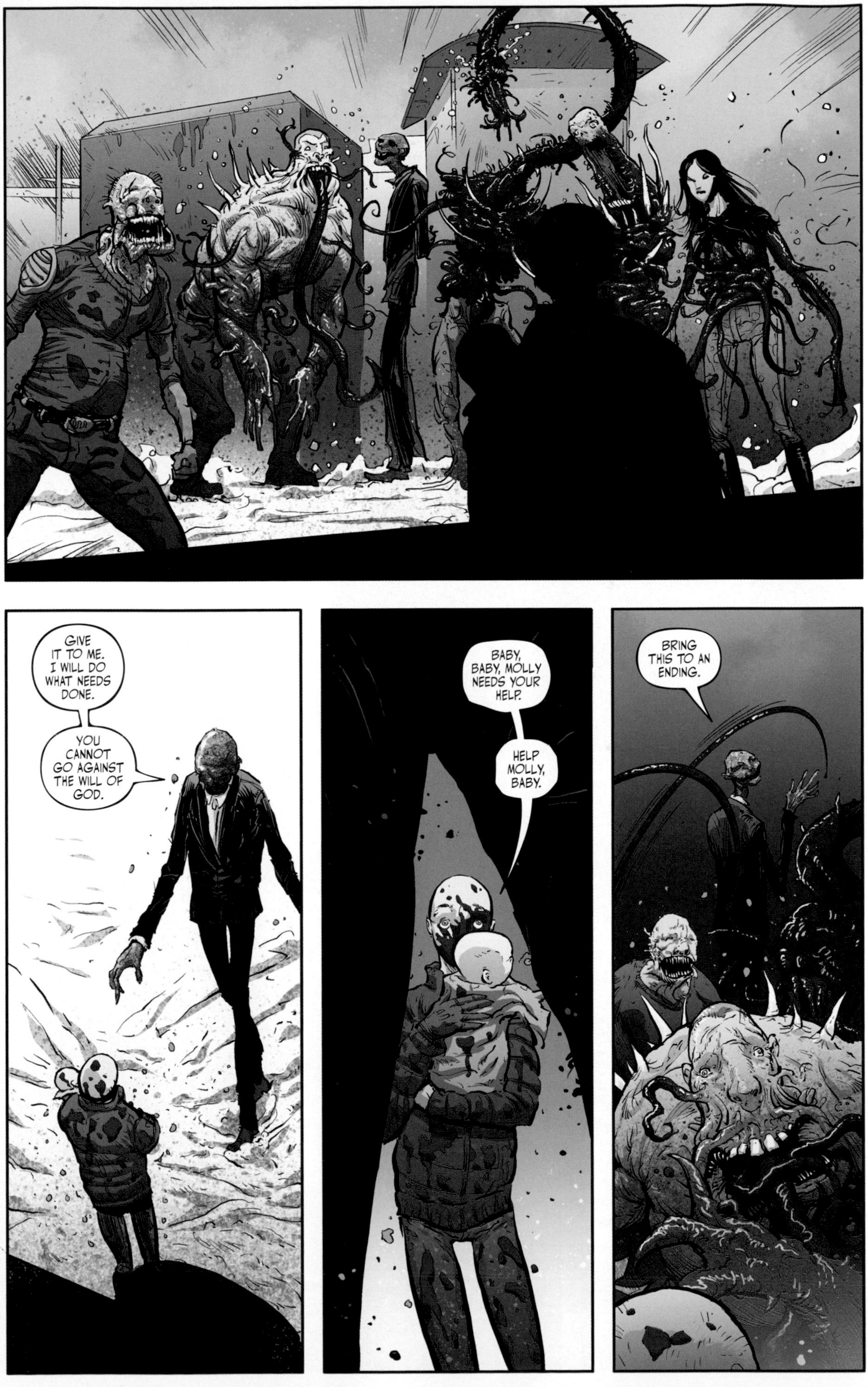
GIVE IT TO ME. I WILL DO WHAT NEEDS DONE.
YOU CANNOT GO AGAINST THE WILL OF GOD.
BABY, BABY, MOLLY NEEDS YOUR HELP.
HELP MOLLY, BABY.
BRING THIS TO AN ENDING.

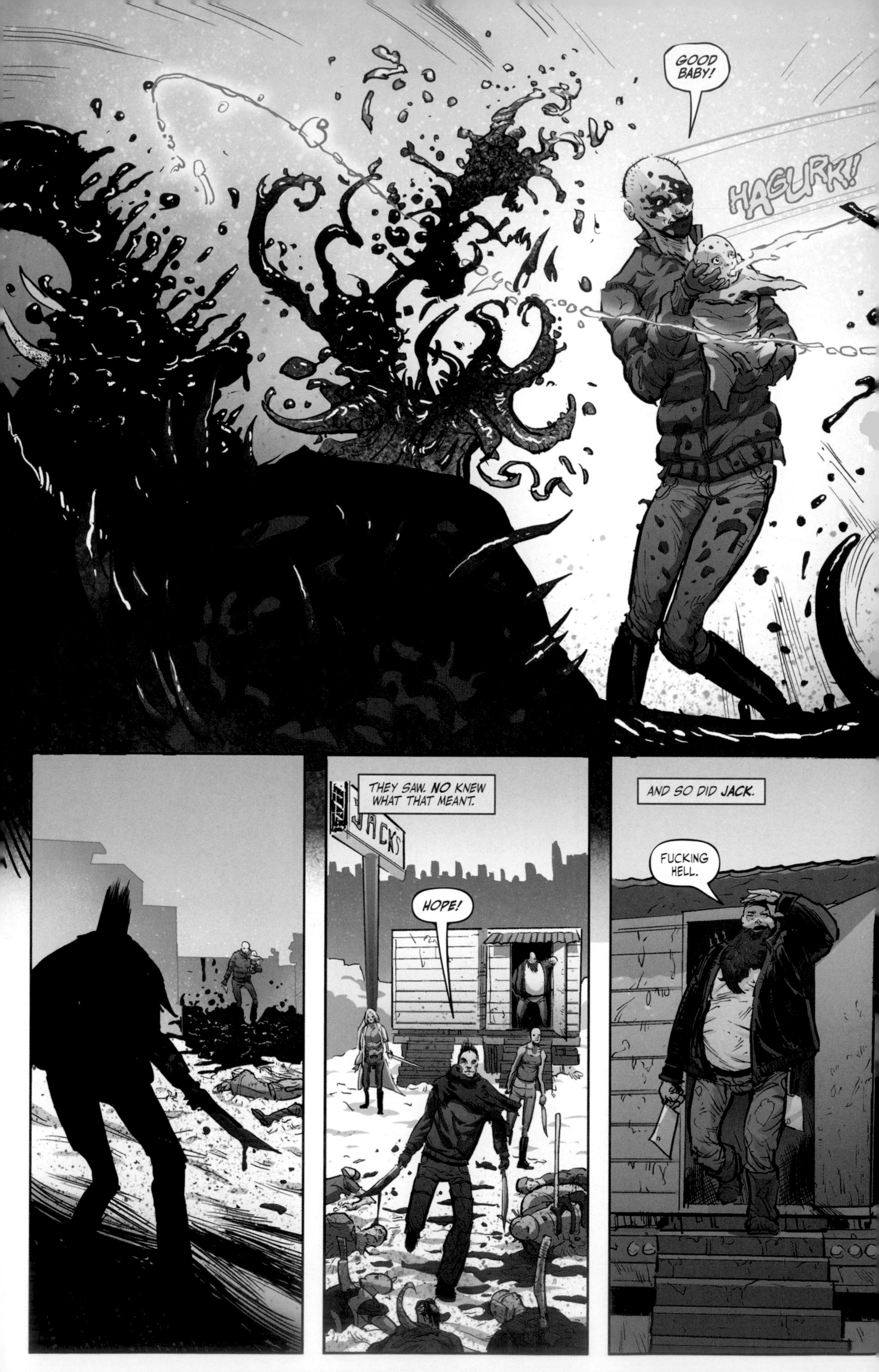
GOOD BABY!
HAGURK!
THEY SAW. NO KNEW WHAT THAT MEANT.
JACKS
HOPE!
AND SO DID JACK.
FUCKING HELL.

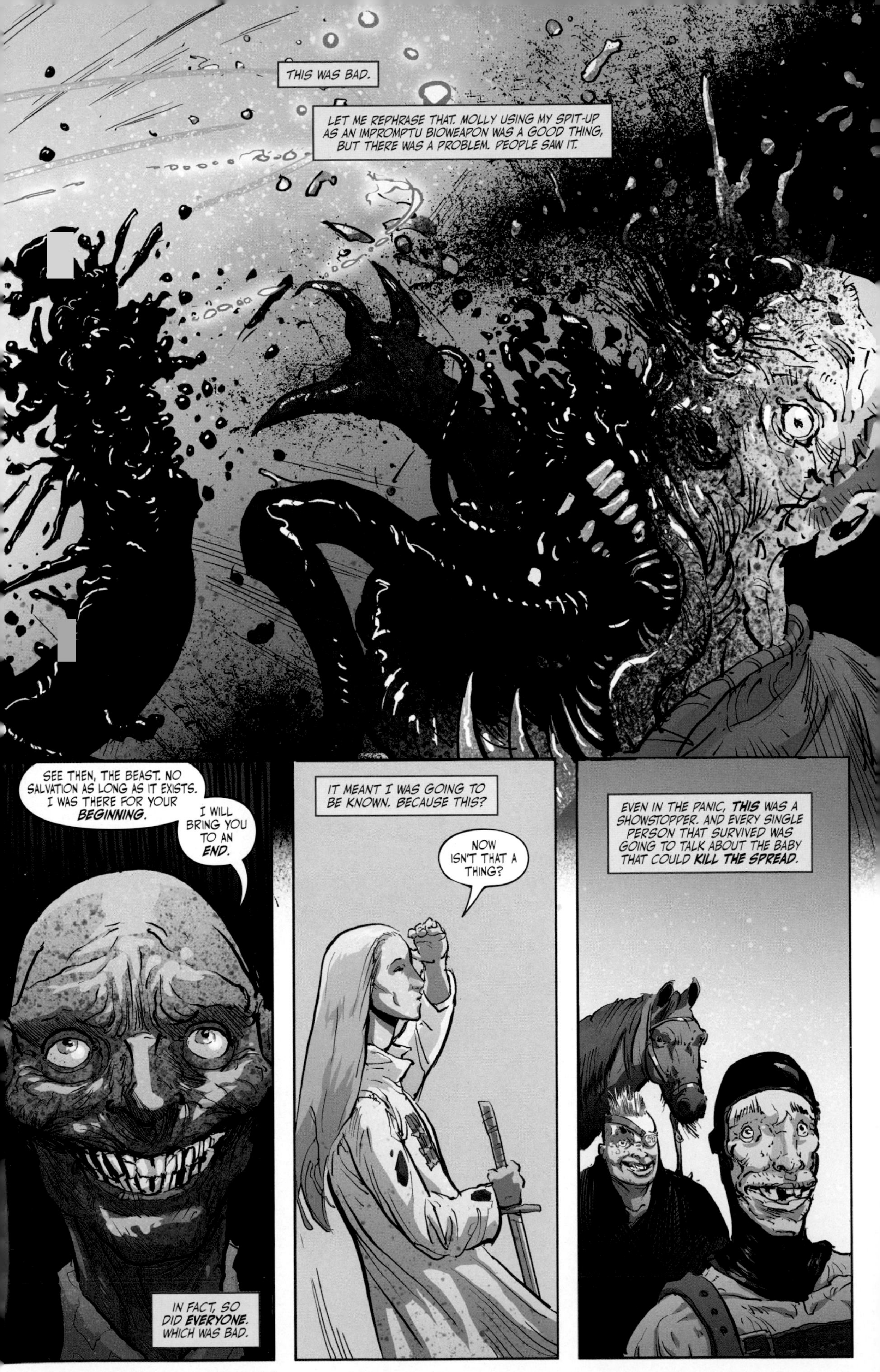
THIS WAS BAD.
LET ME REPHRASE THAT. MOLLY USING MY SPIT-UP AS AN IMPROMPTU BIOWEAPON WAS A GOOD THING, BUT THERE WAS A PROBLEM. PEOPLE SAW IT.
SEE THEN, THE BEAST. NO SALVATION AS LONG AS IT EXISTS. I WAS THERE FOR YOUR BEGINNING.
I WILL BRING YOU TO AN END.
IN FACT, SO DID EVERYONE. WHICH WAS BAD.
IT MEANT I WAS GOING TO BE KNOWN. BECAUSE THIS?
NOW ISN'T THAT A THING?
EVEN IN THE PANIC, THIS WAS A SHOWSTOPPER. AND EVERY SINGLE PERSON THAT SURVIVED WAS GOING TO TALK ABOUT THE BABY THAT COULD KILL THE SPREAD.

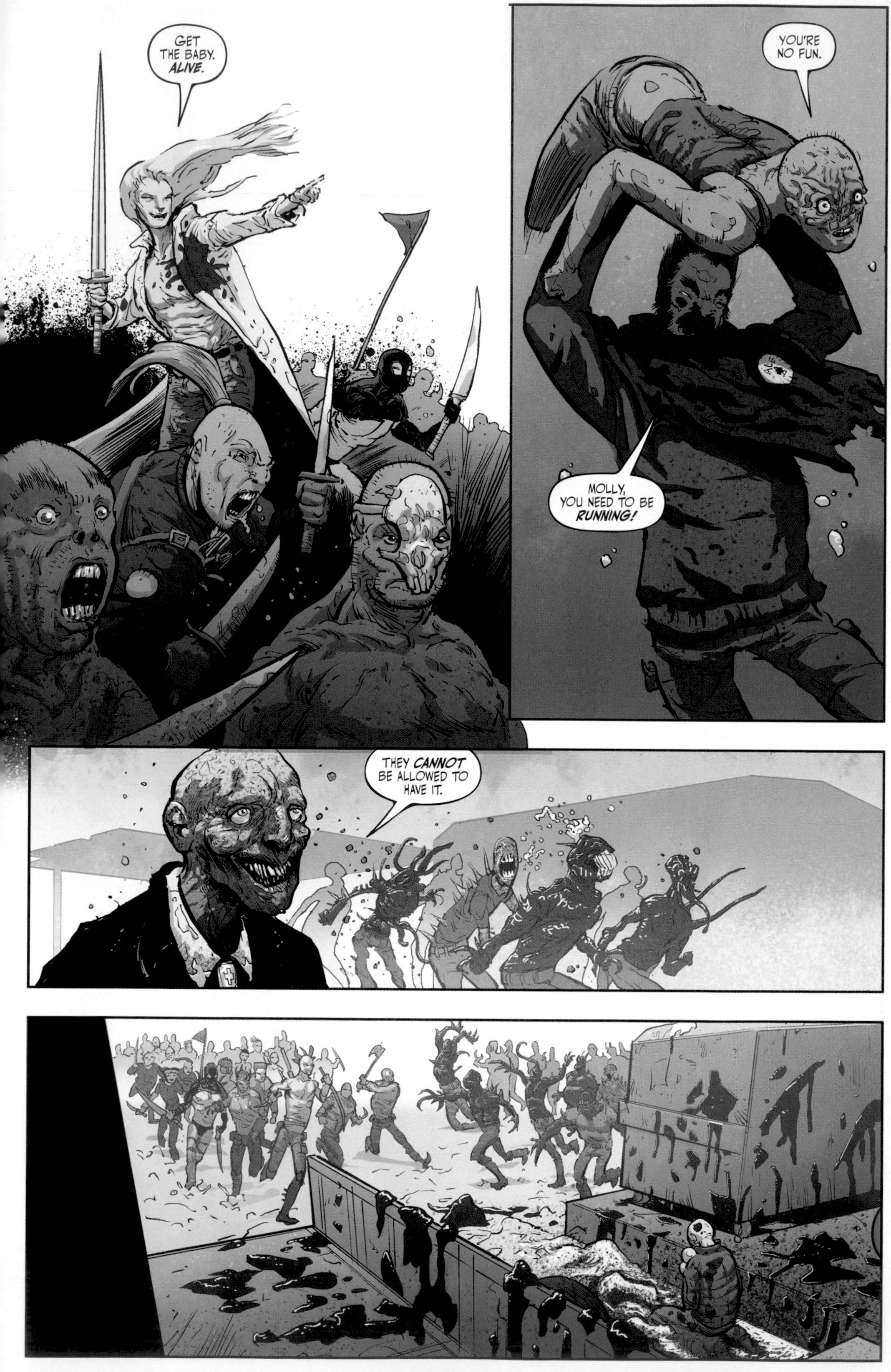
GET THE BABY. ALIVE.
YOU'RE NO FUN.
MOLLY, YOU NEED TO BE RUNNING!
THEY CANNOT BE ALLOWED TO HAVE IT.

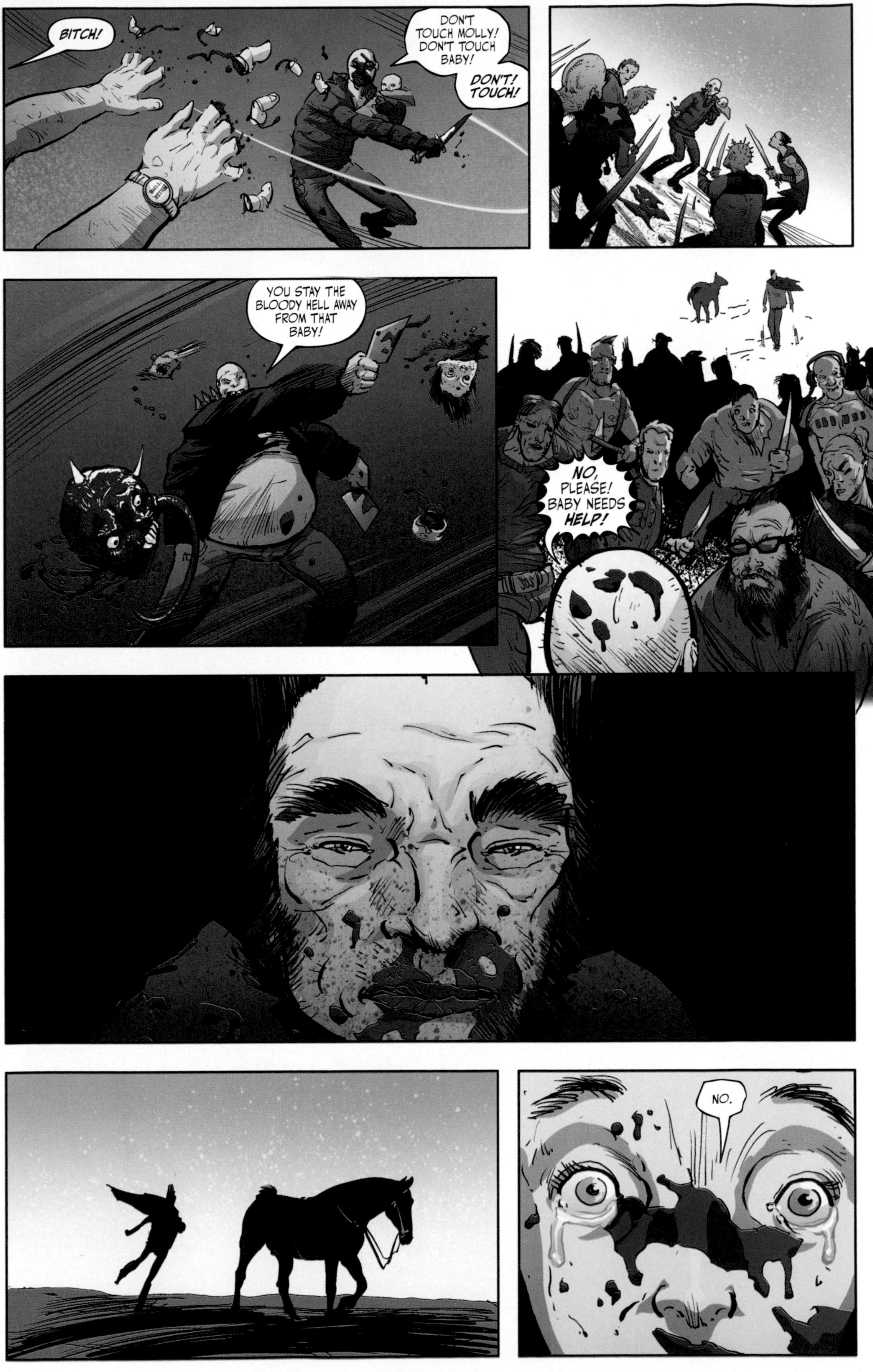

BITCH!
DON'T TOUCH MOLLY! DON'T TOUCH BABY!
DON'T! TOUCH!
YOU STAY THE BLOODY HELL AWAY FROM THAT BABY!
NO, PLEASE! BABY NEEDS HELP!
NO.

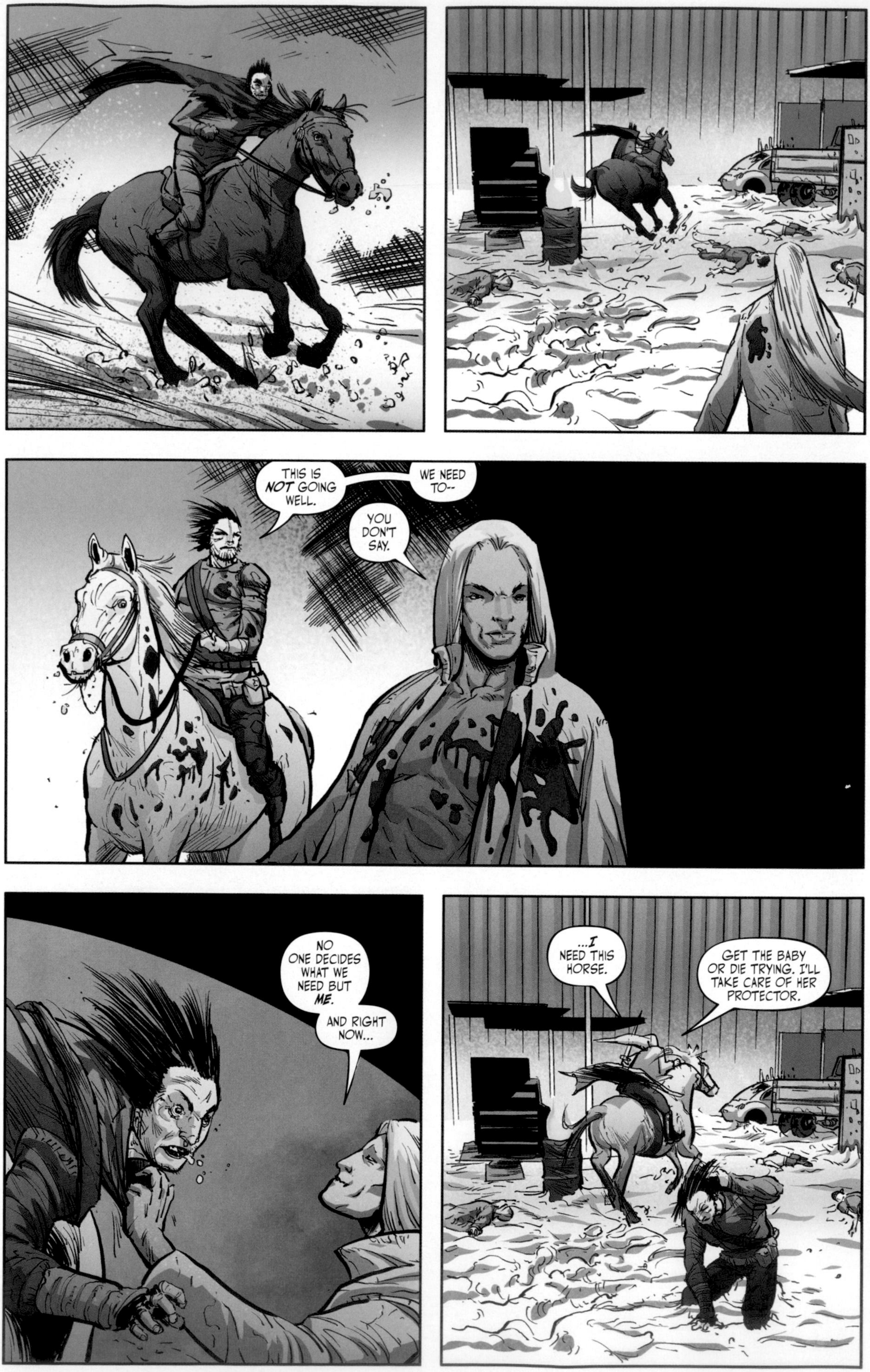
THIS IS NOT GOING WELL.
WE NEED TO--
YOU DON'T SAY.
NO ONE DECIDES WHAT WE NEED BUT ME.
AND RIGHT NOW...
...I NEED THIS HORSE.
GET THE BABY OR DIE TRYING. I'LL TAKE CARE OF HER PROTECTOR.

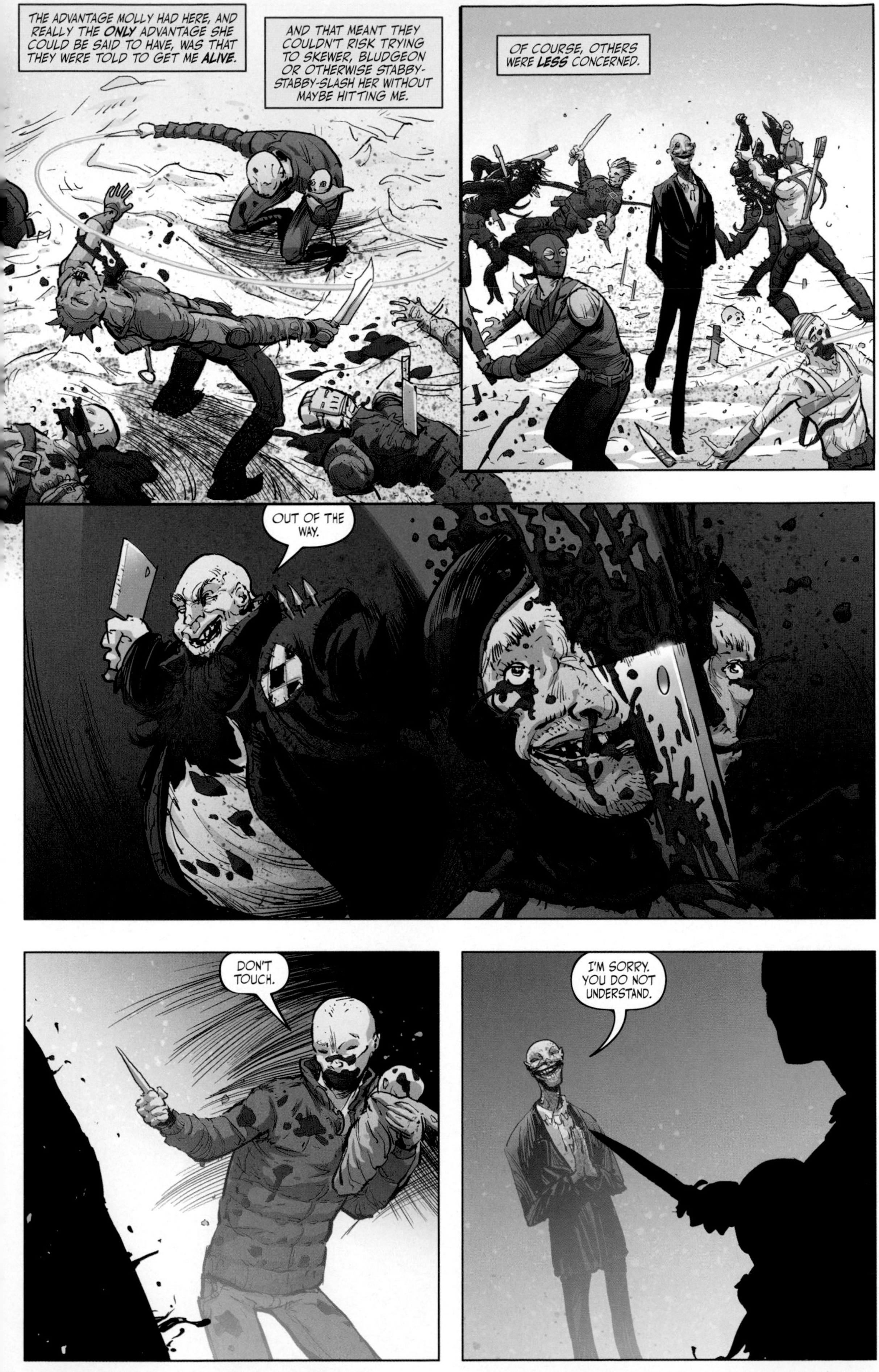
THE ADVANTAGE MOLLY HAD HERE, AND REALLY THE ONLY ADVANTAGE SHE COULD BE SAID TO HAVE, WAS THAT THEY WERE TOLD TO GET ME ALIVE.
AND THAT MEANT THEY COULDN'T RISK TRYING TO SKEWER, BLUDGEON OR OTHERWISE STABBY-STABBY-SLASH HER WITHOUT MAYBE HITTING ME.
OF COURSE, OTHERS WERE LESS CONCERNED.
OUT OF THE WAY.
DON'T TOUCH.
I'M SORRY. YOU DO NOT UNDERSTAND.

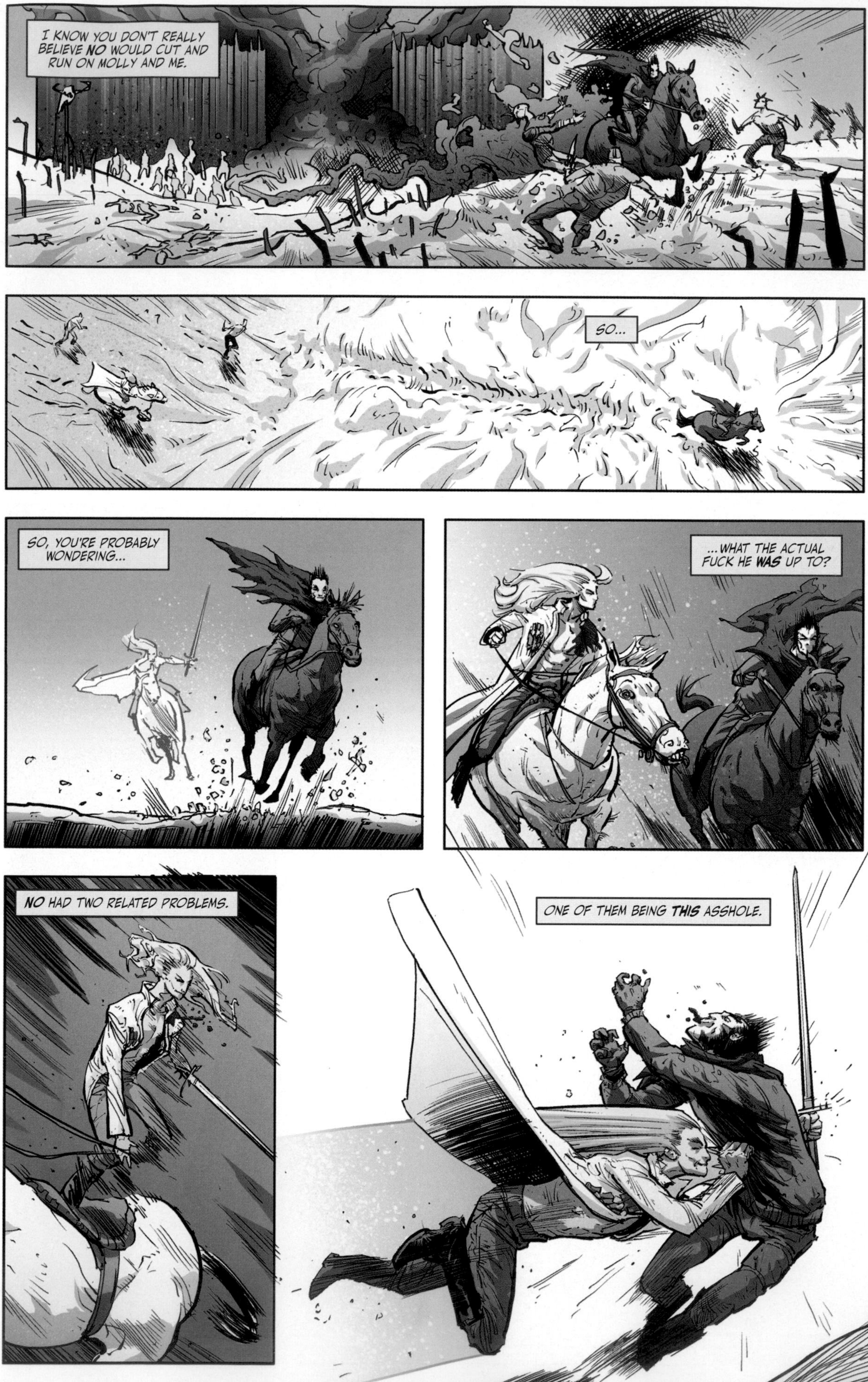
I KNOW YOU DON'T REALLY BELIEVE NO WOULD CUT AND RUN ON MOLLY AND ME.
SO...
SO, YOU'RE PROBABLY WONDERING...
...WHAT THE ACTUAL FUCK HE WAS UP TO?
NO HAD TWO RELATED PROBLEMS.
ONE OF THEM BEING THIS ASSHOLE.

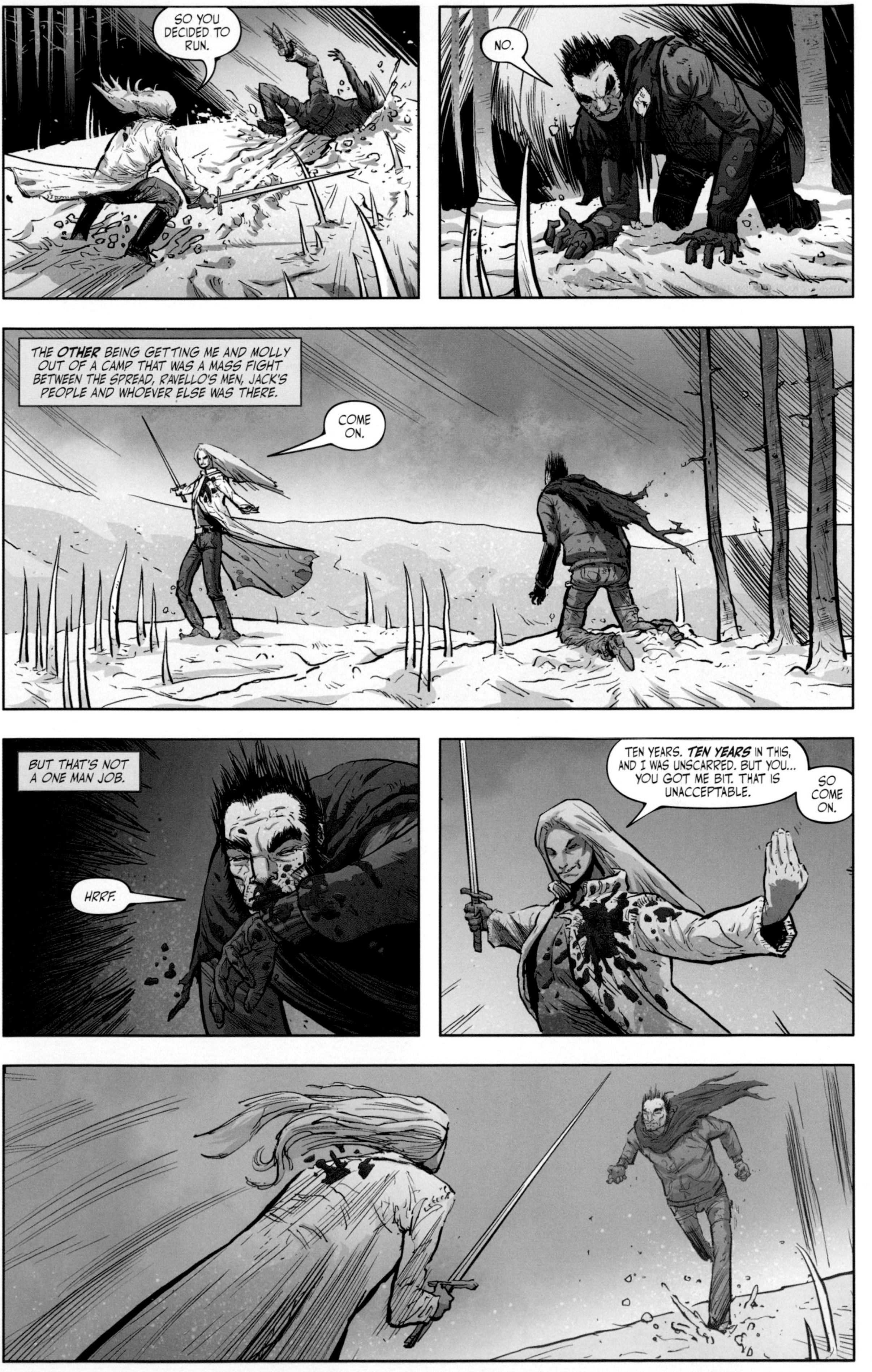
SO YOU DECIDED TO RUN.
NO.
THE OTHER BEING GETTING ME AND MOLLY OUT OF A CAMP THAT WAS A MASS FIGHT BETWEEN THE SPREAD, RAVELLO'S MEN, JACK'S PEOPLE AND WHOEVER ELSE WAS THERE.
COME ON.
BUT THAT'S NOT A ONE MAN JOB.
HRRF.
TEN YEARS. TEN YEARS IN THIS, AND I WAS UNSCARRED. BUT YOU... YOU GOT ME BIT. THAT IS UNACCEPTABLE.
SO COME ON.

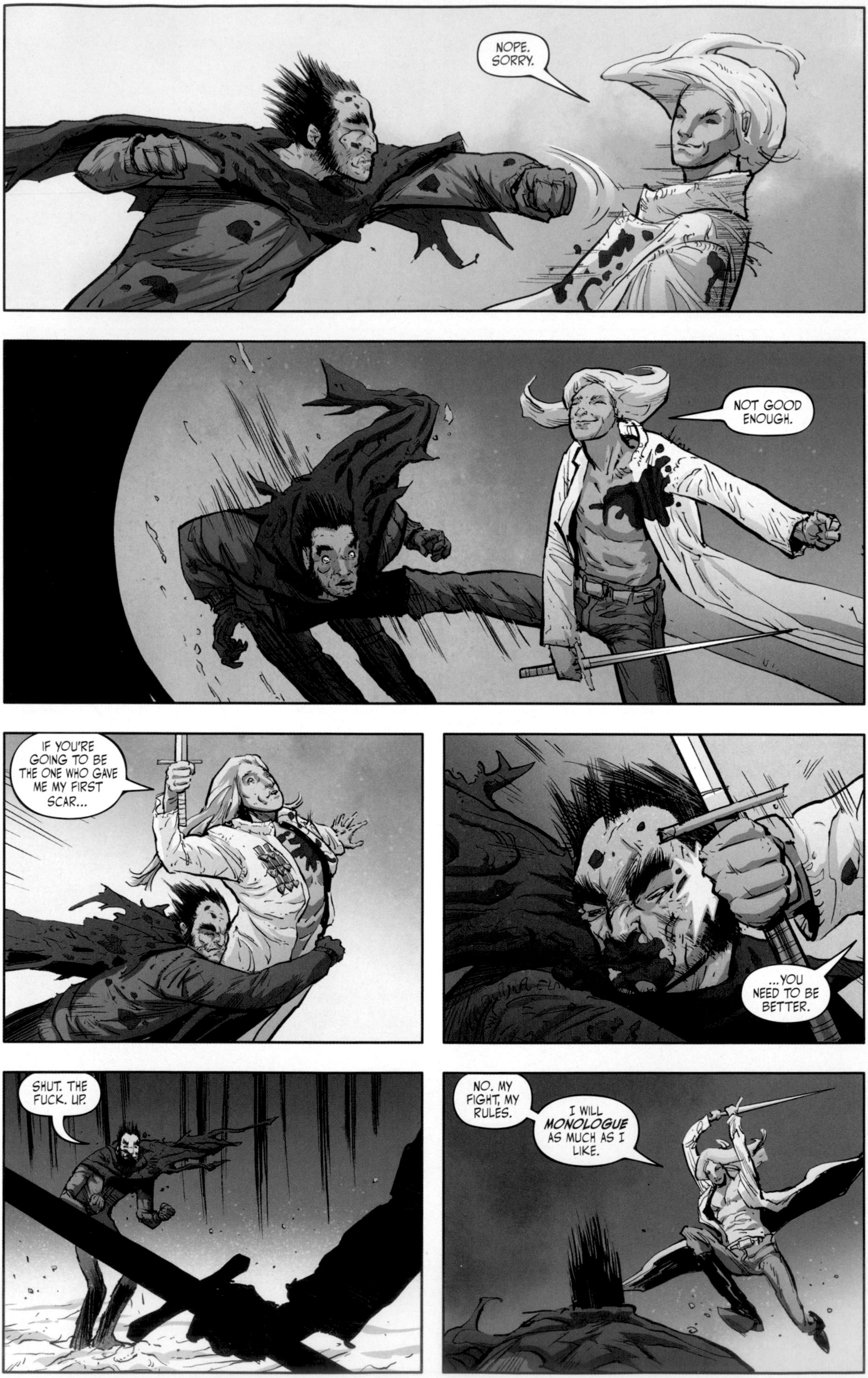
NOPE. SORRY.
NOT GOOD ENOUGH.
IF YOU'RE GOING TO BE THE ONE WHO GAVE ME MY FIRST SCAR...
...YOU NEED TO BE BETTER.
SHUT. THE FUCK. UP.
NO. MY FIGHT, MY RULES.
I WILL *MONOLOGUE* AS MUCH AS I LIKE.

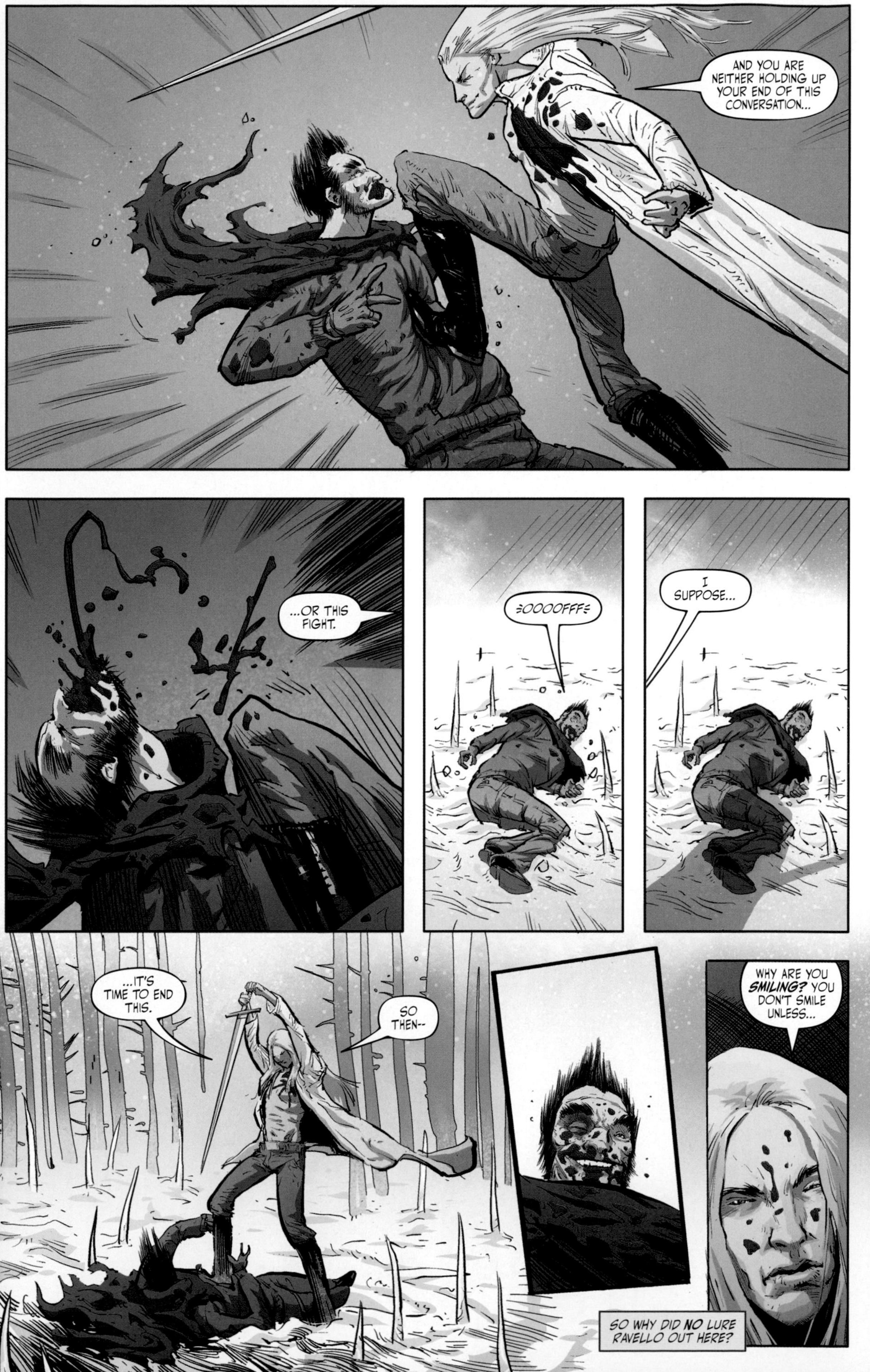
AND YOU ARE NEITHER HOLDING UP YOUR END OF THIS CONVERSATION...
...OR THIS FIGHT.
OOOOFFF
I SUPPOSE...
...IT'S TIME TO END THIS.
SO THEN--
WHY ARE YOU SMILING? YOU DON'T SMILE UNLESS...
SO WHY DID NO LURE RAVELLO OUT HERE?

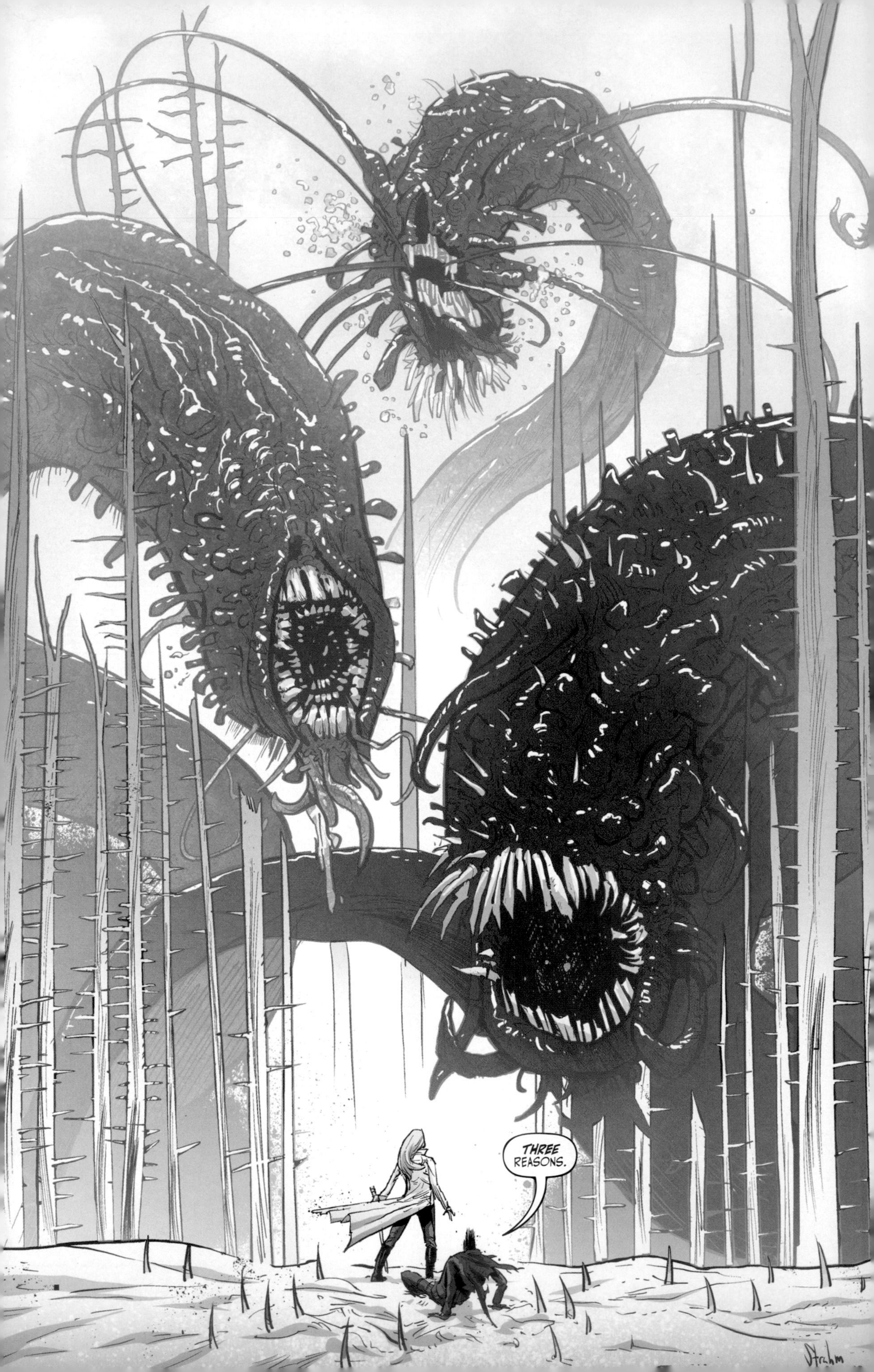
THREE REASONS.

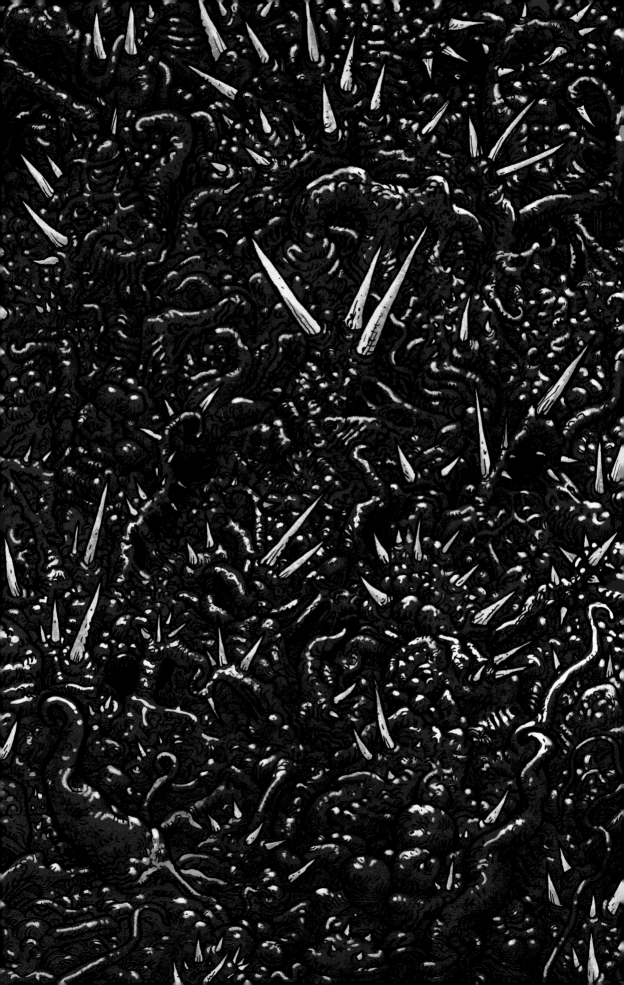

CHAPTER SIX

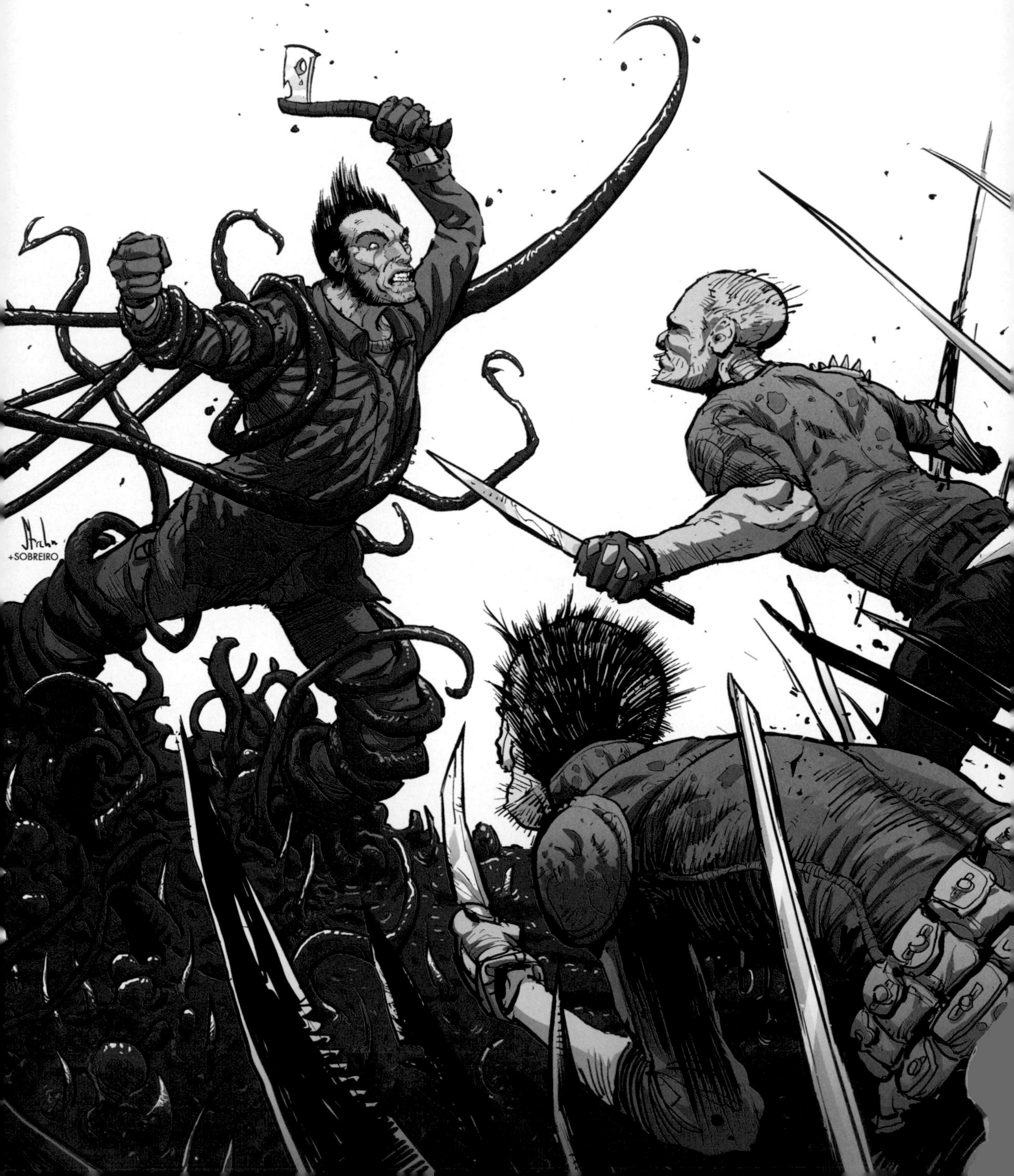
+SOBREIRO

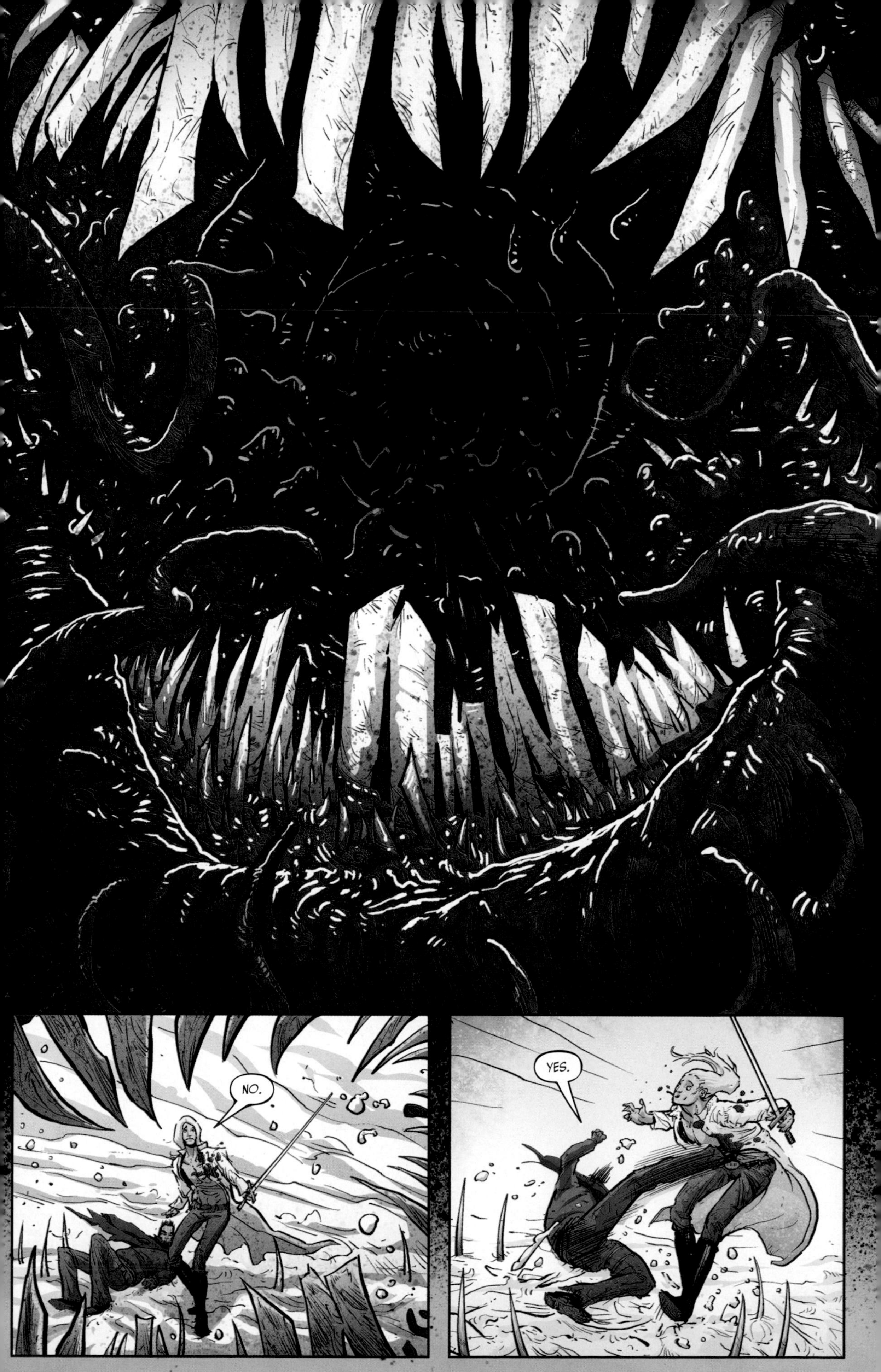
NO.
YES.

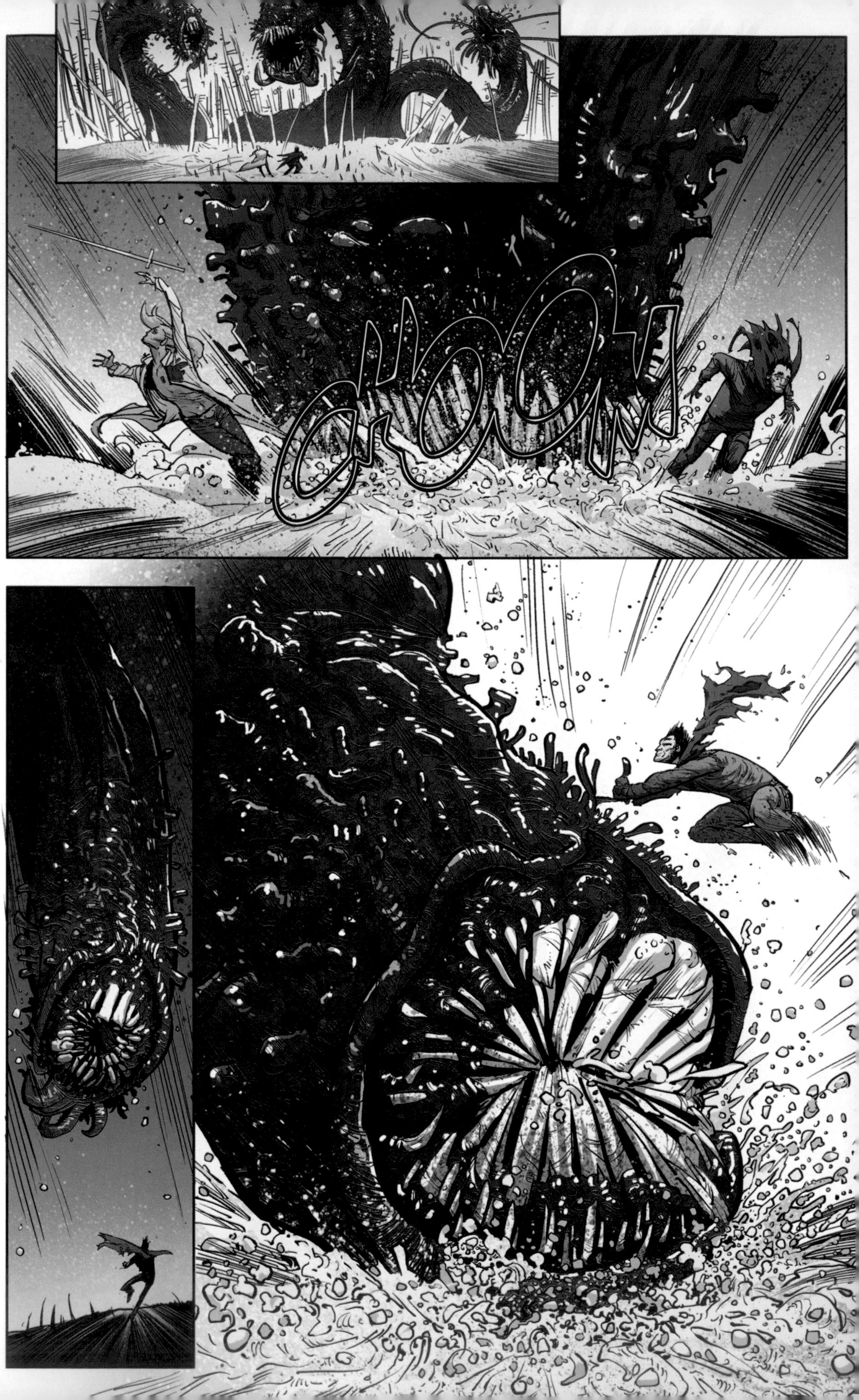
CHOOM

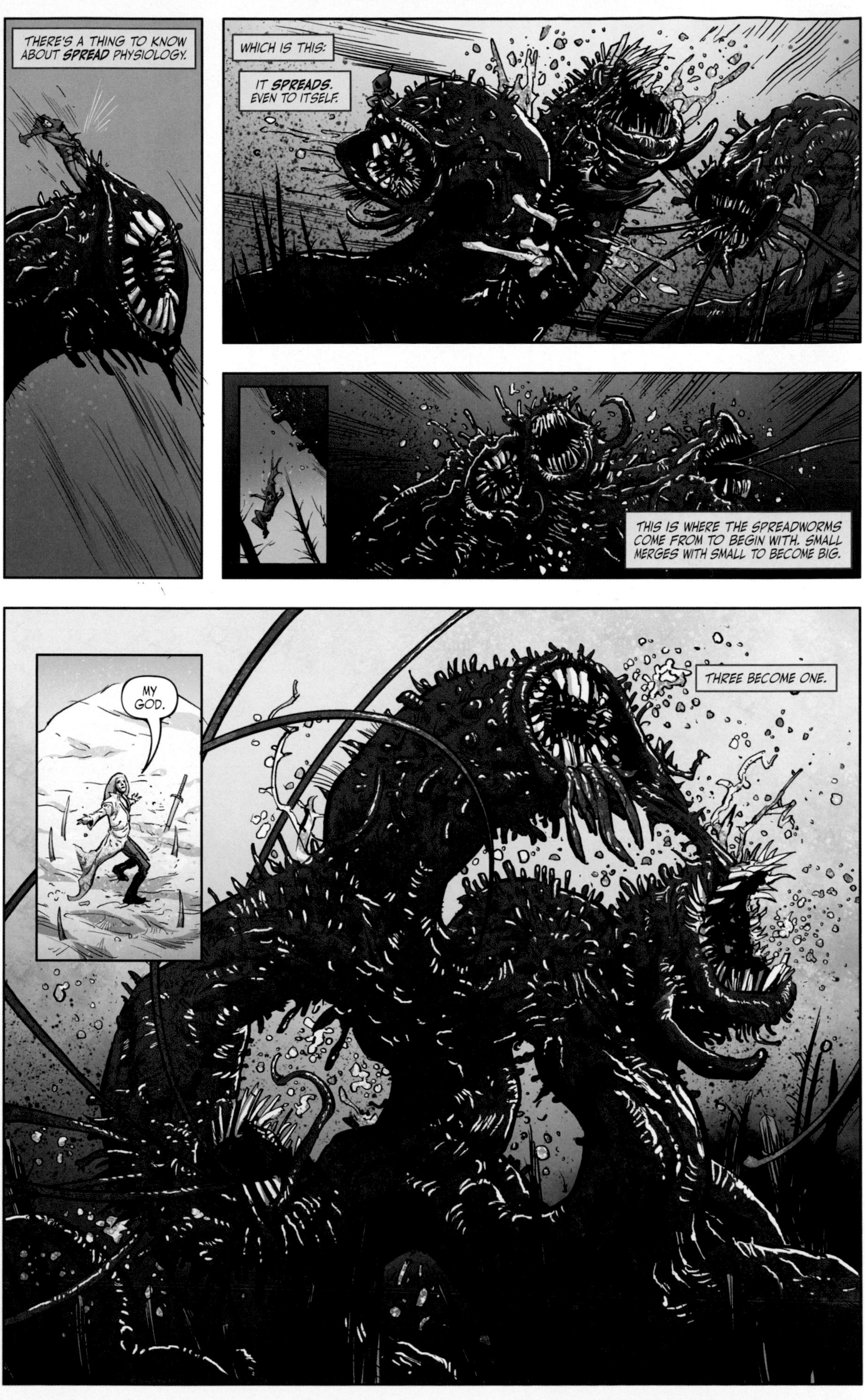
THERE'S A THING TO KNOW ABOUT SPREAD PHYSIOLOGY.
WHICH IS THIS:
IT SPREADS. EVEN TO ITSELF.
THIS IS WHERE THE SPREADWORMS COME FROM TO BEGIN WITH. SMALL MERGES WITH SMALL TO BECOME BIG.
MY GOD.
THREE BECOME ONE.

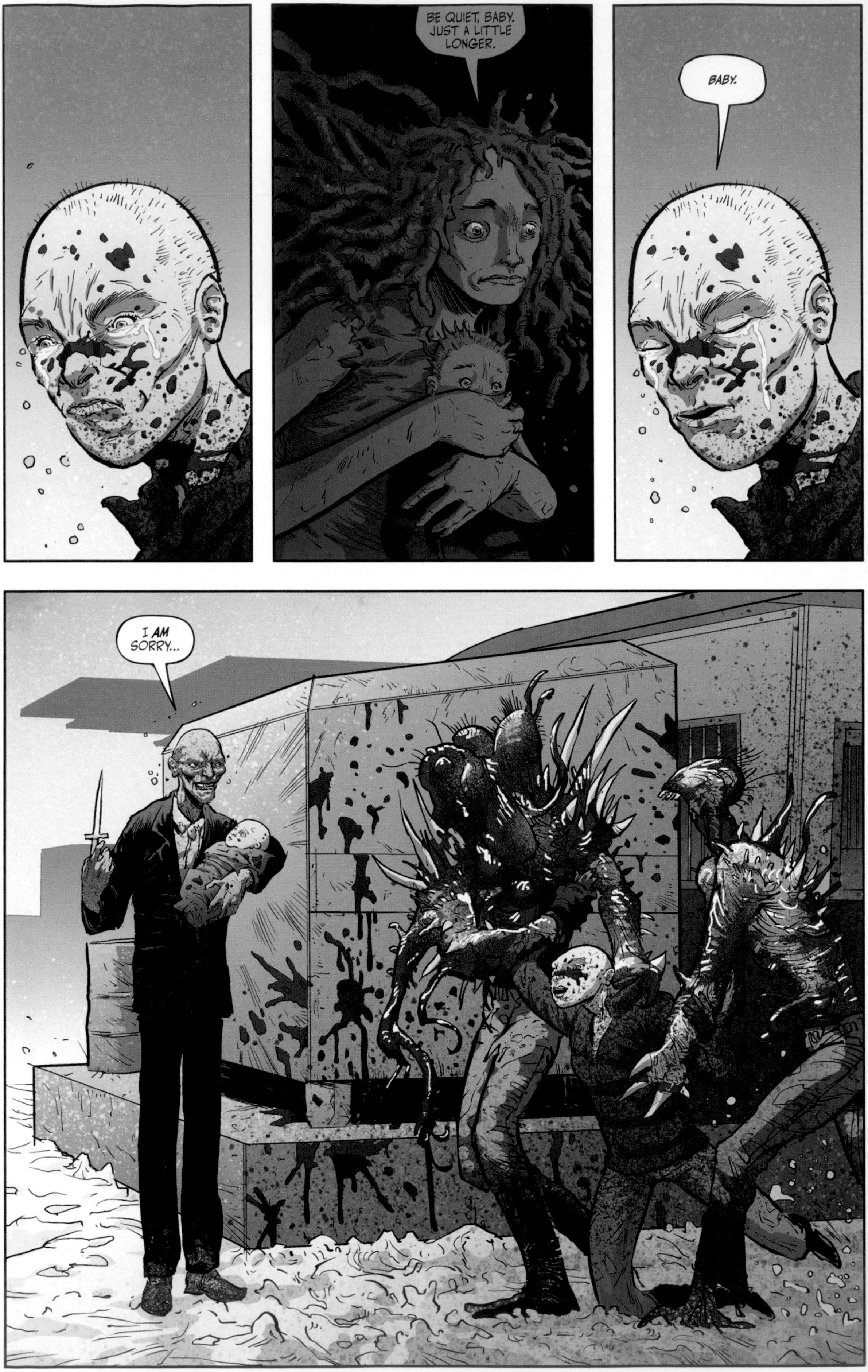
BE QUIET, BABY. JUST A LITTLE LONGER.
BABY.
I AM SORRY...

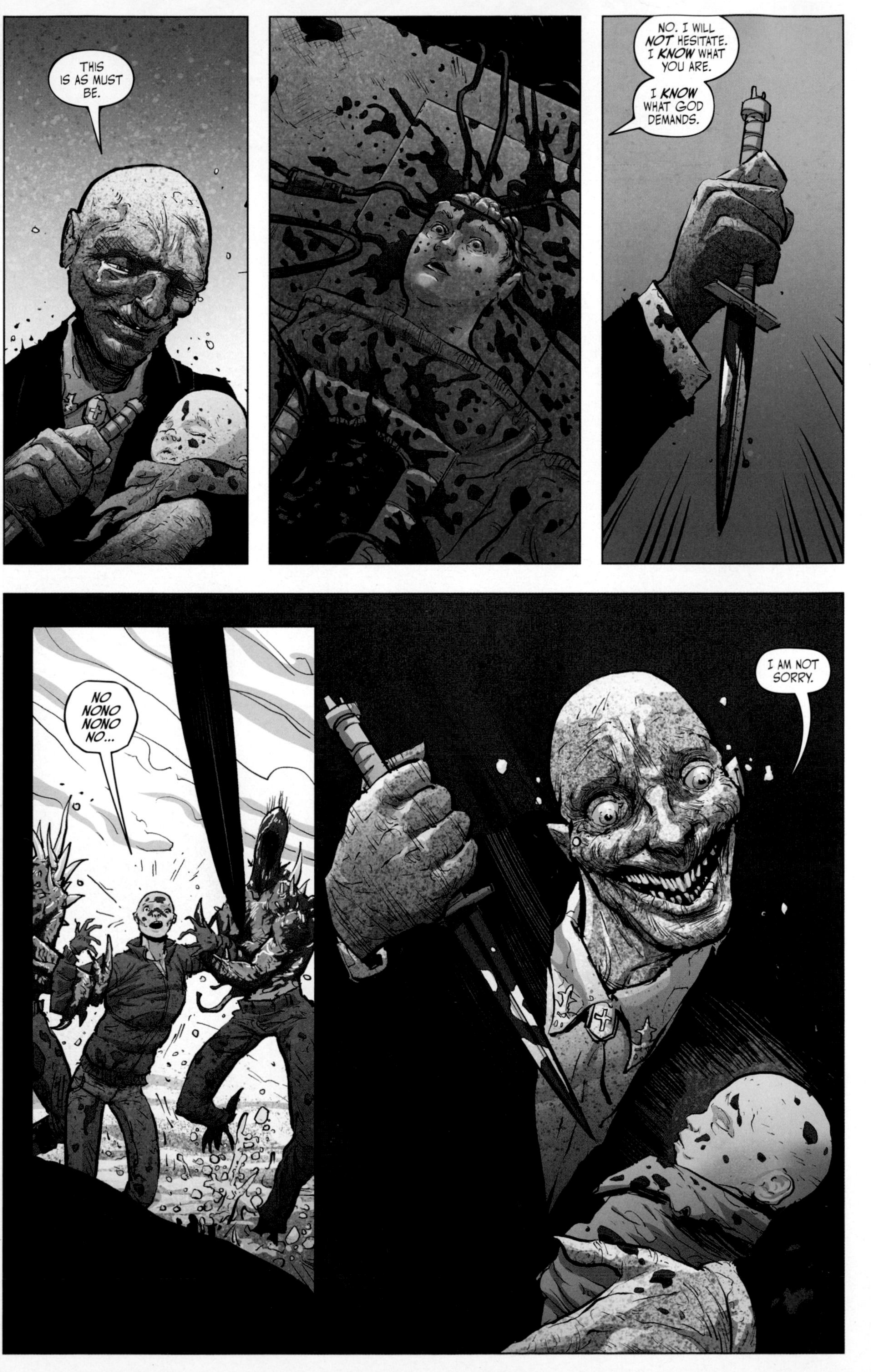
THIS IS AS MUST BE.
NO. I WILL NOT HESITATE. I KNOW WHAT YOU ARE.
I KNOW WHAT GOD DEMANDS.
NO NONO NONO NO...
I AM NOT SORRY.

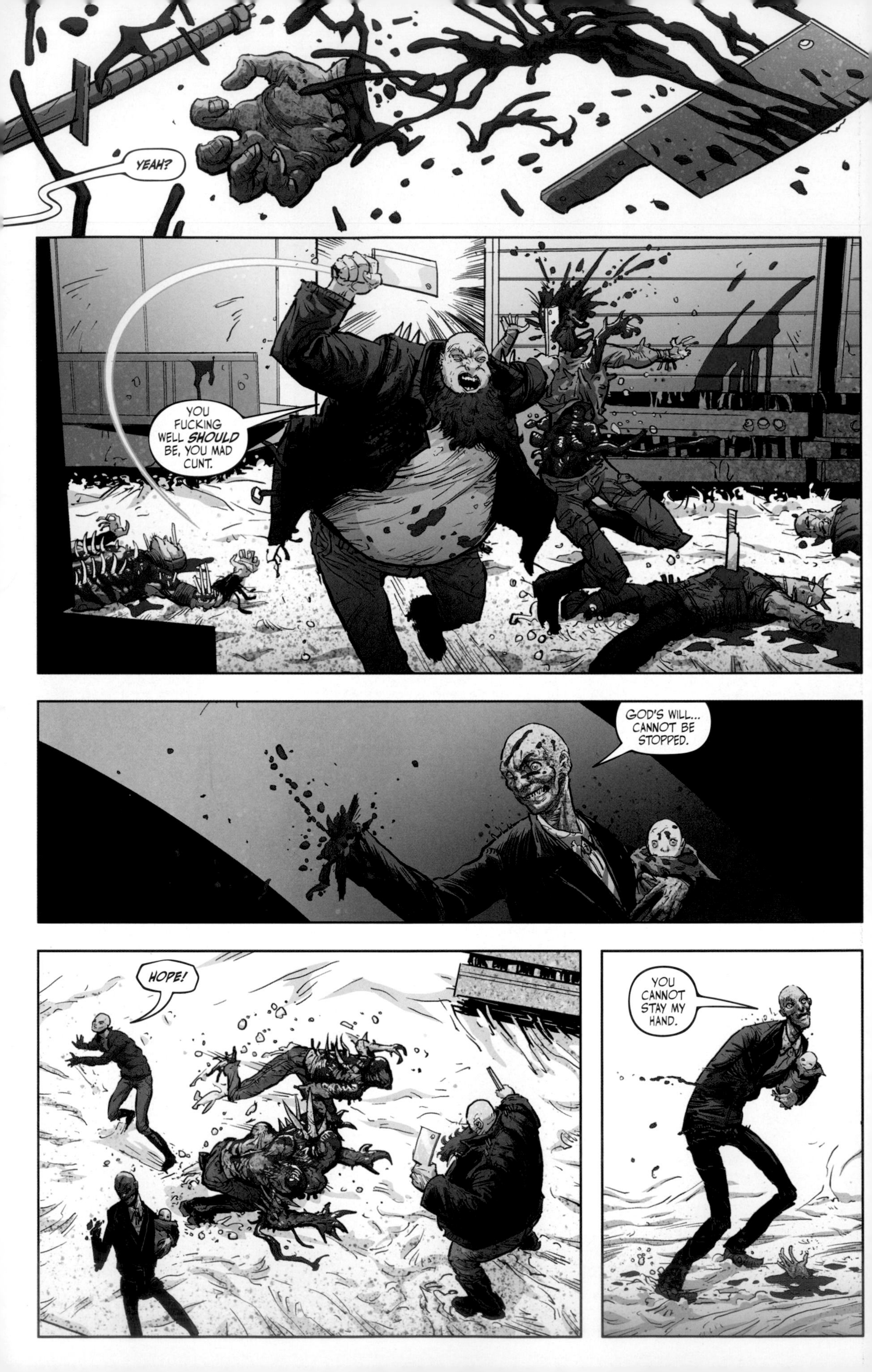
YEAH?
YOU FUCKING WELL SHOULD BE, YOU MAD CUNT.
GOD'S WILL... CANNOT BE STOPPED.
HOPE!
YOU CANNOT STAY MY HAND.

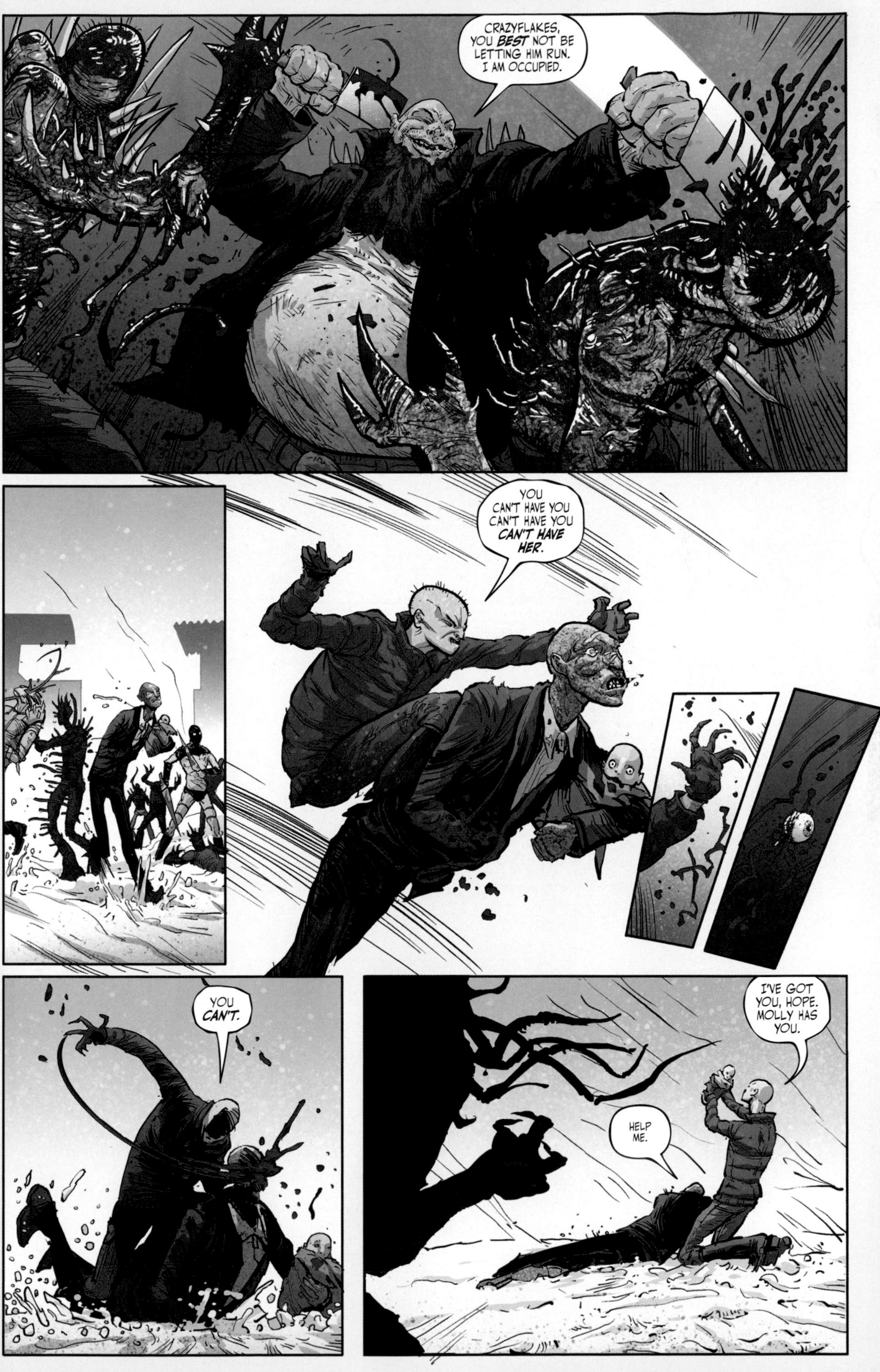
CRAZYFLAKES, YOU BEST NOT BE LETTING HIM RUN. I AM OCCUPIED.
YOU CAN'T HAVE YOU CAN'T HAVE YOU CAN'T HAVE HER.
YOU CAN'T.
I'VE GOT YOU, HOPE. MOLLY HAS YOU.
HELP ME.

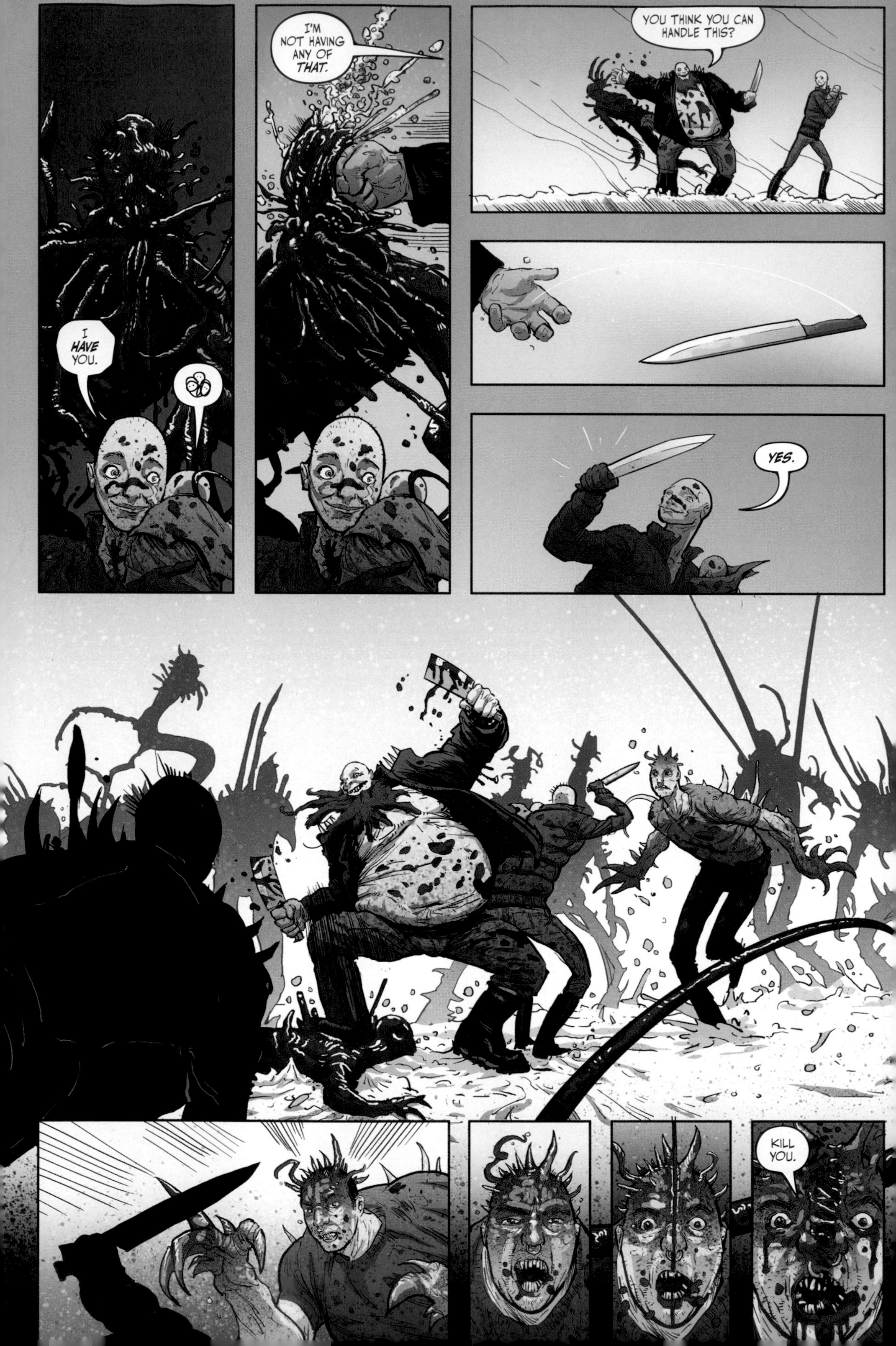
I HAVE YOU.
I'M NOT HAVING ANY OF THAT.
YOU THINK YOU CAN HANDLE THIS?
YES.
KILL YOU.

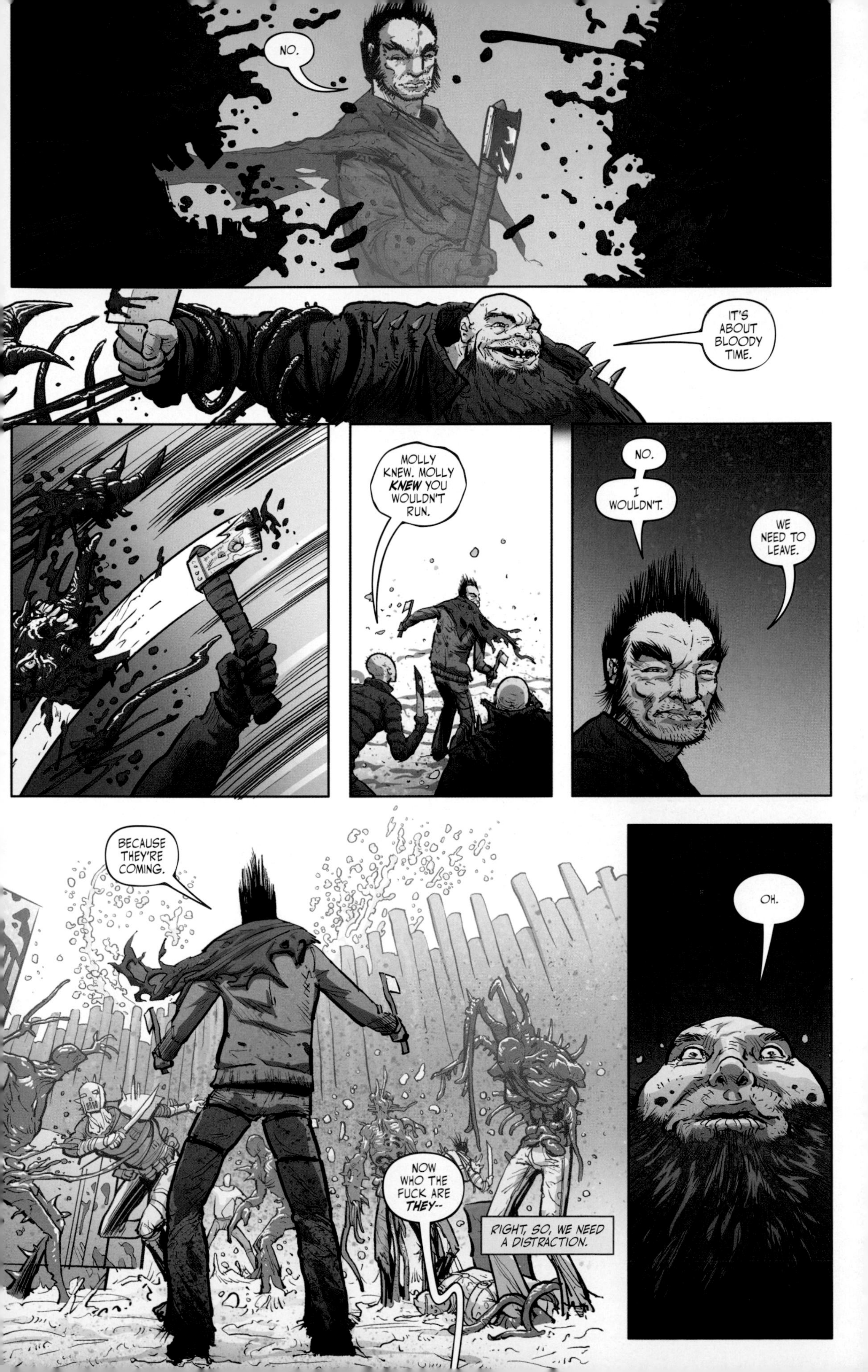
NO.
IT'S ABOUT BLOODY TIME.
MOLLY KNEW. MOLLY *KNEW* YOU WOULDN'T RUN.
NO.
I WOULDN'T.
WE NEED TO LEAVE.
BECAUSE THEY'RE COMING.
NOW WHO THE FUCK ARE *THEY*--
RIGHT, SO, WE NEED A DISTRACTION.
OH.

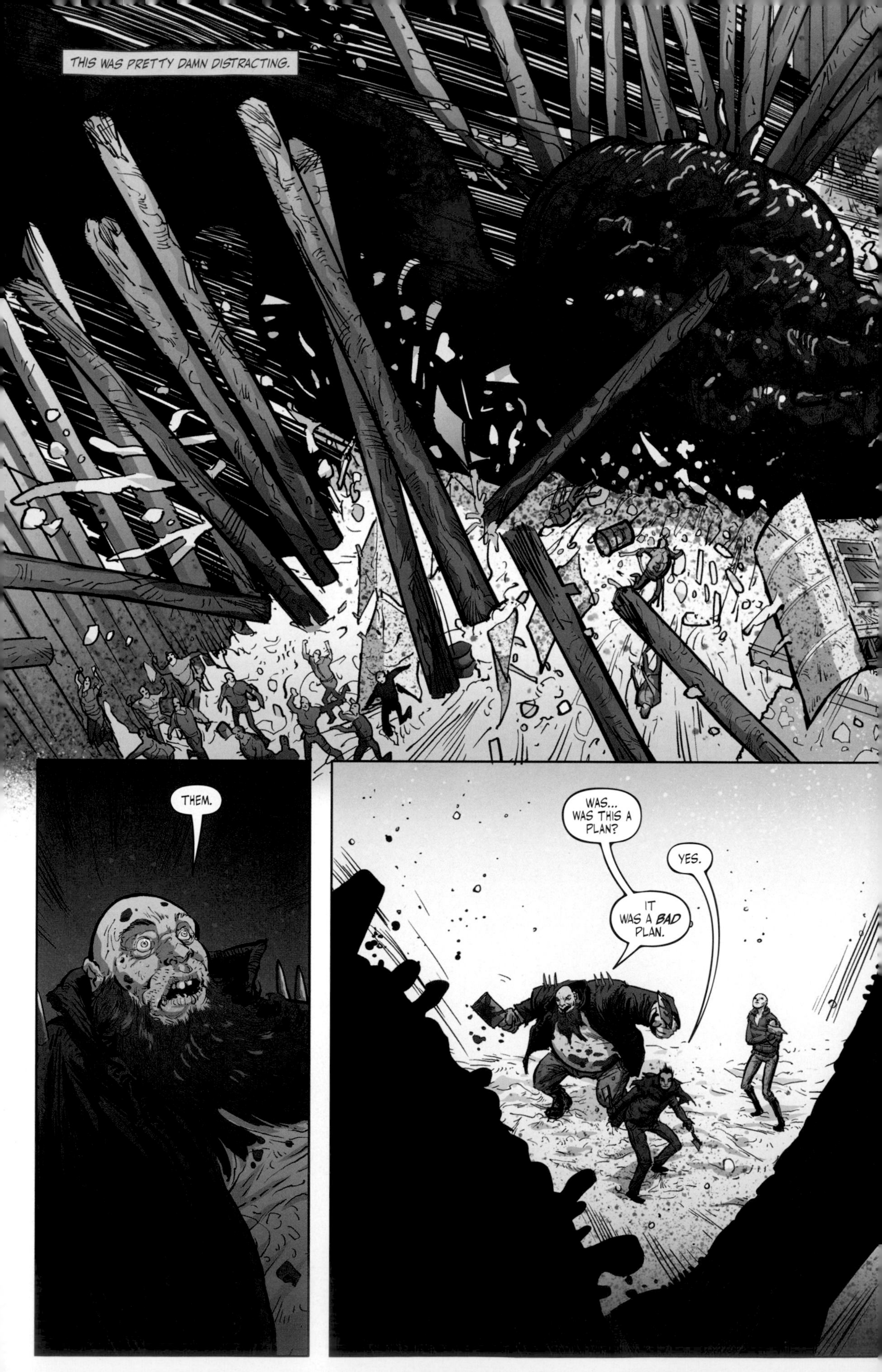
THIS WAS PRETTY DAMN DISTRACTING.
THEM.
WAS... WAS THIS A PLAN?
YES.
IT WAS A *BAD* PLAN.

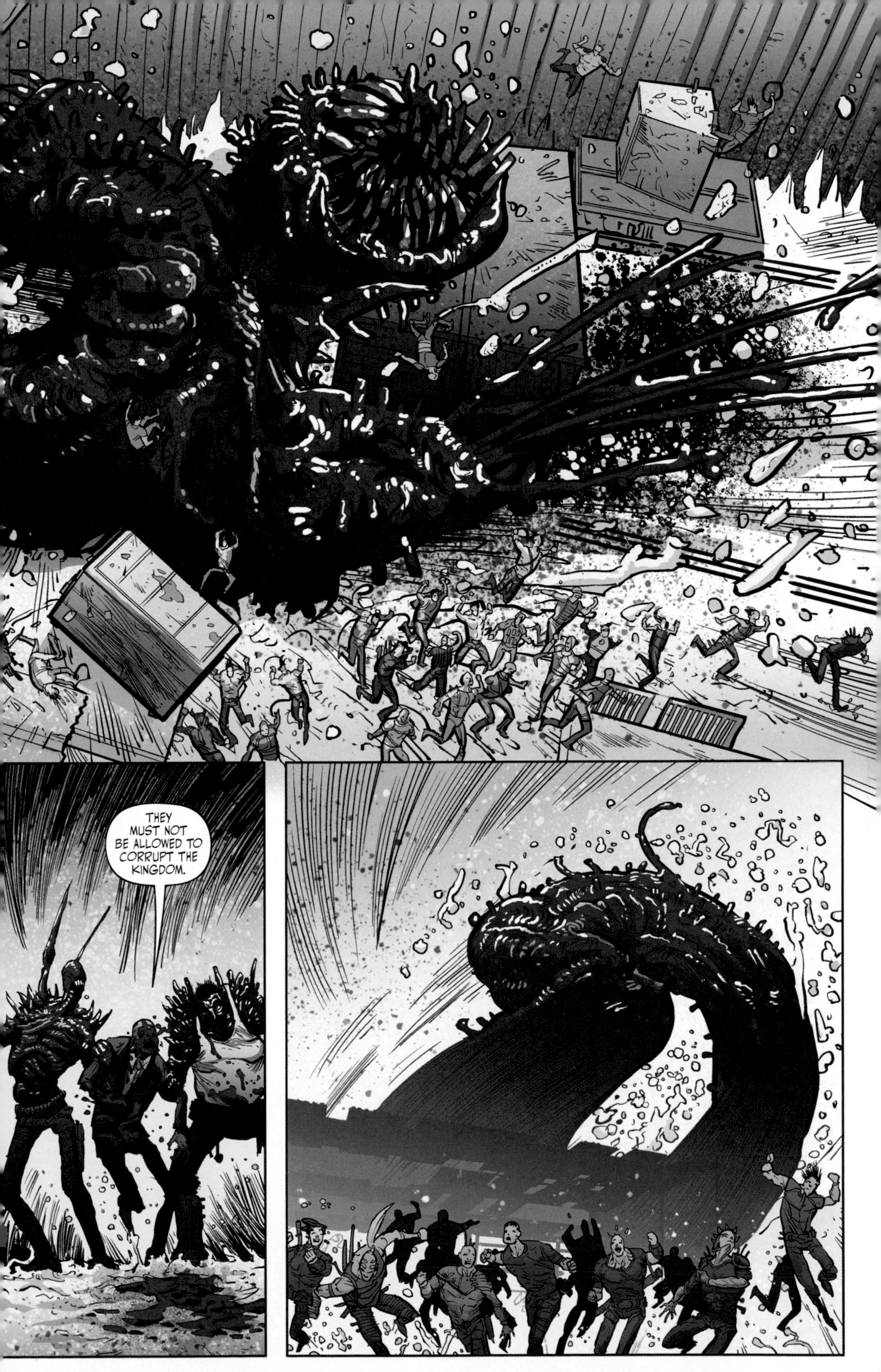
THEY MUST NOT BE ALLOWED TO CORRUPT THE KINGDOM.

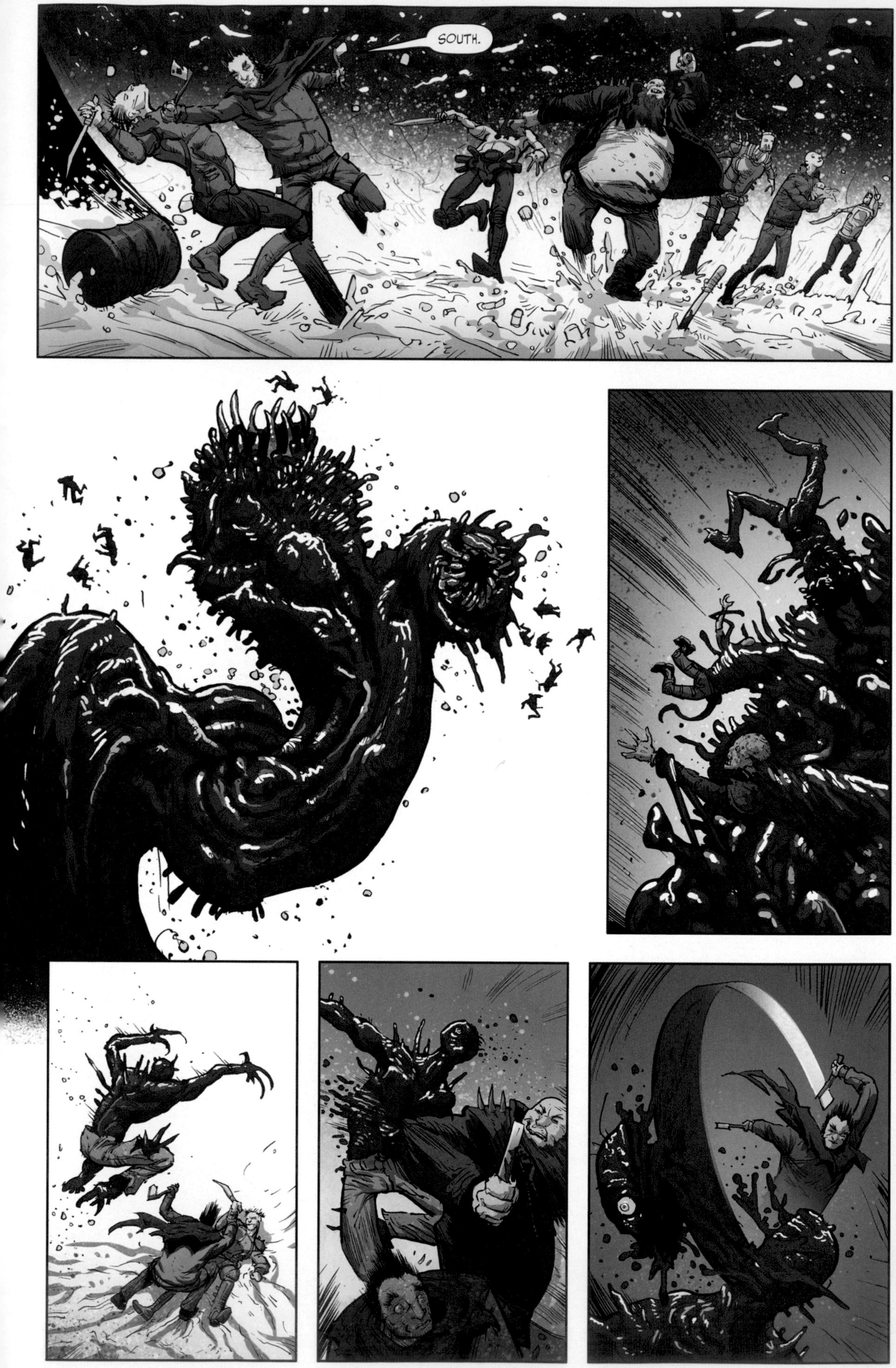
SOUTH.

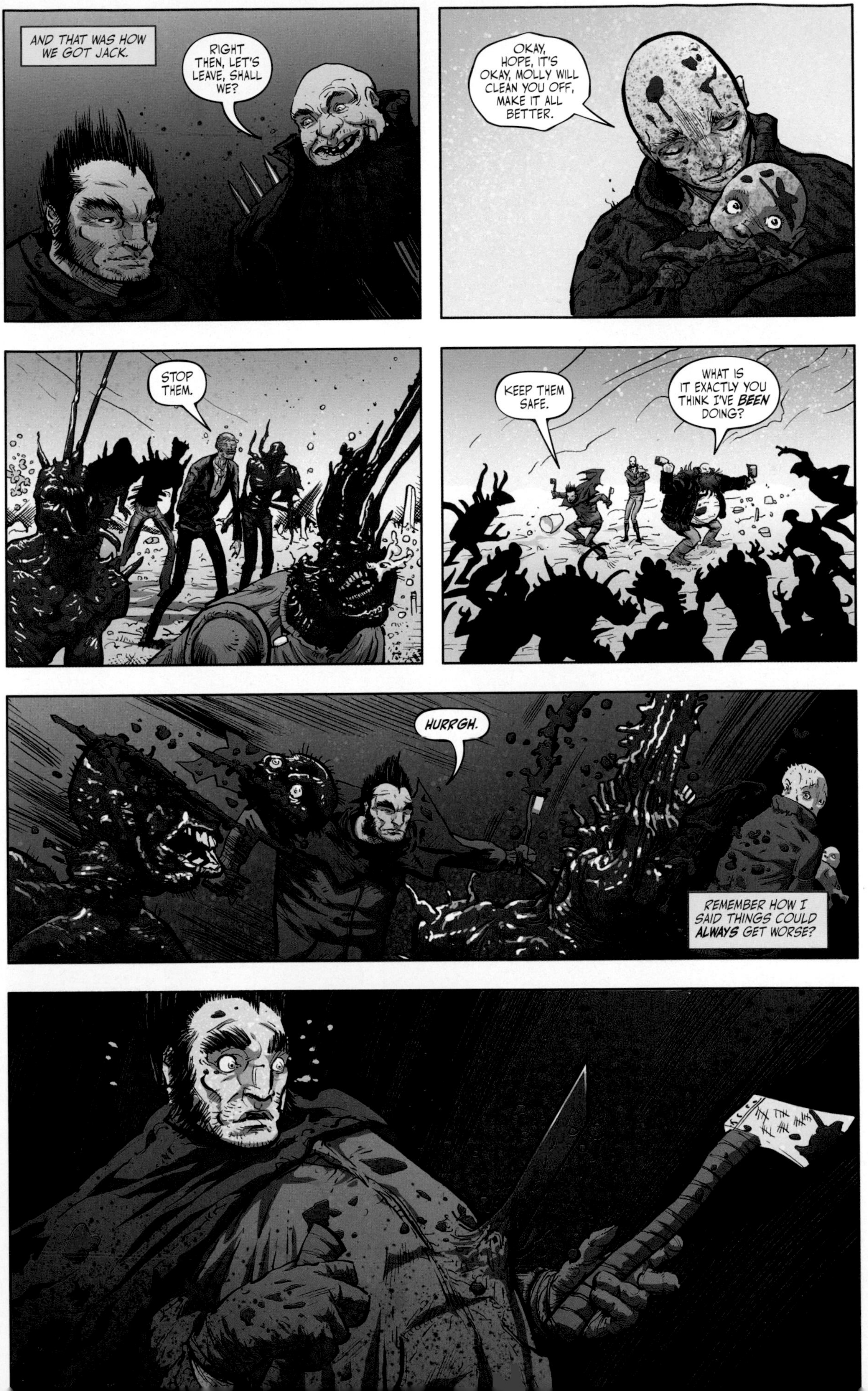
AND THAT WAS HOW WE GOT JACK.
RIGHT THEN, LET'S LEAVE, SHALL WE?
OKAY, HOPE, IT'S OKAY, MOLLY WILL CLEAN YOU OFF, MAKE IT ALL BETTER.
STOP THEM.
KEEP THEM SAFE.
WHAT IS IT EXACTLY YOU THINK I'VE BEEN DOING?
HURRGH.
REMEMBER HOW I SAID THINGS COULD ALWAYS GET WORSE?

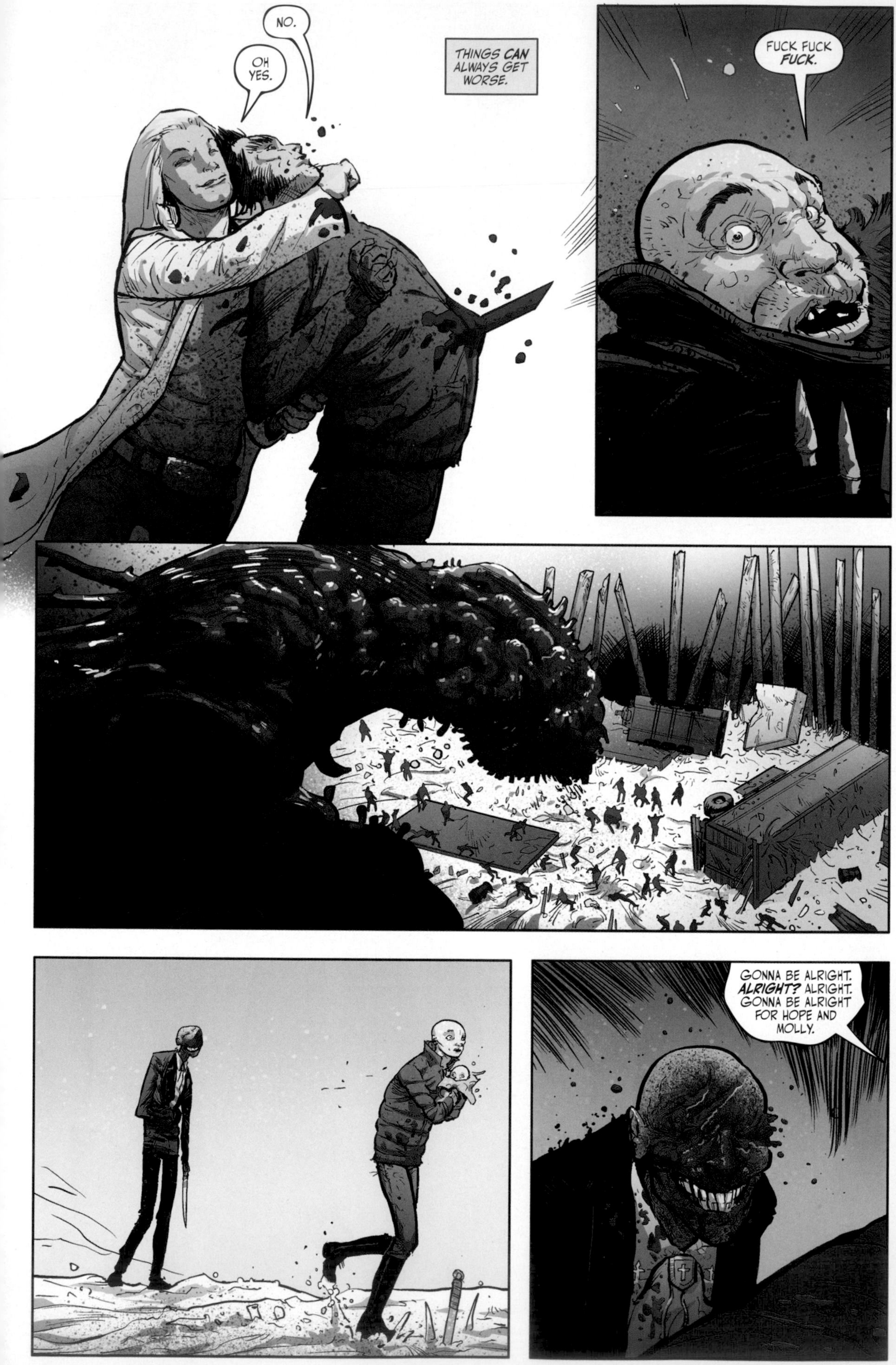
NO.
OH YES.
THINGS CAN ALWAYS GET WORSE.
FUCK FUCK FUCK.
GONNA BE ALRIGHT. ALRIGHT? ALRIGHT. GONNA BE ALRIGHT FOR HOPE AND MOLLY.

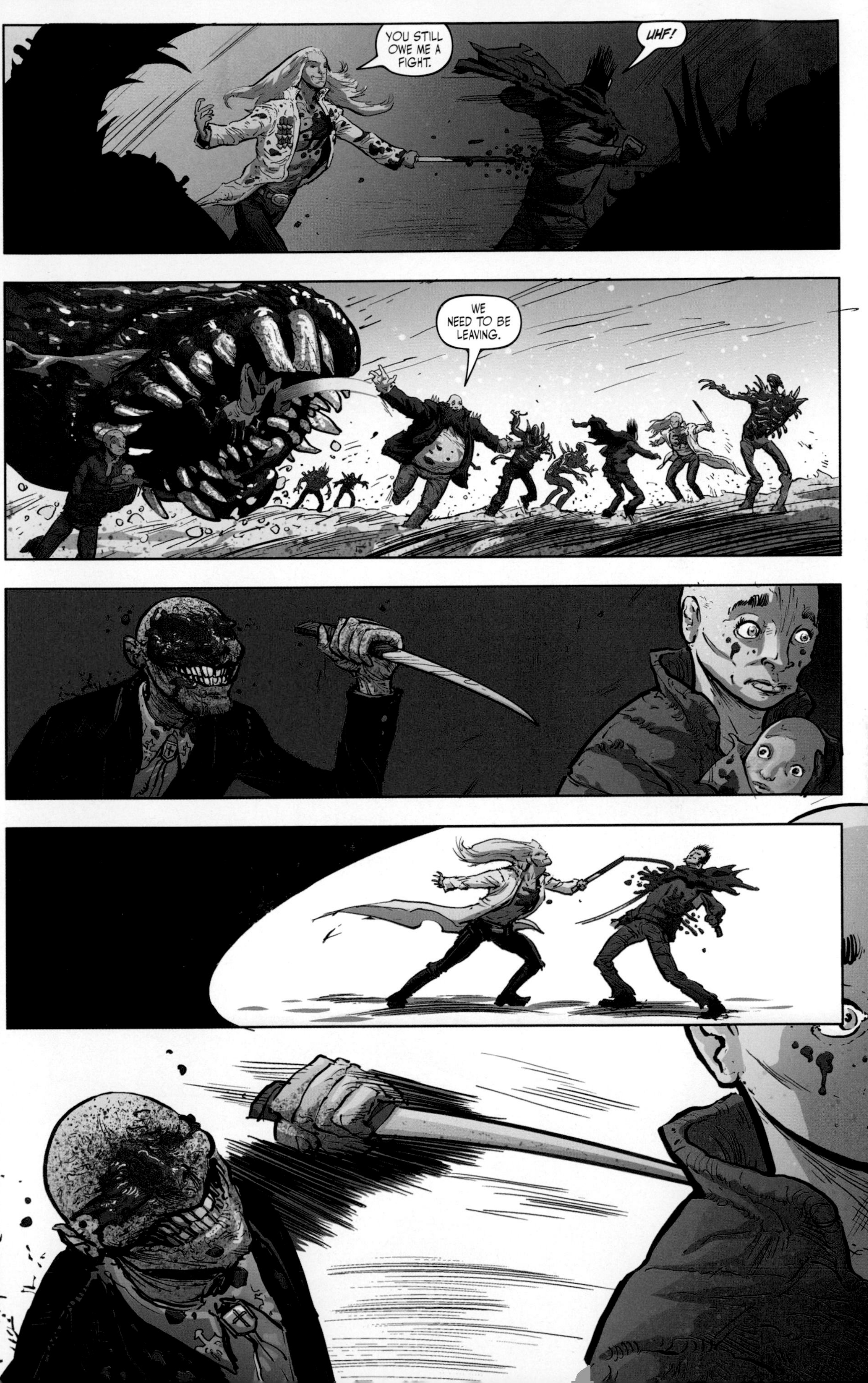
YOU STILL OWE ME A FIGHT.
UHF!
WE NEED TO BE LEAVING.

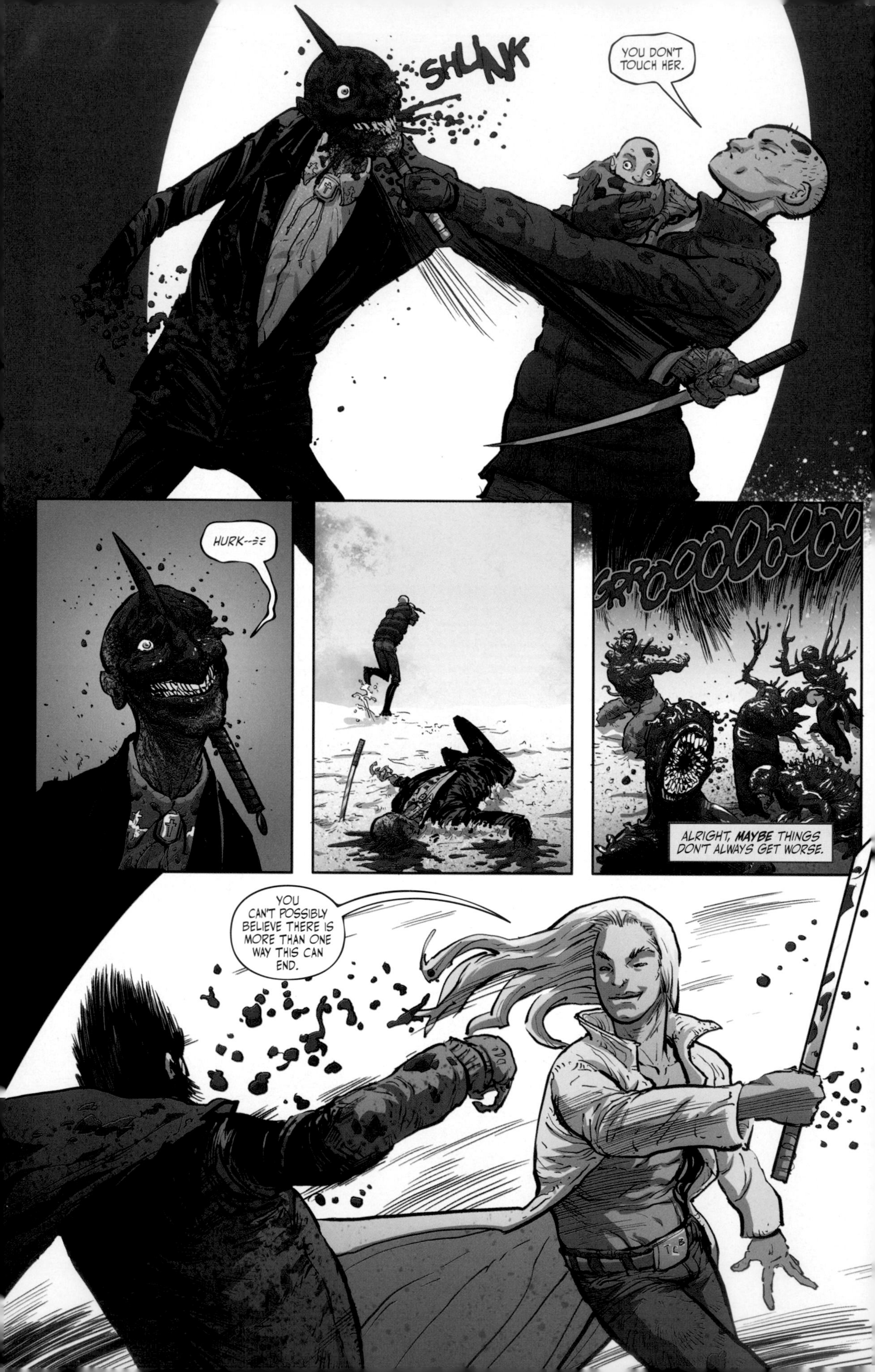
SHUNK
YOU DON'T TOUCH HER.
HURK--
GROOOOOOOOOO
ALRIGHT, MAYBE THINGS DON'T ALWAYS GET WORSE.
YOU CAN'T POSSIBLY BELIEVE THERE IS MORE THAN ONE WAY THIS CAN END.

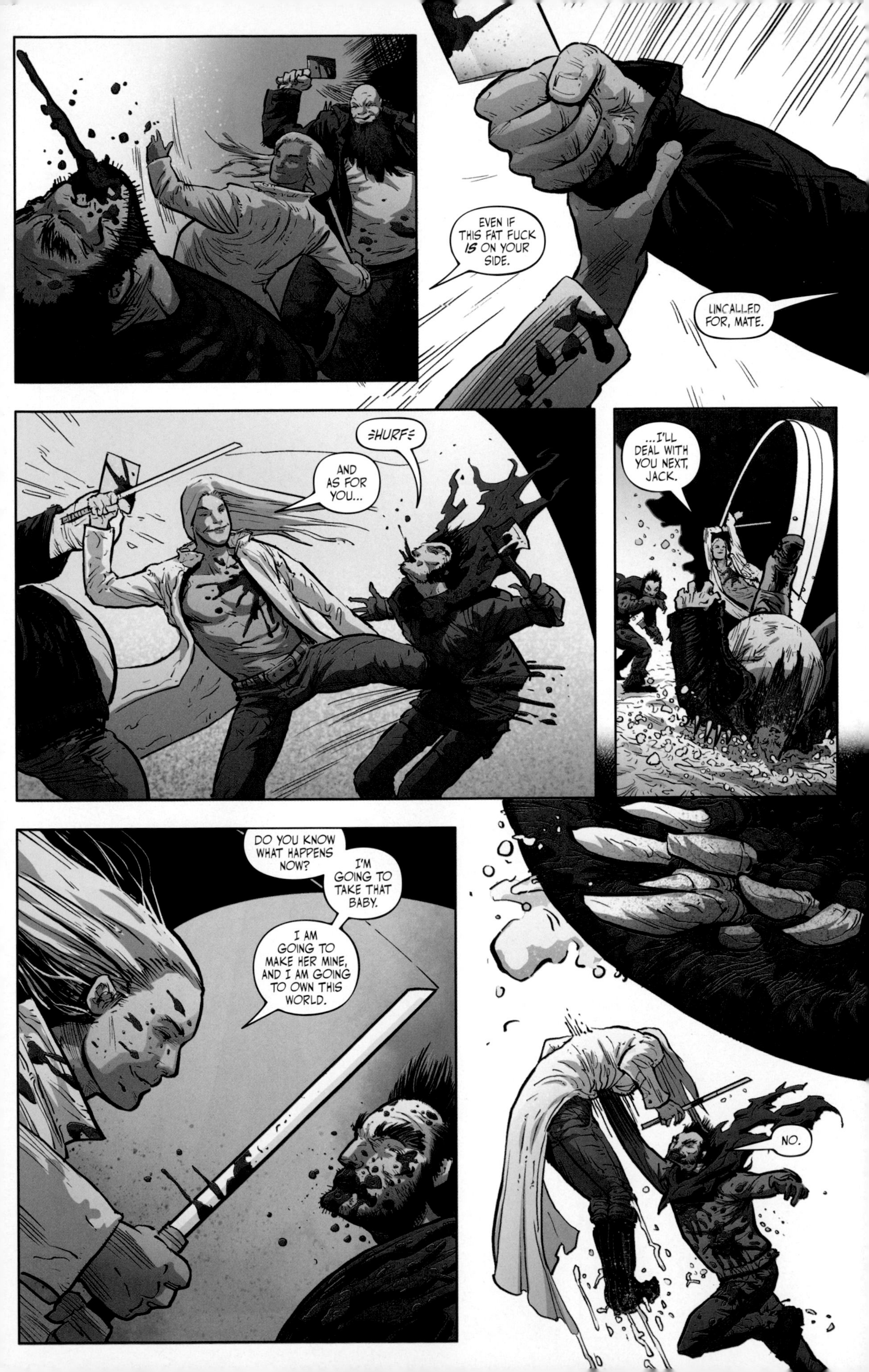
EVEN IF THIS FAT FUCK *IS* ON YOUR SIDE.
UNCALLED FOR, MATE.
HURF
AND AS FOR YOU...
...I'LL DEAL WITH YOU NEXT, JACK.
DO YOU KNOW WHAT HAPPENS NOW?
I'M GOING TO TAKE THAT BABY.
I AM GOING TO MAKE HER MINE, AND I AM GOING TO OWN THIS WORLD.
NO.

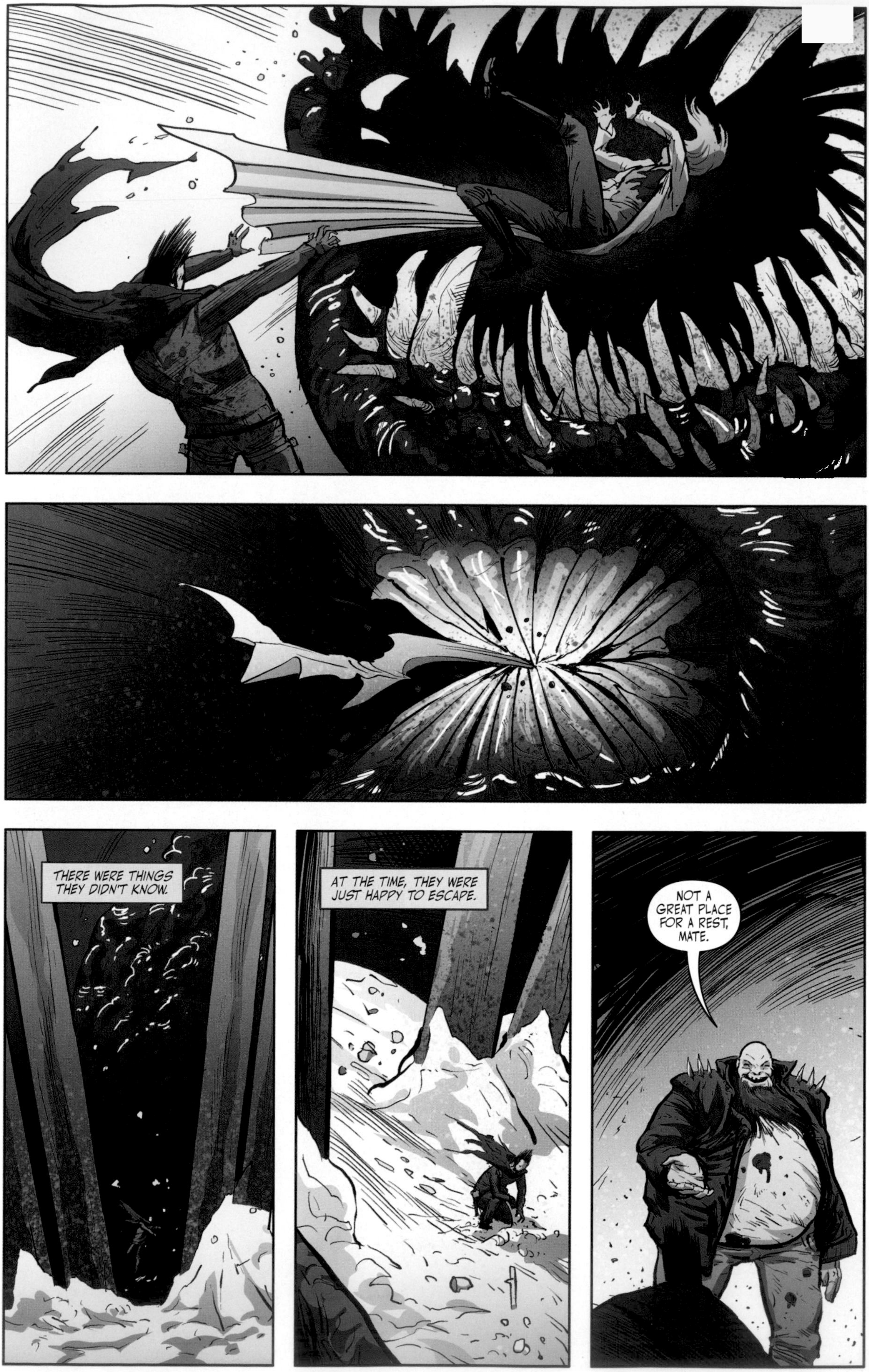
THERE WERE THINGS THEY DIDN'T KNOW.
AT THE TIME, THEY WERE JUST HAPPY TO ESCAPE.
NOT A GREAT PLACE FOR A REST, MATE.

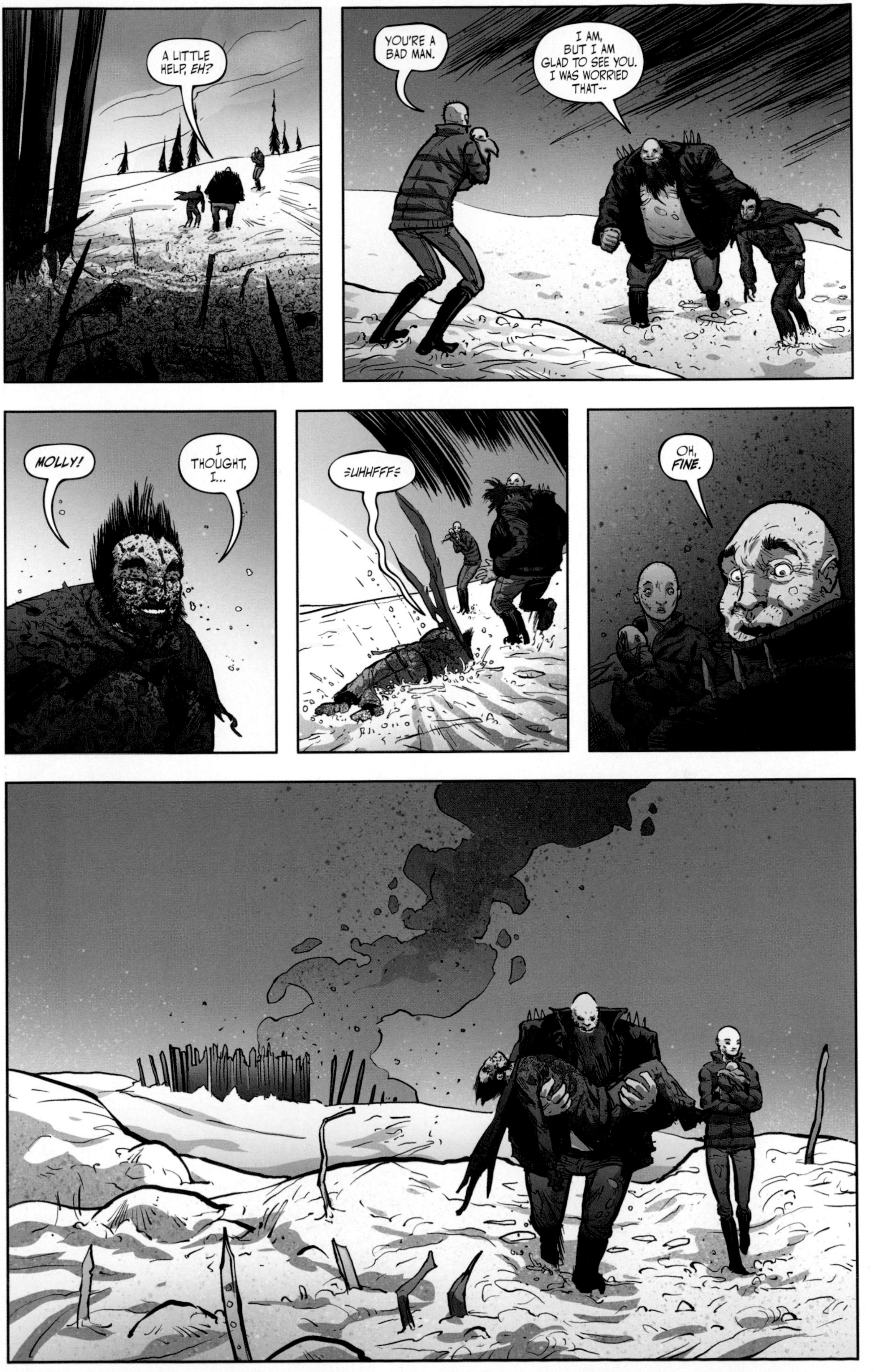
A LITTLE HELP, EH?
YOU'RE A BAD MAN.
I AM, BUT I AM GLAD TO SEE YOU. I WAS WORRIED THAT--
MOLLY!
I THOUGHT, I...
UHHFFF
OH, FINE.

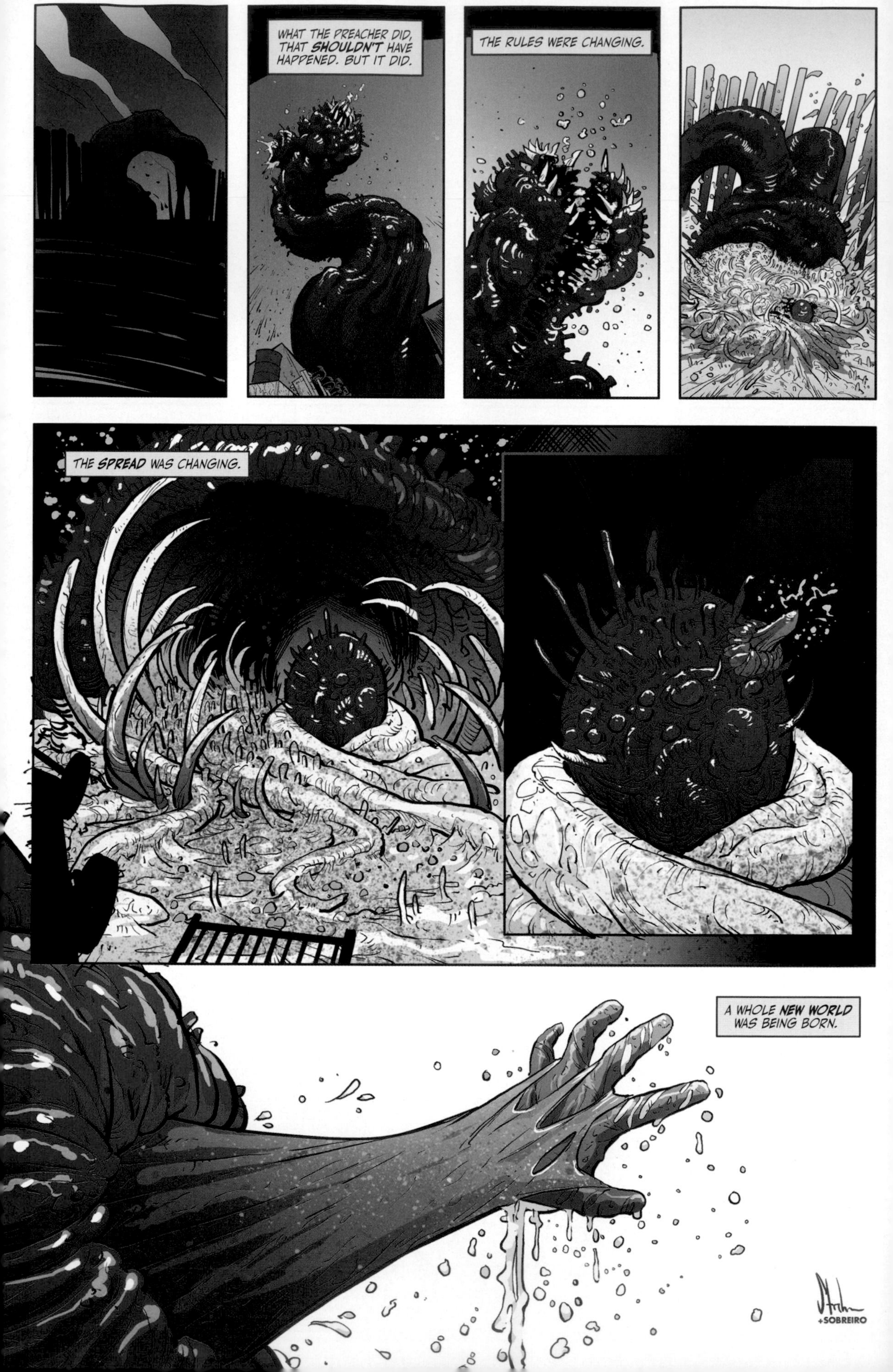

WHAT THE PREACHER DID, THAT **SHOULDN'T** HAVE HAPPENED. BUT IT DID.
THE RULES WERE CHANGING.
THE **SPREAD** WAS CHANGING.
A WHOLE **NEW WORLD** WAS BEING BORN.
+SOBREIRO

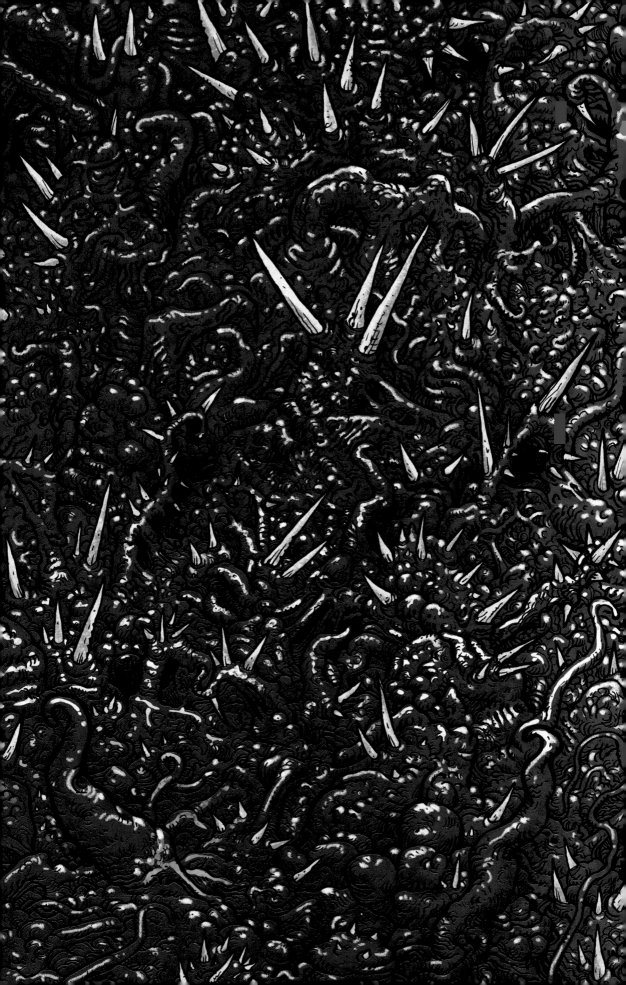

JUSTIN JORDAN

Justin Jordan lives in the wilds of Pennsylvania and writes comics. Lots of comics. Most notably The Luther Strode saga and Dead Body Road for Image.

Twitter: @Justin_Jordan

KYLE STRAHM

Kyle Strahm draws comics and covers for publishers such as Image, DC, Dark Horse, IDW, Boom!, Todd McFarlane Productions and others.
He lives in Kansas City, Missouri just off highway 70.

Instagram: krstrahm
Twitter: @kstrahm
website: www.kylestrahm.com

FELIPE SOBREIRO

Felipe Sobreiro is an artist and colourist from Brazil. His work has been published, among others, by Image, Marvel, DC, BOOM! Studios and Dark Horse. He's the colorist of The Luther Strode saga.

Instagram: sobreiro
Twitter: @therealsobreiro
website: www.sobreiro.com
Facebook: www.fb.com/fsobreiro

SEBASTIAN GIRNER

Sebastian Girner is a freelance editor and writer who has helped creatively guide and produce comics for such publishers as Marvel Entertainment, Image Comics, VIZ Media and Random House. He lives and works in Brooklyn.

COVER GALLERY

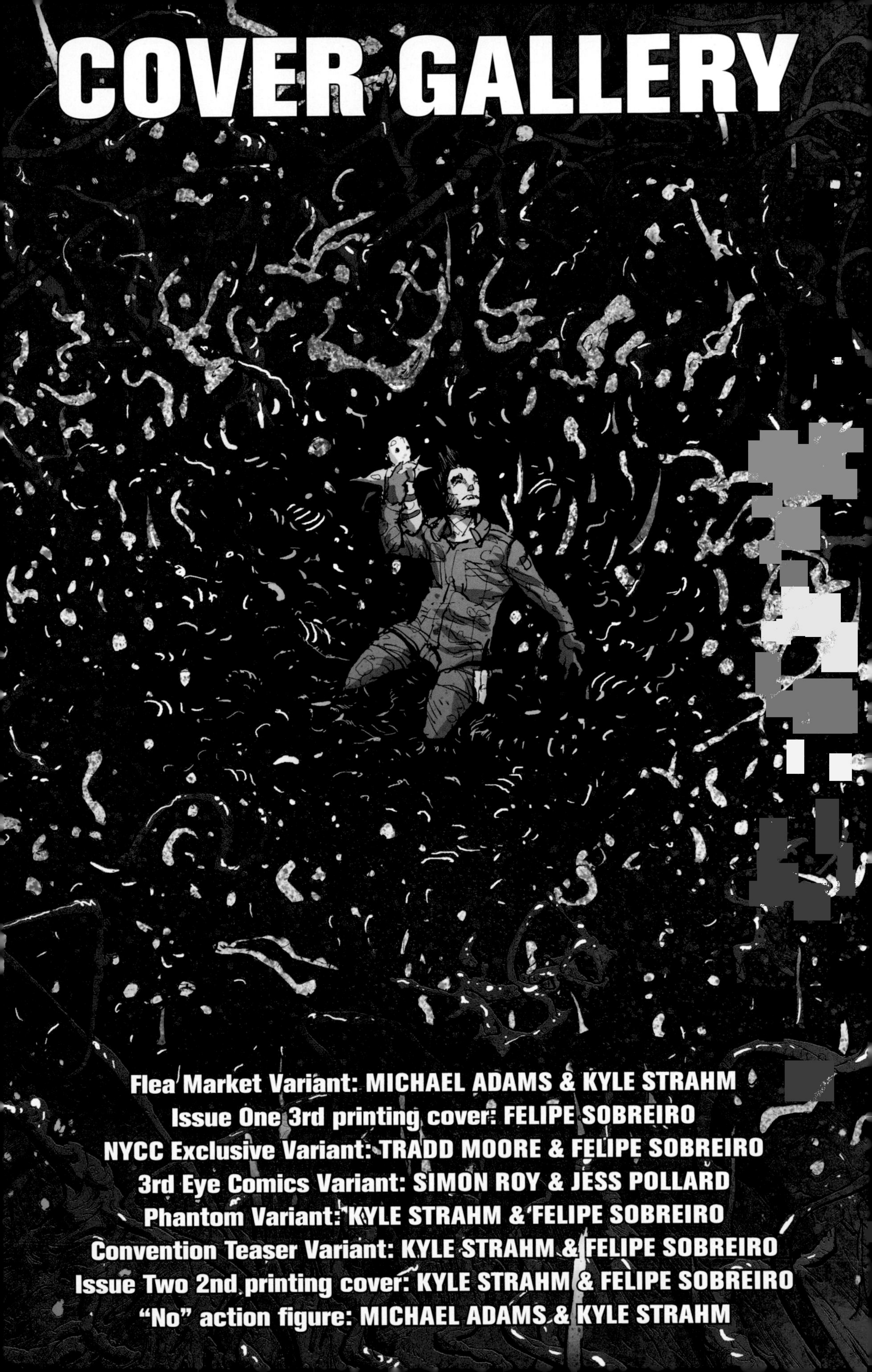

Flea Market Variant: MICHAEL ADAMS & KYLE STRAHM
Issue One 3rd printing cover: FELIPE SOBREIRO
NYCC Exclusive Variant: TRADD MOORE & FELIPE SOBREIRO
3rd Eye Comics Variant: SIMON ROY & JESS POLLARD
Phantom Variant: KYLE STRAHM & FELIPE SOBREIRO
Convention Teaser Variant: KYLE STRAHM & FELIPE SOBREIRO
Issue Two 2nd printing cover: KYLE STRAHM & FELIPE SOBREIRO
"No" action figure: MICHAEL ADAMS & KYLE STRAHM

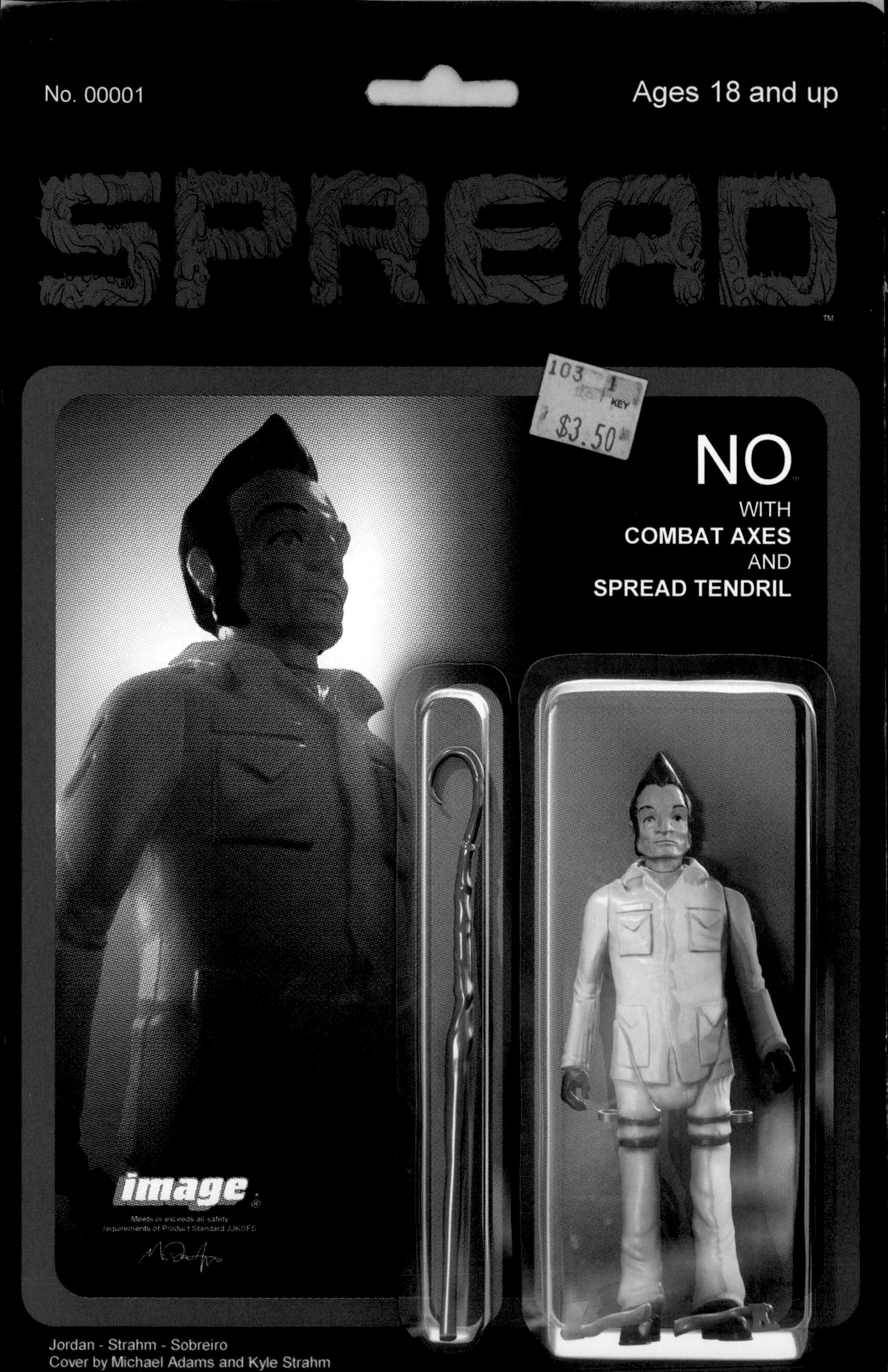
No. 00001
Ages 18 and up
SPREAD
TM
103 1
KEY
$3.50
NO
WITH
COMBAT AXES
AND
SPREAD TENDRIL
image
Meets or exceeds all safety
requirements of Product Standard JJKSFS
Jordan - Strahm - Sobreiro
Cover by Michael Adams and Kyle Strahm

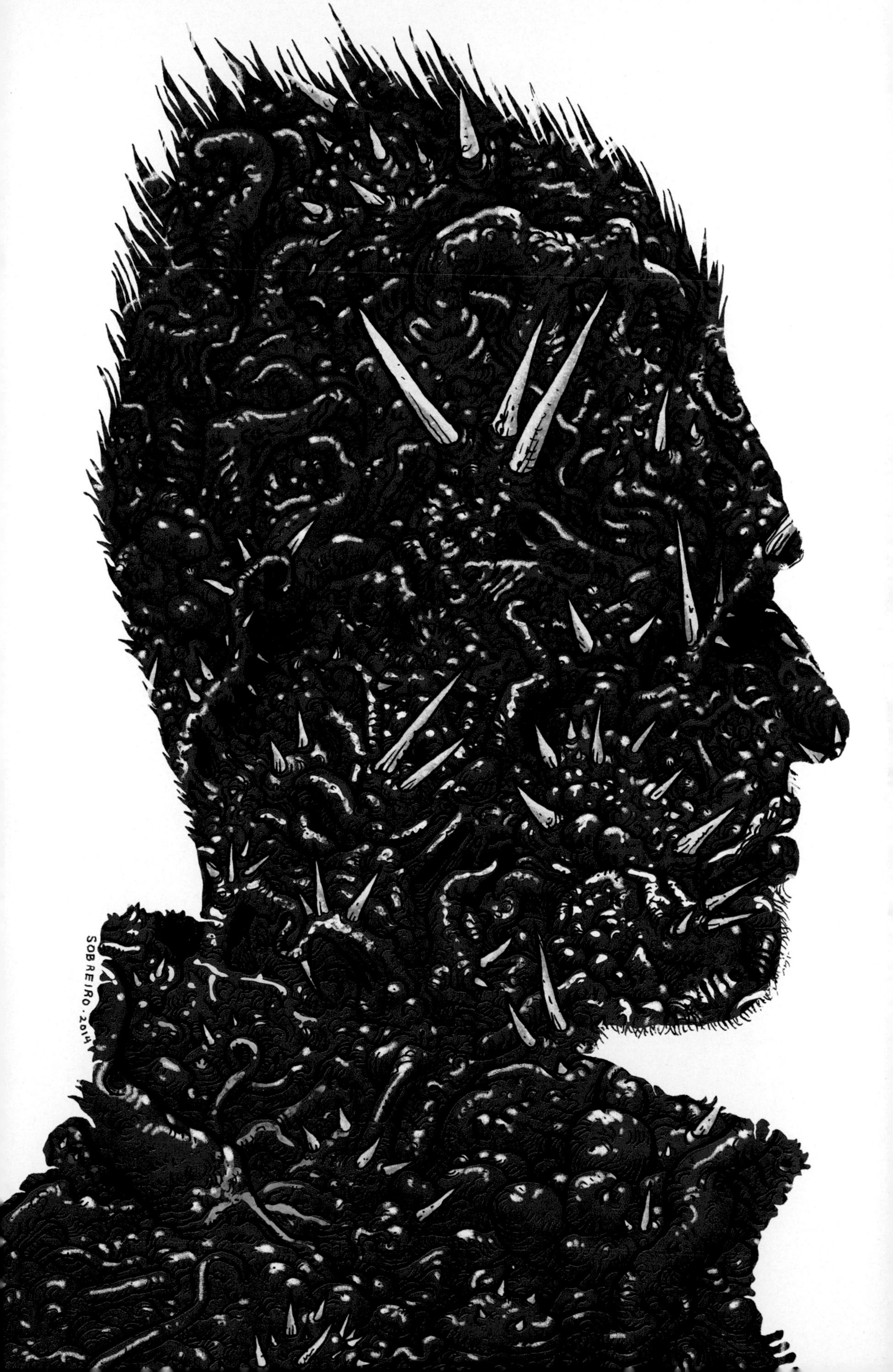
SOBREIRO · 2014

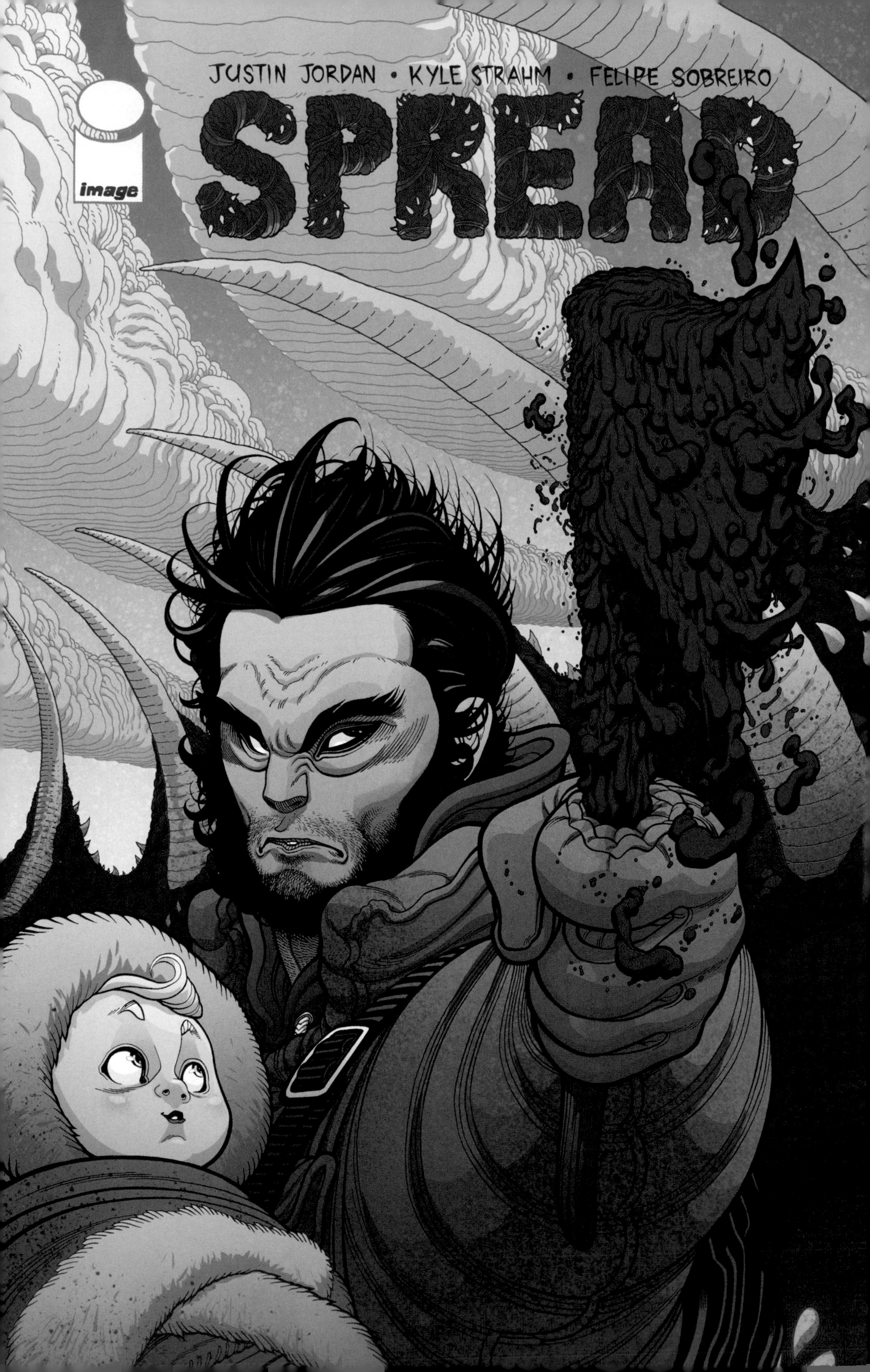
JUSTIN JORDAN • KYLE STRAHM • FELIPE SOBREIRO
SPREAD
image

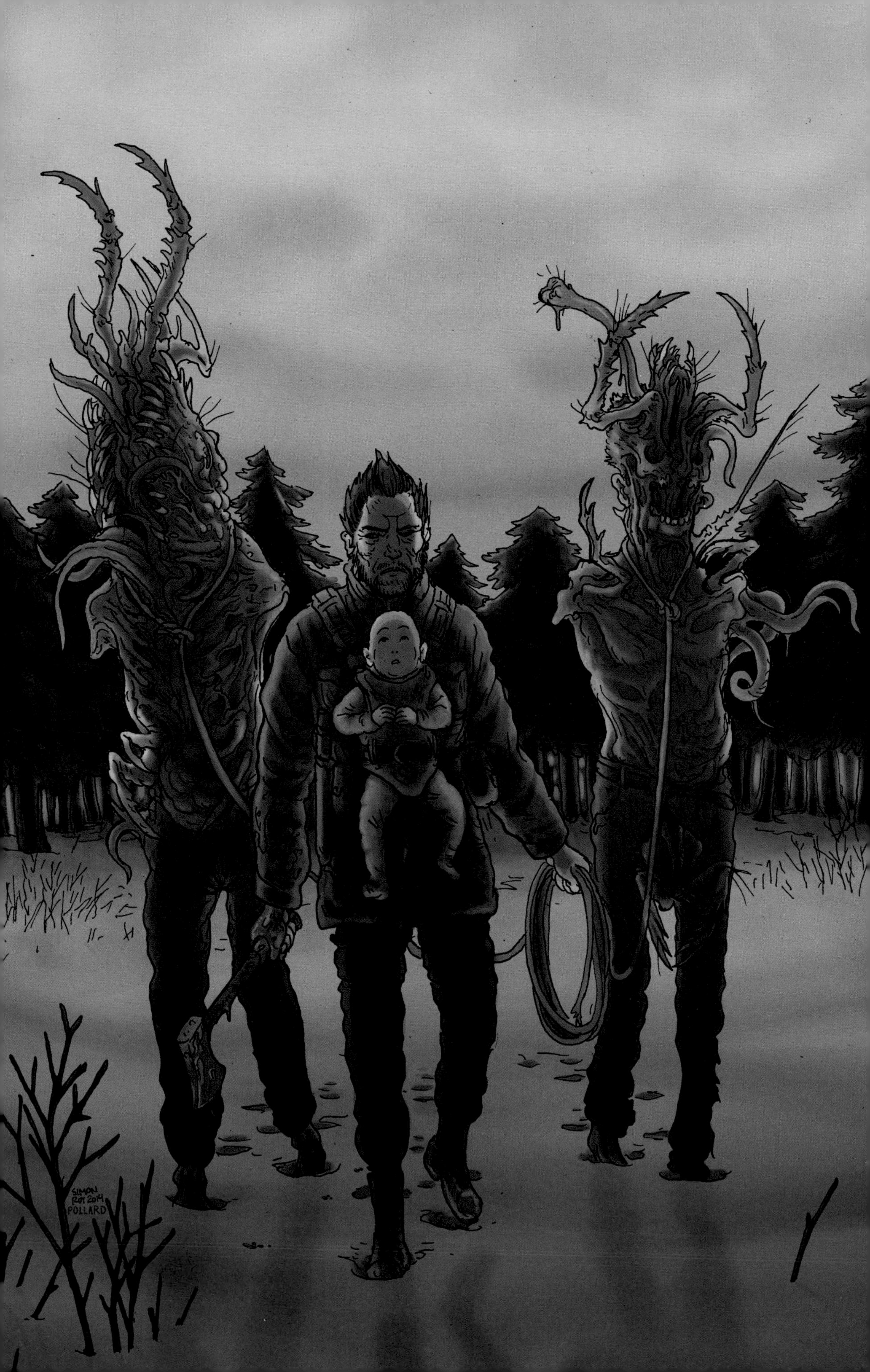
SIMON
ROI 2014
POLLARD

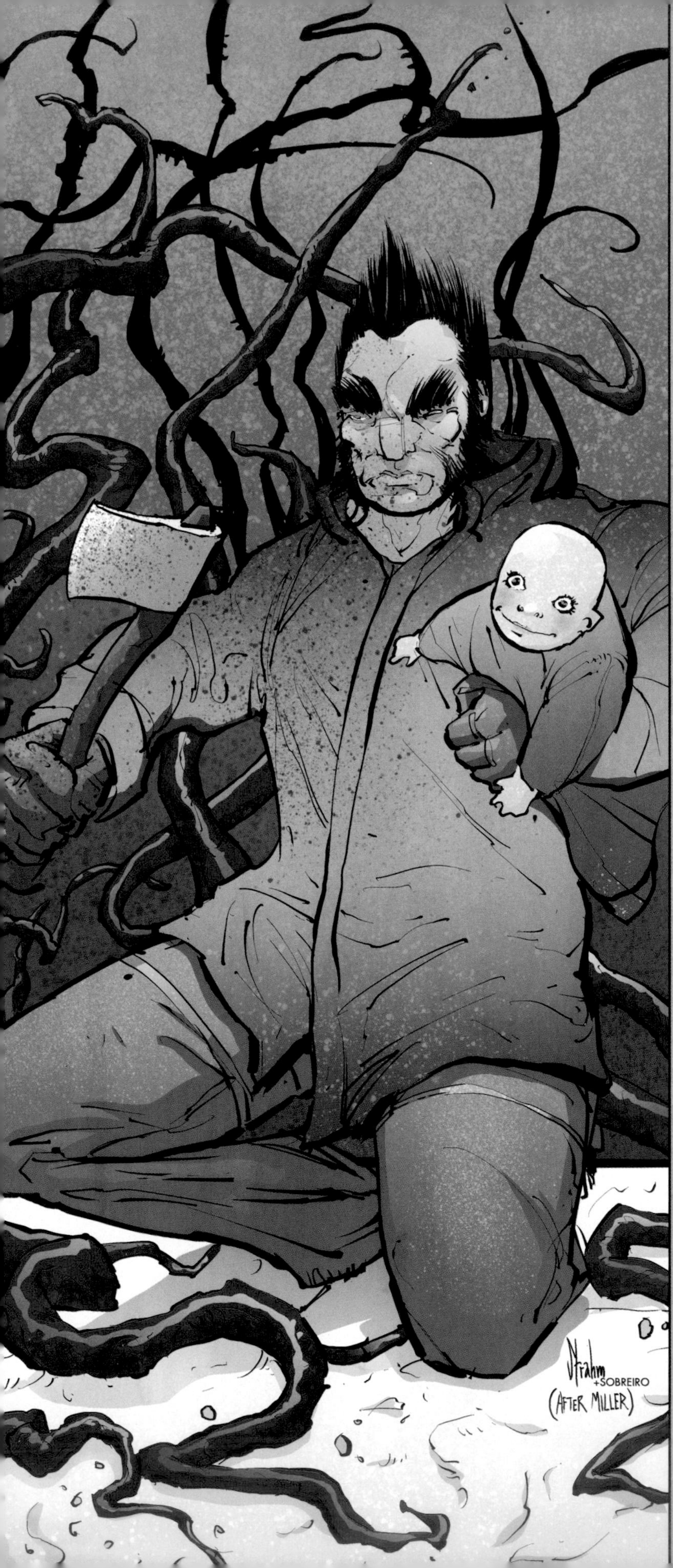
Strahm
+SOBREIRO
(AFTER MILLER)

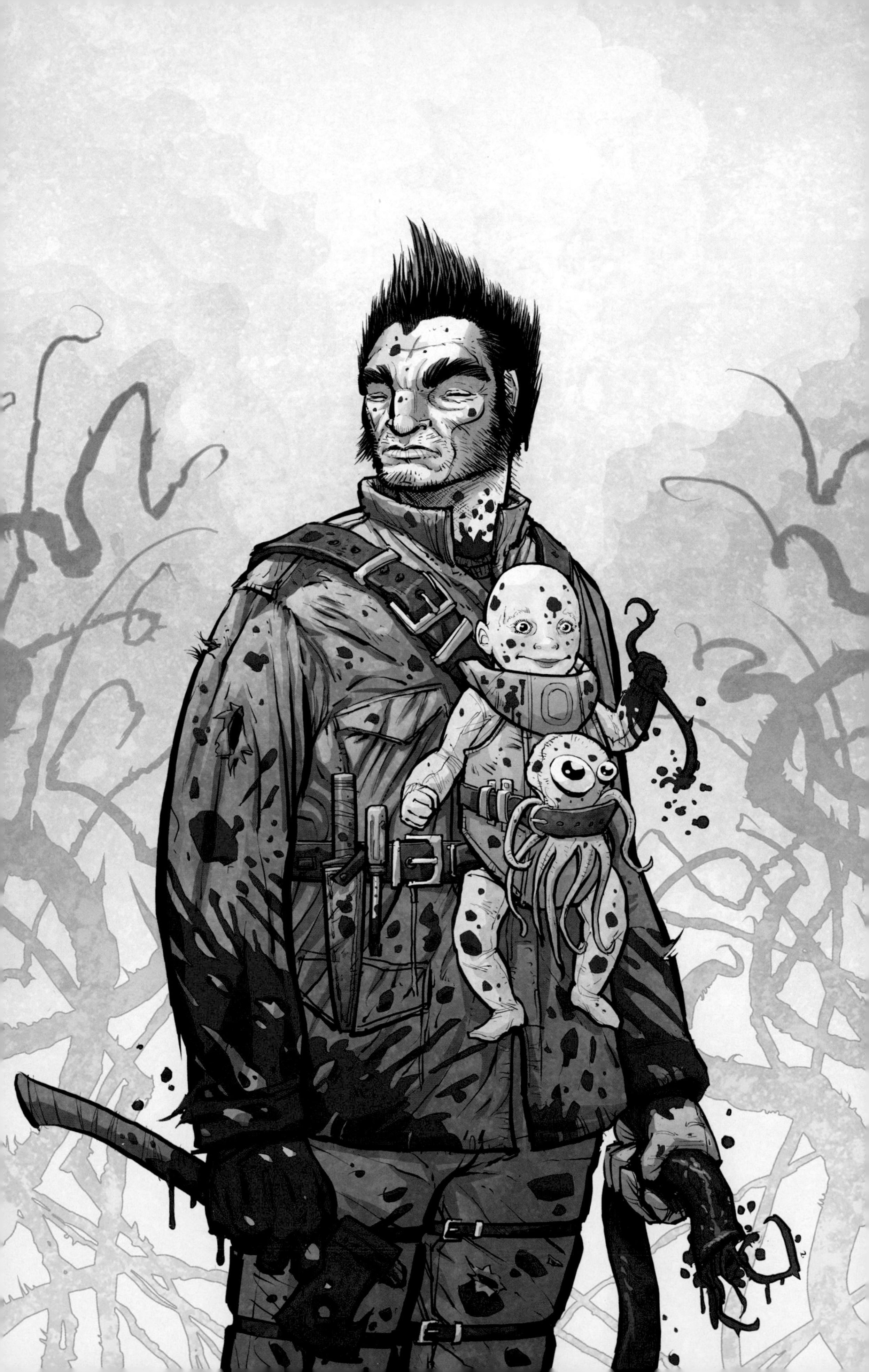

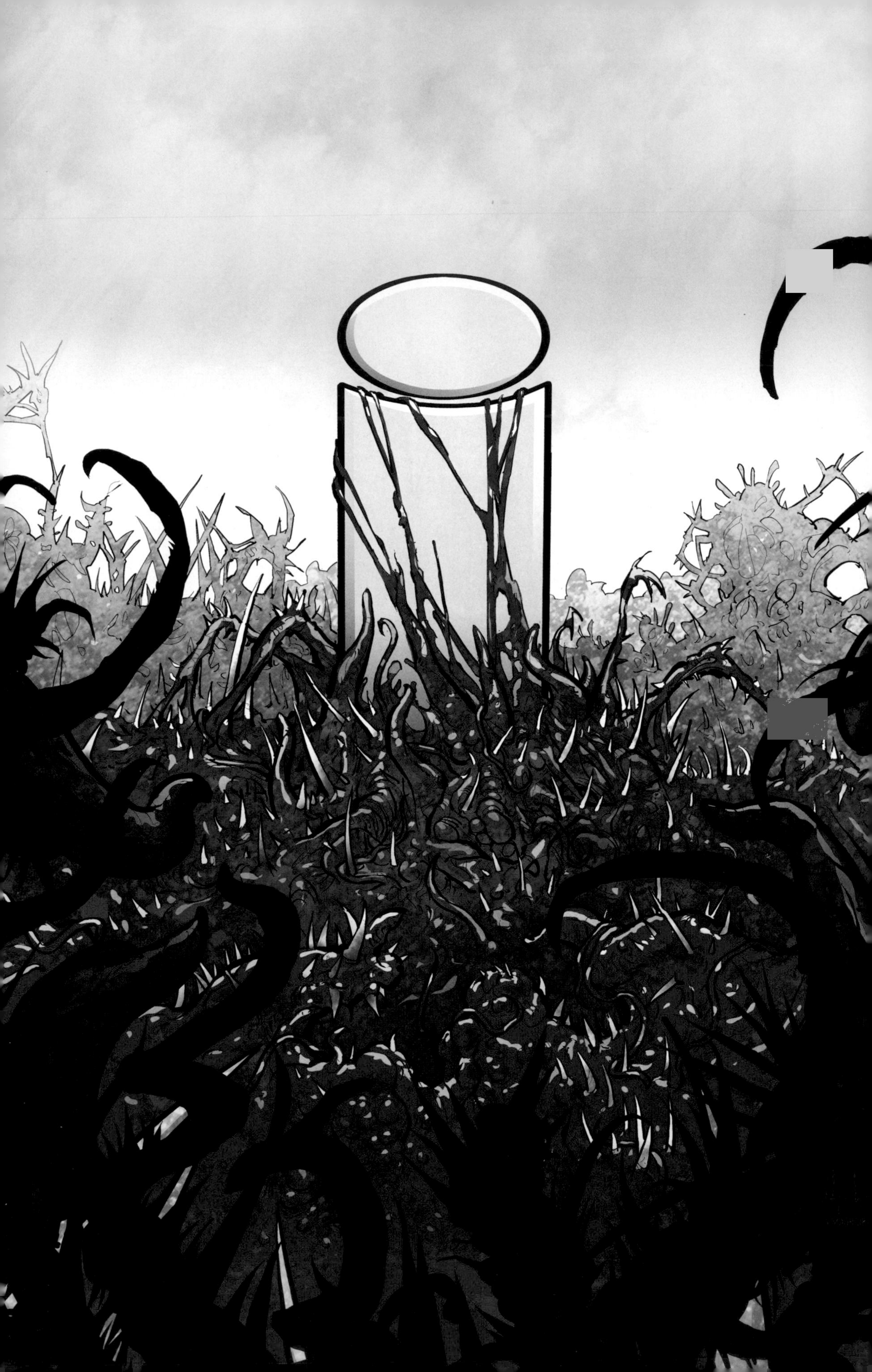

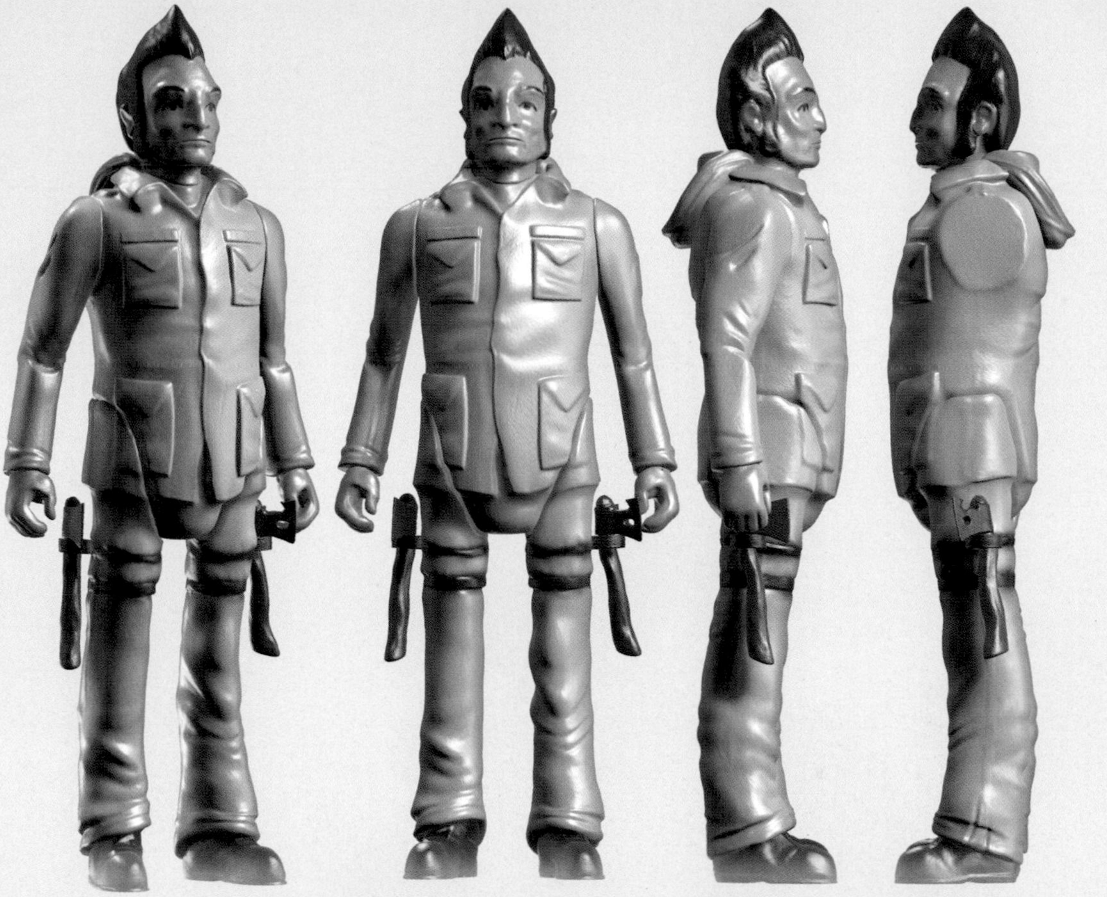

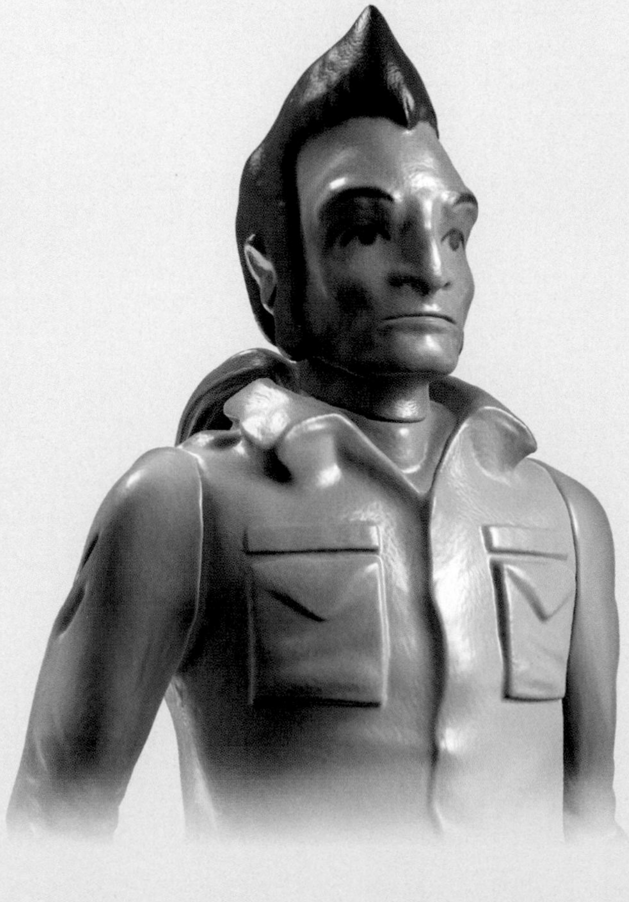

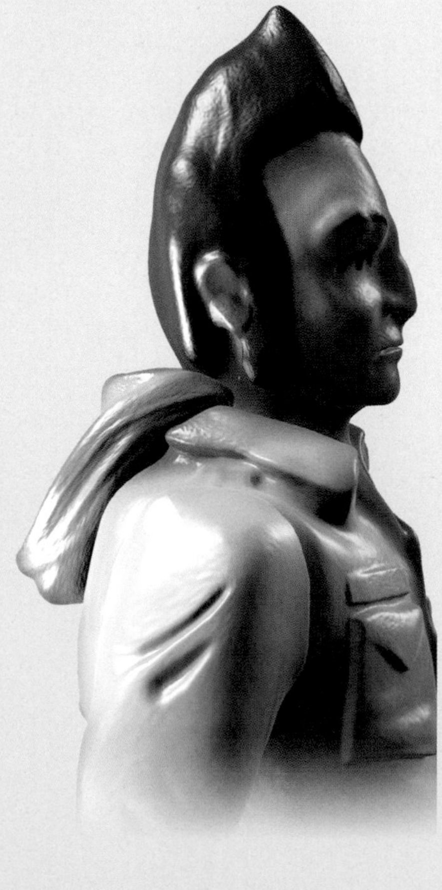

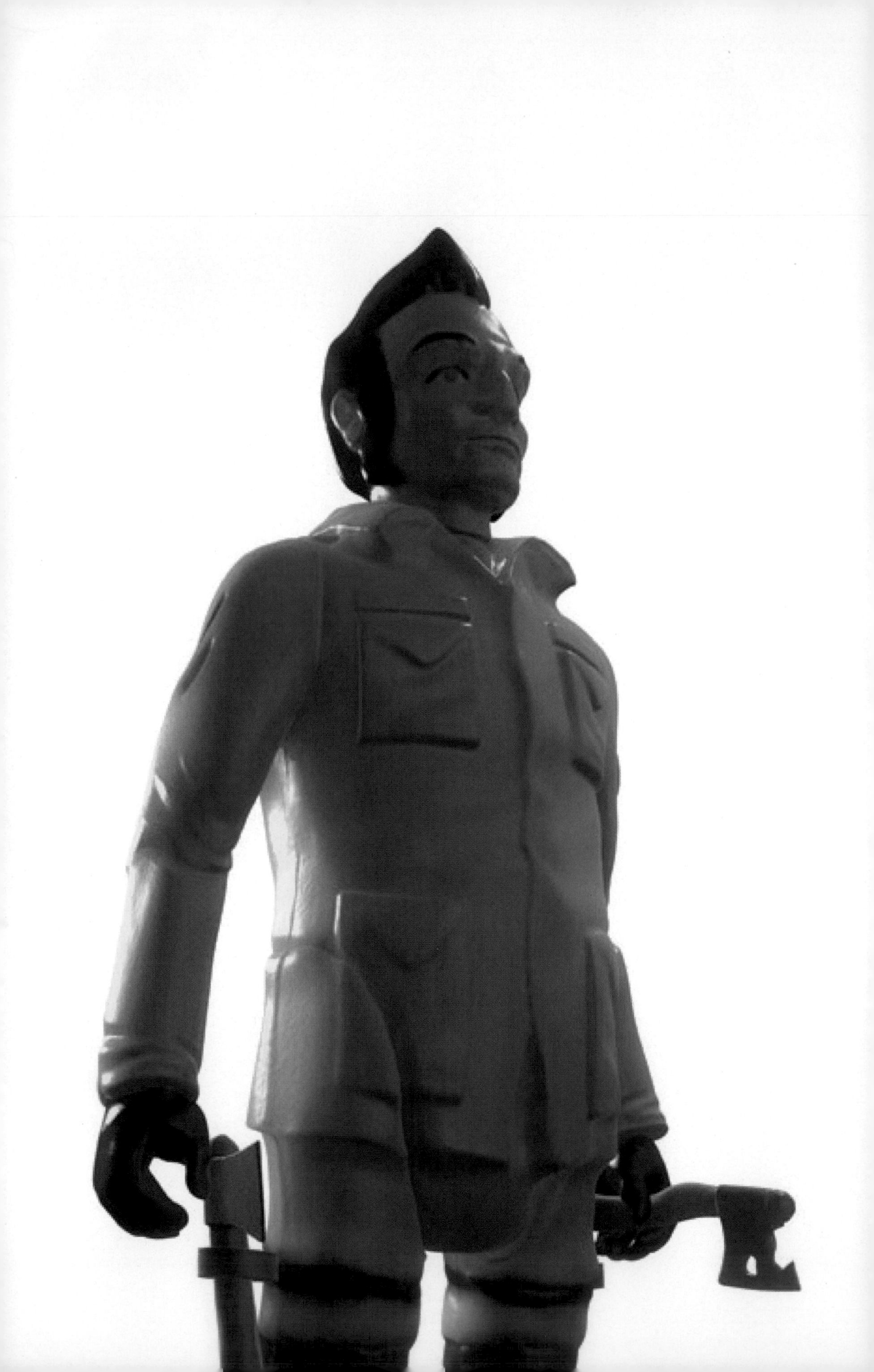

CHARACTER CONCEPTS

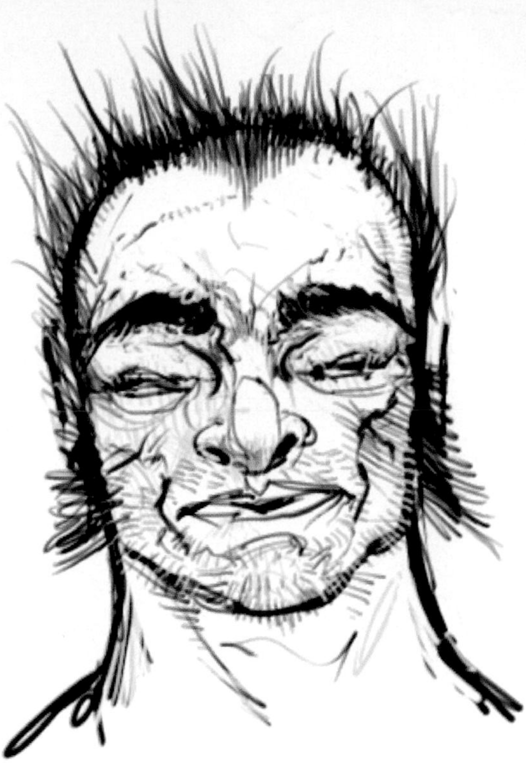

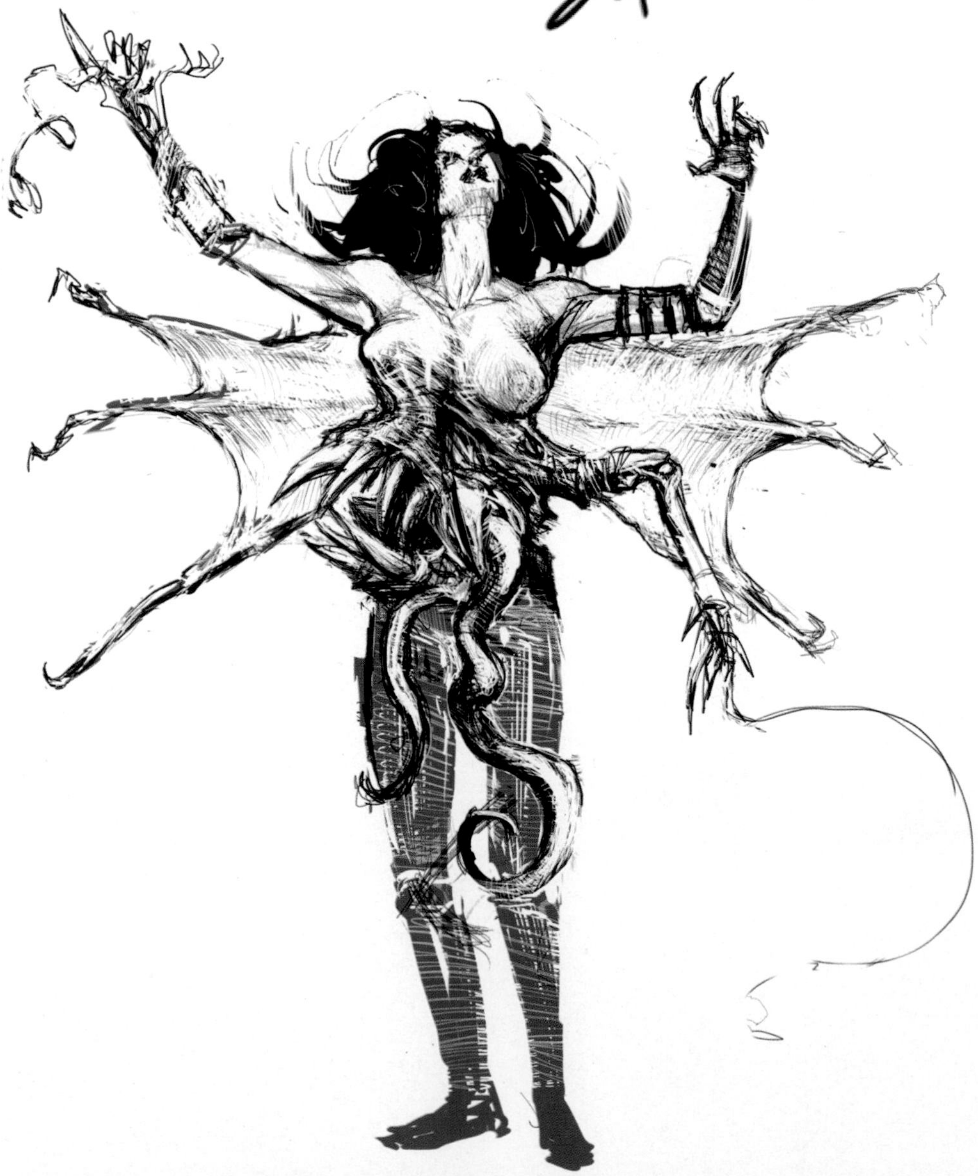

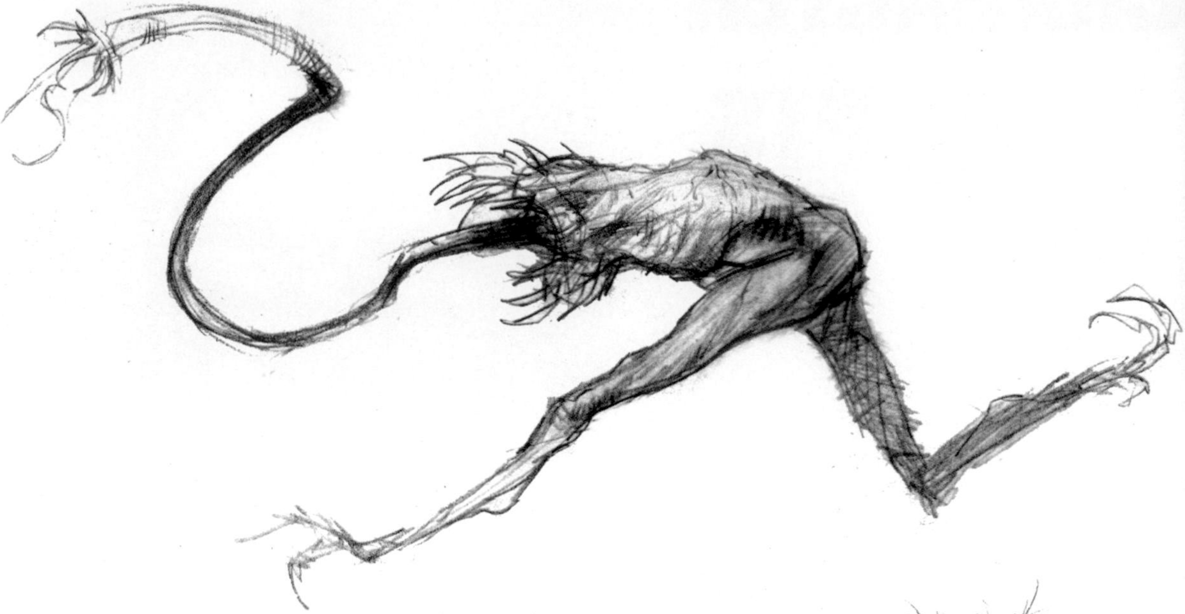

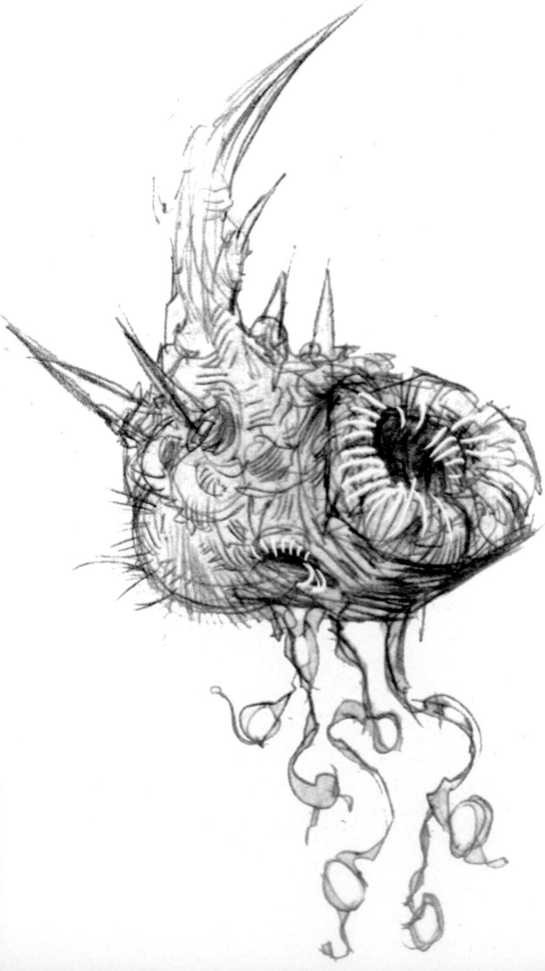

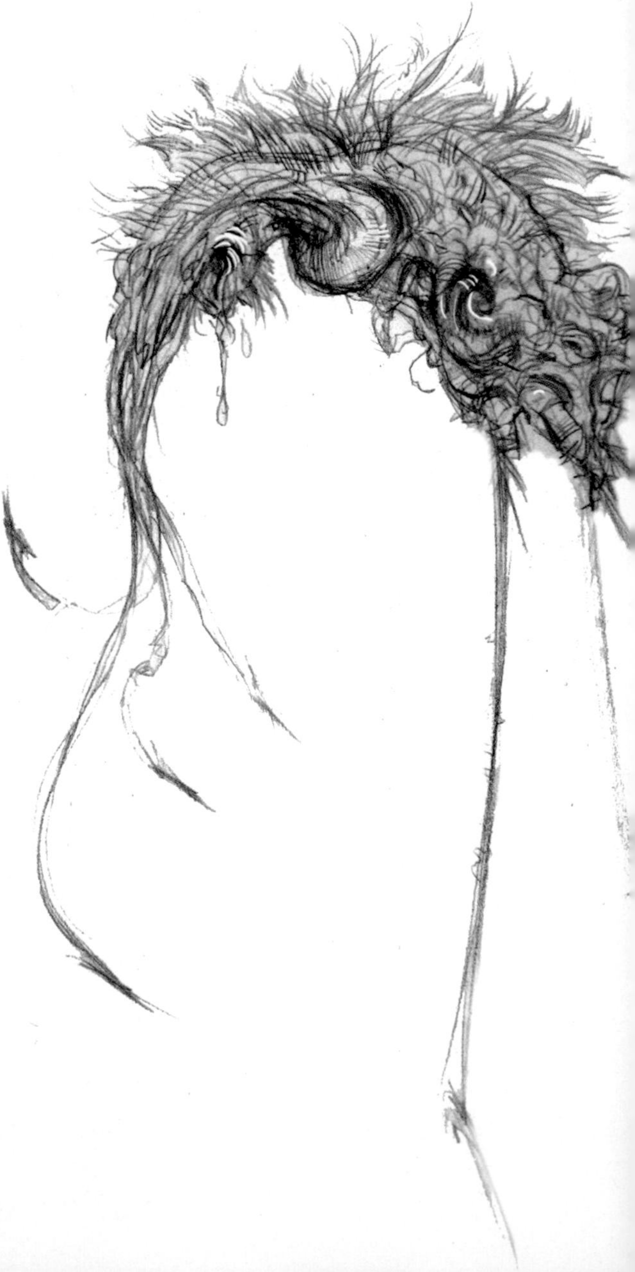

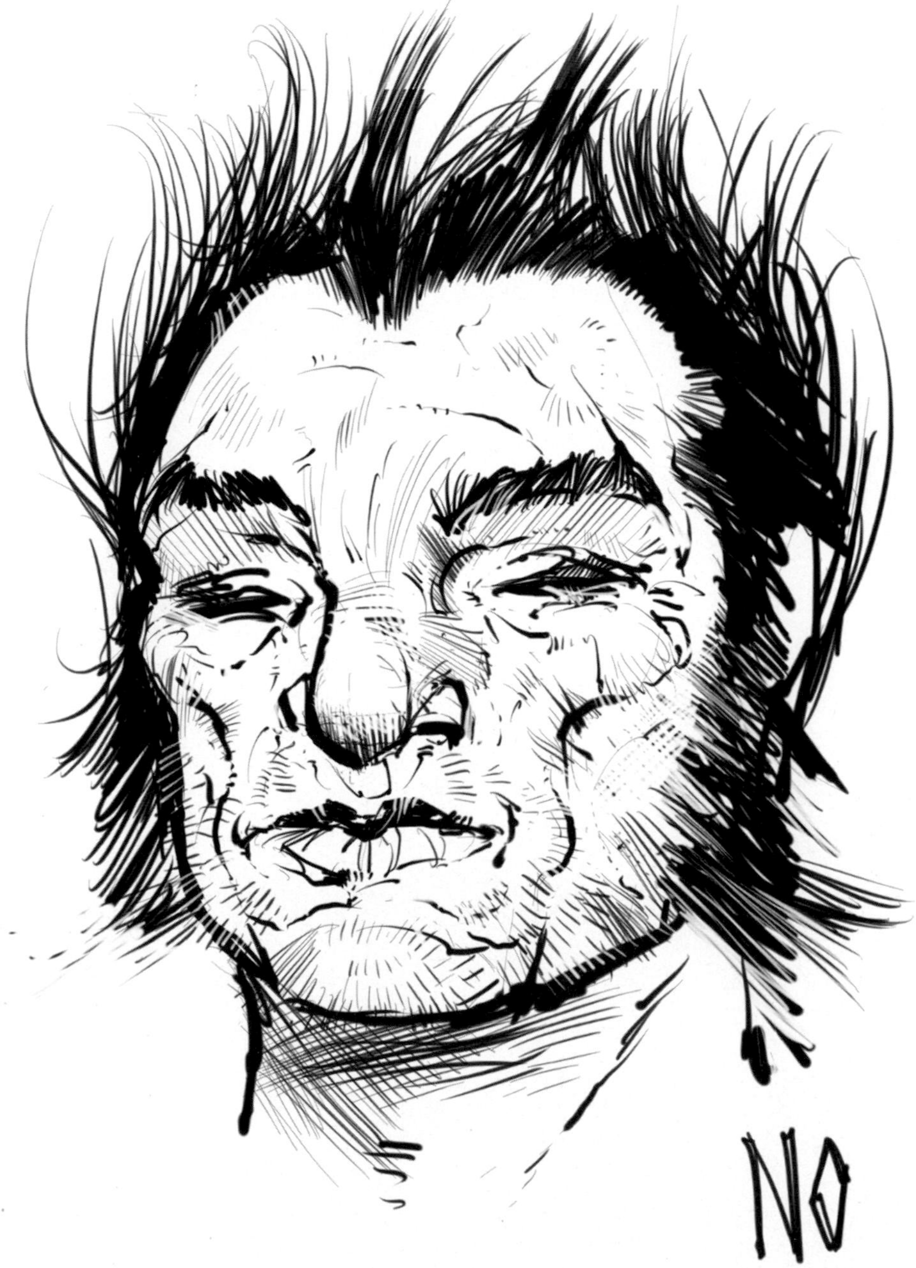
NO

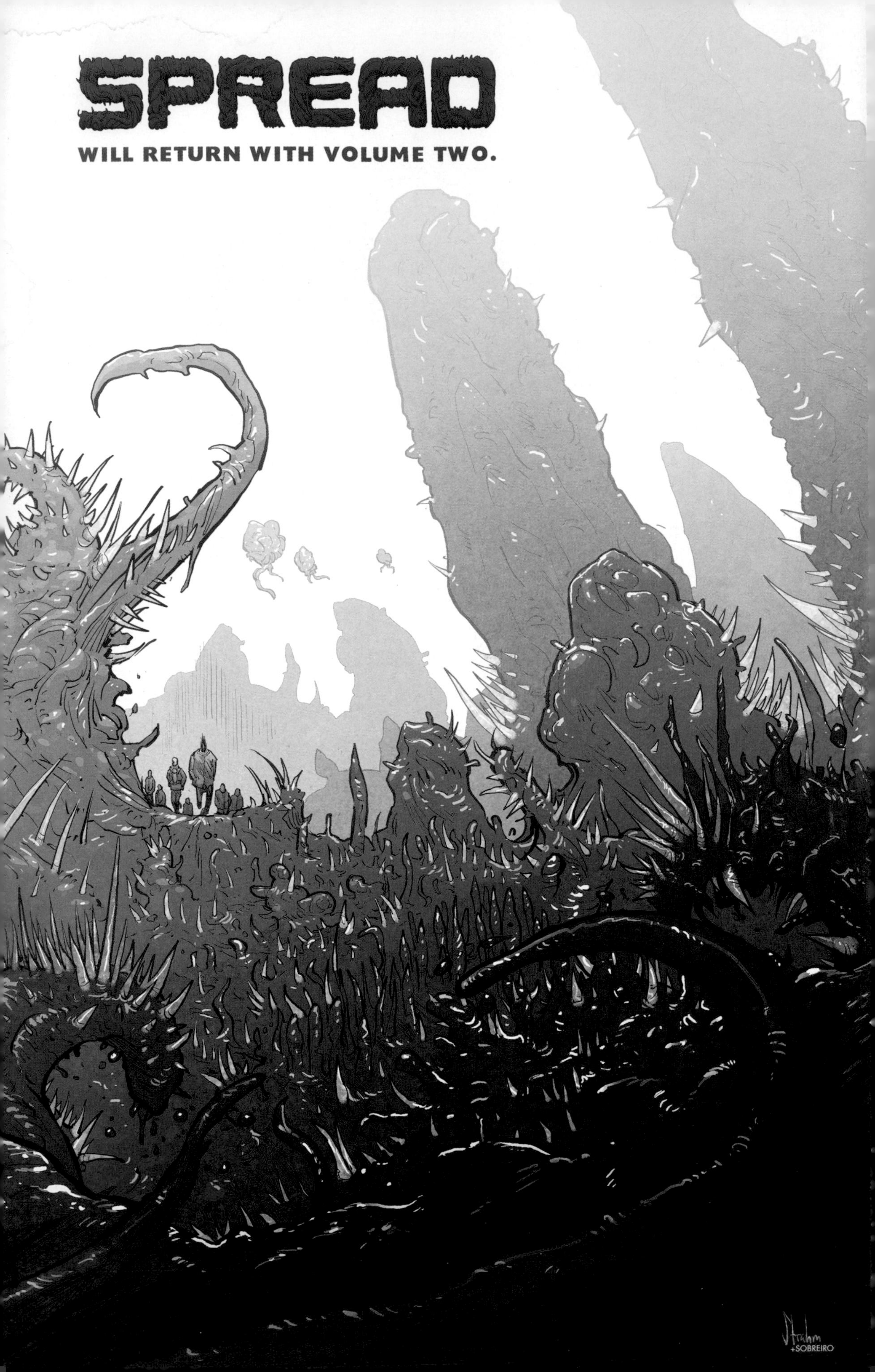
SPREAD
WILL RETURN WITH VOLUME TWO.